Behind
the Tiananmen Massacre

Behind
the Tiananmen Massacre

Social, Political, and
Economic Ferment in China

Chu-yuan Cheng

Westview Press
Boulder • San Francisco • Oxford

Copyright © 1990 by Westview Press, Inc.

Published in 1990 in the United States of America by Westview Press, Inc., 5500 Central Avenue, Boulder, Colorado 80301, and in the United Kingdom by Westview Press, Inc., 36 Lonsdale Road, Summertown, Oxford OX2 7EW

Library of Congress Cataloging-in-Publication Data
Cheng, Chu-yüang.
  Behind the Tiananmen Massacre: social, political, and economic ferment in China/Chu-yuan Cheng.
     p.   cm.
  ISBN 0-8133-1047-4
  1. China—History—Tiananmen Square Incident, 1989.   I. Title.
DS779.32.C46   1990
951.05'8—dc20   90-12384
                                                                                                           CIP

Printed and bound in the United States of America

The paper used in this publication meets the requirements of the American National Standard for Permanence of Paper for Printed Library Materials Z39.48-1984.

10   9   8   7   6   5   4   3

Contents

Tables and Illustrations

Tables

Figures

Maps

Photos (at center of book)

Students demonstrate in Tiananmen Square

A student raises a sign for liberty

Students protest at the front gate of Xinhuamen at Zhongnanhai, headquarters of the Chinese Communist Party

Students and workers demonstrate on April 27, 1989

The sign reads "Long Live the Invincible Mao Zedong's Thought!"

Preface

The 1989 prodemocracy movement in the People's Republic of China and the subsequent crackdown were marked by many dramatic reversals. Supported at first by several thousand Beijing University students, the movement quickly attracted millions of followers and developed into a nationwide mass movement. The jubilant mood during the short-lived freedom in Tiananmen Square turned into despair over the unnecessary bloodshed. The event raised many deeply disturbing questions: Was the massacre necessary and justified? What is the historical significance of this movement? Which path will the PRC follow in the decade ahead?

Although no one had anticipated the tragic outcome, the popular unrest was not totally unexpected. When I read the news of 200,000 Beijing students and residents, in open defiance of the government's order, staging a large-scale demonstration on April 20, I knew a confrontation between the people and the government was inevitable.

In a letter published on May 3 in the *New York Times*, I offered my preliminary assessment of the emerging social and economic crisis. The letter prompted several local and overseas interviews. The most frequently raised questions in the interviews were, Why did the unrest occur after a decade of seemingly successful economic reform? Why did Deng Xiaoping, the pragmatic leader of the reform, side with the hard-liners to purge Party General Secretary Zhao Ziyang, the man Deng had picked as his successor? Did the protests merely represent another episode of the forty-year order-disturbance cycle of the People's Republic of China, or did they signal the beginning of the end of Chinese communism? In order to answer these questions, I embarked on a systematic study of the causes of the unrest from various angles—social, economic, political, intellectual, and military. The June 4 massacre moved me to engage in a broader and deeper analysis, not only to determine the causes of the unrest but also to assess the short- and long-term impacts on the PRC's future development. The aim of this study is thus to provide not a chronological account of *what* happened in Beijing during spring 1989 but rather a comprehensive analysis of *why* this tragedy occurred.

The book draws heavily from many of my earlier publications and the works of other scholars in Chinese studies. In preparing the manuscript, I benefited immensely from the comments of several reviewers. My colleague John Hannaford, associate dean emeritus of the College of Business at Ball State University, read several chapters of the preliminary draft and gave me many insightful comments. Two veteran China experts selected by Westview Press provided detailed reviews of the manuscript and rendered valuable comments and suggestions. James Tu of the *China Times* provided me with photos that he had taken in Beijing, and Congressman Phil Sharp facilitated my use of several U.S. government publications. Judy Lane, editor at the Bureau of Business Research at Ball State, reviewed the final version of the manuscript and helped to improve its readability. To these colleagues, I would like to express my deep gratitude. Needless to say, I alone am responsible for any errors that remain.

Although use of a computer facilitated typing and revising, those tedious jobs were for the most part performed by a group of student secretaries in the Department of Economics, under the capable supervision of Rita Disher, the department secretary. The students who participated in this project were David Bruce, Nancy Dean, Tamara Smith, and Kimberly Wilch. My sincere thanks to them for their enthusiastic and efficient endeavors, which enabled me to meet the deadline set by the publisher.

I would like also to thank Rebecca Ritke, acquisitions editor at Westview Press, for her reviews and valuable comments on the first draft. Marian Safran, copy editor at Westview Press, made a careful review of the final manuscript. Her critical acumen saved me from many errors. I am deeply indebted to both of them for their assistance.

The work could not have been done in such a short span of time without the contributions of members of my family. My son, Andrew, a Yale law school student, initiated the writing of this book and forfeited his entire summer vacation in order to collect and analyze the original materials. Andrew prepared the Chronology and the Profiles of Fifty Major Figures (Appendixes 1 and 2). He also reviewed the manuscript critically and edited the first draft. After Andrew went back to school, my daughter Anita, a medical student at the University of Chicago, edited and typed Chapters 6 and 7. My wife, Alice, a linguist and librarian, besides bearing the burden of the family chores, prepared the documents for Appendix 3 and checked the pinyin transcription of personal and place names. Their unceasing support and encouragement, as always, provided the driving force for my research and writing.

Chu-yuan Cheng
Muncie, Indiana

1

Introduction

Few events in modern Chinese history have drawn such ardent worldwide attention as the 1989 prodemocracy movement and its tragic outcome in Tiananmen Square. Seventy years earlier, the country's first nationwide student demonstration, known as the May Fourth Movement, symbolized a cultural renaissance and ignited a sense of nationalism that inspired Chinese intellectuals for more than half a century. The 1989 prodemocracy campaign far exceeded its forerunner in terms of scale and duration and may well surpass it in terms of significance. Officially labeled a "counter-revolutionary rebellion," the prodemocracy movement was marked by the brutal slaughter of hundreds, perhaps thousands, of its participants. Most of its leaders ended up in exile or in prison. For the millions of eyewitnesses of this cataclysmic event, nothing is more urgent than setting the record straight.

This study seeks to address several salient questions: First, why did China's hard-line leaders choose to attack peaceful demonstrators and citizens? Second, why did Deng Xiaoping, whose pragmatic policies had won him worldwide acclaim, decide to destroy in one day much of what he had accomplished in a whole decade? Third, is the hard-liners' characterization of the prodemocracy movement as "an organized conspiracy" of "a tiny group of people" devoid of all truth? Or was the movement simply a spontaneous protest similar to the May Fourth Movement, but utilized by rival power contenders within the Chinese Communist Party (CCP) hierarchy? And fourth, what is the impact of the bloodshed on Chinese modernization and unification, two major goals Deng had set for the 1990s?

The Social, Political, and Economic Ferment

As in other great historical events, it was the interplay of many social, political, and economic factors that led to the 1989 spring unrest. In brief, there were four major groups of actors: the students who initiated the movement, the people who supported the students, the political leaders who ordered the suppression, and the army that carried out the crackdown. To understand the mounting conflicts between the ruler and the ruled, a brief survey of the Mao-Deng orthodoxy may be useful.

For forty years, since 1949, the People's Republic of China (PRC) has been ruled by a group of autocrats who have attempted to transform the traditional society into a Stalinist totalitarian state. During the first twenty-seven years, under Mao Zedong, there was a continual process of institutional transformation, ideological indoctrination, and political convulsion. The Maoist model in essence involved four peculiar features: (1) emphasis on class struggle and the need for uninterrupted revolution; (2) promotion of mass participation in decision-making and the denigration of intellectuals and experts; (3) use of movements or campaigns to replace normal economic measures; and (4) emphasis on egalitarianism and normative incentives that reject material rewards and profits as motivations for workers and managers. To implement these radical policies, Mao's developmental model required the transformation of the traditional social-economic institutions into a socialist central-planning system based on the Soviet model and the pursuit of a developmental strategy similar to that advocated by Stalin in the Soviet Union during the 1928 to 1953 industrialization process.

Shortly after the founding of the new government, the Chinese Communist leaders began to nationalize all means of production. Private enterprises were basically eliminated by 1957 and all agricultural land was nationalized, with the peasant households organized into communes. The entire economy was guided by a unified plan, with planning authority concentrated at the top. All input and output targets for individual enterprises were decided by the central planners and were passed down through the various levels of the administration. The enterprises were obligated to fulfill the assigned targets regardless of local conditions. Under such a system, there was no room for individual initiative or for entrepreneurial innovations.

The centrally planned and controlled system permitted the government to pursue an unbalanced growth strategy by concentrating all resources on developing capital goods industries, especially steel and defense industries, at the expense of agriculture and consumer goods industries. This strategy resulted in a lopsided industrial structure and an extremely low standard of living. By 1980, some thirty years after the Communist revolution, per capita income in China was only $256, among the lowest in the world. It is against this background that a large-scale economic reform was begun by Deng Xiaoping and his associates in late 1970s.

In the first five years (1979–1984), Deng's program achieved impressive results. The institution of the contract system to replace the ill-conceived rural communes significantly improved agricultural productivity. The revival of millions of individual businesses and the expansion of the tertiary sector greatly invigorated urban life. But reform of the urban economy created more problems than it solved. Since 1985, the negative effects of the reform have appeared to outweigh the positive effects. As a result of excessive investment and huge subsidies for agricultural procurement and for covering the losses incurred by the inefficient state enterprises, the state budget suffered a chronic shortfall, which by 1989 had reached 160 billion yuan ($43 billion). To finance this deficit, the state resorted to issuing currency, triggering rampant inflation. Adding to the demand-pull inflation was a cost-push inflation caused by upward adjustment of raw material and fuel prices. From 1987 to 1989, the annual inflation rate exceeded 30 percent, and food prices rose 40–50 percent a year. In 1988, one-third of urban residents found that their real income had sharply declined.

One revealing economic barometer is the share of consumer expenditure on food. In most advanced countries, expenditure on food in recent years occupied about 25 percent of consumer spending. In 1978, prior to the economic reform, food amounted to 60 percent of the workers' total expenditure in the PRC, the highest among the Asian countries. Between 1979 and 1985, as people's income rose while food prices remained stable, the share for food dropped steadily to only 42 percent, allowing substantial improvement in living standards. After 1985, the situation began to reverse, with food prices climbing rapidly and people's real income falling. In 1987, the share for food rose to 55 percent and by 1988 to 60 percent again.[1] The return to the prereform expenditure structure indicated that the benefits of the reform in the earlier years had been mostly negated. This reversion has frustrated most urban dwellers.

Discontent among urban dwellers was aggravated by widespread corruption practiced by Communist Party members, particularly the children and relatives of high Party officials. The corruption became so prevalent that in 1986, 1987, and 1989, the CCP Central Committee launched three nationwide campaigns to crack down on economic crimes, but the committee's orders went mostly unheeded.

Confronting the increasingly discontented population was a group of aging revolutionary veterans who were intolerant to any challenge and fell automatically back on older, familiar ways of dealing with dissidents. Although Deng intended to revamp many of Mao's economic systems and policies, he refused to encourage reform in the political arena. The Four Cardinal Principles—Communist Party leadership, socialist road, proletarian dictatorship, and Marxism-Leninism and Mao Zedong Thought—which Deng had invoked in 1979, indicated that in politics the Marxist ideology would remain intact. Deng's efforts to maintain a balance between a liberal economic reform and an orthodox political system resulted in the zig-zag course of economy and politics during the 1980s. Deng did not recognize that economic development tends to create pressure for political liberalization. His rigidity on this issue made social unrest inevitable.

Deng's reluctance to initiate political reform was due in part to his personal experience and in part to the Communist power structure. Deng and his veteran comrades had spent the first half of their lives in a China racked by division and chaos. Their abhorrence of disorder became burned into their psyches when the Cultural Revolution began in 1966, causing hundreds of thousands of deaths and countless personal tragedies. The experience of the aged leadership bred the belief that the country needed stability in order to have development. In addition to fearing chaos, Deng, like Mao, could not tolerate any criticism. He read minor dissent as a direct challenge to his ultimate authority.

The conflict intensified as more than 70,000 Chinese students studying abroad sent home information about the outside world. The influx of 1 million Taiwanese and several million overseas Chinese who visited their homeland in the past several years widened people's horizons. Increasing contact with neighboring Asian countries, coupled with more open debates on political and philosophical issues in the official press, caused people to question the very basis of the Chinese political, economic, and social systems. By spring 1989, a political storm was slowly brewing.

Within the Chinese Communist Party hierarchy, a struggle for succession had been going on for several years. When Deng launched China on its modernization path in 1979, the Party hierarchy was divided into three main groups: a moderate group, originally led by Deng, with Hu Yaobang and Zhao Ziyang as two main supporters; a conservative group, led by Chen Yun, including most of the veterans in the Party's Central Advisory Commission; and a neo-Maoist group, led by Hua Guofeng, then chairman of the CCP. After the fall of Hua in 1981, the moderates and the conservatives competed for influence. Deng's dismissal of Hu in 1987 gutted the Party's moderate wing and paved the way for the rise in 1988 of Li Peng (premier), Yang Shangkun (state president), and Wang Zhen (state vice president) as the new strongmen of the conservative faction. Since summer 1988, contention between Zhao and Li Peng had moved toward a showdown. That power struggle, plus the rising conflict between the leadership and the masses, formed two currents that flowed under the 1989 unrest and its subsequent bloodshed.

The year 1989 portended momentous events in China, as it was the fortieth anniversary of the founding of the PRC, the seventieth anniversary of the May Fourth Movement, and the two-hundredth anniversary of the French Revolution. Chinese intellectuals viewed each of these anniversaries as milestones not to be unmarked. They sought to bring attention to the progress of democracy and science since 1919—when science and democracy had been singled out as two national goals for intellectuals to pursue. They also wanted to measure the freedom and human rights they enjoyed against the ideals symbolized in the storming of the Bastille in July 1789. These historical recollections generated emotions that contributed to the spring unrest. Before the death of Hu Yaobang on April 15, 1989, students in Beijing University had already scheduled a demonstration in Tiananmen Square. They wanted to express their resentment toward the corruption and nepotism of high officials and the lack of progress in political reform and human rights. Government threats and security forces forestalled that demonstration.[2] As the political clouds gathered, a severe storm seemed imminent.

Different Interpretations of the Events

Although large-scale demonstrations to mark the May Fourth anniversary were no surprise, few predicted their tragic outcome. In the wake of the Tiananmen bloodshed, two diametrically opposed interpretations of the event have been offered. Both attempt to explain how the movement was used to further differing political causes.

Chen Xitong, the mayor of Beijing, presented the official version of the "turmoil" in a detailed report entitled "Checking the Turmoil and Quelling the Counter-Revolutionary Rebellion," at the eighth session of the Standing Committee of the Seventh National People's Congress, on June 30, 1989 (see Appendix 3). A prominent hard-liner who advocated the imposition of martial law, Chen interpreted the May–June events as the plot of "a tiny handful of people" who "exploited student unrest to launch a planned, organized, and premeditated political turmoil, which later developed into a counter-revolutionary rebellion in Beijing, the capital. Their purpose was to overthrow the leadership of the Chinese Communist Party and subvert the socialist People's Republic of China."[3]

Chen's characterization of the event as a "premeditated political turmoil" and a "counter-revolutionary rebellion" was in fact a restatement of Li Peng's position of April 24, which had been endorsed by Deng on April 25. According to Chen's report, while Zhao was paying a state visit to North Korea, the Standing Committee of the CCP Politburo on April 24, under Li Peng's direction, decided to label the student movement "an anti-socialist attack on the party." Early the next morning, Li and State President Yang Shangkun went to see Deng at his residence. Outraged by Li's and Yang's reports of the ongoing protests and deeply alarmed at the prospect of further unrest, Deng pointed out sharply that "this was not a case of ordinary student unrest, but a political turmoil aimed at negating the leadership of the Communist Party and the socialist system."[4] On Deng's order, a harsh hard-line editorial was prepared for the Party's newspaper, *People's Daily*, condemning the student movement and calling for a crackdown. According to reports, when a draft of the editorial was taken to Deng's residence for approval, he struck out each use of the term "student movement" (*xue chao*), replacing it with "turmoil" (*dong luan*).[5] Deng's assessment of the protest was publicly promulgated in an April 26 editorial of the *People's Daily* (see Appendix 3) and has since become the official interpretation of the spring events.

After the June 4 crackdown, the movement was designated "a counter-revolutionary rebellion" with a "profound international background." Zhao Ziyang was openly identified by the hard-liners as the one "supporting the turmoil, splitting the party, and having the unshirkable responsibility for the shaping and development of the turmoil."[6] Chen's report asserted that a political conspiracy supported by Zhao sought to seize ultimate power. As evidence implicating Zhao in the "plot," Chen alluded to Zhao's meeting with Milton Friedman, an American Nobel laureate in economics, on September 19, 1988, as evidence of Zhao's connection with foreign conservative forces and his intention to turn the PRC into a capitalist country. In Chen's analysis, many publications by liberal writers in Hong Kong and seminars conducted by prodemocracy students and intellectuals in Beijing from summer 1988 to spring 1989 had supported the notion of a premeditated organization engineered by a small handful of people.

Chen then indicated that from the very beginning the turmoil was "manifested by a sharp conflict between bourgeois liberation and the Four Cardinal Principles." Most of the intellectual elite in Beijing and Shanghai, he asserted, were involved in this "plot." Even the "reactionary political forces in Hong Kong, Taiwan, the United States and other Western countries were also involved in the turmoil." He specified the "Voice of America in particular," because it "aired news in three programmes beamed to the Chinese mainland . . . spreading rumors, stirring up trouble and adding fuel to the turmoil."

Chen listed Zhao's many serious mistakes. Notable among them were Zhao's conniving to avoid a crackdown against the prodemocracy movement in April and May, his aides' helping the students in their attempts to overthrow the government, and Zhao's May 4 speech to the annual meeting of the Asian Development Bank, which "created ideological confusion . . . and inflated the arrogance of the organizers and plotters of the turmoil." Henceforth, the situation took an abrupt turn for the worse. According to Chen, Zhao used the opportunity of meeting Gorbachev on May 16 to fire direct criticism at Deng and exacerbate the situation, and Zhao refused to endorse the imposition of martial law on May 19, a refusal that created a schism in the Party. Although Chen did not explicitly identify Zhao as the instigator of the whole event, he did make Zhao responsible "for the shaping and development of the turmoil."

Chen's account of the event represents the official view. On September 26, 1989, in his first press conference as the Party's new general secretary, Jiang Zemin, when asked by a foreign reporter whether the "Tiananmen tragedy" could have been avoided, responded: "We do not believe that there was any tragedy in Tiananmen Square. What actually happened was a counter-revolutionary rebellion aimed at opposing the leadership of the Communist Party and overthrowing the socialist system."[7] Again, in a meeting on October 31, 1989, Deng Xiaoping told Richard Nixon: "Frankly speaking, the U.S. was involved too deeply in the turmoil and counter-revolutionary rebellion which occurred in Beijing not long ago. China was the real victim and it is unjust to reprove China for it."[8] Both Jiang's and Deng's statements clearly indicate that the official interpretation of the crushed democracy movement had two purposes: to justify the brutal crackdown and to find the scapegoat for the tragedy.

Chen Yizi's version of the events sharply contrasts with the hard-liners' account. Director of the Economic Structural Reform Research Institute of the State Council, one of Zhao's brain trusts, Chen fled to France. According to Chen, the whole event had been plotted by the hard-liners. Their immediate target was Zhao's downfall; their ultimate goal was the abolition of the reform program. Chen identified Li Peng as the man at the forefront of this plot. The man behind the scenes was Yao Yilin, deputy premier in charge of economic affairs and a strong supporter of planned economy. The boss was Chen Yun, the eighty-four-year-old chairman of the Party's Central Advisory Commission and mentor of both Li Peng and Yao Yilin.

The strategy of this group was first to provoke Deng. Hard-liners, according to Chen Yizi's report, utilized the students' attacks against Deng, especially the calls for his downfall, to play on his paranoia. Without Li Peng's deliberate provocation, Deng might not have vindictively characterized the student movement as "turmoil." The second step of the hard-liners' plot was to incite the students by belittling their patriotic zeal and labeling their movement a "counter-revolutionary rebellion" manipulated by a small group of people. This label totally distorted the students' motives. By goading both sides, the hard-liners created a situation for which both Deng and the students would have no recourse but confrontation.[9]

From both Chen Xitong's and Chen Yizi's interpretations one can see how the power contenders utilized the student movement. Most independent observers believed that the April–May student protest was a spontaneous campaign. As Zhao Ziyang pointed out in his May 4 speech, the aim of the movement was, not to overthrow the Communist government, but to demand further reform of the political system and correct the current maladies arising from the economic reform. According to Su Shaozhi, who had been director of the Institute of Marxism, Leninism, and Mao Zedong Thought at the Chinese Academy of Social Sciences, the movement arose spontaneously. During the campaign, some student groups emerged, but most of the groups were loosely organized, lacking strong leadership. There was no evidence of any political plot. Even the Beijing Federation of Autonomous Student Unions in Universities and Colleges, the umbrella organization, was poorly organized and could not exert significant influence.

However, as the movement entered the second stage, when millions of Beijing residents joined the students in large-scale demonstrations, both the reformers and the conservatives tried to take advantage of the occasion to strengthen their own positions. Zhao Ziyang saw the movement as an expression of popular demand for reform, which would enhance his standing. Li Peng and other hard-liners saw the unrest as an opportunity to win Deng's support and a weapon to undermine Zhao. At the beginning of May, the student movement became entangled in the power struggle, making a peaceful solution difficult and bloodshed unavoidable.[10]

Setting the Record Straight

Because the prodemocracy movement became entangled in the intra-Party power struggle, official reports about it varied according to the prevailing political current. From April 15 to May 15, there was a blackout of news about the protest. On May 4, several hundred Chinese journalists, demanding freedom of the press, joined the student protest. Among the demonstrators were reporters from the Party organ, the *People's Daily;* the government news agency, Xinhua; and the state-run Central Broadcasting Station. On May 17, official print and broadcast media began to cover the demonstrations factually and prominently. Chinese television also broadcast reports on the action in Tiananmen Square. For the first time, people outside Beijing learned about the demonstrations in the capital. Toward the end of May, the government tightened its grip again. Immediately after the June 4 massacre, the government organizations engaged in a campaign, actually an elaborate cover-up scheme, to mislead the country about the bloodshed. Throughout most of June, national television was turned over to the army and the internal security police. All major newspapers were put under the control of a special propaganda committee set up after the declaration of martial law.

In the second week of June, the army concocted a forty-minute documentary about the event. Night after night, state-run television bombarded viewers with skillfully assembled footage taken by the military and police that featured scenes of students and workers disabling army trucks and armored personnel carries. It also showed the mutilated bodies of three soldiers of the People's Liberation Army (PLA) reportedly killed by the masses. "From this you can see the seriousness of the chaos that the counter-revolutionaries have created," the announcer said to Chinese viewers.[11]

The government cover-up was reinforced by statements from military and Party leaders. At a television press conference on June 6, Yuan Mu, the government spokesman, placed among the dead a few hundred troops and only twenty-three students. Hours later, these figures were revised and turned into good news by Zhang Gong, deputy political commissar of the Beijing Military Region, who declared that "troops did not kill or harm a single person when we cleared Tiananmen Square." To sustain this account, the government arranged for a leader of the hunger strikers who was arrested on June 4 to declare that "he did not see any students, civilians or army personnel killed. Neither did he see anyone run over by the military vehicles."[12]

On June 9, when Deng Xiaoping spoke to the officials of the martial law troops, he maintained that "the PLA losses were great, but this enabled us to win the support of the people . . . they can see what kind of people the PLA are, whether there was bloodshed at Tiananmen, and who were those that shed blood." Deng then asserted: "We should never forget how cruel our enemies are. For them, we should not have an iota of forgiveness."[13] Both Yuan Mu's statement and Deng's speech served to convince people outside Beijing that the members of the PLA were heroic victims, not the perpetrators of violence.

The cover-up was bolstered by a compulsory political-study campaign requiring people in all walks of life to study Deng's speech and express their attitude toward the recent events. Under tremendous pressure, most people bowed to the official line by declaring their resolute support for the quelling of the "counter-revolutionary rebellion." Almost all famous figures in the PRC were requested to issue statements backing the government's actions against the students (see Chapter 6).

After the Fourth Plenum of the CCP Thirteenth Central Committee on June 24, 1989, a torrent of articles and commentaries appeared in the Party's newspapers, accusing leaders of the prodemocracy movement. Zhao Ziyang was named as the villain for splitting the Party, supporting the unrest, tolerating corruption, and causing economic crisis. Many leading intellectuals were condemned as "black hands" behind Zhao; those who had fled to foreign countries were labeled "traitors" to the state. All student leaders became criminal offenders who "incited and organized the counter-revolutionary insurrection in the capital." They were put on a "wanted list." Those who had been seized were shown on television in handcuffs and with their heads brutally pushed down by armed soldiers as a sign of humiliation.

The cover-up was partially exposed by foreign journalists. In early May 1989, when the student movement was beginning to gain momentum, more than 1,200 foreign journalists had assembled in Beijing to report on the historical summit between Soviet President Mikhail Gorbachev and Deng. The presence of international reporters and photographers not only lifted the morale of the protesters but at the same time helped to preserve a trustworthy record of the movement.

Of the reporters sent to the PRC, there were several from major U.S. newspapers and television networks. From May to June, through the talents and efforts of these men and women, the world watched the movement's development.[14] Without their extensive reports and with only the official false account to rely on, it would have been impossible to conduct an independent study of the events.

While the major international news services produced voluminous feature reports about the student movement, the foreign television networks brought the events directly to millions of viewers around the world. The seven-week-long peaceful demonstrations, as shown on the Western networks, provided no discernable evidence of a "premeditated counter-revolutionary rebellion." Many student leaders interviewed by foreign reporters clearly indicated that their goal was to help the government correct its mistakes. They had no intention of getting involved in political power struggles. Nor did they harbor any intention of overthrowing the government. As one veteran U.S. reporter commented: "Many students were surprisingly naïve about the underlying repressiveness of China's leadership. They never guessed that tanks would replace platitudes in the government's arsenal of responses to their demands."[15]

Most journalists, however, were working under extremely difficult conditions. Reliable sources were scarce and rumors swirled around the capital. Foreigners were particularly vulnerable when reporting military affairs or the power struggle of top leaders. Consequently, quite a few widely reported events have proven to be untrue. After the June 4 massacre, there were extensive reports of clashes between army units on June 5 and 6 on the northern outskirts and at the military airport in southern Beijing.[16] It was reported that the 38th Army, based in Baoding, ninety miles southwest of the capital, had refused to attack student demonstrators. As a result, President Yang Shangkun summoned the 27th Army from Inner Mongolia to quell the democracy movement. There were also reports that units from Shanghai, in eastern China, and from the northeastern city of Shenyang had also joined the battle. It was popularly believed that the 38th Army and the units from Shanghai had tenuous connections to Zhao and thus that a conflict between the forces of Yang and those connected with Zhao had developed. Some reports even suggested that Yang, with the support of Li Peng and the backing of key military leaders—some of whom are Yang's relatives—might have been attempting some kind of coup d'état.[17]

These reports gained authenticity when U.S. military specialists and the Bush administration did not contradict the news,[18] which created the impression that the PRC was falling into the abyss of coup, countercoup, and civil war.[19] But later developments showed that the interunit fighting never occurred. According to information from Hong Kong and Taiwan, both the 38th and the 27th armies were in fact engaged in the attack on the demonstrators.[20]

In mid-August 1989, the Associated Press reported from Hong Kong that Defense Minister Qin Jiwei and other high-ranking army officers had been arrested by soldiers loyal to Yang Shangkun. Qin was identified as tied to the deposed Party general secretary, Zhao Ziyang. Others detained were the commanders of Beijing, Guangzhou, and Nanjing military regions who supported Qin and were in the capital for an important meeting.[21] Like the earlier report of civil war, news of the arrest of the defense minister drew worldwide attention, but later investigation showed this news to be untrue as well.

Many stories about personal relationships of top leaders also proved to be groundless. For instance, Jiang Zemin, the new Party general secretary and chairman of the CCP Central Military Commission, was widely reported to be a son-in-law of Li Xiannian, a powerful leader and former president of the state, and Chi Haotian, chief of staff of the PLA, was identified as a son-in-law of Yang Shangkun. It was also reported that the man who commanded the 27th Army was Yang's son or nephew Yang Xiaojun. But apparently none of these identifications was true. Jiang Zemin, on several occasions, denied having any relationship with Li. Jiang's wife came from a family of Wangs, not Lis.[22] In an interview with Chinese reporters, Chi Haotian also denied being a relative of Yang Shangkun. Chi's wife, Jiang Qingping, came from Jiangsu, and his father-in-law was a retired educator. According to Chi, the head of the 27th Army was Qian Guoliang, not Yang's son or nephew Yang Xiaojun.[23]

The examples of misreporting are listed above not to discredit the work of Western journalists but simply to illustrate the difficulty in obtaining reliable information. Although the basic data of this study are mostly derived from the voluminous reports by Western journalists, facts were compared and cross-checked with Chinese sources available in Hong Kong and Taiwan.

My purpose is to provide, not a chronological account of events, but a comprehensive analysis of the causes and effects of the prodemocracy movement and its abrupt and tragic end. In other words, the book is not an eyewitness report of "what" happened in Beijing during spring 1989 but is concerned with "why" this tragedy occurred and what factors are likely to shape the PRC's future and determine the path the country will follow in the decade ahead.

One can draw several conclusions from this study:

1. The 1989 spring unrest, like the uprisings that emerged in Eastern Europe five months later, were the outcome of grievances that had been suppressed for four decades. Even without the death of Hu Yaobang, large-scale protests were bound to occur.

2. The June 4 massacre was completely unnecessary and unjustified. Should the reformers instead of the hard-liners win the power struggle, the 1989 student movement, like those in East Germany and Czechoslovakia, could turn into a formidable driving force for political and economic reform.

3. The crackdown halted the economic reform and demolished Deng's grand plan for an orderly power transition. It also damaged the PRC's international status and destroyed the credibility of the government. The long-term losses to the country's modernization drive are almost incalculable.

4. The future of the country depends on how long the hard-liners maintain their power. In the next three to five years, the hard-liners may continue to dominate. But mounting economic crisis and rapid changes in Eastern Europe and the Soviet Union are bound to undermine the economic base and superstructure of the hard-line leadership.

5. When Deng and his octogenarian colleagues die, sweeping changes may quickly ensue. The collapse of the hard-line regime will pave the way for the resurgence of the reformers. More fundamental changes in political and economic systems will then be pursued. These developments may usher the PRC into a period of stability and prosperity.

Notes

1. Wu Hanzhi, "An Analysis of the Cause of Inflation and Its Control," *Jingji Yu Guanli Yanjiu* [Study on economics and management bimonthly] (Beijing), No. 2 (1989), pp. 1–4.

2. *Wall Street Journal*, June 16, 1989, p. A4.

3. Chen Xitong's 25,000-word report first appeared in *China Daily*, July 7, 1989, pp. 4–6. It was reprinted in *Beijing Review*, July 17–23, 1989. The Chinese version of Chen's report appeared in the *People's Daily* (*Renmin Ribao*), July 1, 1989. An abridged version appears in Appendix 3.

4. Chen, *China Daily*.

5. Nicholas D. Kristof, "How the Hardliners Won," *New York Times Magazine*, Nov. 12, 1989, pp. 65–66.

6. Chen, *China Daily*, and also Li Peng's report to the Fourth Plenum of the CCP Thirteenth Central Committee on June 23, 1989.

7. *New York Times*, Sept. 27, 1989, p. 8.

8. *Wall Street Journal*, Nov. 2, 1989, p. A19.

9. See Chen Yizi's public speech at Columbia University, printed in Sunday supplement, *World Journal* (New York), Oct. 29, 1989, p. 6.

10. Su Shaozhi, "The Origin and Impact of the 1989 Pro-democracy Movement in Mainland China," *Ming Pao* (Hong Kong), Sept. 4, 1989.

11. *New York Times*, June 8, 1989, p. 7.

12. *Beijing Review*, Sept. 11–17, 1989, p. 22.

13. Deng's speech appeared in *People's Daily*, June 28, 1989, p. 1; English version: *New York Times*, June 30, 1989, p. 4.

14. A. M. Rosenthal, "The Reporters of Beijing," *New York Times*, June 9, 1989, p. 37.

15. John Schidlovsky, "Euphoria and Wu'er Kai Xi . . . And the Killing," *Washington Journalism Review*, Sept. 1989, p. 22.

16. *New York Times*, June 6, 1989, pp. 1, 8.

17. *Far Eastern Economic Review* (Hong Kong), June 15, 1989, p. 11.

18. *New York Times*, June 6, 1989, p. 8.

19. *Economist* (London), June 10, 1989, p. 19.

20. *United Daily News* (Taipei), June 12, 1989, p. 2; and *Ming Pao*, July 28, 1989.

21. *Wall Street Journal*, Aug. 18, 1989, p. A6.

22. Su Jin, "The New Party General Secretary as Seen from the Eyes of a Shanghai Reporter," *China Times* (Taipei), July 26, 1989, p. 7.

23. *World Journal*, Nov. 13, 1989, p. 12.

2

From Economic Reform to Social Unrest

The massacre in Tiananmen Square was an event full of great ironies. Deng Xiaoping, the chief target of the demonstrators' anger, had once been hailed as a pioneering reformer whose bold economic programs undid much of Mao's radical legacy, improved the living standards of ordinary Chinese, and sparked a growing prosperity in the economy. In 1976, Deng had utilized similar, smaller demonstrations in Tiananmen Square to consolidate his power. But on June 4, 1989, the paramount leader of the Chinese Communist Party ordered the army to attack the peaceful demonstrators in the square. The sudden interruption of a relatively prosperous economic period by this brutal action points to deeper social and economic phenomena. This chapter analyzes Deng's economic reforms of the prior ten years, examines the positive and negative effects of the reforms, highlights their basic contradictions, and explores those economic and political dilemmas that contributed to the unrest.

The Reform Program

Until 1978, the economic system of the People's Republic of China was modeled primarily on the Soviet Stalinist system. A uniform national plan guided the entire economy. The planning authority, which was concentrated at the top, imposed rigid norms and regulations on various regions and industrial enterprises. The state not only set detailed production plans, supplied materials, and marketed the products but also appropriated most of the profits of the enterprises and made up their losses.

Under this system, the entire nation behaved like a huge corporation, with decision-making power concentrated solely in the hands of governmental departments. The enterprises had no authority to run their own businesses and were mere appendages to the governmental organs. Little attention was paid to the economic performance of the enterprises, which had no bearing on the remuneration of their employees. Moreover, without a voice in management, managers of enterprises lacked the motivation and the means to improve performance. As a result, by 1978, the year Deng came to power, a quarter of the state enterprises had suffered chronic losses.[1]

Capital goods were totally excluded from circulation and were directly allocated according to the state plan. State commercial departments strictly controlled the bulk of consumer goods. Because commodity circulation was organized within administrative divisions, people could not conduct business beyond the boundaries of their provinces, counties, or districts. Excessive linkages in the distribution chain resulted in circuitous transport, high overhead expenses, and a slow turnover rate of commodities. Moreover, because producers and distributors were out of touch with the ultimate consumers of their products, useless goods piled up in warehouses. By the end of June 1978, official statistics showed that unsold products stored in warehouses amounted to 200 billion yuan (about $120 billion at the prevailing exchange rate), equal to half of the country's annual industrial output value.[2]

The employment system also operated irrationally. Labor departments arbitrarily assigned workers to jobs. Because neither the enterprise nor the individual worker had any freedom of choice, a mismatch between employees' training and their jobs often occurred. Furthermore, those employed could not be fired and thus were said to own an "iron rice bowl." The labor system encouraged indolence, stifled the industrious, and resulted in over-staffing and low labor productivity.

In agriculture, between 1958 and 1980, the 170 million peasant households were organized into 54,000 communes, each of which consisted on average of 13 production brigades, 108 production teams, 3,400 households, and 16,000 people. The state appointed commune leaders, who assigned cropping plans as well as yield and delivery quotas to brigades, teams, and peasants. As in the case of the industrial structures, the peasants' rewards did not correspond to their work performance. Apportioning income largely on a per capita basis, with work points accounting for only 10 percent of the calculations, the commune's egalitarian policies weakened peasant incentive.

As a result, the country's agricultural production stagnated. By 1978, twenty years after communization, food grain output per capita was only 318 kilograms (kg), slightly higher than in 1957, but not quite up to the prewar (1936) level of 330 kg. Per capita grain consumption was much smaller than per capita production. The average per capita food grain ration in 1976–1978 for the rural population was even lower than that of 1956 and 1957, before communization had begun.[3]

In view of these problems, the Third Plenum of the Eleventh Party Central Committee, under Deng Xiaoping's initiative, decided in December 1978 to reform the existing planning and management systems in industry and agriculture. From 1978 to 1988, the reform program had four major objectives: (1) the institution of a contract responsibility system in rural areas to replace collective farming; (2) the revival of individual businesses in the cities; (3) the devolution of greater authority to state enterprises; and (4) the reform of the irrational price system. The reforms have had mixed results. Whereas the first two measures generated both positive and negative effects, the latter two not only failed to achieve their proclaimed goals but, in fact, became sources of popular resentment.

Of all the sectors, agriculture has achieved the greatest success in reform. Although land remains collectively owned, plots of land are now contracted to individual farm households for cultivation. By contract, the household surrenders specific crops in specified amounts to the team as payment of agricultural taxes and as contributions to the team's funds for public investment and for welfare. The household is also obligated to sell a portion of its produce to the state. Apart from this, the household may grow any crop and retain the above-quota output for its own use. Under this system, the relationship between the production teams and the farm household became quite similar to the landlord-tenant relationship in traditional China.[4]

Compared to the previous situation, the new farming system displayed several significant improvements: It changed unified management dominated by a few cadres to household management, and each household is responsible for its own profit and loss. In addition, it gave each household some flexibility in allocating its own time and resources and thus was more in step with each family's labor situation and with local conditions. Moreover, because the tax and procurement obligations for each household were fixed at the time of signing the contract, peasants controlled their own income. By establishing a link between reward and effort, the system eliminated the egalitarianism that had stifled the peasants' initiative for more than two decades.

Between 1979 and 1984, agricultural output grew at a rate of 5 percent per annum, double that of the preceding twenty years. Grain output rose from 304.8 to 407 million tons (metric), with an annual growth of 4.9 percent, which was more than double the growth rate achieved between 1957 and 1978.[5] Production of cotton tripled in six years and output of edible oil more than doubled. The rapid growth was partly due to the sharp rise in procurement prices in 1979 that made agricultural production profitable, but it also stemmed from the freedom granted to peasant households to dispose of above-quota products.

Profound changes also took place in the distribution of rural labor. In the late 1980s about 100 million peasants switched from grain farming to other lines of production. Among these, approximately 30 million, or 10 percent of the total labor force in the rural areas, were employed in small factories. The new system expedited the process of commercialization and diversification and brought about sizable increases in peasant incomes. The rise in average annual income for peasants from 133.6 yuan in 1978 to 397 yuan (equivalent to U.S. $107) in 1985[6] reflects the incentive effect of the contract responsibility system.

In urban areas, the reform rapidly revived the private sector. Prior to the reform, the Party leaders viewed private businesses as "remnants of capitalism" and desired their total elimination. In 1978, only about 100,000 private firms still existed, compared to several tens of millions in 1949. After the change of policy in 1980 that reaffirmed the merits of individual business, the number of private businesses soared. By the end of 1983, there were 5.8 million, employing a total of 7.5 million people; by 1985, the private sector employed 17 million people; and in 1988, it employed 24 million. Because most of these workers were in restaurant and repair businesses, the flagging tertiary sector began to boom. Since 1981, the output value of the service sector has increased much faster than that of agriculture or industry. The service sector's share of the gross national product (GNP) rose from 18.7 percent in 1980 to 21.3 percent in 1985 and 23 percent in 1988. Total employment in the service sector reached a record high of 73.65 million. The revival of individual business and the tertiary sector invigorated urban life. The number of retail stores, restaurants, and other service outlets per 10,000 people in the cities rose from 20.6 in 1980 to 102.6 in 1985; the number of people involved in these trades per 10,000 rose from 94.5 in 1980 to 242.9 in 1985.[7]

The mainstay of economic reform, however, rested in the delegation of greater authority to individual enterprises in order to transform them into relatively independent economic units responsible for their own successes and failures. Starting in 1979, the government implemented a series of directives and regulations that included: simplifying administrative structures, lodging more decision-making power at lower departmental levels, cutting the number of state-set mandatory quotas, levying taxes instead of requiring enterprises to hand over profits to the state, allowing enterprises to retain after-tax profits, and instituting the practice of "more work, more pay."[8] Initiated by Zhao Ziyang as an experiment in Sichuan, when he had served there as provincial Party secretary, decentralization of authority was introduced to 100 industrial and transportation enterprises in 1979. By June 1980, the program involved over 7,000 major enterprises throughout the country, accounting for 60 percent of the gross value of the output and 70 percent of the profits of all state-owned enterprises.

The reforms had some short-run stimulating effects on management. But as time passed, the government authorities began to employ various pretexts to recover the power that was to have been delegated to the enterprises. Their most common practice was the conversion of government agencies into control corporations. Numerous corporations that had been set up throughout the country in 1984–1985 began to exercise even tighter control over the enterprises than the state had previously.[9] The bonus system, originally intended to provide material incentives for industrial workers, was gradually converted into a system of subsidies for all workers in the same unit regardless of individual contribution; hence, its incentive function was completely lost. Moreover, the state's continuing subsidies to inefficient plants maintained the old system of "eating from the same big pot." For all of these reasons, ten years after the beginning of the reform, the number of state enterprises operating at a loss remained very high. In 1985, one-fifth of the country's state-owned enterprises operated in the red; the ratio was unchanged in June 1989. The reform, therefore, failed to achieve the goal of promoting efficiency and profitability.

Another major urban economic reform was the revamping of the price structure. A two-tier price system was adopted in 1983. For most industrial intermediates, this system involved a state-planned price for material allocation within the state plan and a negotiated price well above the planned price. For many agricultural products there is also a market price, which is determined by supply and demand. The dual-level price system, while providing some incentive for producers, created unjustified disparities in competitive power among enterprises. Because those with access to official prices secured low-cost materials and made huge profits by selling their goods at higher negotiated prices, no one cared to improve efficiency. The overall effect was a steep rise in the prices of coal, steel, and other raw materials. This, in turn, triggered a series of price hikes throughout the industrial sector and an inflationary spiral in the economy as a whole.[10]

State-planned prices for coal, petroleum, iron ore, and many mineral products continued to be far below their production costs, while prices for processed products remained very high; thus the producers accrued very high profits. The system hampered the development of the energy industry, encouraged the waste of energy and raw materials, and created artificial disparities in profit distribution among and within industries. Because the irrational price system fostered resource misallocation, the formulators of the October 1984 Decision on Economic Reform, which served as the blueprint of urban reform, viewed reform of the price structure as critical to institutional transformation.[11] In 1985, the state took several measures. It replaced the state monopoly on the purchase and marketing of food grains, cottons, and edible oils with a purchase contract system. It lifted price controls on meat, vegetables, and other perishable foods and allowed free markets for these goods. However, the irrational price system remained basically intact for industrial products, raw materials, and intermediate goods.

The country's privileged class took advantage of the relaxation of controls and the dual-price system to engage in illegal activities. Many Party, government, and military institutions and Party and administrative cadres and their children scrambled to do business, forming some 20,000 companies by the second half of 1984. These companies engaged in all sorts of criminal activities, such as speculation, offering or taking bribes, and smuggling. The corruption became so widespread by early 1986 that the CCP Central Committee launched a nationwide campaign to crack down on crime. The committee's orders, however, went mostly unheeded, as the number of speculating companies swelled to 180,000 in 1988.[12] In 1987–1988, many individual businesses (*getihu*) also engaged in speculation, thus further fueling inflation. The increased costs were then passed on to consumers and aroused popular resentment.

The Open-Door Policy

In addition to the reform of the economic system, Deng also initiated an open-door policy to revive the economy. The leadership abandoned Mao's long-standing legacy of self-reliance and replaced it with a set of policies attempting to attract foreign capital and technology to expedite modernization. An array of innovations, from the promulgation of the Joint Venture Law to the establishment of four Special Economic Zones (SEZs)[13] and the opening of fourteen coastal ports to foreign investors, represented a significant departure from the Maoist model. The new policy, while arousing worldwide excitement, became a subject of unceasing controversy within the Party hierarchy.

The urgent need for foreign capital, technology, and management techniques to attain Deng's grand scheme of the Four Modernizations—of agriculture, industry, national defense, and science and technology—was the main motivation for the change from isolationism to the open-door policy. After a hasty start in 1978, the modernization program underwent several adjustments. In September 1982, the Chinese Communist Party at its Twelfth Party Congress put forward a new grand objective of quadrupling the country's gross output value of industry and agriculture (GOVIA) from 710 billion yuan ($426 billion) in 1980 to 2,840 billion yuan ($1.704 trillion) by the year 2000, requiring an average annual growth rate of 7.2 percent.[14] The authorities envisioned a two-stage development scheme, each stage covering a ten-year period. For the first decade, the growth rate of GOVIA was set at only 4 to 5 percent for the first five years (1981–1985) and 7 percent for the second five years (1986–1990). In the subsequent decade the annual growth rate was targeted at over 8 percent. The long-term developmental plan thus anticipated a moderate initial growth period to be followed by accelerated growth.[15] To implement this plan, the PRC required tremendous capital investment, new technology, and management skills, most of which could only be derived from the Western world. According to Hu Yaobang, the former Party general secretary and the architect of the "quadrupling plan," U.S. $50 billion was needed for the first ten years.[16]

Besides lacking the capital needed for renovation, the PRC also is deficient in the technology to produce the capital goods. The country's 400,000 state enterprises are mostly equipped with outdated Soviet machinery and technology from the 1950s and even the 1940s. As one Chinese economist commented, "Due to the prolonged neglect of renovation, existing enterprises in China suffer from 'three olds' and 'two lows'—old technology, old products, old equipment, low quality and low efficiency."[17] Foreign cooperation represents the country's only hope to acquire such technology.

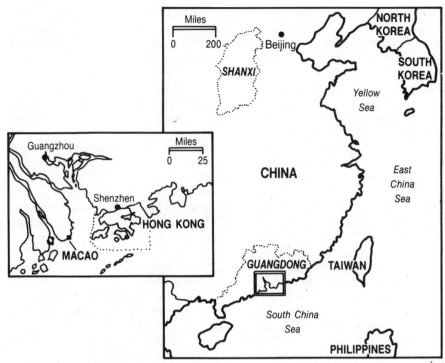

MAP 2.1 Shenzhen Special Economic Zone

To promote foreign interest, Beijing introduced a host of novel measures. The four Special Economic Zones in southern China (see Map 2.1) aroused the most publicity and controversy of all the open-door programs. The idea of building special zones to attract foreign capital has been utilized in various forms throughout the major trading nations of the world. The Kaohsiung processing-export zone, set up in 1960 in Taiwan, represented the most successful example in the Far East. Between 1961 and 1974, total investment in the Kaohsiung zone amounted to $64 million, and foreign-exchange earnings totaled $523.6 million. The success in Kaohsiung may have influenced the Chinese decision to erect the four SEZs in Guangdong and Fujian, where the majority of overseas Chinese have their roots. However, the Chinese leaders envisioned a much broader role for the SEZs than the Kaohsiung zone has had in Taiwan. Besides absorbing foreign capital and technology, the SEZs were also designed to become models of economic reform for the rest of the country.

The operation of the four SEZs, although highly praised by some Party leaders, drew vehement criticism from others. These critics questioned whether a socialist state should set up special zones permitting foreign capitalists to exploit its own labor. Many believed that the four SEZs were a throwback to the concessions existent in the old Treaty Ports, which China had been forced to open to the West in the aftermath of its defeat in the Opium War in 1840.[18] The attacks reached their apex when conservatives launched the anti-spiritual-pollution campaign in late 1983 to check "bourgeois influences." This campaign significantly deterred the influx of foreign capital. To dispel the cloud of opposition, Deng Xiaoping, the author of the open-door policy, made a special inspection tour of three of the four zones in January 1984, and by commenting that "the zones should be developed in a more rapid and thorough manner," he suggested that the PRC should open all coastal areas to foreign investment.[19]

In the wake of Deng's well-publicized visit to the SEZs, the leadership in Beijing decided in April 1984 to designate fourteen cities in the coastal areas plus Hainan Island (which became a province in 1988) in the South China Sea as "open cities," granting the local authorities extensive powers over foreign investment, and offering preferential treatment to foreign inves- tors. The cities involved are Dalian, Qinhuangdao, Tianjin, Yantai, Qindao, Lianyungang, Nantong, Shanghai, Ningbo, Wenzhou, Fuzhou, Guangzhou, Zhanjiang, and Beihai, which represent the most developed areas in the country. Shanghai, Tianjin, and Guangzhou (Canton) are the three leading industrial centers of the country. Together the fourteen cities comprise 78 million people, 7.7 percent of the total population, with a combined investment output value nearly a quarter of the country's total. Moreover, they handled 97 percent of all cargoes exported from China in 1983.[20]

The decision to designate "open cities" stemmed from several consid- erations. First, during the short-lived anti-spiritual-pollution campaign in late 1983, Western investors became concerned that the open-door policy might be abandoned. By opening the fourteen coastal cities, the Chinese leadership sought to reassure foreign investors that its open-door policy would be continued. Second, as the focus of economic reform shifted to the urban sector, the leadership believed that increasing contact with the outside world might enlighten the narrow-minded bureaucracy and help hasten the reshaping of management and economic structures in those cities. Third, because unification with Taiwan is a high priority for Deng, Beijing authorities had been intensifying their efforts to induce Taiwan authorities to enter some sort of negotiation. The opening of the coastal areas directly across the Taiwan Strait represented a part of an overall strategy designed to influence Taiwanese public opinion, for it illustrated Beijing's intention to expand trade with Taiwan and to provide investment opportunity for Taiwanese capital.

In March 1985, the government took a further step by opening three prosperous coastal regions known as the "Golden Coast" to foreign investors. These include the Changjiang (Yangtze) River delta, the Zhujiang (Pearl) River delta, and the Xiamen-Zhangzhou-Quanzhou triangle in southern Fujian Province. In late 1985, the entire Liaodong Peninsula in Shandong Province was added to the list of open areas.

Like the economic reform program, the open-door policy has only partially achieved its goals. By the end of 1988, total pledged direct foreign investment in the PRC amounted to only $19.96 billion, with $7.18 billion actually invested. This amount averaged out to only $700 million a year, representing an inconsequential portion of overall investment needs.[21] Despite all the initial fanfare, both Chinese and foreign investors have become disillusioned. From the Chinese point of view, the open-door policy failed to attract the levels or types of investment it needed for modernization. By the end of 1988, 70 percent of foreign investments had come from overseas Chinese, mostly from Hong Kong, and had been channeled into the adjacent Guangdong Province. U.S. companies had committed just $3.5 billion in equity to some 300 joint ventures—of which two-thirds were worth less than $10 million each.

Conservatives in the PRC have blamed the open-door policy for many social and economic problems. The policy has evoked what Western economists call the "demonstration effect"—the international demonstration of higher consumption standards in more developed countries, which has thereby increased the propensity to consume in the less developed countries. For more than two decades, under the egalitarian principles and Spartan life-style of the Maoist PRC, the standard of living had been kept at a subsistence level. As wages were frozen and all staples were strictly rationed, consumers were denied most modern household appliances. In 1978, when most of the households in Taiwan and Hong Kong owned a color television set, only 1 black-and-white TV was available for every 330 people in the PRC. In 1979, the country produced only 180,000 washing machines and 42,000 refrigerators for a population approaching 1 billion.[22]

The open-door policy brought the population into closer contact with foreigners and overseas Chinese. In 1978, 1.56 million people from Hong Kong and Macao visited the mainland. The number rose to 7.1 million in 1982 and 8.56 million in 1983. In 1987–1988, over a half million Taiwanese visited the PRC. The modern life-styles of the visitors, particularly their access to electric appliances in Hong Kong and Taiwan, were envied and aspired to by those in the PRC. To raise the morale of the people, the leadership decided to loosen its grip on the importation of consumer goods. A flood of consumer appliances sent by relatives and friends in Hong Kong and Southeast Asia (notably Singapore and Thailand) began to fill some Chinese homes. In 1979, Beijing authorities had put development of consumer goods as first priority. Between 1979 and 1983, the Chinese government invested 10.3 billion yuan (about $5 billion) to expand the consumer goods industry. Until the late 1970s, the pinnacle of most Chinese consumers' hopes had been the acquisition of bicycles, wristwatches, and sewing machines. By 1980, TV sets, first black and white, then color, had become the most coveted consumer goods. In recent years, audiocassette and videocassette recorders, washing machines, and refrigerators have been the top items on the consumers' lists. In response to the insatiable demand, output for these items increased dramatically, with a several-hundred-fold increase for certain ones between 1978 and 1988. In 1988, the country produced 24.85 million TV sets, of which 10.28 million were color, 10.46

million washing machines, and 7.4 million refrigerators, ranking it among the largest producers of these products in the world.[23]

The open-door policy facilitated the inflow of some $40 billion of foreign capital (investment and loans) and attracted $10 billion worth of new technology. Yet, simultaneously, it entailed heavy social and economic costs, which were factors in the 1989 unrest.

The Social and Economic Consequences

Although the abolition of the commune system in the rural areas and the termination of the rationing system for staples in the cities brought about a new atmosphere of prosperity and a relaxation of controls, it also brought numerous thorny problems with no easy solutions. The delegation of greater discretionary authority to the enterprises and local government caused a drastic curtailment of state revenues, which in turn seriously affected the structure of the PRC's investment program. First, state revenue as a percentage of national income dropped sharply from 37.2 percent in 1978 to 27.4 percent in 1981 and to only 25.5 percent in 1982. The decrease in state revenue and the increase in state subsidies to agriculture, foreign trade, and state enterprises created huge state deficits. Recent official statistics reveal that between 1979 and 1988 total state subsidies exceeded 500 billion yuan ($135 billion at the 1989 official exchange rate).[24] By the end of 1988, the accumulated deficit exceeded 160 billion yuan. For the year 1988, including internal and external debts, the state deficit was 34 billion yuan; for 1989, 35 billion yuan. To finance the deficit, the state resorted heavily to the issuing of currency, which, in turn, accelerated the process of inflation.

Second, the lax macromanagement also led to the shift of capital investment from central control to local control. During the 1978–1988 period, capital investment outside the central government budget—investment by individual enterprises and local governments—grew from 16.7 percent of total investment to 67 percent. The dispersion of funds caused an overextension of the scale of capital investment. In 1981, the first year of the decentralization, some 71,000 construction projects were started, 11,000 more than the previous year. Of these projects, 34,000 newly constructed factories produced the same kinds of products. In 1982, capital investment rose by 25 percent, resulting in a critical shortage of construction materials. The scale of investment was out of control in 1985, when it rose 42.8 percent over the preceding year, the highest since the Great Leap Forward (1958–1960). Many Chinese economists termed the phenomenon "the hunger for investment."[25]

Third, the dispersal of investment distorted the allocation of capital. Most investment made by local government has been concentrated in light industry, which is concentrated in small plants. Poorly equipped and relatively inefficient, such plants compete with existing large plants for energy and raw materials and thus cause a rapid price rise in those commodities. Although energy and transportation are the two biggest problem areas in the Chinese economy, investment in those two sectors was crowded out by general investment. During the first half of 1985, when investment zeal was at its peak, funds allocated to energy and transportation fell substantially, thus hampering future economic growth.

In sum, the laxity of macrocontrol and the misallocation of capital investment underlay the rapid growth of inflation during those years. The marked economic growth from 1984 to 1988 was constantly fueled by an excessive expansion of aggregate demand from three channels: rising wages and bonuses; capital investment; and banking credit. By the end of 1988, the gap between aggregate demand and aggregate supply grew from 13.6 percent to 16.2 percent. Total excess purchasing power reached a record high of 550 billion yuan ($148.6 billion).[26] The result was the formation of a demand-pull inflation. The official retail price index for large cities shot up from 12.2 percent in 1985 to 31 percent in 1988, but many Chinese economists believed that the inflation rate was really much higher.[27]

Widespread speculation, notably from state-commercial units and government offices, reinforced the inflationary spiral. For more than thirty years, the CCP had been considered a paragon of clean government and egalitarianism. This image has completely disappeared since the inauguration of economic reform. In the process of reform, a new class has emerged, consisting mostly of high government officers and their children. When the CCP reshuffled its Party and government organizations in 1985, a substantial number of children and relatives of influential families were promoted to key positions. Of nine new cabinet ministers appointed in June 1985, at least three were relatives of leading officers. This blatant nepotism has not been limited to government administration but has also spread to upper-echelon positions in state corporations, banking, and trading companies. Referred to as members of the "crown prince party" (*taizi dang*), these privileged Party offspring engaged in all sorts of underhanded practices, enriching themselves at the public's expense.

Official documents and government reports disclose that many Party officials have exploited loopholes in the reform to facilitate illegal financial dealings. Some have set up branch companies enabling fellow cadres, staff members, or their relatives to become shareholders and enjoy the fringe benefits of using the funds, facilities, and personnel of the parent state companies. Others have formed speculating companies that purchase vehicles, steel products, imported consumer appliances, and all kinds of materials urgently needed by society and then resell them at high profits. In one infamous case, the local officials of Hainan Island used their autonomy to engage in collective smuggling.[28] They spent over U.S. $1.5 billion to import 80,000 automobiles and more than 2 million color TV sets as well as tape recorders and motorcycles and resold these goods at considerable profits in other parts of the country.

Chen Yun, former chairman of the Party's Central Commission for Discipline Inspection, summed up the situation in a speech on September 24, 1985:

Whenever we talk about the policy of opening to the world and invigorating the domestic economy, some party, government, and military institutions, party and administrative cadres and their children swarm forward to do business. According to surveys in a dozen provinces and cities, since the last quarter of 1984, some 20,000 various companies have sprung up, a considerable number of which collaborated with law-breakers and unscrupulous foreign businessmen. Taking advantage of reforms, these new companies have been involved in all sorts of criminal activities, including speculating on the rise and fall of prices, engaging in illegal trade, offering or taking bribes and trafficking in smuggled goods. They also have resorted to deception, extortion, evading custom duties, and selling counterfeit medicine and liquor, which are lethal to human lives, just for ill-gotten gains.[29]

Moreover, as we have seen, under the existing multilevel price system, people with special connections could buy one ton of steel at the official price of 700 yuan and immediately resell it at the market price of 2,100 yuan. The price system created many instant millionaires, most of whom were government officials, retired government employees, or the offspring of men in power. The prevalence of "official profiteering" (*guan dao*) has significantly raised the price of raw materials and thereby injected an element of "cost-push" into the rampant inflation.

As a part of the reform, the government encouraged a segment of the population to enrich themselves, hoping that their affluence might stimulate others to emulate them. The rural policy in effect since 1979 allowed specialized households to use their surplus capital to acquire more extensive landholdings, set up transport companies, and invest in local enterprises. These activities led to the emergence of many "10,000-yuan families" (*wanyuan hu*). The rise of an affluent peasant class and the expansion of a new privileged class have markedly widened income disparities. A 1988 official survey revealed that the monthly income of an individual businessman in the Beijing area was about seven times that of a typical middle school teacher; the monthly income of private restaurant owners was ten times that of high school teachers; and many owners of private enterprises had incomes more than ten times that of college professors.[30] Many intellectuals and workers considered the situation unjust and disturbing.

To vent their resentment about poor living conditions, students in several major cities staged large-scale demonstrations in 1985. Workers with fixed incomes also expressed their discontent. In November and December 1985, bus drivers in the Beijing Public Transit System deliberately failed to meet their schedules during the rush hours of a few cold winter mornings in order to dramatize their bitterness about the income gap between public bus drivers and private taxi drivers. More than 10,000 bus drivers openly requested job transfers. Toward the end of 1985, in Henan, several thousand workers in the Loyang tractor plant, the nation's leading tractor producer, staged a sit-in strike to protest the high inflation and the discriminatory apportionment of wages and bonuses among different enterprises. Intentional sabotage also occurred in the railroad system when workers damaged tens of thousands of refrigerators and TV sets, which they themselves could not afford to buy. The social disturbances that erupted had been brewing for several years.

The open-door policy has also produced some unintended casualties. The chief victim has been Communist ideology, ranging from Marxist tenets to Mao's thought, which has suffered general repudiation. For three decades, the leadership has consistently inculcated upon its people "the superiority of the socialist system," maintaining that the capitalist world suffered from decadence and faced imminent collapse. The open door has shown the government's propaganda to be false. When people gradually became aware of the general economic prosperity in Hong Kong, Taiwan, and Singapore as compared to their own primitive and impoverished conditions, they began to distrust socialism, communism, and the leadership of the Communist Party. Many intellectuals openly professed their skepticism about the superiority of the socialist system. Popular disenchantment was reflected in a new trend, in which "foreign" things, ranging from technology, education, and social systems to rock music, blue jeans, and fast foods, were considered superior. The loss of confidence in their own political and economic system and a loss of cultural self-esteem underlay the impending social and economic crises.

The Basic Contradiction

By the middle of 1988, both the economic reform program and the open-door policy had reached a crossroads. The acceleration of inflation and the popular resentment about corruption and speculation forced the reformers to retreat. When the Communist leaders arrived at their beach-resort villas at Beidaihe in summer 1988, the entire program was in disarray. From that time on, the hard-liners gradually began to gain the upper hand, reaching the culmination of their power one year later after the massacre in Tiananmen Square. Some troubles with the reform arose from the program itself, others from the Communist system and from human factors.

The Lack of an Overall Blueprint

From its inception, the reform program in the PRC proceeded on a trial-and-error basis. Tian Jiyun, a vice premier of the State Council, described it as "wading through a river by grasping stone after stone for a solid footing on the river bed" (*mo shi guo he*). The lack of a well-designed, clear, and comprehensive plan undermined the confidence of officials and the people. Because no one knew what the next step of the reform would be, people tended to pursue only immediate gains. In rural areas, peasants adopted the abstraction method of farming (using heavy doses of chemical fertilizers) to maximize their current outputs, ignoring long-term investments. In urban areas, the managers of state enterprises issued bonuses and wage raises indiscriminately to workers and employers. Official statistics showed that between 1983 and 1987, when national income increased 11 percent per annum, workers' wages rose at an annual rate of 16.4 percent; yet labor productivity rose only 5.4 percent. Meanwhile, nonwage income, such as bonuses and other subsidies, rose at an annual rate of 26.4 percent.[31] Because many believed that the reform represented merely a transitional phase that might be rescinded if the political wind changed, they had no incentive for thinking about the long term.

The Lack of Consensus

In Eastern European countries such as Yugoslavia, Hungary, and Poland, economic reforms in the 1950s were partially motivated by nationalism, a desire to resist Soviet suppression and exploitation. A general consensus existed in the ruling hierarchy. No such harmony has developed in the PRC. During its initial stage, the neo-Maoists strongly resisted the reform, claiming that it betrayed Mao's socialist doctrines of egalitarianism, job security, and proletarian dictatorship. In recent years, a schism has opened between the reformers and the conservatives, who desire a return to the policies pursued in the 1950s, a time which they consider the country's golden age. The conservatives have drawn attention to the rising income disparities, widespread speculation, profiteering, and other social evils and have attributed these vices to the economic reform.

The discord in the Party surfaced in September 1985 when Deng Xiaoping and Chen Yun, the two most powerful leaders in the PRC, aired their clashing views at the Party's Congress of Delegates (see Chapter 3). The open split between these two top leaders aroused further skepticism among Party members and the general population. The lack of government consensus was reflected in the publication in an official government periodical of an article asking: "Is socialist China undergoing a crisis of values? Have the economic reforms set off a general scramble for money and material things above all else? Has China's policy of opening to the outside world allowed decadent ideas and habits to creep in?"[32]

The Absence of a Legal Framework

Throughout the entire period under Communist control, the country has been without civil laws. The reform introduced many new changes in the way of conducting business. Economic levers were supposed to replace administrative controls. The relationship among enterprises and between enterprises and the government agents was to be transformed from a vertical to a horizontal relationship, with a chain of command replaced by mutual negotiations. Many of their transactions were to be carried out by bilateral contracts. In rural areas, the contract system replaced unified purchases. A legal framework has become indispensable for the functioning of these new setups as well as for the drafting of new contracts with foreign investors and traders. The lack of a comprehensive legal system in the PRC has been a hindrance to attracting foreign investment and solidifying the reform.

Officials not only disregarded the need for a Western legal system but also demonstrated a general indifference toward existing restraints. Lawbreaking became the symbol of power. The weaknesses of the legal system stimulated many "unhealthy tendencies" (official term for corruption, speculation, and so forth), with the situation worsening during the decade of reform. Bo Yibo, vice chairman of the Party's Central Advisory Commission, lamented that "a rather outstanding problem in our society has been the replacing of law with the individual with power. Many problems in Party style and social behavior are closely related to the slackness in discipline and law." Bo appealed to the Party's leading cadres "to acquire a knowledge of law, study the constitution and all kinds of statutes; and to act according to the law."[33] Bo's statement clearly indicates that the lack of a legal system has become an obstacle to economic reform.

The Influence of Old Ideas and the Old System

The 1980s reforms were carried out in a transitional period; hence, many elements and ideas of the old system were still commonplace in society. The most deep-seated of the traditions, the egalitarian system of "eating from the same big pot," still dominated Chinese thinking and behavior. Thus, as we have seen, the bonus system rewarded good and poor workers alike. In fact, the entire Chinese industrial system has continued to operate this way. Profitable enterprises paid exceedingly high taxes in order to keep the inefficient enterprises afloat. In recent years, because of the increasing income disparity between peasants engaged in rural industries and those engaged in farming, the government began collecting high taxes from industry to subsidize the peasants, another de facto revival of the "big pot" policy. This policy has resulted in the depression of rural industries without any discernible improvement in farmers' productivity.

Another entrenched barrier, the one between different government ministries and between different localities, has also been maintained to the detriment of the development of a nationwide market. Despite numerous regulations, the old structure that separates economic activities in one governmental department or locality from another has not changed. Many mandatory plans continued to be carried out through the original channels in various departments and localities. Decision-making power has remained concentrated either in local authorities or in monopolistic companies. To increase its tax base, each locality in recent years protected its own interests by setting up processing plants in its territory and restricting or banning the movement of raw materials to other places. Local authorities have even set up checkpoints along provincial or district borders to collect duties on goods delivered to other localities. Materials in short supply have not been allowed to move out of their region of origin. These lingering attitudes and behavior stem from the reliance of Chinese society on public support for forty years. Many see the "big pot" as providing a safety net for their lives. At the same time, those in power tend to view their ministry or their locality as their own kingdom and refuse to share their power with others.

The Low Quality of Personnel

Any successful reform, ultimately, can be achieved only through the devoted efforts of large numbers of energetic, well-educated, and sincere people. Of the 47 million Party members and the 27 million government bureaucrats (many are both), fewer than 2 percent received a college education. Although many top leaders and intellectuals see the reform as the only hope for the country, a good number of middle-echelon bureaucrats believe it directly threatens their authority and privileges and have sought to stall the program and sabotage the reform. In some units where reformers were in the minority, interest groups engaged in a variety of schemes to bring the reformers down, such as isolating them or blaming them for all setbacks. In recent years, the official news media have carried reports of reformers having been "shot off their horses" (*zhong jian xia ma*), or outmaneuvered by the interest groups that have seized power.

Some of the reformers are incompetent or lack the willpower to persevere with the reform. Others cannot carry out the policies because of their lack of experience. Deng Xiaoping identified the shortage of qualified personnel as the most critical problem facing the reform. In a 1986 interview with well-known Hong Kong capitalists, Deng concluded: "Our weaknesses and difficulties in carrying out the Four Modernizations are mainly the result of the lack of knowledge and qualified personnel. But sufficient knowledge and qualified personnel cannot be obtained overnight."[34]

Above all, the leaders' ideology and the Party's monopoly on power have been major obstacles to reform. Despite many novel proposals, the Chinese leadership still adheres to the orthodox ideology. In March 1979, Deng declared on behalf of the Party's central leadership, "In order to realize the Four Modernizations in China, we must uphold the four basic political and ideological principles—Communist leadership, socialist road, proletarian dictatorship, and Marxism-Leninism and Mao Zedong thought."[35] Eight years later, the CCP Thirteenth Party Congress adopted a new party line: One Central Task and Two Basic Points. "One Central Task" referred to a focus on economic construction. Of the "Two Basic Points," one called for carrying out economic reform and the open-door policy; the other, for adherence to Deng's Four Cardinal Principles. In the opinion of many young Chinese, the Four Cardinal Principles have been a built-in obstacle, negating the implementation of the reform program.

The leadership is thus caught in a dilemma. To revitalize the economy and modernize the society, the leadership must discard many of Mao's radical and outdated visions. Yet, to legitimize its monopoly on political power, the regime must uphold the four principles, which include Maoism and the doctrine of proletarian dictatorship (later changed to "people's democratic dictatorship"—without altering its content). By simultaneously pursuing two contradictory lines—a pragmatic economic policy and a leftist ideology— the leadership created profound confusion among the cadres and dampened the enthusiasm and shook the faith of the masses.

Like other Communist parties in power, the Chinese Communist Party has wielded considerable influence over the entire population because the Party commands most facets of ordinary life, makes decisions that are above the law, and gives its members a special status in society. In the PRC, members and nonmembers of the Party are not equal before the law. When Party members commit crimes, they are punished by the Party's discipline inspection organizations. Only when so instructed by the Party can judicial organs prosecute Party members for violating laws. The Party has five disciplinary measures: warning, serious warning, removal from Party posts, being put on probation within the Party, and expulsion from the Party. These measures do not adequately deter illegal activities, as collusion and mutual protection exist among cadres at every level of government administration. In most cases, the convicted member merely changes from one job to another or from one locale to another. Seldom have Party members been severely punished. This explains why the Party's frequent rectification campaigns and anticorruption movements have borne very little fruit.

The Mounting Crisis

By the middle of 1988, Deng's reform programs were encountering tremendous difficulties. Foremost was skyrocketing inflation. After thirty-five years of ostensible price stability, inflation began to affect the entire population. By official reckoning, the rate of inflation was relatively moderate. The government retail price index reflected a rise of 12.5 percent in 1985, 7 percent in 1986, 7.2 percent in 1987, and 18.5 percent in 1988. The real effects, however, were far more severe.

In the PRC's statistics system, the official index reflected the overall price changes of both agricultural and industrial products. An especially sharp rise in the price of food was offset by price reductions in certain expensive consumer durable items in the total index calculations. But because consumers spent half or more of their income on food, the food component of the price index was the most important.

In 1987, while the retail price index rose only 7.2 percent, the price of all food increased 10.1 percent, and the price of meat, poultry, and eggs rose 16.5 percent.[36] In the first quarter of 1988, the national retail price index rose another 11 percent. Prices for nonstaple foods went up by 24.2 percent, with a dramatic rise of 48.7 percent in the prices of fresh vegetables.[37] Consumers panicked in mid-May when the government, in order to stimulate production, decided to raise prices for pork, eggs, vegetables, and sugar in state-run stores by 30 percent to 60 percent. To avoid social unrest, the government issued additional subsidies to wage earners of up to 10 yuan (about $3) a month per person.[38] As the subsidies amounted to less than half the price hike, the price rise further strained the already taut family budgets of most urban residents.

As discussed in the preceding section, the causes of the inflation were multiple. Excessive expansion in consumption, investment, and the money supply prompted an upward adjustment of prices for raw materials, fuel, transportation, and public services. During the price reform period, substantial increases in wages and bonuses and the speculative activities of profiteers were also contributing factors. To control the runaway inflation, the conservatives, led by Premier Li Peng, initiated an austerity plan in September 1988 to cut investment and the money supply in the hope that the inflation rate could be kept below 10 percent in 1989. However, government statistics showed that in the first half of 1989 the inflation rate soared 25.5 percent over the preceding period. For major cities, the rate exceeded 40 percent.[39]

Although the inflation rate did come down in the second half of 1989, the annual rate for 1989 still reached 17 percent. The failure to halt the inflationary spiral stems from two basic factors. First, the causes of inflation lie deep in the structure of the economy. Unless the structure is changed, administrative measures can be effective only in the short term. Second, local governments ignore most orders from the central government. Studies on the Chinese economy show that the country has experienced three cycles of inflation in the past decade. In the first cycle (1979–1980), the cause of inflation was primarily overinvestment. A sharp curtailment of investment halted the inflation. The second cycle (1981–1984) brought an inflation caused by both overinvestment and overconsumption. A simple reduction of investment failed to check this inflation. In the third cycle, which began in 1985, the rise of consumption expenditure far exceeded production.[40] In January 1989, when the output value of state-controlled industrial enterprises rose only 3.7 percent, workers' wages rose 61 percent and money supply, 50 percent. The central government's directive to cut consumption and investment was again mostly unheeded.

The persistence of inflation is closely related to agricultural stagnation and the energy crisis. The first affects people's food basket; the latter affects industrial production. The PRC's agriculture made great strides after the institution of the contract system and the boost of procurement prices for agricultural products. Output for all major products peaked in 1984. Since then, although the purchase price of grain has remained relatively low, prices of other agricultural and industrial products have grown, causing many farmers to move out of grain production. Rising prices for chemical fertilizers, diesel oil, and farm tools have further compounded the problem. Moreover, public and private capital investment in agriculture fell steadily from 11 percent of total investment in 1979 to only 3 percent in 1988. Consequently, infrastructure in rural areas deteriorated. Irrigation facilities were not being properly maintained, and floods and drought became more serious with each passing year. Since 1985, output of grain, cotton, and edible oils has stagnated. Per capita production of grains was 33 kg less in 1988 than in 1984. Output of pork and sugar all fell far short of demand.[41] The decline of cotton was even sharper, falling 33 percent from the 1984 peak.

Apart from policy mistakes, the steady deterioration of the land-labor ratio in the PRC has constituted the major obstacle to agricultural progress. During the thirty-one years from 1957 to 1988, the PRC's total acreage of arable land declined by 15 percent, while in the same period, its population rose by more than 80 percent. The decrease in farmland is the result of many factors, notably, the large scale housing construction in rural areas, rapid expansion of construction sites for village industries, and division of farmland. The lost land—1.32 million acres—is equivalent to the total arable area of the three provinces of Liaoning, Sichuan, and Hebei. Between 1957 and 1988, the amount of arable land per capita shrank from 0.427 acres to only 0.22 acres.[42] A continuous decrease of arable land caused farmers to use more fertilizer, substantially raising production costs and dampening the farmers' incentive. The gap between demand and supply of food grains reached a dangerous point in 1988. An official survey showed that in 1953 twenty-one out of twenty-six provinces and autonomous regions throughout the nation were net exporters of grain. By 1988, there were only five in this category. As every province and region has experienced the fear of a grain shortage, the market prices have shot up and there has been panic buying.[43]

No less important than the stagnation of agriculture is the shortage of energy supplies and transportation facilities. In the 1960s, the PRC was seen as a potential exporter of petroleum. The development of the oil fields in Daqing, Heilongjiang, and the projections of offshore oil fields in the East China and South China seas led to sanguine predictions that the PRC would soon replace Saudi Arabia and Iran as the world's chief oil supplier. But the prophecy was never fulfilled. When production at Daqing leveled off after 1978 and discoveries of other oil fields failed to materialize, output of petroleum stagnated. The country's major energy source was still coal. While output of coal rose from 618 million metric tons in 1978 to 970 million metric tons in 1988, an increase of 56.9 percent, with an annual growth rate of 4.6 percent, the value of industrial output grew at more than 10 percent a year. In recent years, the shortage of coal supplies blocked the growth of electricity. Insufficient electricity has idled between 20 to 30 percent of the country's industrial capacity. The loss of industrial output in 1988 was estimated at more than 100 billion yuan ($27 billion). In spring 1989, Beijing suffered a 24 percent shortfall of electricity. In the southern province of Guangdong, the electricity supply can meet only 50 percent of demand and has become the most severe hindrance in industrial development.

Both the agricultural stagnation and sluggishness of energy growth are related to the critical shortage of capital directed to those sectors. As mentioned above, the PRC's state budget has operated at a deficit since 1979; the government has had not only to raise enormous funds for capital investments but also to bear the heavy burden of financial subsidization. Because of backward management, bureaucracy, overstaffing, and an irrational control system, one-fourth to one-third of the state enterprises operate at a loss year after year, and the state subsidizes them. In recent years, the deficit increased markedly when the state raised price subsidies for urban workers and employees; it increased also because of losses from below-cost exports of commodities.

Yearly trade deficits since 1984 have also drained the country's financial resources. Between 1984 and 1988, The PRC's total international trade deficit reached $39.57 billion. Most of the deficit was financed through foreign borrowing. During the period 1985–1988, foreign debts grew at an annual rate of 38 percent and accumulated debts totaled $40 billion by the end of 1988. About 50 percent of the debt was financed by Japan and denominated in Japanese yen. Because the PRC's foreign trade is calculated in U.S. dollars, the 50 percent appreciation of the yen against the dollar in that period substantially increased the debt burden, which must be repaid in 1992 and 1993. It is officially estimated that by 1993 the repayment of principle and interest on foreign debt will account for 25 percent of the PRC's total exports, surpassing the 20 percent warning level set up by the International Monetary Fund. This will further limit the country's capacity to invest in infrastructure and energy development.[44]

Unemployment is yet another intractable problem confronting the PRC. Officially, unemployment has been a taboo subject because it can only exist in capitalist countries. For years, the government used the term "awaiting employment" (*dai ye*) to refer to the unemployed. Recently, government statistics began to report an unemployment rate that was so low (1.5–2 percent) that no one believed it was reliable. In 1988, the official news media began publishing a series of surveys that showed that in Shanghai and many major industrial centers, at least 14 to 25 percent of the total work force was "latently unemployed." This referred to superfluous personnel, many of whom were in state enterprises. One official report gave a figure of 20 million surplus workers in state enterprises throughout the country. Others raised the number to 30 million.[45] The cost to the state of those people who are officially employed but lack job assignments and who spend their work time playing cards or watching television is 60 billion yuan per year. The existence of this huge disguised unemployment in the state economic orbit prevents any improvement in labor productivity. According to a survey of several hundred factories in sixteen industries in Shanghai, without overstaffing, labor productivity could be increased by 26 percent. Paying salaries and bonuses to superfluous personnel prevents the reform of the wage system and the enterprises.[46]

While the PRC's labor force has been increasing at a rate of 20 million per year, those who have not been able to get into the state enterprises could only be hired as low-paid temporary workers. Unemployed people travel from one city to another seeking job opportunities, creating a 50-million-strong "fluid population," with neither job nor home. Most of them sleep in railway stations, parks, and urban slums, causing problems for public traffic and social order.

In contrast to the unemployed and fluid population, people with official connections can easily locate high-paying jobs. Once a person occupies such a position, his family members and relatives will slip in and form a net of personnel who protect each other and engage in unchecked corruption. The system of personal connections has also bred extravagance. Government officials spent large portions of public funds to construct administrative buildings, resort hotels, and guest houses. Almost all government departments and Party organizations purchased expensive imported cars. They also indulged in endless lavish banquets. When the National People's Congress convened its annual session in March 1989, Beijing residents were shocked by the hundreds of expensive, foreign luxury cars in the parking lot of the People's Assembly Hall. A *People's Daily* reporter identified 495 out of 556 automobiles as expensive cars, such as Mercedeses and Cadillacs. Only 37 were made in the PRC.[47] On March 27, 1989, the very day that the premier appealed to the Chinese people to tighten their belts for several years, 150 state enterprises jointly staged a fashion show that featured Parisian models wearing evening gowns costing $10,000 apiece. The contrast between the extravagant life-style and conspicuous consumption of the nouveau riche and the subsistence-level existence of most of the population has generated popular resentment, especially in the face of inflationary budget strains.

The Popular Demand for Change

Events prior to summer 1988 indicated that the positive results of the reform in the initial years (1979–1984) had been gradually overtaken by negative effects in the later years. As inflation accelerated and official corruption and speculation ran rampant, social discontent was brewing. Zhao Ziyang, then Party general secretary, in October 1988, delivered a speech in which he frankly admitted: "The vast majority of the people are in favor of the reforms. The concerns that are troubling them are related to three main problems: (1) escalation of commodity prices; (2) unjust remuneration for their work in society; (3) certain manifestations of corruption in the organs of Party and government."[48]

The ruling authorities lacked a consensus on how to deal with these problems. The reformers contended that unless reforms were carried on more vigorously, the efforts of the previous ten years would have been in vain. Believing that all social and economic maladies were rooted in the state ownership of industries and in the one-party system, they proposed privatization and democratization.

In spring 1989, three economists associated with Zhao Ziyang presented a bold proposal in which they stated that public ownership would no longer be the premise of socialism. A new definition of socialism, focusing on broad issues of social justice, such as equality of opportunity, instead of public ownership of the means of production, was needed. They argued that when companies are owned by the state, the government interferes with their efficient management and the companies themselves try to maximize benefits for the employees rather than concentrating on profits and productivity. In the long run, they believed, society and workers suffer because the economy is unable to grow robustly. The companies would do better if they had owners whose sole interest lay in seeing them perform efficiently and profitably.[49] In the wake of the publication of this proposal, several other proposals were made regarding the sale of farmland to the tillers and a move toward a system of share-holding ownership.[50]

In the political realm, demands for democracy became open and widespread. On March 23, 1989, Xu Simin, an outspoken delegate from Hong

Kong to the Seventh National Chinese People's Political Consultative Conference, directly appealed to the CCP for democracy in a strongly rhetorical speech. He challenged Deng to imitate the later years of Chiang Ching-kuo, the late president of the Republic of China in Taiwan, in promoting political liberalization. Xu lauded Chiang's abolition of the law forbidding opposition parties and his permission for the publication of new newspapers. Xu also blasted the official slogan "stability and unity" as an excuse for prohibiting people to speak their minds. He stated emphatically:

> The present situation of unchecked corruption is extremely dangerous. Unless we make urgent plans to establish a democratic political system, unless we are able to stir up the enthusiasm of the millions of the masses to join in a common effort to overcome the present difficulties, then it will be very difficult to keep the Chinese Communist Party, which I have supported, from continuing to sink further and further into corruption, even to the point of final self-destruction.[51]

Several Chinese newspapers in Hong Kong and North America published editorials in support of Xu Simin and applauded him as the most forthright delegate at the conference, one who spoke with the genuine voice of the Chinese people.

The hard-liners viewed the social and economic chaos in a different light. They believed it resulted from lax central control and the failure of ideological indoctrination. They fiercely attacked Zhao's overheated economic policy and his neglect of ideological education. The hard-liners' solution to the economic maladies included: (1) a sharp curtailment of capital investment by 20 percent in 1989 and 1990 by eliminating tens of thousands of construction projects; (2) the suspension of all price reforms and a partial resumption of price controls; (3) the recovery of partial control over taxes, finance, pricing, and foreign exchange from local governments; (4) the regularization of the economy and the reestablishment of party discipline.

To counter popular demands for democratization, the hard-liners advanced the theory that what the PRC urgently needed was not democracy but stability and unity. On March 10, 1989, the Party organ *People's Daily* launched a propaganda offensive to push the new line. The paper claimed that "if we want to carry out regularization of our economic order and the deepening of the economic reform, the most important condition is the maintenance of political stability. Without a stable political environment, nothing can be accomplished."

In support of the call for stability there were articles and symposia promoting "neoauthoritarianism," a theory derived from the ideas of Samuel P. Huntington. Huntington took the countries of East Asia and Southeast Asia, especially the "Four Little Dragons"—Taiwan, South Korea, Singapore, and Hong Kong—as a case study to advance his thesis that in a period of transition from an agrarian economy to that of an industrial society, a country must be ruled by a relatively strong central government. The authoritarian governments of the countries cited were made up of a mixture of political elites and technocratic specialists. The centralization of political powers enabled those governments to achieve social stability and rapid economic development. It also allowed them to postpone a number of phenomena that regularly accompany modernization, such as the rise of labor unions, development of a multiparty system, and growth of environmental movements.[52]

The core of this new campaign urged the establishment of an authority to deal with the economic failure and political chaos. The proponents of neoauthoritarianism maintained that economic reforms developed into chaos because they lacked strong central authority. Only a political elite or a political strongman could form a governing body with a degree of authority high enough to guarantee the orderly development of the economy.[53]

Although some of the original proponents were supporters of Zhao Ziyang and there was a wide split in the liberal camp over the issue, the majority of the reformers rejected neoauthoritarianism. They pointed out that the PRC was a de facto totalitarian state. The people did not enjoy even the limited freedoms existing in authoritarian East Asian countries, such as the publication of independent newspapers, the existence of opposition parties, the selection of government officials at provincial and local levels through general elections, and the guarantee of private property. According to the reformers, the problem the PRC was facing was the abuse of power by a Communist Party unchecked by an independent legislature, judiciary, or public opinion. The government, they maintained, exercised arbitrary power over all aspects of life. Further centralization of power would be futile because the current disorder arose, not from the absence of central power, but from the misuse of the existing power without scientific analysis or democratic consultations. In their view, neoauthoritarianism was a regressive approach. It advocated government by the will of an individual and the function of the strongman. It overlooked the fact that such a transformation could only lead to a dictatorial regime.

The popular demand for freedom and openness, for curtailing the special privileges of the new class,[54] versus the rulers' emphasis on stability and the promotion of neoauthoritarianism, constitutes a sharp clash of views. The interaction of these currents presaged an enormous social and political storm that finally erupted from mid-May to early June in Beijing's Tiananmen Square and in several other Chinese cities.

Notes

1. Chu-yuan Cheng, "Economic Reform in Mainland China: Consequences and Prospects," *Issues and Studies* (Taipei) 22, No. 12 (Dec. 1986), pp. 13–44.

2. He Jiangzhang, "Problems and Direction of Reform for the Planning and Management System in the Public Ownership of our Country," *Jingji Yanjiu* [Economic research] (Beijing), No. 5 (May 1979), pp. 35–36.

3. Liu Baifu, "The Way of Agriculture," *Beijing Review* 26, No. 4 (Jan. 24, 1983), pp. 14–17.

4. Jan S. Prybyla, "*Pao-kan Tao-hu:* The Other Side," *Issues and Studies* 22, No. 1 (Jan. 1986), p. 66.

5. PRC State Statistical Bureau, *Statistical Yearbook of China* (Hong Kong: Jingji Daobao Shi, 1984).

6. *New York Times,* Feb. 21, 1987, p. 26.

7. Li Rongxia, "Tertiary Industry Takes Off in China," *Beijing Review* 30, No. 5–6 (Feb. 9, 1987), pp. 18–19.

8. For details see Chu-yuan Cheng, "China's Economic Reform at the Crossroads," in Shao-chuan Leng, ed., *Changes in China: Party, State and Society* (New York: University Press of America, 1989), pp. 147–174.

9. *World Economic Herald* (Shanghai), July 7, 1986.

10. *Beijing Review* 29, No. 11 (March 17, 1986), p. 4.

11. "Decision of the Central Committee of the Communist Party on Reform of the Economic Structure," *Beijing Review* 27, No. 44 (Oct. 29, 1984), pp. i–xv.

12. *China Daily* (Beijing), March 8, 1986, p. 1.

13. The four SEZs are Shenzhen, near Hong Kong; Zhuhai, located directly opposite Macao; Shantou, in the eastern part of Guangdong; and Xiamen, located in southeast Fujian.

14. Chu-yuan Cheng, "Economic Development in Mainland China Since the Twelfth Party Congress," *American-Asian Review* (New York), Summer 1983, pp. 47–48.

15. Ma Hong, "On Steps to Achieve the Strategic Objective," *People's Daily* (Beijing), Oct. 28–29, 1982, p. 5.

16. See Hu's interview with Japanese newspapers, reported by Reuters, Tokyo, June 4, 1984.

17. Xue Yaozhong, "A Vital Decision Meets Reality," *Liao-wan* [The outlook weekly] (Beijing) 45 (Nov. 5, 1984), p. 4.

18. Xu Dixin, "China's Special Economic Zones," *Beijing Review,* No. 50 (Dec. 14, 1981), pp. 14–16.

19. *Jingji Guanli* [Economic management], No. 9 (1984), pp. 53–59.

20. *Guangming Ribao* (Beijing), June 11, 1984.

21. Yin Ruxiang and Li Ronglin, "On the Problems of Investment Environment in China," *Nankai Economic Journal* (Tianjin), No. 2 (Apr. 1989), p. 21.

22. Li Chaochen, "Consumer Revolution in Domestic Appliances," *China Reconstructs* (Beijing), No. 6 (June 1984), pp. 33–35.

23. PRC State Statistical Bureau, "Consequences for 1988 Economic Development," *People's Daily,* March 2, 1989, p. 3.

24. *People's Daily,* July 24, 1989, p. 8.

25. Fang Gungwen, "Correctly Evaluate the 1985 Reform of the Economic Structure," *Guangming Ribao,* March 22, 1986, p. 3.

26. *Qiushi* [Seeking truth] (Beijing), No. 6 (1989), p. 14.

27. For instance, Qian Jiaju, a noted Chinese economist, has criticized the official price indexes as grossly understating the real inflation rate, *China Daily News* (New York), Apr. 14, 1986, p. 2.

28. *China Reconstructs,* No. 5 (1986), p. 28.

29. *Beijing Review* 28, No. 41 (Oct. 4, 1985), pp. 15–16.

30. *Jingji Ribao* [Economic daily] (Beijing), Feb. 22, 1988.

31. *Qiushi,* No. 6 (1989), p. 16.

32. I Hsu, "Corruption: Why It Occurs, What's Being Done?" *China Reconstructs,* No. 5 (1986), p. 26.

33. Foreign Broadcast Information Service (FBIS), Apr. 4, 1986, pp. K15–K16.

34. *Ta Kung Pao* (Hong Kong), Apr. 20, 1986, p. 1.

35. *Selected Works of Deng Xiaoping* (in Chinese) (Beijing: Renmin Chubanshe, 1983), p. 150.

36. PRC State Statistical Bureau, "Statistics for 1987 Socio-Economic Development," *People's Daily*, Feb. 24, 1988.

37. *Beijing Review* 31, No. 18 (May 2–8, 1988), p. 12.

38. *New York Times*, May 10, 1988.

39. *People's Daily*, July 13, 1989.

40. *Zhongguo Jingji Tizhi Gaige* [Reform of China's economic system] (Beijing), No. 1 (1989), pp. 16–19.

41. Ji Yicheng, "Renewed Emphasis on Agricultural Reform," *China Reconstructs* 37, No. 6 (June 1988), pp. 11–15.

42. Xinhua News Agency, Beijing, Apr. 2, 1989.

43. Ibid. The incentive effect of the contract responsibility system is quite evident.

44. Zhang Pingbeng, "Could China Avoid a Debt Crisis?" *Guoji Maoyi* [Intertrade monthly] (Beijing), No. 1 (Jan. 1989), pp. 36–38.

45. *Jingji Ribao*, Sept. 7, 1988, p. 1, and *People's Daily*, July 29, 1988, p. 5.

46. *People's Daily*, July 29, 1988, p. 5.

47. *People's Daily*, Apr. 4, 1989.

48. *People's Daily*, Oct. 28, 1988, p. 1.

49. Nicholas D. Kristof, "In China, a Bold Proposal to Ease State Ownership," *New York Times*, Jan. 10, 1989, pp. 1, 4.

50. See Li Yining, professor of economics at Beijing University, speech delivered to the University of Hong Kong in January 1989, published in *Pai Hsing* [The people] (Hong Kong), Jan. 16, 1989.

51. *Pai Hsing*, Apr. 16, 1989, pp. 9–10.

52. Samuel P. Huntington, *Political Order in Changing Societies* (New Haven: Yale University Press, 1969).

53. *Pai Hsing*, March 16, 1989, pp. 48–49.

54. The widespread discontent of the reform and popular demand for change is fully reflected in a detailed study by the All-China Federation of Trade Unions released for internal circulation in 1987. The study based on 770,000 questionnaires collected from 29 provinces reveals an "uneasy public mood" toward the reform beginning in 1985 and accelerating over the next few years. For details see Stanley Rosen, ed., "The All-China Federation of Trade Union's Survey of China's Workers and Staff," *Chinese Economic Studies* (Armonk, N.Y.) Summer 1989, pp. 1–110.

3

Ideological Schism and Power Struggle

The demonstrations in Tiananmen Square can be interpreted as a reflection of the mounting popular discontent of the people. But the decision to crack down on the protesters can be understood only as having occurred within the framework of an intra-Party power struggle. Power alignments, personal influences, and ideological disputes had led to fierce behind-the-scenes contention in the top hierarchy of the CCP, and prodemocracy demonstrators became the pawns of the two rivals for power—Zhao Ziyang and Li Peng. The downfall of Zhao, who had been Deng's heir apparent, the rapid ascent of Li Peng and Yang Shangkun, and the appointment of the relatively unknown Jiang Zemin as Party general secretary all came out of the stormy struggle that occurred in the top hierarchy during spring and summer 1989. This chapter focuses on the power structure of the CCP, the oscillations of the party line, the Machiavellian power plays of Deng Xiaoping, the intensified factional strife for Deng's succession, and the showdown between Zhao Ziyang and Li Peng that directly triggered the brutal slaughter of the demonstrators.

The Power Structure

Power in the CCP is centered in the Party's Central Committee, particularly the Political Bureau (Politburo). At the Party's thirteenth congress, which convened from October 25 to November 1, 1987, the Central Committee selected seventeen members for its Politburo—Zhao Ziyang, Li Peng, Qiao Shi, Hu Qili, Yao Yilin, Wan Li, Tian Jiyun, Jiang Zemin, Li Tieying, Li Ruihuan, Li Ximing, Yang Rudai, Yang Shangkun, Wu Xueqian, Song Ping, Hu Yaobang, and Qin Jiwei—and one alternate, Ding Guan-gen. Five of the Politburo members (Zhao, Li Peng, Qiao Shi, Hu Qili, and Yao Yilin) served on the Standing Committee, responsible for major decision-making. The day-to-day decisions were entrusted to the Central Secretariat, with Zhao, the general secretary, serving as the de facto chief of the Party. Four secretaries—Hu Qili, Qiao Shi, Rui Xingwen, and Yan Mingfu—and one alternate secretary, Wen Jiabao, assisted Zhao in the business of the Party.

Under the Central Committee are three major power bases, in which most of the Party veterans are concentrated. The Central Military Commission, headed by Deng Xiaoping until November 1989, is the most powerful organization because of its control of the army. The Central Advisory Commission, headed by Chen Yun, is the headquarters of the conservatives. The Central Commission for Discipline Inspection, headed by Qiao Shi, lost much of its prestige after Chen Yun left his post as its head in 1987.

Of the existing power holders, the most influential were eight octogenarians. In spring 1989, at the peak of the power pyramid were Deng Xiaoping (85) and Chen Yun (84). Next to Deng and Chen were Yang Shangkun (83), state president and permanent vice chairman of the Central Military Commission; Wang Zhen (82), state vice president; Li Xiannian (86), former state president and chairman of the Chinese People's Political Consultative Conference; Peng Zhen (83), former chairman, Standing Committee of the National People's Congress (NPC—the parliament); Bo Yibo (82), vice chairman, Central Advisory Commission; and Song Renqiong (80), military leader and also vice chairman of the Central Advisory Commission. These men (with the exception of Yang Shangkun) were no longer members of the Politburo but had not been deprived of their authority.

The party elders, although each supports his own protégés, share some common experiences and have a common outlook: (1) They all participated in the historic Long March of 1934–1935, in which more than 100,000 Communists set out on a march of over 6,000 miles, with the Kuomintang (KMT) (Chinese Nationalist) forces in hot pursuit. Because only 8,000 survived the Long March, participation became a valuable qualification for the top leadership. (2) They all experienced persecution during the turbulent years of the Cultural Revolution. (3) They joined forces in the struggle against the Gang of Four and took part in the maneuver to oust Mao's appointee Hua Guofeng. (4) They all adhere to the Four Cardinal Principles proclaimed by Deng in 1979. (5) With the exception of Deng, they are conservatives. Sharing these common ties, the octogenarians tend to band together when the Party confronts any severe crisis. Their solidarity during the 1989 upheaval was characteristic.

The daily functions of the Party and the state machine are carried out by the second and third echelons of the leadership. Most of the officials in the second echelon are in their late sixties and early seventies and fought in the Sino-Japanese War and in the civil war against the KMT. Since most have Party and administrative experience at the provincial level, they tend to be less dogmatic and more adaptive to changing circumstances than the old veterans. However, they lack the cohesiveness of the veterans and have been inclined to engage in building their own power bases. Notable among them have been Hu Yaobang, who served as Party chief (general secretary) from 1982 to 1986 and whose death on April 15, 1989, triggered the student protests; Zhao Ziyang, who served as premier between 1982 and 1986 and as Party general secretary between 1987 and June 1989; Yao Yilin, vice premier in charge of economic affairs; Wan Li, chairman of the National People's Congress; Jiang Zemin, the new general secretary and former mayor and Party secretary of Shanghai; Li Ruihuan, a new member of the Standing Committee of the Politburo, who served as mayor of Tianjin; Qin Jiwei, the defense minister and former commander of the Beijing Military Region; Li Ximing, Party secretary of the CCP's Beijing Committee; and Song Ping, another new member of the Standing Committee of the Politburo.

The third echelon consists of many of the Party's rising stars, such as Li Peng (premier), Hu Qili (close associate of Zhao Ziyang and former member of the Standing Committee of the Politburo), Qiao Shi (chairman of the Central Commission for Discipline Inspection), Tian Jiyun (vice premier), Li Tieying (Politburo member and councillor of the State Council in charge of education), and Yan Mingfu (former member of the Secretariat and director of the CCP United Front Department). Most of these men are in their fifties and hail from the post–1949 revolution generation. The majority of them are college educated and technocratic by training.

At the time of Mao's death, leaders in the first and second echelons promoted political and economic reforms that repudiated the policies of the later years of Mao's life and precluded the recurrence of an episode like the Cultural Revolution. Within this context, all of them could be considered reformers. However, in the wake of the downfall of Hua Guofeng and his associates, a gap emerged between two wings of the reform movement. In this book, the emergent two wings have been classified as "conservatives" and "reformers."[1] Prior to the Tiananmen incident, leaders gradually became aligned with one of the two wings. The power alignment is illustrated in Tables 3.1 and 3.2.

Chinese officials have never admitted the existence of these two cliques. Zhao Ziyang, at his press conference after the Thirteenth Party Congress, replied very sharply to a question from a journalist about "conservatives" and "reformers," categorically denying that any factions existed in the Chinese Communist Party. However, policy disputes, personal connections, and various institutions all point to the fact that the cliques or factions do indeed exist.[2]

Newspapers and periodicals provide more evidence. During the period when Hu Yaobang and Zhao Ziyang controlled the Party center, the *People's Daily* became the mouthpiece of the reformers. On December 7, 1984, the *People's Daily* carried a commentary that implicitly denounced Marxism as

TABLE 3.1
Power Alignment in the PRC (April 1, 1989)

Sphere of Influence	Reformers	Conservatives	Undetermined
Politburo			
Standing Committee	Zhao Ziyang	Li Peng	Qiao Shi
	Hu Qili	Yao Yilin	
Members	Wan Li	Yang Shangkun	
	Tian Jiyun	Li Ximing	
	Jiang Zemin	Song Ping	
	Li Ruihuan		
	Qin Jiwei		
	Yang Rudai		
	Li Tieying		
	Hu Yaobang		
	Wu Xueqian		
Alternate		Ding Guan-gen	
Central Secretariat			
General secretary	Zhao Ziyang		
Secretaries	Hu Qili		Qiao Shi
	Rui Xingwen		
	Yan Mingfu		
Alternate	Wen Jiabao		
Central Military Commission			
Chairman	Deng Xiaoping		
First vice chairman	Zhao Ziyang		
Vice chairman		Yang Shangkun	
Secretary-general		Yang Shangkun	
Central Advisory Commission			
Chairman		Chen Yun	
Vice chairmen		Bo Yibo	
		Song Renqiong	

Note: This is the power alignment before and during the student demonstrations of May–June 1989.

an obsolete theory and that reflected Hu's personal views but not the Party's. When Zhao advanced his strategy of opening the coastal areas to foreign investment and turning them into huge export-processing zones in spring 1988,[3] the conservatives equated his policy to capitalist practices that would restore colonialism and invite an economic invasion by foreign nations.[4] To defend Zhao's strategy, the *People's Daily*, from May 19 to June 25, 1988, published seven commentaries on this issue, an extraordinary number.

Another stronghold of the reformers has been the Shanghai-based *World Economic Herald*, the PRC's most influential weekly newspaper. From 1984 to 1988, the *Herald* was the main forum for outspoken intellectuals whose views were representative of those of the reformers. The *Herald* was even more critical than usual during spring 1989. In the April 10 issue, the *Herald* carried an article by the prominent economist Qian Jiaju criticizing Premier Li Peng by name for not explaining the failure of the prior year's price reform in his report to the National People's Congress. In its April 24 issue,

TABLE 3.2
Power Alignment in the PRC (December 1, 1989)

Sphere of Influence	Reformers	Conservatives	Undetermined
Politburo			
Standing Committee	Jiang Zemin	Li Peng	Qiao Shi
	Li Ruihuan	Yao Yilin	
		Song Ping	
Members	Wan Li	Yang Shangkun	
	Tian Jiyun	Li Ximing	
	Li Tieying	Ding Guan-gen	
	Wu Xueqian		
	Qin Jiwei		
	Yang Rudai		
Central Secretariat			
General secretary	Jiang Zemin		
Secretaries	Li Ruihuan	Ding Guan-gen	Qiao Shi
		Yang Baibing	
Central Military Commission			
Chairman	Jiang Zemin		
First vice chairman		Yang Shangkun	
Second vice chairman	Liu Huaqing		
Secretary-general		Yang Baibing	
Central Advisory Commission			
Chairman		Chen Yun	
Vice chairmen		Bo Yibo	
		Song Renqiong	

Note: This table reflects personnel changes that were made by the CCP fourth and fifth plenums, convened respectively in June and November 1989.

the *Herald* devoted six pages to comments on Hu Yaobang by dissident intellectuals, including several scholars and writers, such as Su Shaozhi, Yan Jiaqi, Yu Guangyuan, and Dai Qing. These intellectuals praised Hu highly and called for a positive reassessment of both the student demonstrations in 1986–1987 (see Chapter 4, "The New Student Movement") and Hu's forced resignation. When he saw the content of the issue, Jiang Zemin, then Party secretary of the CCP Shanghai Committee, immediately ordered the censorship of the *Herald* and the suspension of Qin Benli, the editor-in-chief. Zhao Ziyang, upon receiving the news of Qin's suspension, attempted to intervene but failed to get Qin returned to his position. Jiang's success in silencing the *Herald* won him much goodwill from conservative leaders who had failed to subdue the *Herald* in past purges. After Zhao's downfall, Jiang was deemed an acceptable choice as the Party's new general secretary.[5]

Supporting the conservative camp are publications such as *Beijing Ribao* (Beijing daily), the organ of the conservative CCP Beijing Committee, and until 1987 *Hongqi* (Red flag), the Party's theoretical journal. For years, Deng Liqun and Hu Qiaomu, two leading conservative theoreticians, had supervised *Hongqi*. Upon assuming the post of Party general secretary in 1987, Zhao

Ziyang ordered the shutdown of *Hongqi*. He reorganized the journal in summer 1988, changing its name to *Qiushi* (Seeking truth) and turning it into a mouthpiece of the reformers. When one compares the views published in *People's Daily, Jingji Ribao* (Economic daily), and the *World Economic Herald* with those in *Beijing Ribao, Jiefang Ribao* (Liberation daily), the CCP Shanghai Committee's journal, and *Hongqi*, one sees a contrast so stark that the existence of two contending political cliques is beyond any doubt.

Power bases in the central and provincial Party organizations are also discernable. Hu Yaobang's influence in the Communist Youth League (CYL) was profound because of his past service as head of the organization. When Hu became the Party general secretary in 1982, a large number of former associates from the league were promoted to key positions in the Party center and to provincial committees. Because Zhao Ziyang had served as Party first secretary of Guangdong and Sichuan, and Wan Li as Party first secretary of Anhui, their connections in these provinces were widespread and deep-seated. Chen Yun, the czar of Chinese economic affairs for more than forty years, has had no rivals in terms of influence in economic planning, banking, and trade. In the Politburo Standing Committee formed in late 1989, both Yao Yilin and Song Ping were Chen's subordinates. Chen had nominated Li Peng to the post of minister of Electric Power in 1985 and has been his staunch backer in recent years.[6] Peng Zhen, the mayor of Beijing before the Cultural Revolution, had served as the chairman of the National People's Congress (1983–1987) and possesses great influence in public security matters and the legal system. Qiao Shi, the chairman of the Central Commission for Discipline Inspection, is a protégé of Peng Zhen. Thus, although the reformers dominated the Party Secretariat as well as many coastal provinces and have had the popular support of intellectuals and students, they have been much weaker than the conservatives in matters of public security and economic affairs. Deng and Yang Shangkun possess the greatest control over the army. Although Zhao was promoted to be first vice chairman of the Central Military Commission in 1987, his connections with the field armies were not close. His lack of military backing was evident at the time of the showdown when the conservatives, with the support of Deng Xiaoping, exerted their military muscle and won the power contest. Both the downfall of Hu Yaobang in early 1987 and the dismissal of Zhao Ziyang in late May 1989 demonstrate the strength of the conservatives' military backing.

Ideological Tenets and the Party Line

The Chinese Communists consider themselves devout Marxist-Leninists. In theory, all policies regarding social, economic, and political affairs must be formulated in accordance with Marxist-Leninist doctrine. In practice, Mao Zedong's Thought dominated policy-making until his death in September 1976. To many Chinese Communists, Mao's Thought is more important than Marxism-Leninism because it offers an interpretation of the latter that the mostly uneducated officials can accept without reservation. As early as 1945, Mao's Thought was incorporated into the Party constitution as its guiding doctrine. Although Mao intended to have his concept of socialism define the economic system, not all of the Communist leaders shared his views. Arguments for and against his doctrine underlay a continuing struggle between two lines within the Chinese Communist Party, culminating in the Cultural Revolution, which affected Chinese economic development for more than a decade.[7]

The essence of Mao's economic thought is embodied in his vision of "Communist man," whose counterpart is the "economic man" of classical economic theory. Classical economics, since the time of Adam Smith, has viewed man as a creature of inherent self-interest whose behavior is always guided by economic forces. The whole structure of Western economics is based on the assumption that man, a rational being, will deliberately subordinate means to the attainment of definite ends. If man is allowed to pursue his own rational self-interest and government function is confined to the protection of private property, resources will be allocated most efficiently. This, in essence, is the doctrine of laissez-faire, a cornerstone of capitalism.

In contrast, Mao believed that the transformation of men's souls into selfless parts of an organic whole was the key to an ideal society. According to Marx and other socialists, unselfishness characterized people under communism. In Mao's Thought, unselfishness was also the basis for achieving a metamorphosis of the state. Thus, Mao envisaged the Communist man as an ideal type with some unique characteristics. First, he possessed the capacity for total self-denial as well as a wholehearted willingness to overcome material limitations. Second, he was solely concerned with benefiting the commonwealth, as opposed to merely maximizing personal gain like Smith's "economic man." Third, in contrast to Smith's model, in which the harmony between individual self-interest and the good of the commonwealth was achieved through competition, the Communist man replaces the mechanism of competition with a fervently religious pursuit of the common goals of the community.

Having developed the concept of the ideal Communist man, Mao formulated a corollary proposition that singled out man as the most powerful factor in shaping economic development. He assumed that labor and capital were interchangeable and that ideological indoctrination and mass mobilization could take the place of capital equipment and technological expertise. Realizing that poverty was the prevailing condition in the PRC and that no overnight cure existed, Mao concluded that the best way to enlist mass support was through the pursuit of egalitarian policies. A series of campaigns during the first decade after the revolution was launched to eradicate private enterprises (1956) and establish the communization of farm households (1958). To ensure a minimum subsistence level of consumption for every citizen, a rigid system of rationing food grains, cotton fabrics, and edible oils was introduced in 1955. These policies resulted in an equal allotment of basic staples to the entire population and became known as "everyone eating from the same big pot."[8]

Although many of the leaders associated with Mao shared his ideas of the Communist man and the egalitarian spirit, Mao diverged from the others in several major aspects of ideology. The most crucial one concerned the concept of class struggle, which he borrowed from Marx and which became a pillar of his thought. According to Marx, every society, except the final classless society under communism, consists chiefly of a ruling class and an oppressed class. Marx saw human history as a series of class struggles until the ultimate Communist victory. Mao advanced Marx's belief one step further by maintaining that even after the bourgeois class had been removed from power, it would retain some of its traditional influence on society. Thus, a continuing class struggle would be required after the socialist victory in order to combat lingering bourgeois, revisionist influences as well as pressures from foreign imperialist powers.[9] In his later years, Mao emphasized class struggle as the "key link" upon which everything hinged. His obsession with class struggle, at the expense of economic reconstruction, led to his open split with many Party leaders, including his appointed successor Liu Shaoqi and Liu's close associate Deng Xiaoping. This split and the power struggle that ensued precipitated the Cultural Revolution (see Chapter 4).

After Mao's death and the downfall of the Gang of Four,[10] Deng and his supporters immediately forged a new party line. At the Third Plenum of the Eleventh Party Central Committee in late 1978, under Deng's initiative, the new leadership declared that the "main concentration of party work and the full attention of the people of China would shift toward socialist modernization and construction." In other words, the Party would no longer make class struggle its primary task, but instead would concentrate on the "forces of production." In this context, the Four Modernizations became the popular catchwords for foreign and domestic audiences.[11]

The party line promoted by the third plenum, however, was not fully worked out. Many components were added at a later stage. In summer 1978, when Mao's successor Hua Guofeng was still in power, the leaders in the second echelon, such as Hu Yaobang and Hu Jiwei, staged a systematic campaign in which they criticized almost every major policy Mao had initiated in his twenty-seven-year reign. Many other people, particularly in the younger generation, began to disparage Mao's thought as practically worthless. When this creed—for which the Chinese people over a period of several decades had fought and made many sacrifices—was cast aside and repudiated, the country experienced a severe crisis of faith in which a lack of respect for authority and a rapid erosion of the Party's standing occurred.[12] It was against this background that Deng announced the Four Cardinal Principles in 1979 as a component of the new party line. In his essay explaining this doctrine, Deng argued that the country's numerous problems would be solved only if the Party could achieve the Four Modernizations. But that action would succeed only if the Party adhered to correct ideology and political actions, namely, the Four Cardinal Principles:

adhering to the socialist road; upholding the dictatorship of the proletariat; upholding the leadership of the Communist Party; and adhering to Marxism-Leninism and Mao Zedong Thought.[13]

When Deng promulgated the Four Cardinal Principles, the reform and open-door policies still had not been incorporated into the party line. At the CCP's Thirteenth Party Congress in September 1987, there was a division of opinion between the conservatives and the reformers regarding those policies. The report of the Central Advisory Commission, the power base of the conservatives, insisted that the CCP make "economic development the central task [and] adhere to the Four Cardinal Principles and preserve them." The commission stressed that these two elements were "the main aspects of the Party's basic line in the initial stage of socialism."[14]

In contrast, Zhao Ziyang's government report to the congress introduced the components of the party line: One Center and Two Basic Points. As we saw in Chapter 2, the central task was economic development; the two basic points were adhering to the Four Cardinal Principles and persevering in reforms and the open-door policy.

The discrepancy between the Central Advisory Commission's and Zhao's reports illustrates the basic contradiction between the conservatives and the reformers. Whereas the reformers have made the open-door and reform policies an integral part of the party line, the conservatives have limited the party line to "economic development." Reform and the open door remain relegated to party policy, not party line. The conflict was temporarily resolved when the Thirteenth Party Congress adopted Zhao's new approach on the "primary stage of socialism." On October 25, 1987, Zhao told the delegates at the congress: "A correct understanding of the present historical stage of Chinese society is of prime importance for building socialism with Chinese characteristics, and it is the essential basis on which to formulate and implement a correct line and correct policies. Our Party has already made a clear and definite statement on this question: China is now in the primary stage of socialism."[15]

Zhao admitted that despite its socialist structure, the PRC still had one of the lowest per capita GNPs in the world. Out of a population of more than 1 billion, 800 million lived in rural areas and for the most part, worked the land manually to make a living. Nearly one quarter of the population was illiterate or semiliterate. The principal problem at that time was the contradiction between the growing material and cultural needs of the people and the low productivity in industry and agriculture. According to Zhao, under the new guidelines, the PRC should pursue the following goals: (1) vigorously expand the commodity economy and raise labor productivity; (2) reform the relationship between production and the political superstructure because the latter was inhibiting the growth of the productive forces; (3) adhere to an open and flexible policy to attract foreign technology and capital; (4) develop diverse sectors of the economy and diverse forms of distribution to encourage some people to become financially well-off first; and (5) build democracy on the basis of stability and unity.

According to Zhao, the primary stage of socialism was not a short-term phenomenon but would last at least 100 years, starting from the 1950s to the middle of the twenty-first century. The new concept represented a formal repudiation of Mao's policies while simultaneously providing a theoretical justification for many economic policies attacked by the conservatives as violating Marxist tenets.

The Thirteenth Party Congress reconfirmed the Party's commitment to economic reform and the open-door policy, reassuring intellectuals and foreign investors that the ideological crackdown of early 1987 had ended. Yet, many of the social and economic problems facing the new leadership still defied easy solution. Toward the end of 1987, inflation moved into double digits. In the first quarter of 1988, prices of nonstaple foods rose by 24.2 percent, with a dramatic increase of 48.7 percent in the price of fresh vegetables. As consumers panicked, the economy fell into disarray.

With the economic crisis worsening, conservatives stepped up their attack on the hasty price reform. The reformers were forced to choose between pushing the price reform a step further or retreating. When the Party leaders gathered at Beidaihe in summer 1988, Zhao offered a bolder plan for a "new order for the socialist commodity economy." The new plan called for the end of state control of prices within four or five years and a major currency devaluation to boost exports and fill an empty treasury. It also called for a gradual decontrol of wages and labor, as well as the establishment of rules to enforce and institutionalize free competition for money, labor, and raw materials. Compensation for workers and employees would be based on merit, with intellectuals receiving substantial pay hikes, which would put their incomes above those of manual laborers.

To check the widespread corruption, Zhao proposed new laws to curb kickbacks and commissions. The plan also called for a reduction of the civil service and for pay raises to the remaining government employees in order to obviate their need for under-the-table deals. The entire blueprint ran counter to the unceasing conservative pressure to retreat.

Zhao's proposal drew fierce criticism from conservatives, who denounced it as a "word-facade behind which China was careening toward capitalism." They convinced Deng and other veteran leaders that if Zhao's plan were implemented, it would lead to worsening inflation and would push the economy to the brink of total collapse. They also maintained that the only way to save the economy was to suspend price reform and adopt an austerity program to reduce aggregate demand. In the wake of the Beidaihe Conference, the decision-making power on economic affairs was wrested from Zhao and put in the hands of Li Peng and Yao Yilin, marking a decline in Zhao's power and the rise of Li's influence.[16]

The Unique Role of Deng Xiaoping

Of all the post-Mao Communist leaders in the PRC, Deng Xiaoping has undoubtedly played a unique role, rivaled by few others. Deng, an extremely shrewd and capable manipulator, lost and regained power several times during his colorful political career. Although popularly credited as being the architect of the reform and open-door programs, Deng is also the author of the dogmatic Four Cardinal Principles. He handpicked Hu Yaobang and Zhao Ziyang as his potential successors but then abandoned each of them in the face of conservative pressure. In 1985, when his popularity was at its apex, *"Xiaoping hao"* (How are you, Mr. Xiaoping) was an expression of the affection in which the younger generation, particularly university students, held their leader. On June 4, 1989, this leader ordered the People's Liberation Army to crush the unarmed prodemocracy demonstrators. When he appeared on TV on June 9, 1989, to endorse the suppression openly and to praise the brutal soldiers, many of those watching felt outraged and bewildered. The big question became, Who is the real Deng Xiaoping?

One salient characteristic of Deng Xiaoping is his multifaceted nature. He is a man of both great flexibility and rigidity, a reformer and an ideologue, a proponent of the open door but also an ardent nationalist. Above all, he is a survivor who has managed to rebound from successive purges and who wields power ruthlessly whenever he deems it to be necessary.

Before the Cultural Revolution, Deng was already the fourth-ranking leader after Mao, Liu Shaoqi, and Zhou Enlai. At the outset of the Cultural Revolution, the Maoist radicals identified him as the number-two "capitalist roader" (Liu was number one) and stripped him of all his posts, except for his Party membership. Deng was sent to Xinqian County in Jiangxi Province, where he was ordered to perform manual labor at a tractor plant.

The turning point of Deng's ordeal came on September 12, 1971, when Defense Minister Lin Biao, Mao's new heir apparent, died in an air crash in Outer Mongolia. Supposedly, Lin was attempting to escape to the Soviet Union after an abortive coup d'état.[17] Immediately after learning the news, Deng wrote a letter to Mao and the CCP Central Committee, pledging his support to purge the Lin Biao clique, demonstrating his willingness to correct his past "mistakes," promising not to reverse past verdicts against him (during the Cultural Revolution Deng had been condemned for being a "capitalist roader" and guilty of revisionism), and expressing his hope to serve the Party and the people.[18] With the help of Zhou Enlai, Deng was rehabilitated in August 1973, when Mao selected him as a CCP Central Committee member. Later that year Mao appointed him to the CCP Central Military Commission and as chief of staff of the army. In January 1975, Deng was named one of the twelve vice premiers of the State Council. Later, when Zhou Enlai became seriously ill, Deng substituted for him and acted as premier. By then, he had reemerged as the PRC's strongman.

During this period, however, the radical Gang of Four, led by Mao's wife Jiang Qing, still held power. To reduce their influence, Deng helped to reestablish many purged officials, one of whom was Hu Yaobang. Deng asked Hu to draft a series of documents on the subject of overhauling the Party and the government. The resulting documents included: "A General Outline of All Work of the Party and the State," "Some Questions Concerning the Acceleration of Industrial Development," and "An Outline of the Report on the Work of the Academy of Sciences." Each of these documents criticized radical policies advocated by the Gang of Four. As a result, Deng was counterattacked by the radicals for restoring capitalism and attempting to reverse the past verdicts against him.[19] In February 1976, a *People's Daily* editorial criticized Deng as an "unrepentant capitalist-roader within the Party."

To mark Zhou's death, which had occurred in January 1976, a large number of mourners gathered in Tiananmen Square on April 5. This triggered the first spontaneous demonstration against the regime. Deng was blamed by Mayor of Beijing Wu De for having instigated the Tiananmen incident. On the evening of April 7, the CCP Politburo dismissed Deng from all Party and government posts. Allowed to retain only his Party membership, he was informed that he would be monitored closely to ensure that he behaved himself in the future.[20] Ironically, the fate Deng suffered in 1976 was the same experienced in 1989 by Zhao Ziyang—in the same theater (Tiananmen Square), but with different actors.

According to internal documents of the CCP, prior to the downfall of the Gang of Four, Deng had been escorted by senior military leader Xu Shiyu, then commander of the Guangdong Military Region, to south China, where he met secretly with Ye Jianying, one of the ten marshals of the PLA and then vice chairman of the Central Military Commission, who had also returned to Guangdong. In Guangdong, they plotted the steps for bringing down the Gang of Four. Deng was quoted as saying: "If we win, everything will be solved. Even if we fail, we can lie low and wait for another opportunity either by taking to the hills (meaning, engaging in guerilla warfare) or by going abroad. . . . If we don't seize this opportunity, we may lose our stakes altogether."[21]

Deng's plot to topple the Gang of Four was carried out with the assistance of Ye Jianying, Wang Zhen (one of the eight powerful old-timers), and Mao's bodyguard, Wang Dongxing, the director of the administrative office of the CCP Central Committee and head of the 8341 unit, which protects the CCP central leadership. Less than a month after Mao's death, Hua Guofeng had the Gang of Four arrested.

The downfall of the "Gang" did not immediately result in Deng's second return to power, as Hua Guofeng had became Mao's successor. Hua was elected chairman of the Party and its military commission and simultaneously served as premier. Having risen from an obscure position in Mao's hometown to a provincial position and then to the head of the State Public Security Ministry, Hua had been appointed first vice chairman of the CCP Central Committee and premier of the State Council after Deng's April 7 purge. Aware of Deng's prestige and ability, Hua certainly did not want to see him back in power.[22]

In order to regain power, Deng had to bide his time and feign meekness and subservience before Hua. In a letter to Hua written shortly after the ouster of the radicals, Deng pledged his support for Hua's appointment as chairman of the Party and its military commission and praised him as the most suitable successor of Mao, both politically and ideologically. Deng also noted that Hua, in the prime of his life, would be able to ensure a proletarian dictatorship for at least fifteen to twenty years.[23] On April 10, 1977, Deng wrote to Hua again, admitting his own shortcomings and the mistakes he had made in his work in 1975 and expressing his willingness to accept whatever work the Party Central Committee assigned to him. He also affirmed "the necessity of using Mao's Thought to lead the Party, the army, and the people."[24] Deng's efforts finally were rewarded when the Third Plenum of the Tenth Party Central Committee, on July 16, 1977, decided to reappoint him as a member of the Politburo and its Standing Committee, vice chairman of the CCP Central Committee, vice chairman of the military commission, vice premier of the State Council, and chief of staff of the PLA.[25] Deng thus recovered all the posts he had relinquished after the 1976 Tiananmen incident.

As soon as he had consolidated his power base, Deng began to criticize Hua Guofeng's "two whatevers theory." Hua, a devoted loyalist of Mao's, upon assuming the Party leadership, had pledged "to support firmly whatever decisions Chairman Mao had made and to follow persistently whatever directives Chairman Mao had given."[26] Deng argued that such a position was not Marxist. Nothing like it had been mentioned in the works of Marx, Engels, Lenin, Stalin, or Mao Zedong.[27] Deng then endorsed a position presented by his associates: Practice is the sole criterion of truth. The new slogan established the groundwork for the reform programs he proposed at the historic Third Plenum of the Eleventh Party Central Committee, which convened in December 1978.

The ups and downs of Deng's political fortunes reveal his flexibility. Whenever he faced adversity, he tended to adopt an extremely humble, obedient, and subdued posture. This low-key behavior made him acceptable to his rivals. However, once he regained power, he wielded it ruthlessly and shrewdly. His subsequent treatment of Hu Yaobang and Zhao Ziyang reflects this Machiavellian side of his character.

Deng's diverse personality has been fully exhibited in the programs he has promoted. Deng was the sponsor of the open-door policy. As early as 1975, in a major Party document outlining a strategy for industrial development, he advanced the idea of exchanging Chinese petroleum resources for Western equipment and technology. He warned Party leaders that the PRC should not adopt an isolationist attitude, refusing to learn from the experiences of foreign countries. On several occasions, Deng has attributed the slow pace of China's modernization to its international isolation—from the middle of the Ming Dynasty through the Opium War and from the Sino-Soviet split of the late 1950s to the end of the Cultural Revolution.[28] He not only personally endorsed the establishment of the four SEZs but also encouraged the opening of fourteen coastal cities for foreign investors. He firmly supported sending large numbers of students abroad to study.

However, his reformist enthusiasm has been tempered by a stern adherence to ideology. When Hua Guofeng was still in power, to counter Hua's "two whatevers theory," Deng, at a CCP Work Conference in November 1978, called for the "emancipation of people's minds." His speech inspired the first post-Mao democracy movement in late 1978 and early 1979. But just a few months later, he reversed his position completely and ordered a crackdown on the 1979 "Democracy Wall" movement: The young dissident Wei Jingsheng, because of openly criticizing the Communist government, was sentenced to lengthy imprisonment. Deng then proclaimed the Four Cardinal Principles, which have provided the conservatives ample ammunition to attack the reform.

Moreover, Deng's modernist and cosmopolitan tendencies are balanced by a strong sense of nationalism. Deng started the war to punish Vietnam in 1979, brutally suppressed Tibet in 1987 and 1989, and insisted on the return of Hong Kong and Macao to the PRC. He wants students to learn Western science, technology, and management skills, but not Western principles and ideals. His position evokes the spirit of the late nineteenth-century reformers. For example, Zhang Zhidong and his contemporaries espoused the concept of "Chinese learning as the essence, Western learning for utility" (*zhong xue wei ti, xi xue wei yong*). The *ti yong* dichotomy is still alive and well, the Four Cardinal Principles having replaced "Chinese learning" as the essence. Deng's conservative ideological and nationalistic sentiments partially explain why he joined the hard-liners in suppressing the students.

Among the party veterans, Deng is the most dynamic and capable. Mao on several occasions openly commended him. In December 1974, in a conversation with Zhou Enlai and Wang Hongwen, Mao asserted that "Deng Xiaoping has a strong political-ideological consciousness and is a person of extraordinary ability."[29]

A master of the tactics of manipulation and balancing, Deng utilized several stratagems in his power plays. First, because he joined the Red Army in his early twenties, he has fully understood Mao's well-known axiom: "Political power comes from the barrel of a gun." As soon as he resumed power in 1978, he wasted no time in consolidating his control over the army. By 1987 he had given up all Party posts except for the chairmanship of the CCP Central Military Commission and the State Military Commission. With control over the army, he has wielded great power even without formal membership in the Politburo. Second, he has adopted a detached position, never directly committing his personal prestige to any particular reform program. As Harry Harding rightly observed, Deng has attempted to preempt and co-opt potential criticism.[30] When the Central Committee adopted a comprehensive program of urban reform in 1984, Deng indicated that he approved of the document, but he also pointed out that he had neither added nor deleted a single word, thereby avoiding any criticism.[31]

Third, he has always struck a balance between the two cliques. For more than a decade, Hu Yaobang was his closest aide and his first choice for successor. Yet, when the Party elders fiercely attacked Hu, Deng sacrificed him to appease his peers. When the hard-liners tried to alter the power balance, however, Deng immediately moved to strengthen the weaker side by promoting Zhao Ziyang not only to the position of Party general secretary but also to the position of first vice chairman of the Party's military commission. After Zhao had been relieved of his duties as Party general secretary in June 1989, instead of promoting the hard-liner Premier Li Peng to that post, Deng selected Jiang Zemin for the job. The manipulative skills he employed in the past two decades have rendered him the most formidable leader since Mao.

The Ideological Confrontation

In a Communist state, ideology or theoretical formulations confirm the legitimacy of the leadership and shape the political climate and economic policies. Often since the founding of the PRC, ideological conflicts have been the first indication of a fierce power struggle. In factional strife, the contending parties seldom admit that their goal is to seize political power. Instead, they attempt to cloak their convictions by arguing about Marxism-Leninism. In most cases, the oscillations in ideology reflect shifts in power balances.[32]

During the post-Mao era, the first ideological conflict occurred in spring 1978, when the emerging reformers took the offensive against Hua Guofeng's "two whatevers theory" and presented their approach—practice is the sole criterion of truth. This ideological battle played a crucial role in preparing public opinion for the Third Plenum of the Eleventh Party Central Committee. Without this fight, it would not have been possible to change the balance of power within the top leadership or to reshape the prevailing intellectual climate.[33] Had the reforming leaders failed to persuade the Party members and the population to repudiate Hua's "two whatevers," Mao's radical doctrines would still prevail.

In the aftermath of the third plenum in December 1978, the general political climate appeared to favor further liberalization in order to restore the people's morale and the country's dynamism, which had been damaged by the Cultural Revolution. In late 1980, Deng Xiaoping put forth the concept of "socialist spiritual civilization" as an integral part of his blueprint for a new China. In a speech delivered on December 25, 1980, to a Party work conference, Deng expressed this idea: "What I call spiritual civilization refers not only to education, science and culture (although these are essential), but to Communist thought, ideals, beliefs, morality, discipline, a revolutionary standpoint and principles, comradely relations between people, and so on."[34]

In short, Deng hoped to create a social and political environment that possessed both centralism and democracy, discipline and freedom, unity of purpose and room for the individual, ideals Mao had first conceived of early in 1957. From mid-1982 to mid-1983, the political climate in the PRC was calm. In summer 1983, the *Selected Works of Deng Xiaoping* was published, further consolidating his authority in both ideology and politics.

The first crack in the united front of the reformers occurred in spring 1983 when an ideological debate suddenly erupted among the Party theoreticians. Su Shaozhi, director of the Institute of Marxism-Leninism and Mao Zedong Thought, part of the Chinese Academy of Social Sciences, presented a keynote paper at an academic conference on the occasion of the centenary of Marx's death. In this paper Su argued that the theories that advanced the notion of Marxism's obsolescence were "a punishment for having treated Marxism in a dogmatic fashion. . . . Only by creatively developing Marxism," he argued, "can we truly uphold it."[35] In alluding to the futility of a dogmatic reassertion of Marxism, Su challenged the Chinese Marxists to address the vital theoretical problems confronting Marxism. These included dealing with the consequences of extremely rapid technical and scientific change in modern times and discovering the source of the class force in an advanced industrial society needed to overthrow capitalism. He also mentioned numerous new problems of world Communist governments, including Stalin's "revolution from above," errors committed by Stalin and Mao in building socialism, and problems of the relationship between the young and the mature Marx.[36]

Following Su Shaozhi's provocative paper, Zhou Yang, a veteran CCP member and the former deputy director of the CCP Propaganda Department, presented a theoretical paper contending that the concept of alienation in Marxist theory was in fact also applicable to the socialist state:

> Because democracy and the legal system were unsound, the servants of the people were able at times to misuse the power bestowed upon them by the people, and to become the master of the people. This is alienation in the political domain. . . . As for ideological alienation, the best example is the cult of the individual, which was similar in some respects to the religious alienation criticized by Feuerbach . . . only if you recognize that alienation exists can you overcome it.[37]

Before Zhou's article had appeared, back in August 1980, Wang Ruoshui, deputy editor-in-chief of the *People's Daily*, had argued that the transition of the CCP from being in opposition to being a ruling party had led to the phenomenon of ideological and political alienation. The problem of cadres who acted like "high and mighty officials" existed at all levels of the leadership and had not yet been solved.[38]

Both Zhou Yang and Wang Ruoshui also promoted the theory of humanism, which had previously fallen into the category of issues that no one in the PRC dared to discuss openly. The fact that Zhou Yang's article had appeared in the Party organ, the *People's Daily*, indicated that it had the sanction of some Party leaders, particularly General Secretary Hu Yaobang.

The new approaches of Su Shaozhi, Zhou Yang, and Wang Ruoshui drew nationwide attention and angered the conservatives. On October 24, 1983, Wang Zhen, a leading hard-liner, member of the Politburo, and at that time president of the Central Party School (in 1989 he was the vice president of the state) gave a speech firing the first salvos against the Marxist "heresies":

There are people who say that our country is not yet socialist, or that ours is agrarian socialism. There are also those who are constantly propagating so-called socialist alienation, saying something to the effect that socialism suffers not only from ideological alienation, but from political alienation and economic alienation. They even go so far as to say "the roots of alienation are to be found in the socialist system itself." These views are entirely opposed to Marxist scientific socialism.[39]

Wang's accusations paved the way for a nationwide anti-spiritual-pollution campaign. Articles written by members of the conservative wing flooded official newspapers. The social and political climate decisively turned in a conservative direction. Party officials began to criticize people's dress and hairdos. The CCP Beijing Committee, a conservative stronghold, decreed that beginning October 1, 1983, those whose dress and decorum failed to comply with the set standards would be barred from entering government premises. In rural areas, cadres and activists who had been disgruntled for years as a result of the rise of 10,000-yuan households took out their resentment by harassing, persecuting, and intimidating those who they deemed were lacking in "revolutionary purity." People feared that another Cultural Revolution was on the way.

As peasants halted investment and foreign capital began to dry up, Deng intervened, ordering the termination of the campaign. The ideological pendulum once again swung back in a reformist direction. On April 1, 1984, the *People's Daily* published an editorial identifying "leftist" influences, instead of bourgeois influences, as the country's major threat, and announcing that the Party would take measures to "eliminate the residual 'leftist' [antireformist] poison." The new political climate facilitated the adoption of a broader reform program for the urban sector during the Third Plenum of the Twelfth Party Central Committee, which took place in September 1984.[40]

The check to the conservatives did not stop them from opening another offensive. The period between 1985 and 1986 witnessed the second assault against the reformers. As prices of foodstuffs soared and corruption became rampant, attacks on the reform intensified. The most vocal criticism came from the provincial press, with Party newspapers in the northeast regions leading the campaign. In November 1985, right after the CCP National Party Congress of Delegates, the secretary of Liaoning's provincial Discipline Inspection Commission used terms reminiscent of the Cultural Revolution in warning Party members against "the vicious inflation of individualism" and "the sugar-coated bullet of the bourgeoisie."[41]

Sharp criticism of the reform was heard also from Party leaders in the hinterlands, indicating the increase in polarization along regional lines. During the 1960s, as a step in preparation for war with the Soviet Union, less developed provinces in the northwest and southwest had received large proportions of state funds. With the reform, investment priorities had shifted back to coastal areas. The gap in economic growth between these two parts of the PRC became more apparent, increasing the resentment from these regions.[42]

In the central Party and government organizations, the conservative leaders accused the reformers of seriously damaging the institutional integrity and organic solidarity of the CCP. The ideas of "liberalism" and "individualism" were felt to be hazardous to the institutional loyalties of Party members. Reform also weakened command and control in the CCP, as Party members increasingly "disregarded organizational discipline and failed to enforce orders and prohibitions."[43]

Moreover, conservatives also condemned the destructive effects of the "commodity exchange" relations in the CCP. Li Ximing, one of the stern conservative leaders and the first secretary of the CCP Beijing Committee, warned that "the principle of exchange of equal value" had "seeped into the political life of the Party," so that many members now operated on a basis of "no money no work" and "work according to the amount of money." He contended that the instrumental values and commodities relations fostered by the reform had seriously undermined Party traditions of "unpaid labor" and "arduous struggle." Young officials especially ignored Communist ideals and considered revolution something "empty and soft."[44]

Conservative attacks focused on several outspoken intellectuals, such as Liu Binyan, a well-known journalist and vice chairman of the China Writers' Association; Wang Ruowang, a noted writer; Liu Zaifu, editor-in-chief of the *Wenxue Pinglun* (Literary review) and director of the Institute of Literature of the Academy of Social Sciences; Fang Lizhi, the well-known dissident astrophysicist; and the three "Marxist heretics" and "spiritual polluters": Su Shaozhi, Zhou Yang, and Wang Ruoshui. Thus, a new campaign of "anti-bourgeois liberalization" gradually gained momentum in the PRC.

The first open confrontation between the two top CCP leaders, Deng Xiaoping and Chen Yun, occurred at the CCP National Party Congress of Delegates in September 1985. In his closing remarks, Chen Yun reiterated his earlier warnings about the effects of overheating the economy and hasty reforms and reaffirmed the value of central planning. He also criticized the program for inducing peasants to take up nonagricultural activities. Chen quoted Mao to warn of possible social disorders if the population exodus from the farms was not arrested. He also reminded Party members that since "we are a communist country, the economy should continue to be based on central planning, not on market regulations." Moreover, he said that he considered the downgrading of party propaganda and ideological work a grave mistake and supported Hu Qiaomu and Deng Liqun, the two top conservative ideologues, in their bid to stay in the Politburo and the Central Secretariat respectively.[45]

In the wake of the Party's Congress of Delegates, factional jousting in the Party hierarchy intensified. In order to rally popular support, the reformers extended their program into the political arena. In spring and summer 1986, Deng declared on many occasions that without changes in the political system, economic reform could no longer proceed. Although Deng's idea of political reform was to bring the tightly hierarchical political structure into step with economic reform rather than to reduce the monolithic power of the Communist Party, the conservatives saw even this limited reform as a direct threat to their authority and privileges and tried to sabotage it.[46]

At the same time, the reform-minded intellectuals agitated for more freedom and democracy. With the blessing of Hu Yaobang, there was extensive academic freedom during summer and autumn 1986. Newspapers and scholarly journals published a profusion of essays and articles discussing the ideals of Western political and economic thinkers, from Aristotle to Adam Smith and from Jeremy Bentham to Friedrich Von Hayek. The atmosphere led intellectuals to believe that the PRC was entering a period of academic freedom despite the increasing recalcitrance of the ultraconservatives. However, the Sixth Plenum of the Twelfth Party Central Committee, convened in September 1986, came under strong pressure from the hard-liners to adopt a resolution reinforcing "spiritual civilization" instead of endorsing political reforms, as the intellectuals expected. The plenary session also called for bolstering ideological defenses against foreign cultural influences and for reinforcing the anti-bourgeois-liberalization campaign. The resurgence of conservative forces triggered the first nationwide student demonstration in early December 1986, which led to Hu Yaobang's downfall in January 1987.

The Struggle for Succession

Unlike transitions in Western democracies, shifts in power in Communist states do not follow an established procedure but are often dictated by the power holders, and contention for succession either before or after the death of the power holder becomes almost inevitable. The power struggles that plagued the Soviet Union after the deaths of Lenin and Stalin and the PRC before and after Mao's demise were typical of this phenomenon. After consolidating his leadership, Deng conceived a plan for grooming his own successor to prevent the recurrence of intra-Party struggle. Like Mao and other authoritarian leaders, Deng hoped his successor would share his ideas and ensure a continuation of his programs. As early as 1981, Deng publicly stated that the problem of succession "will determine our fate. If we fail to solve the problem within three to five years, chaos may ensue."[47]

The first stage in Deng's succession plan involved placing capable and energetic associates in key positions in Party and government organizations. First he picked Hu Yaobang to be the Party general secretary and subsequently Zhao Ziyang and Wan Li, two outstanding provincial Party secretaries, to be premier and vice premier respectively. Both Hu and Zhao quickly became members of the Standing Committee of the Politburo. In September 1980, Zhao was formally appointed premier of the State Council. In the following year, Hu was selected as the chairman of the Central Committee. By that time, Deng's succession plan had achieved its initial goal.

To consolidate Hu's position, the second stage of Deng's strategy was to weed out the remaining extremists left over from the Cultural Revolution. Beginning in 1983, a party rectification campaign began. The campaign aimed to rid the Party of "three types of people": those who had risen to prominence during the Cultural Revolution, those who had engaged in faction building, and those who had committed violent acts during the Cultural Revolution.[48] Several million cadres fit this description and were expelled from the Party and the government.

Deng noted publicly the fact that most remaining officials were old and poorly educated. In 1983, he flatly declared, "In order to ensure the stability of the state, and the continuity of the directions and policies of the Party and the State for a long period of time, it has become necessary to start to build up the third echelon."[49] He began promoting younger officials to leadership positions in 1982. In November 1983, Hu Yaobang revealed the plan to "cultivate about 1,000 middle-aged and young officials for ministerial and district-level positions."[50] Later on, Hu disclosed that more than 70 percent of the heads of 107 departments and ministries under the direct control of the CCP Central Committee and the State Council would be replaced by officials under the age of 60, with only 20 percent to be filled by persons above the age of 60.[51]

Deng's plan to rejuvenate the Party leadership achieved noteworthy results. Between 1982 and 1984, about 20,000 officials under 55 years of age with specialized knowledge and long experience were promoted to leadership positions at various levels.[52] In addition, about 100,000 officials entered the third echelon, approximately 1,000 for provincial and ministerial leadership positions, 20,000 for jobs at the bureau and district levels, and the rest for county-level positions. But the most important change was at the central level. At the Fourth Plenum of the Twelfth Party Central Committee, 64 members and alternate members of the Central Committee, 37 members of the Central Advisory Commission, and 30 of the Discipline Inspection Commission resigned and were replaced by younger officials. At the fifth plenary session, 6 members of the Politburo and 5 of the Central Secretariat also were replaced. As a result, the average age of the members in the Politburo dropped from 75 to 65, and that of members of the secretariat from 65 to 60.[53]

The plan, however, encountered stiff resistance. At the central level, the conservative wing carried out a counterattack to undermine Hu's position. The anti-spiritual-pollution campaign blamed Hu for being too lenient toward Party heretics, thus having disqualified himself for the role of Party general secretary. In addition, the conservative veterans strongly recommended that hard-liner theoreticians Hu Qiaomu and Deng Liqun remain on the Politburo and the Secretariat despite their having passed the age limit. The conservatives hoped that these two hard-liners would become potential contenders for power and rivals of Hu and Zhao. Moreover, the conservative veterans refused to retire at the September 1985 National Party Congress of Delegates. Bo Yibo even openly advocated the return to Mao's model of "three combinations" (*san jie he*), leadership by a coalition of old, middle-aged, and young officials.[54]

At the local and provincial levels, the reaction to the succession plan was mixed. Those middle- or low-ranking officials 50 to 55 years old considered themselves victims of the plan. Most of them came from peasant backgrounds and had little formal education. Starting their careers at the bottom of the bureaucratic hierarchy in the 1950s when they were in their early twenties, they had engaged ardently in political activism. As loyal supporters of the regime, they had carried out whatever the Party ordered. However, their role in the reform has been limited because they lack the ability and knowledge to contribute to the Four Modernizations. Too old to be considered as third-echelon material and lacking the title of "liberation cadres" (those who participated in the civil war), these officials have become frustrated and resentful. This unhappy group—several million strong—has become a retarding force in Deng's reform program. In recent years, whenever the central authorities enacted a new policy, these local bureaucrats adopted countermeasures to nullify it.

The beneficiaries of the succession plan have been the children and the former secretaries of high-ranking officials as well as former leaders of the Communist Youth League.[55] Most of the Party officials' children met the official requirements of age and education and were suitable for promotion. Thousands of high officials' offspring and relatives were placed in the third echelon, earning them their nickname—the "Crown Prince Party" (*taizi dang*). In the 1989 student demonstration, wall posters (*da zi bao*) on the Beijing University and Qinghua University campuses publicized alleged "family ties in the government." Examples of some famous names follow:

- Deng Pufang—son of Deng Xiaoping; ex-president of Kang Hua Company, a giant corporation.
- Deng Nan—daughter of Deng Xiaoping; bureau director, State Science and Technological Commission.
- Zhao Baojiang—son-in-law of Deng Xiaoping; mayor of Wuhan city.
- Li Peng—foster son of Zhou Enlai; premier of the State Council.
- Li Yang—son of Li Peng; vice president of Hainan Development General Company.
- Zhu Ling—wife of Li Peng; president of a state enterprise in South China.
- Zhao Dajun—son of Zhao Ziyang; president of Hainan Huahai Company.
- Yang Baibing—brother of Yang Shangkun (state president); director, General Political Department, PLA.
- Ye Xuanping—son of Ye Jianyin (former chairman of the NPC); governor of Guangdong Province.
- Wu Xiaolan—wife of Ye Xuanping; deputy mayor, Shenzhen Special Economic Zone.
- Zhou Jiahua—son-in-law of Ye Jianyin; minister, Machinery and Electronic Industry, new minister, State Planning Commission, State Council.
- Liu Yuan—son of Liu Shaoqi (former state president); vice governor of Henan Province.
- Ding Henggao—son-in-law of Nie Rongzhen (former vice chairman of the military commission); director, Defense Scientific and Industrial Commission, State Council.

- Bu He—son of Ulanfu (vice chairman, NPC); chairman, Inner Mongolian Autonomous Region.
- Utchur—son of Ulanfu; mayor of Baotou city.
- Bo Xilai—son of Bo Yibo (vice chairman, Central Advisory Commission); deputy mayor of Dalian city.
- Wang Jun—son of Wang Zhen (vice president of the PRC); deputy political director, Chengdu Military Region.
- Chen Yuan—son of Chen Yun (chairman, Central Advisory Commission); Party secretary, CCP Beijing Committee.
- Li Tieying—son of Li Weihan (former director of CCP United Front Department); member of CCP Politburo.
- Song Ruixiang—son of Song Renqiong (vice chairman, CCP Advisory Commission); governor, Qinghai Province.[56]

The promotion of large numbers of high-ranking officials' children and relatives into the third echelon has obstructed Deng's succession plan by generating immense discontent, even among university students, with the reform program.

The contest for succession reached its first climax when, in January 1987, Deng abruptly forced Hu Yaobang to resign as chief of the Chinese Communist Party. Hu's ouster not only dealt a severe blow to economic reform but also shook up Deng's entire plan of succession. Although the mounting pressure from the hard-liners was the ostensible cause of Hu's removal, his inability to gain the support of the senior military leaders and his loss of Deng's trust probably were the real reasons. Although Hu had built quite a strong base in the Party Secretariat and in many provincial committees, he lacked liaisons with the military.[57]

More important, when Deng announced on several occasions that he would seek retirement from the Party and state positions, experienced politicians knew that he was only soliciting pleas for him to stay. In September 1986, in an interview with CBS correspondent Mike Wallace, Deng reiterated his wish to retire at the Thirteenth Party Congress. However, he immediately added that this suggestion had been met with a chorus of opposition. In any case, Deng said, as a Party member he was bound to abide by the Party's decision,[58] which suggested that he had no intention of retiring. But when Hu was consulted by Deng about his retirement plans, Hu heartily endorsed Deng's proposal to retire instead of begging him to stay. That was deemed a lack of loyalty and may have precipitated Deng's decision to remove him.

To minimize the adverse effects of Hu's removal, Deng immediately picked Zhao Ziyang as interim successor. Aware of the precarious nature of the Party post and the history of disgrace for its holders, Zhao was extremely reluctant to accept the new assignment. On several occasions, he expressed the preference to keep his position as premier. But under Deng's persuasion, Zhao finally accepted the Party general secretary post. During this period, the conservatives endorsed Li Peng as Zhao's contender. As Deng was in his mid-eighties, a final showdown for succession was imminent.

The Final Showdown of the Contenders

The fall of Hu Yaobang was followed by a nationwide campaign, orchestrated by the hard-liners, against "bourgeois liberalism." From spring to summer 1987, the conservatives continued to gain the upper hand, prompting fears of another reversal in the reform policy. But the tide turned as Deng decided to keep his reform program in high gear. Through skillful maneuvers during the Thirteenth Party Congress, which met in late October and early November 1987, Deng and his associates removed many staunch hard-liners from the Party's Central Committee and replaced them with a group of younger reform-minded technocrats. As a tactic to force elderly conservatives to step down, Deng himself resigned from the Central Committee. Among those who joined him were a dozen powerful and venerated aged leaders, including Chen Yun, Li Xiannian, and Peng Zhen. Zhao Ziyang was officially named as Party general secretary and proposed the theory that the country was at that time in the "primary stage of socialism."

From late 1987 to early 1988, Zhao was extremely active, conducting three inspection tours of the southeastern coastal provinces, including Zhejiang, Fujian, Jiangsu, and Guangdong. During his tours, Zhao proposed an export-oriented economic development strategy for the coastal areas, patterned after the successful Taiwan experience. Deng immediately supported this new strategy and personally issued an instruction that "the chance of winning a battle should not be bungled." However, the proposal met with strong opposition from the conservatives within the Party. In early February 1988 Zhao published an article entitled "Further Emancipate the Mind and Further Liberate the Productive Forces," to attract popular support and to refute the arguments of conservatives such as Li Peng and Yao Yilin who contended that economic stability instead of bold strategies should be the key objective of economic reform at that stage. As inflation burgeoned out of control, Zhao gradually lost his authority over economic matters. In an interview with U.S. publisher Frank Gibney on September 6, 1988, Zhao admitted that he no longer was involved in economic decisions and would henceforth concentrate on research and investigation of economic reform and development.[59]

However, because Zhao was the only remaining high-ranking leader possessing the will to implement large-scale economic reforms and the open-door policy, Deng continued to support him. On several occasions, Deng made it known that Zhao was still his chosen successor. To strengthen Zhao's connection with the army, Deng let Zhao preside over a rally in celebration of 1988 Army Day. At a PLA ceremony on September 14, Zhao, in his capacity as first vice chairman of the CCP Military Commission, granted the rank of general to seventeen senior PLA officers on behalf of Deng. All of these developments indicated that up to autumn 1988, Deng still placed great confidence in Zhao. Had Deng disappeared from the political scene, Zhao, as Party general secretary and as first vice chairman of the Military Commission, would have been positioned as Deng's successor—if Zhao had been able to rally support from the army.

Aware of this possibility, the conservatives stepped up their campaign to discredit Zhao. On March 20, 1989, in his lengthy government work report to the Second Session of the Seventh National People's Congress, Li Peng offered an unprecedented critique of serious economic mistakes made over the past year. Although his review masqueraded as self-criticism, the real target was Zhao, who had been in charge of economic decisions during that period. Li implicitly accused Zhao of seeking quick results in economic and social development and overlooking the country's vast population, shortages of natural resources, and unbalanced economic structure. Li stressed mistakes of the price reform, especially its unpopularity with enterprises and the population and the failure to establish a macroeconomic control mechanism, "thereby deepening the fear of the people for inflation and inducing panic buying and lowering savings in many places."[60]

Li Peng's attacks on Zhao's economic policy signaled the imminence of the final showdown between the reformers and the conservatives on the problem of succession. When Deng announced in March 1989 that he was seriously considering complete retirement after the May Beijing summit meeting with Soviet President Mikhail Gorbachev, he helped to hasten the denouement. The sudden death of Hu Yaobang on April 15 and the ensuing large-scale student demonstrations for democracy both occurred at this critical juncture. While reform leaders desperately needed popular support to keep the program alive, conservatives also urgently sought an excuse to uproot Zhao and his group. A fight between Zhao and Li Peng took place behind the walls of Zhongnanhai while young students fasted in Tiananmen Square. Li later openly accused Zhao about his statements downplaying the Four Cardinal Principles except for Party leadership. He also blamed him for inciting the student unrest.[61]

One can draw several conclusions from the political drama in the PRC since the end of the Cultural Revolution. First, Chinese politics from Mao Zedong to Deng Xiaoping can be portrayed as a cycle of purges involving almost all of the heirs apparent. In 1961, when British Field Marshal Montgomery visited the PRC and interviewed Mao about his successor, Mao stated that Liu Shaoqi was his choice.[62] The fact that Mao allowed Liu to replace him as state chairman in 1958 verified his statement. But at the beginning of the Cultural Revolution in 1966, Liu was labeled by Mao as "China's Khrushchev" and the "number one representative of the capitalist-roaders in power within the party." Later on Liu was further accused of being a "renegade, traitor and scab." In October 1968, according to a resolution of the Twelfth Plenum of the Eighth Party Central Committee, Liu was expelled from the Party irrevocably. He was separated from his family and tortured to death in jail in Kaifeng, Henan.[63]

Following the purge of Liu Shaoqi, Mao designated Lin Biao, the defense minister, as his successor and even wrote the decision into the CCP constitution adopted by the Ninth CCP National Congress. Soon afterward, Mao began to feel that Lin posed an even greater threat to his power than Liu had, despite Lin's launching of large-scale campaigns to advance the cult of Mao throughout the whole country. As Mao stepped up arrangements for the purge of Lin Biao, Lin allegedly attempted a coup. When it failed, he and his wife and son died in a plane crash while they were trying to escape to the Soviet Union in September 1971.

After Lin's death, the members of the Gang of Four established themselves as Mao's successors, but they were arrested and put in prison less than one month after Mao's death. The man who carried out the arrest, Hua Guofeng, became Mao's successor. However, Hua lost real power after two and a half years, even though his rule lasted four years. In 1980 Deng Xiaoping and other reformers forced him to step down.

Deng had attempted to cultivate Hu Yaobang and Zhao Ziyang as his own successors, but both suffered the fate of their predecessors and ended up in tragic disgrace. Although each of the purges has occurred in different circumstances, the underlying reasons for them all are almost the same: The dictator cannot tolerate anyone threatening his absolute authority. Mao's purge of Liu Shaoqi and Lin Biao and Deng's sacrifice of Hu Yaobang and Zhao Ziyang both evince the despot's mentality.

Second, power struggle at the top always takes place under the guise of ideological schism. In the purges of the designated successors, the explanation most often offered was that they had deviated from the party line. Liu Shaoqi, Hu Yaobang, and Zhao Ziyang all were accused of neglecting the basic principles of Marxism-Leninism and Mao's Thought. They were attempting to lead the country toward the revival of capitalism to betray the socialist revolution. In contrast, Lin Biao, the Gang of Four, and Hua Guofeng were condemned as "leftist/dogmatist," hindering the country's cultural and economic development. Only the supreme leader is above ideological labels. In each case, ideology became the most effective weapon for disarming opponents.

Third, because intellectuals are responsible for the development of ideas for society, they are the guilty parties in any ideological deviation. Most political storms were presaged by a purge of leading intellectuals.

The purge of Liu Shaoqi started with Yao Wenyuan's attack on Wu Han's historical play *Dismissal of Hai Rui* in 1964, spread gradually to the purge of Peng Zhen and, ultimately, of Liu.[64] Likewise, the criticism of the novel *Water Margin* (*Shui Hu Zhuan*) preceded the struggle against Zhou Enlai and Deng Xiaoping.

The purge of Hu Yaobang started with the expulsion from the Party of several famous writers, including Liu Binyan and Wang Ruoshui, and especially with the "Ma Ding" and "Liu Zaifu" affairs. The former was a controversy over economic theories and the latter, a debate over theories of literature and art. Ma Ding (a pseudonym of Song Longxiang), a young professor of philosophy at Nanjing University, published an article in the November 2, 1985, issue of *Gongren Ribao* (Workers' daily) contending that Marxist theory could be regarded only as a theoretical guide but not a practical solution to problems in economic reconstruction. He suggested that Western economic theories be introduced to supplement Marxist theories.

Upon the publication of the paper, Hu Qiaomu and Deng Liqun, two conservative theorists, immediately accused Ma Ding of advocating a commodity economy, violating Marxist principle, and deviating from the socialist road. The Ma Ding affair went on for five months until Zhao Ziyang (premier) and Zhu Houze (director of the CCP Central Committee Propaganda Department) intervened on behalf of Hu Yaobang to defend Ma Ding, ending the controversy.

As the Ma Ding affair subsided, the conservative attack moved to Liu Zaifu, director of the Institute of Literature of the Chinese Academy of Social Sciences. Liu had asserted in an article that in the past, Chinese theorists of literature and art had neglected the nature and values of human beings. They tended to substitute politics for art and interpret the personality of characters from political viewpoints, thus transforming aesthetic appraisal into political trials. His call for restoring humanism to a great extent repudiated Mao's basic theories of literature and the arts. Liu's article enraged the conservatives. The "Ma Ding" and "Liu Zaifu" affairs are considered by many China experts as a prelude to the final downfall of Hu Yaobang.[65]

Zhao's eclipse was preceded by the conservatives' criticism of the six-part TV documentary "River Elegy" (see Chapter 4) as well as attacks on Qin Benli, editor-in-chief of the Shanghai *World Economic Herald*. Despite the fact that most intellectuals considered "River Elegy" a critical study of Chinese culture and a valuable reflection of the roots of the country's poverty and backwardness, Wang Zhen, vice president of the PRC, ordered its ban. When Singapore's prime minister, Lee Kuan Yew, visited the PRC in early September 1988, Zhao Ziyang presented him with a tape of the film to show his personal support of the film. The deep schism over the "River Elegy" was the harbinger of the greater power struggle.[66]

Finally, under the Chinese Communist tradition, whoever controls the army holds ultimate power. Both Mao and Deng derived their power from the wide connections with the army. The fatal weakness of both Hu and Zhao rested in their inability to control the army, the instrument of power in a proletarian dictatorship. Many military leaders, while supporting Deng, refused to accept either Hu or Zhao as commander-in-chief because neither had commanded a field army nor fought in a battle.

As can be seen from this survey, the political storm that broke out in spring and summer 1989 was not an accident triggered by the sudden death of Hu Yaobang and the student demonstrations but a continuation of a struggle for succession. It also involved a deep schism about the party line between two groups of leaders. During the power contention, both intellectuals and the army were actors. Whereas most intellectuals tended to support the reformist wing of the Party leadership, the army backed the conservative wing. In the next two chapters, the role of intellectuals and the military in Chinese society will be subjected to closer scrutiny.

Notes

1. There are different categorizations of these two wings. Harding used the terms *moderate reformers* and *radical reformers*. See Harry Harding, *China's Second Revolution:*

Reform After Mao (Washington, D.C.: Brookings Institution, 1987), pp. 77–82. Some others have used *conservatives* and *reformers*. See Lawrence R. Sullivan, "Assault on the Reformers: Conservative Criticism of Political and Economic Liberalization in China, 1985–86," *China Quarterly*, No. 114 (June 1988), pp. 198–222. Schram used the term *conservative leftist*. See Stuart R. Schram, "China After the Thirteenth Congress," *China Quarterly*, No. 114 (June 1988), pp. 177–197. In this book I use the terms *reformers* and *conservatives*.

2. Stuart R. Schram argued that "there are no organized cliques, but it is evident from the public record, and is denied by no one in China, that there are substantial differences of opinion." Schram, op. cit., p. 179.

3. "Zhao on Coastal Areas' Developmental Strategy," *Beijing Review* 31, No. 6 (Feb. 8–14, 1988), p. 9.

4. Yu Yu-lin, "Change and Continuity of the CCP's Power Structure Since Its Thirteenth National Congress," *Issues and Studies* (Taipei) 25, No. 6 (June 1989), p. 25.

5. For details, see *Far Eastern Economic Review*, June 1, 1989.

6. Fox Butterfield's article in the *New York Times*, June 16, 1989.

7. For details, see Chu-yuan Cheng, *China's Economic Development: Growth and Structural Change* (Boulder, Colo.: Westview Press, 1982), Chapter 2.

8. Ibid., pp. 32–34.

9. Mao Zedong, "On the Correct Handling of Contradictions Among the People," *Selected Works*, Vol. 5 (Beijing: Foreign Languages Press), pp. 363–402.

10. The "Gang of Four" refers to Jiang Qing (Mao's wife), Wang Hongwen, Zhang Chunqiao, and Yao Wenyuan (head of the Party's Propaganda Department). After Mao's demise and Hua Guofeng's ascension, they plotted to assassinate Politburo members and seize power. On October 6, 1976, Hua invited the four to an "emergency Politburo meeting," where he had them arrested. After a lengthy trial four years later, Jiang Qing and Zhang Chunqiao were sentenced to death; Wang Hongwen was given life imprisonment; and Yao Wenyuan received a twenty-year sentence.

11. Ramon H. Myers, "Does the CCP Have a 'Line'?" in Shao-chuan Leng, ed., *Changes in China: Party, State and Society* (New York: University Press of America, 1989), p. 19.

12. *Wen Wei Pao* (Hong Kong), Apr. 14, 1981, p. 3.

13. Myers, op. cit., p. 20.

14. Report of Central Advisory Commission, FBIS, Nov. 4, 1987, p. 12.

15. Zhao Ziyang, "Advance Along the Road of Socialism with Chinese Characteristics," *People's Daily*, Nov. 3, 1987, pp. 1–4.

16. *Wall Street Journal*, June 16, 1989, pp. 1, A4.

17. For details see Ying-Mao Kau and Pierre M. Perrolle, "The Politics of Lin Piao's Abortive Military Coup," *Asian Survey*, No. 6 (1974), pp. 558–577.

18. Han Shan-pi, *Teng Hsiao-ping chuan* [A critical biography of Teng Hsiao-ping] (Hong Kong: East-West Cultural Publishing Co., 1985), p. 32.

19. Zheng Derong et al., eds., *Xin Zhongguo Zhi Shi* [Chronicles of new China] (Jilin: Northeast Normal University, 1986), p. 576.

20. Ibid., pp. 580–581.

21. This inside information is from a speech by Zhang Pinghua, director of the CCP's Propaganda Department. The full text of the speech appears in the *Chinese Communist Affairs Monthly* (Taipei) 21, No. 5 (Nov. 1978), pp. 72–73.

22. Chu-yuan Cheng, "Hua Kuo-feng, Really Not an Enigma," *New York Times*, Feb. 28, 1976, Op-ed. page.

23. Deng Xiaoping, "A Letter Passed on to Comrade Hua Guofeng by Comrade Wang Dongxin," in *Deng Xiaoping Yan Lun Ji* [Collections of Deng Xiaoping's speeches] (supplement), 1957–80, compiled by General Political Department of the Ministry of National Defense (Taipei, Dec. 5, 1983), p. 108.

24. Ibid., pp. 109–110.

25. Zheng Derong et al., op. cit., p. 608.

26. See "Study the Document Well and Grasp the Key Link," a joint editorial of *People's Daily, Hongqi*, and the *Liberation Army Daily*, Feb. 7, 1977.

27. Zheng Derong et al., op cit., p. 606.

28. Xinhua News Agency, Beijing, Dec. 31, 1984, in FBIS, Jan. 2, 1985, p. 4.

29. Zheng Derong et al., op cit., p. 555.

30. Harding, op. cit., p. 92.

31. Xinhua News Agency, Dec. 31, 1984, in FBIS, Jan. 4, 1985, p. K1.

32. For a detailed study of this topic, see Stuart R. Schram, "Economics in Command? Ideology and Policy Since the Third Plenum, 1978–1984," *China Quarterly*, No. 99 (Sept. 1984), pp. 417–461; and Frederick Teiwes, *Leadership, Legitimacy and Conflict in China: From a Charismatic Mao to the Politics of Succession* (Armonk, N.Y.: M. E. Sharpe, 1984).

33. Schram, "Economics in Command?" p. 419.

34. Deng Xiaoping, "Carry Out the Adjustment of the Orientation, Guarantee Stability and Unity," in Deng's *Wen xuan* (Beijing: Renmin Chubanshe, 1983), pp. 313–333.

35. Schram, "Economics in Command?" p. 435.

36. Ibid., p. 435.

37. Zhou Yang, "A Discussion of Some Theoretical Questions in Marxism," *People's Daily*, March 16, 1983, pp. 5–6.

38. Schram, "Economics in Command?" p. 441.

39. Wang Zhen, "Guard Against and Remove Spiritual Pollution on the Ideological Front; Raise High the Banner of Marxism and Socialism," *People's Daily*, Oct. 25, 1983, p. 1.

40. This refers to the "Decision of the Central Committee of the Communist Party of China on Reform of the Economic Structure." The English version of the decision appeared in *Beijing Review* 27, No. 44 (Oct. 29, 1984), pp. i–xv.

41. Liaoning Provincial Radio Service, Nov. 29, 1985, in *JPRS* (Joint Publication Research Service), Jan. 2, 1986, p. 105.

42. For details of regional criticism of the reform, see Sullivan, op. cit.

43. See *Gongchan dangyuan* [Communist Party member] (Beijing), No. 3 (March 10, 1986), p. 6.

44. Quoted from Sullivan, op. cit., p. 208.

45. *New York Times*, Sept. 24, 1985, p. 8.

46. China News Service, Beijing, Apr. 9, 1986, and FBIS, Apr. 30, 1986, pp. K1–K2.

47. Deng Xiaoping, "The Primary Task of Veteran Cadres is to Select Young and Middle-aged Cadres for Promotion," in *Selected Works of Deng Xiaoping (1975–1982)* (Beijing: Foreign Languages Press, 1984), p. 361.

48. *People's Daily*, Nov. 27, 1984, p. 1.

49. Hong Yung Lee, "China's Future Leaders: Third Echelon," in Shao-chuan Leng, op. cit., p. 66.

50. Ibid.

51. Chang Chen-pang, "Teng Hsiao-ping's Succession Problem," *Issues and Studies* 21, No. 8 (Aug. 1985), p. 1.

52. *Liaowang* [Outlook], Oct. 5, 1984.

53. Chang Chen-pang, "Rejuvenation of the CCP Central Leadership," *Issues and Studies* 21, No. 10 (Oct. 1985), pp. 1–4.

54. Chang Chen-pang, "Some Observations on Possible Changes in Peking's Top Leadership," *Issues and Studies* 23, No. 5 (May 1987), pp. 1–2.

55. Hong Yung Lee, op. cit., pp. 77–78.

56. *Asian Outlook* 24, No. 3 (May-June 1989), pp. 11–12. The Chinese version of the name list is in *Chao-liu* [Tide monthly] (Hong Kong), May 15, 1989, pp. 42–43.

57. In 1985, Hu candidly confided to some friends, "with the military under the control of Deng Xiaoping, a single sentence of his will always work; under us, we have to say five sentences" (*Issues and Studies* 21, No. 8 [Aug. 1985], p. 3).

58. *Issues and Studies* 23, No. 5 (May 1987), p. 2.

59. Yu Yu-lin, "Chao Tzu-yang's Political Future," *Issues and Studies* 24, No. 10 (Oct. 1988), pp. 1–2.

60. *Issues and Studies* 25, No. 4 (Apr. 1989), pp. 1–4.

61. *China Daily News* (New York), July 17, 1989, p. 2.

62. See Field Marshall Montgomery, "China on the Move," *Sunday Times* (London), Oct. 15, 1961.

63. For details, see Chu-yuan Cheng, "Power Struggle in Red China," *Asian Survey*, Sept. 1966, pp. 469–483, and "The Roots of China's Cultural Revolution: The Feud Between Mao Tse-tung and Liu Shao-chi," *Orbis* 11, No. 4 (Winter 1968), pp. 1160–1178.

64. Chu-yuan Cheng, "Power Struggle in Red China," pp. 475–476.

65. Yu Yu-lin, "The Ma Ting Affair and the Liu Tsai-fu Affairs," *Issues and Studies* 22, No. 6 (June 1986), pp. 5–8.

66. Chang Chen-pang, "The Controversy over the River Elegy," *Issues and Studies* 24, No. 12 (Dec. 1988), pp. 8–11.

4

Intellectual Challenge and Student Movements

The prodemocracy movement that kept the attention of the world focused on Tiananmen Square from mid-April to early June 1989 was shaped by the moral commitment and sense of mission that have long been a part of the Chinese intellectual heritage. Traditionally, Chinese people have regarded scholars and university students as members of a social elite whose responsibility was the articulation of the grievances of the people and the formulation of better alternatives for society. From the Han Dynasty (206 B.C.–A.D. 221) to the Song (960–1280) and Qing (1644–1911), student movements championed lofty goals, ranging from national survival and territorial sovereignty to honest government and social justice.

In modern times, student unrest frequently precipitated great political upheavals. The May Fourth Movement of 1919 inspired the eventual over-throw of the corrupt northern warlord regime. Students constituted the vanguard in calling for the KMT's downfall in 1949. More recently, the April 5, 1976, Tiananmen demonstration led to the later arrest of the Gang of Four. Like their historical predecessors, the student demonstrators in 1989 acted spontaneously. The most recent student protest may mark yet another turning point in Chinese history.

To a large extent, student demonstrations have reflected prominent intellectuals' ideas about the need for change in society and the state. By challenging the political establishment, leading writers, philosophers, and theoreticians, primarily in the social sciences, have catalyzed student activism. These intellectuals, therefore, are the real masterminds behind the student unrest. This chapter will examine the role of intellectuals in Chinese society, explore the causes and effects of the May Fourth Movement, analyze the changing relationship between state and intellectuals under the forty years of Communist rule, and probe the intellectual challenges to the Communist government that presaged the current political storm.

The Role of Intellectuals

For more than 2,000 years, Confucianism dominated Chinese society. Essentially, Confucianism is an ethical code concerned with human relationships. It advocates moral principles such as loyalty, filial piety, benevolence, love, trust, righteousness, peace, and harmony. The ruling class of the Confucian system was comprised of scholar-officials. Because only a small fraction of the population had the chance to become educated, traditional Chinese society was stratified into a hierarchy of the learned to the illiterate. Those who were uneducated could lead a moral life only by following the guidance of the sage. Even the position of the ruler was considered a popular trust in which he should elevate the moral status of the ruled and further their material well-being.

Under the Confucian system, Chinese intellectuals performed moral, political, and socioeconomic functions. They were expected to be standard-bearers of morality, preserving traditional ethical values. If given the opportunity, they might serve in government. However, as government positions were very limited, many of them remained in their hometowns, forming a local gentry that protected local interests against government exactions.[1] Some Western scholars have written that Chinese intellectuals functioned as ideological spokesmen, servants of the state, and moral critics of the ruler.[2] Because of their pivotal and prestigious positions, intellectuals ranked at the top of the four social groups in Chinese society.[3] They became the chief targets of tyrannical suppression under Qinshi Huangdi, the first emperor of China (221–206 B.C.), and during Mao's Cultural Revolution (1966–1976), but also served as the beacons of the uneducated masses during times of great confusion and chaos, as in the recent campaign against corruption and inflation.

As the standard-bearers of morality, intellectuals possessed a strong sense of mission. Fan Zhongyan, a renowned scholar in the Song Dynasty, expressed this sentiment in one of his often quoted statements: "A scholar worries over the world before the world worries itself; a scholar is happy only after all mankind has achieved happiness."[4]

To uphold moral principles, the intellectual needed to live frugally and avoid the accumulation of personal wealth. Confucius once praised highly his beloved disciple Yan Hui for enduring a subsistence-level of consumption and concentrating his attention on studying.[5] Before Fan Zhongyan became a government official, he had lived in a monastery because he could not afford anything else; he had barely kept himself alive on lean rations of rice-porridge.[6] Both Yan and Fan became models for Chinese intellectuals to emulate.

As defenders of the Confucian doctrine, traditional scholars showed astounding fortitude, sometimes sacrificing their very lives. When Prince Yan of the Ming Dynasty (1368–1644) proclaimed himself emperor, Fang Xiaoru (Fang Hsiao-ju), a Han-lin scholar (the highest degree in the civil examination) not only refused to draft the accession edict but also denounced the conqueror as a usurper, knowing that his action would bring punishment to himself, all his relatives, and his pupils.[7] In traditional culture, the scholar-moralist's determined defense of his beliefs has been considered one of his most glorious roles.

The scholar-moralists also functioned as critics both of government policies and of the power holders. The censorial system was specifically designed to check royal caprice. Censors were required to criticize the court and the officials but had to avoid making unsubstantiated charges, which could lead to their own dismissal. Because determined efforts won populist acclaim, the censors often became antibureaucratic heroes.

As government officials, Chinese intellectuals exerted great influence. Most of the civil servants were recruited through an elaborate civil examination system, which provided a practical and impartial means of recruiting government officials. The system reduced favoritism to a minimum, broadened the base of power by opening officialdom to all educated men, and thus helped to promote political stability.[8]

To a large extent, the promotion of officials was independent of the royal will. During the Ming Dynasty, personal appointments were the exclusive concern of the Board of Civil Officers. Regular promotions took place according to a detailed merit-rating system, and additional promotions depended largely on the highest officials, who were required to make specific recommendations from time to time. Thus, contrary to the common perception that the Chinese emperor was an absolute despot with unlimited powers over his ministers, the traditional bureaucrats actually enjoyed substantial influence.[9]

Because the emperor's role was to teach the masses and direct them to the righteous path, his personal behavior was far more important than his administrative skill. Moreover, as 90 percent of the population lived in rural areas, visible government beyond a certain minimum was deemed unnecessary. The restriction of government activities went hand in hand with limitations of the number of officials dealing directly with the masses. The authority of the central powers usually stopped at the county (*xian*) level. Below that level, the intellectuals residing in the district became the natural leaders.

Although the scholar-gentry did not hold official titles, they performed a variety of important functions, ranging from organizing schools, raising funds, subsidizing promising students, and initiating famine relief to arbitrating civil disputes. Most important, because rulers were economically supported by their subjects in Confucian society, the gentry protected the masses by ensuring that they received fair treatment.[10] The traditional role of Chinese intellectuals remained basically unchanged throughout the numerous dynasties.

Under the influence of the leading intellectuals, student movements became an effective outlet for younger scholars to articulate their views and the views of the masses. Although large-scale student protests can be traced back to the Later Han period (25–220), when 30,000 students once gathered at the Imperial College to criticize government corruption,[11] the most famous instance occurred much later in the Northern Song Dynasty (960–1126). According to historical records, the student leader Chen Dong (Ch'en Tung) began in 1125 to send petitions to the emperor and did so on several occasions. On May 2, 1126, Chen led his fellow students in presenting another petition, protesting the dismissal of Li Gang, an advocate of war against the Jurched. On this occasion, the petition of students from the Imperial University (Tai Xue) was strongly supported by members of the public. Over 100,000 men gathered within one day to take up the cause of the students.[12] With public emotions highly charged, the crowd rioted and killed several eunuchs.

Emperor Qin Zong (Ch'in-Tsung) was frightened into reinstalling Li Gang as defense commissioner. Realizing that student leaders could not be suppressed by force when they had support of the masses, the government resorted to offering bribes and official positions to the students to induce them to end their protests. However, student leaders rejected the bribes and Chen Dong was sentenced to death by Emperor Gao Zong (Qin Zong's son) in 1127. Subsequently, in the second month of 1129, the emperor expressed his remorse over the execution by granting Chen Dong an official rank posthumously.[13] For almost half a century during the Ming Dynasty, the Dong Lin scholars, a group of powerful intellectuals who advocated morality, led a movement of political criticism of the imperial court. These incidents illustrate the long heritage of student and intellectual dissent.

Several characteristics of Chinese intellectuals emerge from this brief overview of their traditional role. First, up to the end of the Qing Dynasty, intellectuals occupied a unique place in society, as they circumvented the power of the emperor, directed the masses, and served as intermediaries between the emperor and the people. However, despite their social eminence, they lacked the economic base for an independent life. Possessing only two major employment prospects—government work or teaching—many could barely survive on their pay as private tutors and usually had to be separated from their families. Employment in government positions was rather scarce because only 10 percent of those who passed the civil examinations were eligible. The intellectuals' precarious financial position significantly tempered their moral commitment and undermined their role as independent political critics.

Second, imbued with the Confucian mantle of defenders of morality, the intellectuals were sensitive to the people's welfare and became infuriated with oppression and corruption of the power holders. To voice their resentment and to castigate the powerful, their most effective weapon was literature—novels, essays, poems, and historical plays. The time-honored plays by the great playwright Guan Hanqing during the Yuan Dynasty (1290–1368), the social novel *Lao Can Youji* (Travels of Lao Can) in the late Qing, the essays by Lu Xun during the 1930s, the "Wild Lily" by Wang Shiwei during the Yanan period (1942), the historical play *Dismissal of Hai Rui* by Wu Han right before the Cultural Revolution, and the controversial novel *Kulian* (Unrequited Love) by Bai Hua in the post-Mao era are outstanding examples of attacks on authorities under the guise of literature. As a result, the purge of a famous writer usually antedated the arrival of political crises (see Chapter 3, "The Final Showdown of the Contenders").

Third, as the intellectuals became aware of their vulnerability and more circumspect in periods of suppression, the role of students became more pronounced. Not entrenched in social and government positions, they have had fewer personal interests at stake than the intellectuals. Consequently, students have tended to be more outspoken and radical, expressing their demands for social and political reform more forcefully and their discontent more bluntly than the intellectuals were able to. The first organized student movement in modern times, popularly known as the May Fourth Movement, unfolded in May 1919. It was a patriotic campaign mixed with a New Culture Movement.

The May Fourth Movement and Its Legacy

The May Fourth Movement, the most significant student uprising in modern Chinese history, paralleled the student protests in the Song Dynasty, when students advocated war against the Jurched. An angry intellectual response to Western and Japanese imperialist exploitation of China, the movement had a strong nationalistic imprint. But unlike previous protests, which seldom touched cultural affairs, the new movement called for the abolition of "traditional culture" and the building of a new culture based on Western science and democracy. Many Chinese liberals proclaimed the new movement a "Chinese Renaissance."[14]

Before the Opium War in 1839–1842, China had been basically isolated from the Western world. The Confucian system had reigned supreme. China in the middle of the Qing Dynasty (mid-eighteenth century) was enjoying a period of relative prosperity. The war, however, terminated the country's isolation, shattered its self-esteem, and ushered in a long period of national humiliation. The first intellectual response to the Western challenge was the self-strengthening movement (*zi qiang yun dong*), which advocated the adoption of Western technology to strengthen national defense. Arsenals and shipyards were soon established and students were sent off to learn modern science and technology in the United States and Western Europe. But the traditional cultural system and its political institutions remained intact. The self-strengthening campaign was summed up in Zhang Zhidong's famous phrase: "Chinese learning as the essence, Western learning for utility." Consequently, the piecemeal reform failed to halt national decline. As China suffered one military setback after another, intellectual demands for institutional changes mounted. In 1898 Emperor Guang Xu, advised by Kang Youwei (K'ang Yu-wei), one of the greatest scholars in modern Chinese history, proclaimed a series of reforms in preparation for a constitutional monarchy. The Hundred Days of Reform abruptly ended with the coup d'état of the Dowager Empress Ci Xi, who ordered the execution of six leading reformers and imprisoned Emperor Guang Xu until his death in 1908.

The failure of the institutional reform set the stage for the 1911 revolution, which not only brought the Manchu Dynasty to a close but also marked the end of the dynastic era of Chinese history. The revolution, however, failed to bring about a curtailment of imperialist encroachments and exploitation. By 1911, most imperialist powers had acquired concessions[15] in major Chinese cities and the country had a "subcolonial" status. By a treaty concluded in 1898, China had been forced to lease Jiaozhou (Kiaochow) in Shandong Province to Germany. In the first year of World War I, Japan declared war on Germany and occupied the leased territory despite Chinese protests. A few months later, Japan presented the infamous Twenty-One Demands to China, which, among other things, sought to legitimize Japanese interests in Shandong.

When the peace conference opened in Versailles in 1919, Chinese intellectuals harbored high hopes that the major powers, in accordance with President Woodrow Wilson's Fourteen Points of National Self-Determination, would give China sovereignty over its territory seized by Japan. These hopes were dashed by a series of secret treaties in which England, France, and Italy pledged their support to Japan.

Frustrated by international injustice and indignant about the ineptness of their government, some 3,000 students from thirteen universities staged a demonstration in Beijing on May 4, 1919. They carried white flags bearing such inscriptions as "International Justice," "Return our Qingdao," "Abolish the Twenty-One Demands," and "Down with the Traitors." Three officials in the Beijing government incurred the students' wrath: Cao Rulin (Ts'ao Ju-lin), a principal negotiator of the treaties relating to the Twenty-One Demands; Lu Zongyu (Lu Tsung-yu), president of the Sino-Japanese Exchange Bank; and Zhang Zongxiang (Chang Tsung-hsiang), Chinese minister to Japan. All of these men had been educated in Japan and appeared to the public to be sympathetic to Japanese interests. The demonstrators stormed Cao's residence and severely injured Zhang despite police intervention. When some thirty-two students were subsequently arrested, the public demonstrated its support: Workers staged nationwide sympathy strikes and many merchants closed their shops.[16] The student movement had developed into a nationalistic, anti-imperialist campaign. A month later, the government accepted the popular demands and dismissed all three officials from office.

Whereas the Versailles Peace Conference had sparked the May Fourth incident, the movement's roots lay in the cultural influences of the West.

During the two decades before 1919, various Western philosophical ideas had been popularized in China. Empiricism, utilitarianism, and the theory of evolution were introduced in Yen Fu's translations of Thomas Huxley's *Evolution and Ethics*, Adam Smith's *The Wealth of Nations*, John Stuart Mill's *On Liberty* and *System of Sociology*, Edward Jenks's *A Short History of Politics*, Montesquieu's *L'esprit des lois*, and William Stanley Jevons's *Primer of Logic*. These works had had great influence on Chinese intellectuals.[17] Their interest in politics rose in tandem with their increased awareness of Western ideology.

As Chow Tse-tsung observed, every major student movement in Chinese history, and certainly the May Fourth incident, represented a shift from traditional apathy toward political action.[18] Since the turn of the century and particularly during the first decade of the republic, as China succumbed to warlordism, the intelligentsia had been extremely restless. After comparing the Confucian system with Western political and economic systems, many intellectuals blamed the poverty and backwardness on the traditional culture and called for a wholesale Westernization as the cure. Democracy and science, touted as the sources of Western strength, became the catchwords of the movement. The introduction of democracy and science required a total discarding of the old culture, especially the Confucian ethical system. Under the leadership of Chen Duxiu (Ch'en Tu-hsiu), a fierce anti-Confucian campaign had begun before the May Fourth incident.

Writing in the radical new magazine *Youth* (*Qing Nian*), which he founded in Shanghai in September 1915, Chen Duxiu denounced Confucianism as "incompatible with a new society, a new nation, a new faith" and indicated that "unless the old [society] is demolished, the new one will not arise."[19] In several subsequent articles, Chen attacked the Confucians for advocating superfluous ceremonies, preaching the morality of meekly complying with authority, and disparaging struggle and competition. These attitudes, he argued, debilitated the Chinese people, making them too passive to survive in the modern world. Moreover, Confucian ethics imposed the burdens of filial piety in the family and loyalty to one's ruler, without providing people with individual rights. These outmoded principles were incompatible with a modern individualistic society. In addition, Confucianism upheld a caste system that condoned the unequal status of individuals. This hierarchy could not be retained in a republic. Finally, Confucianism demanded a sexual double standard, which was impractical for everyday life.[20]

Chen's criticism of Confucianism, though cogent, was rather perfunctory compared with the real champion of anti-Confucianism, Wu Yu (1871–1949). Wu, a scholar who had studied law and political science in Tokyo, not only criticized Confucianism as an overly abstract philosophical and ethical system but also attacked its application to "the teachings of proprieties" (*li jiao*), the law, institutions, customs, and the evaluation of historical events. He concluded that China's ethical system, particularly the principle of filial piety and unquestioning obedience to the ruler, fostered despotism.

A campaign to reform the literary language represents one major part of the New Culture Movement. In early 1917, Hu Shi (Hu Shih) published his celebrated article, "Some Tentative Suggestions for the Reform of Chinese Literature," which appeared in the January issue of *New Youth* (the new name of the magazine *Youth*). In this article, Hu introduced the idea of replacing the traditional language (*wen yan*) with the vernacular (*bai hua*). He argued that the vernacular was not as vulgar as traditionally believed. Hu proposed an "eight-point program" of reform, including the avoidance of classical allusions, stale phrases, and imitation of the writers of antiquity, all of which were the common practices of traditional literature. Chen Duxiu, the editor of the *New Youth* and the leader of the radicals, endorsed Hu's proposal and went one step further in condemning not only the classical writing style but also classical literature as a whole.

The novel nature of Hu's thesis aroused enthusiastic responses from the students and young intellectuals; soon, the *bai hua* movement flourished. In 1918, all the articles in *New Youth* appeared in the vernacular. Over 400 tabloid newspapers soon followed suit and eventually even the supplements of the country's most influential newspapers switched to that idiom.

During the May Fourth incident, most intellectuals agreed that reevaluating tradition and promoting new learning were the fundamental means to reform China. However, this unanimity ended after they turned to the more formidable task of finding solutions to the urgent political and economic problems. In the early years of the movement, the leading leftists had been idealistic and democratic socialists, anarchists, guild socialists, and syndicalists. Led by Chen Duxiu and Li Dazhao (Li Ta-chao), they gradually moved from advocating various forms of democracy to advocating Marxism-Leninism. But except for a common hostility toward private property, they had widely different notions regarding how to realize socialism in China.

The evolution of Chen Duxiu from liberal to Marxist is instructive. In the beginning of the New Culture Movement, Chen called for science and democracy without precisely understanding what those words meant and how they could be introduced. When faced with the daunting task of implementing his proposals, he turned to John Dewey's concept of democracy for inspiration. Dewey, in a series of lectures in China a few months before the May Fourth Movement, had stressed the importance of local self-government at the county level in the United States and suggested that China might utilize its old guild system[21] to build a democracy. Soon after Dewey's lectures, Chen published an article echoing Dewey's views. However, when Chen finally discovered that these proposals also defied easy implementation in rural China, he forsook liberalism for Marxism-Leninism.[22] Chen's shift to Marxism-Leninism was inspired by the success of the Russian Revolution more than by conviction that the theory was valid. Few Chinese intellectuals possessed a thorough understanding of Marxism-Leninism at that time.

A liberal, or moderate, reformist wing of the May Fourth Movement, led by eminent intellectuals like Cai Yuanpei, Wu Zhihui, and the younger scholars Hu Shi and Jiang Monlin, did not undertake any systematic exposition of liberalism but, in varying degrees, advocated freedom of thought and expression. Generally, the liberals tended to avoid political entanglement and stressed that reform should be achieved through educational and cultural movements. In contrast to various leftists who had become obsessed with ideology and models, the liberals felt that solutions could be achieved only gradually, not through a "basic solution." Hu Shi, on July 20, 1919, called for more study of problems, less talk of "isms." In Hu's view, the formulations of a doctrine, or ism, should be based on and should grow from the study of specific, practical problems. High-toned, all-embracing isms might be facilely advocated by anybody but would ultimately provide no practical solutions. Hu maintained that only if one tackled China's maladies individually, could one effect a cure.[23]

These intellectual groups were joined by the two major political parties of that time, the Guomindang (Kuomintang, or KMT) and the Jinbudang (Chinputang, or Progressive Party). A number of the intellectual leaders of the Jinbudang associated with Liang Qichao (Liang Ch'i-ch'ao) and under the influence of Bertrand Russell and Henri Bergson came close to guild socialism. Many intellectuals involved in the KMT, while supporting the May Fourth incident in the main, attacked both liberals and Communists on the grounds that they did not give due respect to traditional civilization and therefore undermined the self-confidence of the Chinese people.[24]

In the wake of the May Fourth Movement, on the one hand, the liberals and conservatives tried in vain to demand moderate reforms under the warlord rule and, on the other, the leftists and nationalists accelerated their organizational activities under the rising influence of Soviet Russia. On August 1, 1920, the liberals Hu Shi, Jiang Monlin, Tao Menghe (T'ao Mengho), Gao Yihan (Kao I-han), Wang Zheng (Wang Cheng), and Zhang Zuxun (Chang Tsu-hsun) joined with the new Marxist convert Li Dazhao to publish a "Manifesto of the Struggle for Freedom." In this manifesto, they demanded the abolition of police oppression, the enforcement of laws and regulations governing the press and publication enacted in 1912 and governing emergencies enacted in 1914. They also demanded freedom of speech, publication, assembly, and association; secrecy of communications; the writ of habeas corpus; and supervision of elections by nonpartisan organizations.[25] When one compares the students' demands of April–May 1989 with those put forward by the Chinese intellectuals in 1920, one must conclude that despite a seventy-year interval, the appeals for basic human rights—freedom of speech, press, assembly, communication, and security—have remained virtually unchanged and unaddressed.

From a historical perspective, the most significant effect of the May Fourth Movement was the rise of communism in China. In the months following the incident, socialism attracted great interest among the new intellectuals. The Society for the Study of Socialism, organized at Beijing University in December 1919, had a membership of over one hundred college students and professors. Socialism study groups were also established in many other major cities. In view of the rising interest in socialism, the international Communist organization, Comintern, sent a representative, Gregory Voitinsky, to China to promote communism. He first contacted Li Dazhao in Beijing and then met with Chen Duxiu in Shanghai. The Society for the Study of Marxist Theory was set up in March 1920 under Li's initiative.

In the same period, the founder of the 1911 republic, KMT leader Sun Yat-sen, was also in Shanghai. Frustrated in his dealings with the southern warlords and politicians, Sun left Canton after May 1918 and set up his headquarters in Shanghai. Sun was inspired by Lenin's success in the October Revolution and disappointed by the Western countries' lack of financial support for his reconstruction plan and their continuous recognition of the Beijing warlord regime; thus he established contact with Lenin. When Voitinsky arrived in Shanghai, Chen Duxiu introduced him to some of Sun's associates, such as Dai Jitao (Tai Chi-t'ao), Shao Lizi (Shao Li-tzu), and Zhang Dongsun (Chang Tung-sun). In May 1920, a Chinese Communist Party was founded secretly in Shanghai. Among the members were Dai Jitao, Li Hanzhun, Shen Dingyi, Shao Lizi, Chen Wangtao, Li Da, Shi Cuntong, Yu Xiusong, and Yuan Xiaxia; Chen Duxiu was the leader.[26]

In the initial period of Chinese communism, Mao Zedong was not a leading figure. From spring 1913 to summer 1918, Mao was a student at Hunan Province First Normal School (equivalent to high school) in Changsha, where he began to read *New Youth*. Mao went to Beijing in September 1918 but returned to Changsha in March 1919 after failing to meet with leading intellectuals. In Changsha, Mao joined the local students who supported the May Fourth Movement in Beijing; and he edited the magazine *Xiang River Review* (*Xiangjiang pinglun*). Mao's excellent analysis of the May Fourth Movement brought the magazine national attention and placed him among the foremost Communist activists in the nation.

The May Fourth incident set a precedent for future young intellectuals. University students in China no longer confined their attention and activities to their campuses but became deeply involved in national affairs by participating in organized protests. Student movements after 1919 became entangled with Sino-Japanese relations as Japanese imperialists stepped up their efforts to dominate China. In some events, such as the May 30 incident in 1925, anti-Japanese protests by students resulted in arrests and deaths and provoked national outrage, countrywide protests, and strikes. As the students' interest in politics increased, they began to develop closer relations with political parties. During the war with Japan (1937–1945) and especially during the civil war period (1945–1949), student movements became aligned with the Communists, whose superior organizational techniques, propaganda skills, and attractive programs captured student support. The large-scale hunger strikes organized by left-wing students in Nanjing, Shanghai, Beijing, and Tianjin in 1948 partially contributed to the demise of the KMT the following year.

Based on these historical highlights, it is fair to say that the Chinese Communists were the chief beneficiaries of the May Fourth Movement. Most of their future leaders participated actively in the movement. Leftist intellectuals, expecting that the CCP would champion their freedom and welfare, thoroughly supported the Communists during the showdown with the KMT. Even the majority of the liberals also leaned toward Mao's cause. However, the intellectuals, regardless of political affiliation, as soon as Mao and his associates had consolidated their control over China, began to suffer a prolonged period of humiliation and persecution, unparalleled in modern history.

Intellectuals Under Communism

In the context of cultural tradition, Marxism-Leninism is an ideology alien to most Chinese intellectuals. Before 1919, none of the leading thinkers regarded socialist doctrine as a possible solution to the country's woes. A glance at the contents of *Youth* and *New Youth* published between 1915 and 1918 reveals much discussion of Adam Smith, John Stuart Mill, Darwin, and a host of other Western thinkers but none regarding Marx.[27] Until the end of 1919, even Chen Duxiu, founder of the CCP, was a democrat, not a Communist.[28]

The lack of interest in Marxian theory before the formation of the CCP stemmed partially from the content of the theory itself. According to Marx, socialism necessarily followed capitalism. In 1920, the number of workers in China totaled 1.5 million, only 0.37 percent of the total population. The economy was in a condition remote from the capitalist stage. Socialism, therefore, was rather irrelevant by Marx's own terms.[29]

In essence, the doctrines developed by Marx constituted the antithesis of Confucianism, which was still deeply embedded despite the New Culture Movement. Whereas family is considered the basic social unit of traditional Chinese society and the state a mere extension of family, Marx saw class as the key social unit. Confucian doctrine emphasizes social harmony; Marxist doctrine stresses class struggle as the driving force behind historical progress. In the Confucian system, intellectuals, the standard-bearers of morality, are the natural leaders of the masses; for Marx, workers constitute the vanguard of society.

In view of these fundamental differences, few Chinese intellectuals embraced Marxism wholeheartedly. Moreover, most intellectuals in the 1920s and 1930s saw France and the United States as the ideal models for China to follow and tended to accept without question the virtues of liberty and democracy. There was little room for any other political ideal.

To introduce an alien doctrine and particularly to convince liberal and conservative intellectuals of the sole truth of Marxism, the Communist leadership under Mao needed to impose its authority over virtually every sphere of intellectual life. Mao formulated the policy of organizational control—using organizations such as the Party, youth movements, and student associations to control individuals—and periodic thought reform, which became the means of fettering the intellectuals. Having received only a high school education and having been belittled by some scholars in his early career (e.g., Hu Shi), Mao harbored visceral anti-intellectual feelings. In his

New Democracy, the society would be composed of four classes—workers, peasants, petite bourgeoisie, and the national bourgeoisie (Chinese, as distinguished from foreign, capitalists). Intellectuals, no longer recognized as a separate, privileged class, would lose their traditional leadership role.

Moreover, Mao believed that all useful knowledge came from practice, rather than from books. According to Marx's materialistic interpretation of history, only labor possesses creative power. Mao deliberately downplayed the contribution of mental labor in comparison with manual labor. Teachers, students, and other intellectuals were required to devote a large part of their time to work on farms, in factories, and in mines in order to reform their outlook. In line with this idea, Mao preferred lay leadership over experts and "redness"[30] over "expertise." Under these general guidelines, during the twenty-seven years of Mao's reign, the Communist government launched periodic campaigns to remold the Chinese intellectual.

The first period of trial started in 1951 as a thought reform campaign. Although the campaign attempted to instill new Communist ideology in the minds of the whole population, the main targets were a group of prominent intellectuals in the liberal and conservative camps, notably Hu Shi, the eminent liberal scholar and leader of the literary revolution during the May Fourth period, and Liang Suming, a defender of Confucian doctrine and the leader of the cultural conservatives. Thousands of articles denounced these two venerated scholars. Hu was branded a reactionary who spread "bourgeois ideals" to poison the youth and a cultural comprador of the imperialists. Liang was denounced as an archconservative defending the feudal Confucian system. Later on, the purge extended to some famous leftist writers such as Hu Feng, who had criticized the Party's oppressive controls over literature and the arts. A sense of trepidation gripped the intellectuals, and even those not singled out as targets felt threatened and intimidated. Numerous tedious meetings were convened in which intellectuals were compelled either to conduct self-criticism or to receive criticism from their peers. Most of the victims had to denounce themselves in public in order to get through the ordeal. As Yang Shizhan, professor of accounting at the South Central Institute of Finance and Economics, indicated in a 10,000-character letter to Chairman Mao in early 1957:

> We have applied to the intellectuals methods of punishment which the peasants would not apply to the landlords, and which the workers would not apply to the capitalists. During the social reform campaigns, unable to endure the spiritual torture and humiliation imposed by the struggle . . . innumerable intellectuals chose to die by jumping from tall buildings, drowning in rivers, swallowing poison, cutting their throats, or other methods . . . compared with the massacre methods adopted by the Fascists at Auschwitz, the latter appears more clumsy and childish, but more prompt and "benevolent."[31]

The thought reform combined with the policy of disgracing intellectuals aroused widespread resentment and discontent among those affected. In his 1956 report to an enlarged conference on intellectuals convened by the CCP

Central Committee, Zhou Enlai, then premier, admitted that only 40 percent of the upper intelligentsia (professors, writers, researchers) actively supported the government, while 40 percent took a middle road, and 20 percent were "reactionaries" strongly opposed to socialism.[32] Confronted with governmental antagonism, many prominent scholars simply ceased all academic and research activities.

Intellectual inactivity undermined the government's plans for industrialization. After the enlarged conference, the Party took steps to alleviate the situation. Addressing the Supreme State Conference on May 2, 1956, Mao announced the attractive slogan, "Let a hundred flowers bloom; let a hundred schools of thought contend."[33] Mao's dictate was elaborated by Lu Dingyi, director of the CCP Central Committee's Propaganda Department. At a Beijing meeting of leading intellectuals on May 26, 1956, Lu explicitly promoted Mao's policy for the "luxuriant development of literature, art, and science" and explained that the slogan referring to a hundred schools of contending thought meant: "freedom of independent thinking, freedom of debate, freedom of creative work, freedom to criticize, freedom to express and to maintain one's own views in literature, art, and science."[34]

Although the new policy represented a drastic modification of the party line, it was initially received very coolly by the intellectuals, who had learned to be wary of political traps. As Lo Longji, a leading social scientist, indicated: "During the past year, few flowers bloomed and few schools of thought contended in the academic and ideological fields. The basic cause lies in the fact that the higher intellectuals are still suspicious."[35]

Mao responded to this distrust with a speech to the Supreme State Conference, on February 27, 1957, "On the Correct Handling of Contradictions Among the People." Mao frankly admitted that contradictions still existed in China and recognized the existence of widespread discontent and internal conflict. In advocating corrective measures, he once again recommended the "blooming and contending policy."[36] In the wake of this historic speech, the Party leadership launched a rectification drive for Party and state personnel, proclaiming that the Party would welcome suggestions from the higher intellectuals on ways to improve the CCP leadership.

After years of quiet, the higher intellectuals, deceived by the Party leaders' statements, responded with a storm of outspoken criticism, which shook the Communist government to its foundations. In May 1957, at least one-third of the 100,000 higher intellectuals in Beijing, Shanghai, and other major cultural centers, led primarily by social scientists, openly denounced the regime. They charged the Party with being dictatorial, conducting a lopsided foreign policy, treating intellectuals inhumanely, and dogmatically worshiping Marxist-Leninist works.[37] The hostility of the higher intellectuals was so widespread that even professors teaching at the China People's University, the highest institution for training Marxist social scientists, attacked the regime. The multitudinous complaints voiced by the intellectuals during the short-lived "blooming and contending" period indicated that the conflict between the government and the intellectuals defied easy reconciliation.

The public criticism of the regime triggered a flurry of anti-Communist activities. Students in Beijing, Tianjin, Shanghai, Hankou, Lanzhou, and Guangdong conducted their own crusades for the abolition of Party controls over the universities and the implementation of democratic principles in academic circles and elsewhere. Popular emotions seemed to reach an explosive stage quite similar to the April–May demonstrations in 1989. Suddenly, in June 1957, the CCP stemmed the tide of criticism by introducing an "antirightist" campaign. All who had denounced the regime during the "blooming and contending" period were summarily labeled "rightists." Thousands of meetings were held in universities, government offices, and elsewhere for the suppression of those alleged deviants. Once again, the technique of self-criticism was employed to force confessions. After repeated confessions and public accusations, most of the "rightists" were removed from their assignments and marked for labor reform. According to official reports, some 450,000 higher intellectuals, including most of the nation's top social scientists, were removed from political and academic positions. Late in 1957, the government initiated a large-scale campaign called *xia fang* (sending down), in which rightists were assigned to do physical labor in the villages as punishment. Most of them did not return to normal life until Deng and Hu Yaobang rehabilitated them in 1980. By that time, most of the victims had reached retirement age, were already completely incapacitated, or had committed suicide. The country's intellectual elite had suffered the loss of twenty years. As a result, stagnation and backwardness persisted during Mao's rule.

The mass dismissals of higher intellectuals created a void in the fields of politics and economics. Economic planning became the sole prerogative of dogmatic Party officials, who lacked proper economic training. A series of policy mistakes, such as the hasty establishment of people's communes and the disastrous Great Leap Forward pushed the economy toward the brink of total collapse. (The Great Leap Forward was a radical program to catch up to industrial countries through mobilization of the masses; the utilization of primitive techniques resulted in sharp declines in agricultural output and starvation of 20–30 million people.) Early in 1961, the government began to pardon some social scientists, such as Fei Xiaotong and Wu Wenzao, both sociologists, and Pan Guangdan, a psychologist, and once again promoted a new "blooming and contending" policy. Late that year, the regime convened hundreds of "forums of higher intellectuals" throughout the country for the alleged purpose of "seeking the opinions of the higher intellectuals, consolidating their unity, developing their activism, and mustering their working enthusiasm." The response, however, was unenthusiastic. Some leading Party intellectuals, such as Sun Yefang, director of the Institute of Economics at the Chinese Academy of Sciences, Yang Xianzhen, a top Party ideologist and president of the CCP Higher Party School, and Jian Bozan, a prominent Marxist historian and vice president of Beijing University, did come forward to voice their views. Sun's criticism of the Great Leap Forward and his proposal to reform the financial and economic system, especially in delegating authority to the enterprises and basing planning on potential profits rather than material output, went against the conventional Stalin-Mao approach and subsequently became the first target of a new attack.[38]

In summer 1964, Party officials denounced Yang Xianzhen. Yang, who had received ideological training in the USSR, had served as vice president of the CCP Central Marxist-Leninist Institute in the 1950s. Beginning on May 29, 1964, Yang was subjected to severe criticism for advocating a theory of "class reconciliation," which stood in opposition to Chairman Mao's views that class struggle must be carried through to the end. This campaign soon involved many eminent philosophers, theoreticians, novelists, and playwrights and was transformed into a nationwide rectification campaign among highly placed intellectuals, including Jian Bozan and three well-known novelists, Xia Yan, Tian Han, and Meng Zhao. The extension of the purge in November 1965 to Wu Han, a historian and vice mayor of Beijing, marked the prelude of the Cultural Revolution.[39]

Although the Cultural Revolution was basically a power struggle between Mao and his rivals Liu Shaoqi and Deng Xiaoping, this aspect was camouflaged by an assault on bourgeois, feudal, and Western influences. During the turbulence, almost all intellectual elites of the 1920s and 1930s were victimized. To defeat the Liu-Deng group, which controlled the Party and state machines, Mao encouraged the Red Guards (mostly high school and college students) to act as his "shock force." Under the aegis of Mao and the army, the Red Guards indiscriminately attacked almost every established intellectual, including scientists and engineers. Denounced for elitism, arrogance, ivory-tower mentality, and isolation from the masses and labeled the "stinking old ninth" type (a class at the bottom of the society, below even landlords, capitalists, reactionaries, outlaws, and other class enemies), the intellectuals suffered yet another painful period.

As intellectuals were now considered the dregs of society, everyone had license to humiliate them. Scholars were paraded about in dunce caps and in excruciatingly painful handcuffs while hostile crowds denounced, hit, and spat on them. They were compelled to engage full-time for several years in demeaning labors like cleaning latrines. Some were even locked up in bathrooms and small dark rooms ("cow pens") for months or years. During this decade, more than 100 million people suffered. Many gifted novelists, such as Lao She, and famous scientists, like Liang Sicheng, were either tortured to death or committed suicide.

Mao's personality cult was extended during the Cultural Revolution, and the "Thought of Mao Zedong" was praised as the acme of Marxism-Leninism. Red Guards and other zealots burned millions of copies of Chinese classics, and the publication of most periodicals was suspended in order to devote all available facilities to printing Mao's works. According to an official report, between 1949 and 1965, before the Cultural Revolution, only 10 million sets of the *Selected Works of Mao Zedong* had been published. Under the new campaign to popularize Mao's Thought, the regime printed 15 million sets before the end of 1966 and another 86 million sets in 1967.[40] Such extensive publication of a single work was unprecedented. In the high tide of the Cultural Revolution, the nation's broadcasting network spent more than two-thirds of its air time reading from "The Little Red Book," *Quotations from Chairman Mao*. Red Guards took as their highest obligation the study, dissemination, application, and defense of Mao's Thought. Propaganda teams infiltrated factories, government agencies, schools, and army units in order to turn all major forms of organizations into schools of the Thought of Mao Zedong. The innumerable symbols of his personality cult made the entire Cultural Revolution appear as if Mao's grand design was to assume complete personal dominance, to take revenge upon those who had opposed him after the Great Leap Forward, to establish himself as an unrivaled leader in the CCP, and to transform his doctrine into sacrosanct dogma. Chinese communism was so identified with Maoism that any expression or action against it automatically became an object of struggle.[41]

The Relaxation and Repression Cycles

The cost of the Cultural Revolution was immeasurable. As high school and college students formed Red Guard units and labeled their teachers as "reactionaries" or "rightists," the entire educational system fell into disarray. Key schools and most universities shut down for several years. When some universities reopened in the early 1970s, high school graduates were unprepared for entrance. After several years of absence from school, these students could absorb few intellectual concepts more complex than those provided by Mao's Thought. Moreover, there was a dearth of qualified teachers. As the guardians and communicators of culture, teachers had been most vulnerable to the Red Guards' accusations of perpetuating a feudal and elitist culture. Many had been driven from their classrooms, beaten up, humiliated, and even murdered. When the survivors returned to their schools, they no longer possessed any authority. Students and factory workers began teaching many classes. Experiments in the countryside and in factories replaced laboratory experiments. The 120 research institutes of the Chinese Academy of Sciences, the pacesetters for scientific research and theory, had been virtually dismantled during the Cultural Revolution.[42] It is popularly believed that an entire generation of educated citizens was lost during the "ten bad years."

The economic loss was equally devastating. As Hua Guofeng reported to the Fifth National People's Congress in February 1978, between 1974 and 1976, the radicals had caused losses worth 100 billion yuan ($53 billion) in industrial output, and 40 billion yuan ($21 billion) in state revenues. As a result, Hua indicated, "the national economy was on the brink of collapse."[43] Later official reports assessed the total loss for the period (1966–1976) at 500 billion yuan (or $260 billion at the prevailing exchange rate).[44]

When Deng Xiaoping took power in 1978, the toughest obstacle facing the new leadership was rekindling the enthusiasm of intellectuals, who were needed for the country's modernization. The Third Plenum of the Eleventh

Party Central Committee introduced policies aimed at rectifying the mistakes committed by Mao. Yet at the same time, Deng shared Mao's conviction that the Party's legitimacy rested with the upholding of Marxism-Leninism. Intellectuals, important for the PRC's modernization, should remold their thinking along Party lines and prove their loyalty by subordinating their interests and endeavors to the Party. Once the intellectuals stepped beyond the boundary permitted by the Party, they would be suppressed. During Deng's years, intellectuals have experienced a new cycle of relaxation and repression, with the policy pendulum swinging three times through 1989.

Deng first moved to accommodate Chinese intellectuals by removing the "rightist" label from those persecuted during the 1957 antirightist campaign and those who were denounced during the Cultural Revolution. By 1980, more than 400,000 people had had their "rightist" stigmas removed. In thirty-five ministries, committees, and institutes of the State Council, which employed half of all high-level intellectuals in state organs in Beijing, over 90 percent of the rightists were freed of their opprobrious designation.[45] Of the 1,000-plus intellectuals in the Chinese Academy of Social Sciences who had run into political trouble during the antirightist campaign and the Cultural Revolution, 800 had been rehabilitated by the middle of 1979.[46]

Following the removal of their rightist labels, some older intellectuals were given leadership positions to improve the morale of the intelligentsia. For example, the positions of president of Wuhan University, Fudan University, and the Chinese Academy of Sciences were filled by rehabilitated intellectuals. Intellectuals began to be admitted into the Party despite the opposition of hostile midlevel Party functionaries.[47]

Improvements in living conditions and better housing for reunited intellectual couples were signs of the new policy. More important, the leadership in the reform faction began to revive scientific freedom by advocating "seeking truth from facts." The new atmosphere, however, did not last long. When the film version of Bai Hua's novel *Kulian* (Unrequited Love) was banned by the military leaders because its dismal picture of the PRC undermined the government's efforts to lure overseas Chinese investment, intellectuals sensed that the policy was changing.

When Su Shaozhi and Zhou Yang extended their criticism to Marxian theory in 1983, an anti-spiritual-pollution campaign immediately ensued (see Chapter 3). Although this campaign was initiated by Deng Liqun and other hard-liners, Deng Xiaoping in his speech at the Party plenum in October 1983 gave the green light to Deng Liqun to clamp down on intellectual expression. Deng Xiaoping spoke of "rightist" laxity among Party officials in dealing with "bourgeois liberal" trends in the arts and social sciences and agreed with the hard-liners that intellectuals had exceeded the limitations of freedom he had allowed them. The Bai Hua and Su Shaozhi affairs were further illustrations of Deng's orthodoxy despite his perceived image as a reformer.

With Deng's endorsement, conservative leaders who controlled the Party propaganda machine wasted no time in hurling political charges of "anti-

Party activity" against a wide range of intellectuals in the arts and social sciences. By the end of October 1983, Zhou Yang had been forced into self-criticism for his "irresponsible" handling of the humanism issue and Hu Jiwei (publisher of the *People's Daily*) and Wang Ruoshui (deputy editor-in-chief) had lost their posts. Once again, the Party press was inundated with articles and reports denouncing "capitalist mentalities," "degenerate lifestyles of the youth," and "unabashed worshipping of the West" among the economic and scientific scholars. By early November 1983 the anti-spiritual-pollution campaign had become a major part of the Party's rectification program, creating a political climate similar to that of the 1957 antirightist campaign.[48]

Aware that the anti-spiritual-pollution campaign could damage his economic reform program, Deng gradually steered his policy course to the right. By mid-1984, the Party's rectification campaign was redirected toward explicit repudiation of the Cultural Revolution, targeting "leftist deviation." When the National Congress of the Writers' Association met in December 1984–January 1985, Hu Qili, Hu Yaobang's chosen successor, delivered a major speech on behalf of the reform camp promising full support for "freedom of creativity" in artistic work. In contrast to previous congresses, many young reformers were elevated into the leadership of the association. Hu Qiaomu and Deng Liqun, two leading figures in the conservative camp, seemed to have lost their influence among these people. With this atmosphere prevailing, media articles called for a more liberal publications law and for academic freedom in all spheres of intellectual life, not just the arts.[49] After the September 1985 Party Congress of Delegates, Hu Qili and other reformers were promoted to the Politburo, but Hu Qiaomu and Deng Liqun, with the support of Chen Yun, retained their top positions. As the power contention reached a stalemate, the Party's policy toward intellectuals had the potential to shift in either direction.

In the wake of the September Party congress, intellectuals staged a major offensive. Taking advantage of the celebration of the thirtieth anniversary of the Hundred Flowers policy and marking the tenth anniversary of the conclusion of the Cultural Revolution, dozens of books were published in 1986. Some eminent scholars and writers gave personal accounts of their travails and humiliation during the Cultural Revolution; others reflected on the socialist revolution in the PRC and posed soul-searching questions: How could a traumatic event like the Cultural Revolution occur in the PRC and what should the country do to prevent a recurrence?

Of the numerous publications, two received special attention. The first was memoirs, *The Passage of My Seventy Years*, by Qian Jiaju, who had joined the Communist Party when he was a college student and had devoted his life to the study of Marxian doctrine. A prominent left-wing economist, Qian was an ardent supporter of the Communist cause. However, during the Cultural Revolution, radicals labeled him a reactionary "rightist" and subjected him to all kinds of torture. Unable to endure the prolonged humiliation and physical abuse, Qian attempted to commit suicide by jumping from a cliff, but failed to die. Believing that he would never be rehabilitated, he set down a frank account of his personal suffering, without any expectation that it would be published. In the book, Qian characterized the brutality of the Maoists as unprecedented in human history. He asserted:

When Hitler's fascists ruled Germany, he ordered the large-scale massacre of the Jews; in Chinese history, Empress Wu Zetian [of the Tang Dynasty] appointed cruel officials to slaughter the innocent. In the Ming Dynasty, the wicked prime minister Wei Zhongxian, a eunuch, also murdered thousands of people. But none of these historical events can compare with the Cultural Revolution. During the Cultural Revolution, the radicals entertained themselves by savagely killing. Its ferocity therefore surpassed all past records.[50]

The book rekindled the bitter memories of millions of intellectuals who had shared the fate of Qian during the Cultural Revolution. It became an immediate best-seller.

The second controversial book was the two-volume *Ten-Year History of China's "Cultural Revolution"* by Yan Jiaqi and his wife Gao Gao. Yan, at forty-five, had become the youngest director of the Institute of Political Science, a new organization under the Chinese Academy of Social Sciences. A rising star in the post-Mao era, Yan and his wife spent several years collecting data to produce the most comprehensive analysis of the Cultural Revolution. Based on official documents, the book unraveled the intricate power struggle between Mao Zedong and Liu Shaoqi and between Mao and Lin Biao and exposed the cruel ways Mao and his followers had dealt with their enemies. Before being published as a book, Yan's account of the Cultural Revolution appeared for eighty-one days in serial form in *Ta-Kung Pao*, a Beijing-supported newspaper in Hong Kong, and drew worldwide attention.

Both Qian's memoirs and Yan's documentary analysis constituted a direct attack on Mao, his ideology, and the dictatorship he established. Yan, in an interview with foreigners, indicated that "if another Cultural Revolution occurred in China, or if the country could not learn a lesson from the Cultural Revolution, it would be a catastrophe. If after summarizing the lesson, China was still unable to establish democracy, it would also be a catastrophe."[51]

Based on this deep conviction, Yan and his young associates wrote articles, gave interviews, and organized symposia to promote the idea that reform of the political structure must be carried out simultaneously with reform of the economic structure. He also openly called for the participation of all citizens in political activities and decision-making, the introduction of checks and balances to protect against errors in political leadership, and strong legislative and judicial oversight of administration.[52]

The intellectual offensive reached its peak in summer 1986 and provoked strong responses from the hard-liners. The united force of conservative and military leaders, such as Bo Yibo, Chen Yun, and Wang Zhen, exerted pressure on Deng Xiaoping, who responded by reversing the political course back to the left. In less than six months, the hard-liners had gained the upper hand, culminating in their crackdown on student demonstrations of December 1986–January 1987, the forced resignation of the reform-minded leader Hu Yaobang from the position of Party general secretary, and the nationwide anti-bourgeois-liberalization campaign in spring 1987.

The reversals in the post-Mao policy toward intellectuals partly reflected the power contest between Party conservatives and reformers but also were dictated by the conflict between the Party leadership and intellectuals. The latter, whose concern is with matters of the mind, require freedom as a prerequisite for creativity. But in the eyes of the Party veterans, from Mao Zedong to Deng Xiaoping, scholars should behave like manual workers, serving as cogs in the Party machine. When politics is in command, those in the arts, humanities, and social sciences must follow the party line. Creativity must be confined within the boundaries of political acceptability, defined by the people in power. As Lu Xun, the most influential writer in the 1930s, observed, politicians cannot stand people who think and speak out, and this is where politics and literature become opposing forces. According to Lu Xun, "once the revolutionaries gain power, they no longer tolerate a "revolutionary" literature."[53]

Responding to the limitations imposed by the Party, some writers decided to cut down or cease working. For instance, the playwright Cao Yu, who produced many masterpieces, such as *Leiyu* (The thunderstorm) and *Richu* (The sunrise) in the pre-1949 era, has not written any plays on a par with his previous works. Another prolific author, Shen Congwen, shifted to the study of the history of apparel and stopped writing novels. Among those still struggling to keep their writings within the acceptable boundary, many have become frustrated and antagonistic. Whenever an opportunity has presented itself, they have come forward to speak their minds, as in 1956–1957 and more recently in 1986–1989. But as long as the Chinese leaders continue to uphold Marxism-Leninism and Mao's Thought, the tension between the leadership and the intellectuals will not subside.

Challenges from the Intellectuals

Since mid-1980s, Chinese intellectuals have directly challenged Communist authorities, a phenomenon that appeared for the first time since the 1957 antirightist campaign. Factors contributing to this new tide include the rising role of social scientists in policy-making, the increasing influence of Western ideologies, and the deterioration of the living standards of intellectuals.

When Zhao Ziyang ascended to the new post of premier responsible for preparing a comprehensive reform program and new strategies of development in 1980, he began to create policy-research organs patterned after U.S. think tanks such as the Rand Corporation and the Brookings Institution. By 1983–1985, several new institutions under the State Council had sought the advice of well-known social scientists, especially theoretical economists like Xue Muqiao and Yu Guangyuan of the older generation, Li Yining and Wu Jinglian of the middle generation, and Hua Sheng of the younger generation.

The most important of the organizations established are the Rural Development Research Center of the State Council; the Economic Structural Reform Research Institute of the State Council; and the Economic, Technical, and Social Development Center of the State Council. Each employs hundreds of economists, statisticians, sociologists, and engineers. Under the Academy of Social Sciences, the Institutes of Political Science, Economics, and Marxism-Leninism–Mao Zedong Thought all established close ties with the State Council and engaged in research into ideology and political reform. The recruitment of thousands of social scientists to government policy research organizations greatly enhanced the prestige of this group and revived their traditional role as government advisers and critics.

The open-door policy led to the reestablishment of cultural links between the PRC and the West, particularly the United States and Western Europe. Tens of thousands of Chinese scholars visited these countries under various exchange programs or were sent by the government. Hundreds of Western social scientists were invited to lecture in the PRC. The intellectual exchange injected new Western ideas and stimuli, significantly widening horizons of Chinese social scientists.

However, although the Chinese intellectuals assumed a higher social status, their material well-being did not keep pace. They suffered a relative decline in income compared with individual businessmen and corrupt government officials as well as an absolute decline. In a speech to the People's Congress of Beijing Municipality's Second Electoral District, Li Shuxian, wife of Fang Lizhi and associate professor in the Department of Physics of Beijing University, compared salary scales for university professors in 1956 and 1985. According to the 1956 pay scale, a professor in the Grade 1 (the highest) had a salary almost on par with a minister of the State Council (about 345 yuan per month). A Grade 2 professor received 287 yuan, a Grade 6 associate professor, 149.5 yuan; Grade 7 teaching assistants, 62 yuan; and college graduates who had just joined the staff, 56 yuan. In that period, academic compensation was more or less in line with pay in other careers. The wage reform in 1985 was adopted under the pretext that because the number of professors had expanded, the state could not afford to keep the old scale. Monthly pay for a Grade 1 professor fell 45 percent to only 255 yuan and that of a grade 6 associate professor to 122 yuan— despite a 45 percent rise in the cost of living during this time span. Li pointed out that after teaching at the university for thirty-one years, she was paid only 122 yuan a month, or a salary lower than that of an average construction worker, who could earn 154 yuan a month.[54]

The subsistence-level income of most scholars caused them to suffer from malnutrition and a general deterioration in their health. A 1987 Chinese Medical Association investigation reported that 81.6 percent of middle-aged Chinese scientists and technologists in eleven research institutes in Beijing were suffering from chronic diseases. Another government investigation, conducted by the state Scientific and Technological Commission and involving 37,000 intellectuals, showed that 60.1 percent of them were victims of chronic ailments. In 1983, the death rate of middle-aged intellectuals was more than double that of nonintellectual, old-aged citizens. In the two years 1985 and 1986, the death rate of middle-aged intellectuals in the Beijing area was twenty times that of other middle-aged workers and staff.[55] These reports alarmed the intellectuals.

But the reasons that intellectuals staged a challenge to the regime lay more in their moral convictions than in the paucity of their personal incomes. With a strong commitment to revitalizing the country, many middle-aged intellectuals felt it incumbent upon themselves to stand up and voice their views. Some proposed bolder reform plans for the political system; others used literary works to articulate their ideas. A new configuration of forces gradually emerged.

Prominent among the intellectual leaders have been Yan Jiaqi, Su Shaozhi, and Fang Lizhi. Yan, the energetic political scientist who was identified by the Beijing government as the number-one anti-Party element inciting the 1989 student demonstration, advocated the "division of powers" and the "checking of power with the people's power" in 1986. He also suggested the adoption of a Western-style parliamentary government.[56] Su emphasized the importance of legislative and judicial independence, the separation of Party and government functions, and the rule of law instead of men.[57] Fang has maintained that freedom, equality, and fraternity are the products of historical development and that true democracy can be obtained only through struggle, rather than bestowed by authority. Fang also has emphasized the importance of knowledge, asserting that "China's greatest tragedy is that its intellectuals have not been recognized as a leading force in promoting social programs."[58]

With the Party leaders stubbornly clinging to the Four Cardinal Principles, explicit pleas in favor of Western democracy have been extremely rare. On July 25, 1989, the *People's Daily* published a long article identifying Fang Lizhi, his wife Li Shuxian, and Yan Jiaqi as those who had incited the recent unrest. On August 3, the same Party organ carried another long article blasting Yan Jiaqi and calling him a traitor who had played a significant role in the "rebellion." The paper identified Yan as the brain behind Zhao Ziyang's anti-Party activities and accused Yan of attempting to woo the protesting students and to force the central authorities to accept their "democratic demands." Since the middle of July 1989 all publications of Yan, Fang, and Su Shaozhi have been banned in the PRC.[59]

Other prominent intellectuals who have implicitly criticized the regime are the novelist and essayist Liu Binyan and Wang Ruowang. Liu began to participate in Communist underground activities in 1943, becoming a Party member in 1944, and joining the editorial board of the *China Youth Daily* in 1951. As early as 1939, he had already won a prize for his first short story. In 1957, Liu was labeled a "rightist" and his works were denounced as "poisonous weeds." During the Cultural Revolution, he was dispatched to a "May 7 Cadre School" for labor reform and was not rehabilitated until October 1976. He then worked at the *People's Daily* as a reporter. Liu has used his writings as a means of exposing injustice. Convinced that under the repressive Communist system, literature that reflects real life has become scarce while that which praises the status quo abounds, he vowed to write the truth. Liu has played the role of social investigator and articulator of popular grievances, contending that when unsightly and unpleasant things are reflected in a mirror, one should not blame the mirror but should investigate and deal with the unpleasant facts themselves. Liu has published several works along these lines, such as "Between People and Monsters" (*Ren yao zhi jian*), "My Diary," and "The Second Kind of Loyalty" (*Di er zhong zhong cheng*). The immediate and widespread impact of these works made him the most prominent Chinese writer of the 1980s.[60] Whereas the people welcomed his candid works, the authorities believed they tarnished the socialist state and expelled Liu from the Party in January 1987.

Like Liu Binyan, Wang Ruowang joined the Communist Youth League in 1933 when he was fifteen. He was soon arrested by the KMT, sentenced to ten years in jail in 1934, but served only three years before being released. Subsequently, he went to Yanan and joined the Communist Party the same year. In 1943, his "Mao Zedong Story" was serialized in the Shandong *Da Zhong Ribao* (Masses daily). In 1950, he supported the PRC's participation in the Korean War and strongly condemned U.S. imperialism. His loyalty prompted him to respond to Mao's call to offer criticism during the Hundred Flowers movement. Becoming a target of attack, he was jailed during the antirightist campaign and again during the Cultural Revolution. He finally was rehabilitated in 1979.

Through investigations, interviews, examination of evidence, and reports of his findings, Wang has also exposed cases of injustice. He has vigorously opposed both the subordination of literature to politics and the use of art for political ends. In his article "A Broad View on Speaking Falsehood," he openly railed against "the lie that the whole Party and country have entertained for more than ten years—the lie about the Red Flag of Dazhai [Mao's model for agriculture] which brought calamity to the country and the people and became the laughing stock of history."[61] In the short stories "Hunger Trilogy" and "A Magic Flute," he reflected on the cruelty of the Cultural Revolution. Toward the end of 1986, he sent letters to various intellectuals suggesting that a meeting be convened in February 1987 to commemorate the thirtieth anniversary of the Hundred Flowers movement. Wang was denounced as "attacking and defaming the socialist system, negating the Party leadership, and opposing the Party's policy under the guise of advocating reforms." Wang shared the fate of Liu Binyan and was expelled from the Party in January 1987.

The punishment of Liu Binyan and Wang Ruowang failed to deter other intellectuals from speaking out. In June 1988, a group of young writers unleashed a more powerful offensive. The six-part television documentary "River Elegy" (*He Shang*), shown on Beijing's Central Television, immediately shook the country. The script was written by Su Xiaokang, a noted journalist, and Wang Luxiang, a lecturer at Beijing Normal University, with two well-known scholars serving as consultants—Li Yining and Jin Guantao. "River Elegy" used the death of the Yellow River, the cradle of Chinese culture, to symbolize the retarding effect of traditional culture on the country's development. It strongly endorsed the idea that overcoming China's weakness and backwardness required Westernization. In "River Elegy," China's agrarian culture symbolized by the Yellow River represented conservatism; the Great Wall symbolized China's confinement and isolationist mentality; and the dragon, the worship of authority. Although the ostensible target was Chinese traditional culture, the documentary implicitly denounced the Chinese Communist Party. The TV series openly attacked the Cultural Revolution and railed against the privileged class, whose acquisition of wealth did not come from fair competition.

> The official departments' and privileged class's domination of commodities has destroyed the socialist ownership system and poisoned the ruling Party's working style as well as the general atmosphere in society. This enabled those with power to employ it for private gains. As a result, the right of use and the right of administration would be alienated into the right of possession, and things owned by the state would consequently be seized by departments or individuals. Aren't the startling corruption practices of graft, receiving bribes, and robbery a clear indication of this?[62]

In another segment, the documentary alludes to the fundamental flaw of the system:

> In a dark room in Kaifeng Henan, the chairman of the republic [Liu Shaoqi], the man who was in charge of drafting the constitution for both the state and the Party, was secretly confined there to spend his last twenty-eight days. When he died, his white hair stretched one foot long. When the law cannot protect a common citizen, it eventually cannot protect the chairman of the republic either. If China's social structure cannot be revamped and its politics, economy, culture, and ideas cannot be modernized, who can guarantee that the same tragedy [Cultural Revolution] will not be repeated again?[63]

When Wang Zhen, the hard-liner vice president of the PRC, saw this powerful indictment of the Communist system, he condemned it as propagating national nihilism and opposing the CCP and socialism. He immediately suggested that the series be banned. After the Tiananmen massacre, "River Elegy" was openly condemned as negating socialism and promoting bourgeois ideas. An article that appeared in the *People's Daily* asserted that the documentary contained ten important errors and grossly insulted the Chinese nation.[64] One of the authors of "River Elegy," Wang Luxiang, was arrested, while the other, Su Xiaokang, was put on the premier's wanted list.

Chinese intellectuals—from Yan Jiaqi, Su Shaozhi, Fang Lizhi, Liu Binyan, Wang Ruowang, and Li Shuxian to the authors and filmmakers of the "River Elegy"—have ended their long period of passivity and subordination to the Party "priesthood." Like their forerunners of the May Fourth generation, they have assumed the mantle of the traditional moral critics, endeavoring to put the PRC on the right track of modernization. The resurrection of the intelligentsia has meant a renewed challenge to the authoritarian power holders.

The New Student Movement

Student movements in China have always been the convergence of various currents—the effects of intellectual fermentation and developments in the domestic and international spheres. In the post–Cultural Revolution era, the surface tranquility belied the latent discontent that became channeled into two vehement protests that ushered in the spring 1989 unrest. The first originated in grievances about the Japanese economic invasion.

Since the first Sino-Japanese War (1894–1895), China's relationship with Japan has been a major concern of the students. Students staged mass demonstrations on December 9 and 16, 1935, in response to Japanese demands for an autonomous region in northern China. These demonstrations represented a call for a national salvation movement and were the first step in pushing the KMT and CCP into a United Front to fight the Japanese. Therefore, CCP historians view the December 9 incident as a key event in Party history.[65]

On September 12, 1985, when Japanese Prime Minister Yasuhiro Nakasone paid an official visit to the Yasukuni Shrine to honor the Japanese war dead of World War II (most of whom had participated in the invasion of China), students at Beijing University immediately lodged a protest. Posters appeared on the campus demanding that henceforth the date September 18 be set aside as "National Humiliation Day" to commemorate the "Mukden Incident," when Japan occupied China's northeastern provinces and established Manchukuo. They also called on all students to rally in Tiananmen Square on that day. Their demands were immediately echoed by students of Qinghua University, People's University, and Beijing Normal University. Soon afterward, posters went up on the campuses of these schools demanding the overthrow of "Japanese imperialism" and calling for more democracy and an end to dictatorship in the PRC.

Despite preventive measures taken by university authorities, over 1,000 Beijing University students demonstrated in Tiananmen Square. The protesters were dispersed by police forty minutes later. The Beijing demonstration was followed on October 1 by a similar but much larger scale action in Xi'an in which more than 10,000 students from ten universities participated. Besides voicing their indignation over the revival of Japanese militarism and Beijing's subservience to Japan, students also expressed their discontent with the domestic political situation, especially government corruption, nepotism, and price hikes following the economic reform.

Students at Beijing and Qinghua universities planned another round of protests for the fiftieth anniversary of the December 9, 1935, incident. To prevent possible unrest, the authorities rushed into action with a series of mediating measures: (1) High-ranking CCP officials personally received student representatives and paid pacifying visits to campuses. Both Hu Qili and Li Peng received student representatives at Zhongnanhai (the residence of Party leaders). At the end of September and in early October, Party committee secretaries at the provincial and municipal levels also visited universities and colleges to listen to complaints. (2) The authorities promised to improve the students' living and studying conditions and provide more coal for heating the dormitories and classrooms and more vegetables and rice for university dining halls. (3) To defuse campus discontent, the CCP took the initiative in commemorating the December 9 incident. (4) Students of eighteen universities in the Beijing area formed an investigative team to visit Shanghai's Baoshan Iron and Steel Works (built by the Japanese) to see whether the Chinese government had spent over 10 billion yuan ($5 billion) to buy worthless equipment from Japan, as students had alleged.[66]

The prompt responses of the CCP authorities assuaged the anger of the students but did not eliminate the roots of student dissatisfaction. One year later, on December 5, 1986, in Hefei, the capital of Anhui Province, in east China, protests broke out among students at the University of Science and Technology, a key institute of scientific training. Four days later, demonstrations resumed to commemorate the December 9 incident, a replay of the previous year's demonstrations in Beijing, and spread to seventeen additional cities and 150 campuses. The protests originally stemmed from some specific local issues, but soon the protesters paraded under banners calling for reform and democracy. In this respect, the demonstrations differed significantly from the smaller and more short-lived ones that had begun in September 1985.

In Hefei and Wuhan, where the demonstrations coincided with local elections to the provincial People's Congress, students demanded the right to participate in the nominating process, hitherto dominated by the CCP. The issue was brought to a head when Fang Lizhi, professor of astrophysics and vice president of the University of Science and Technology, supported this demand. He arranged to have elections in Hefei postponed to allow student participation in the nominating process. As the momentum of the protest mounted and workers began to join the demonstrations, local authorities became alarmed. In Shanghai from December 19 to 22, more than 70,000 people participated in the demonstrations. A few banners reading "Down with the Communist Party" and "To Hell with Marxism–Leninism–Mao Zedong Thought" were raised.[67] According to Hong Kong's Ta-Kung Pao (a Beijing-supported newspaper), students in Shanghai made four demands: speedier democratic reforms, greater press freedom, recognition that their protests were lawful, and a guarantee of their personal safety. Jiang Zemin, then mayor of Shanghai, after engaging in dialogue with the students, promised to recognize the demonstrations as legitimate and agreed not to punish or arrest the participants. However, he made no concessions regarding the first two demands.[68]

The tidal wave of protests finally hit Beijing on the morning of New Year's Day 1987. Defying a ban on unauthorized demonstrations and stern warnings in the official press, several thousand students and their supporters assembled in Tiananmen Square. About 300 of them broke through a police cordon and began shouting slogans and unfolding banners calling for democracy, freedom of the press, and reform. More than 20 students and several nonstudents were arrested.[69]

The resurgence of student protests and particularly their explicit defiance of the Communist Party's absolute authority were taken by the hard-liners and the Party veterans as an ominous sign of a recurrence of the Red Guard nightmare, one that posed a fundamental threat to the Party and its system. The hard-liners took advantage of this opportunity to blame Hu Yaobang for not taking stern measures against the students and forced him to resign from the post of general secretary of the Party, an action that sowed the seeds of further unrest. Next, Fang Lizhi, Liu Binyan, and Wang Ruowang were all expelled from the Party. Fang was accused by the CCP Anhui Provincial Committee for "sowing discord between the Party and the young intellectuals, encouraging bourgeois liberalism, ridiculing Party leadership, and going against the fundamental interests of the Party and the people," connecting him with the outbreak of the student movements.[70]

Prior to the June 1989 Tiananmen massacre, three undercurrents appeared in Chinese society. The mounting discontent of the masses arising from inflation, corruption, income disparities, and nepotism stimulated the consciences of students and intellectuals and called them back to their traditional duty as moral critics of the state. Reflections on the Cultural Revolution and growing Western stimuli strengthened demands for democracy and human rights. Ideological disputes and the contest for succession intensified the power struggle within the Party's top hierarchy. All of these undercurrents converged in 1989 to create an explosive situation. To defuse the imminent crisis, the top leadership had two alternatives: to accept part of the students' and intellectuals' demands or to suppress the demonstrators. The choice of the latter option by the power holders led to an enhanced role for the army. The decision to impose martial law and to use field armies to suppress demonstrators not only destroyed Deng's plan to relegate the soldiers to the barracks but also reintroduced the military as a significant player in politics, prompting fears of a military ascendancy similar to that during the Cultural Revolution.

Notes

1. These three functions are adopted from Y. C. Wang, *Chinese Intellectuals and the West 1872–1949* (Chapel Hill, N.C.: University of North Carolina Press, 1966), Part 1.

2. Merle Goldman et al., eds., *China's Intellectuals and the State* (Cambridge: Harvard University Press, 1987), "Introduction."

3. There are four social groups in traditional Chinese society: scholar-official, peasant, artisan, and merchant (*shi, nong, gong,* and *shang*).

4. From Fan's essay in *Ku-wen kuan chih* [A compilation of ancient famous essays], Vol. 9 (Taipei: Commercial Press, 1956), p. 138.

5. "How admirable Hui is! Living in a mean dwelling on a bowlful of rice and a ladleful of water is a hardship most men would find intolerable, but Hui does not allow this to affect his joy. How admirable Hui is!" *Analects*, trans. D. C. Lau (New York: Penguin Books, 1979), Bk. 4, p. 82.

6. Wang, op. cit., p. 23.

7. Fang's biography in *Ming-shih* [History of the Ming Dynasty].

8. Wang, op. cit., pp. 12–13.

9. Ibid., pp. 19–20.

10. Fei Xiaotong, "Peasantry and Gentry," *American Journal of Sociology*, July 1946, pp. 1–17.

11. Wen-han Kiang, *The Chinese Student Movement* (New York: King's Crown Press, 1948), p. 8.

12. For details of this event, see Gong Wei Ai, "Government Policy of Accommodation and Decline in Students' Morale during Southern Sung China 1127–1279," in *Chinese Culture* 18, No. 2 (June 1977), pp. 49–69.

13. Ibid., p. 53.

14. For details, see Chow Tse-tsung, *The May Fourth Movement* (Cambridge: Harvard University Press, 1960), pp. 338–342.

15. Concessions were foreign-controlled settlements protected by extraterritorial rights. They were set up in Shanghai, Tianjin, Hankou, Guangzhou, and other coastal treaty ports under the unequal treaties China signed with imperialist powers after the Opium War and other wars.

16. Wang, op. cit., pp. 306–308.

17. Chow, op. cit., p. 294.

18. Ibid. p. 227.

19. *La Jeunesse* [Chinese title, first *Qing Nian*, then *Xin Qing Nian* (Hsin Ch'ing Nien)] 11, No. 3, 1916.

20. Chow, op. cit., pp. 302–303.

21. Guild systems (*tong ye gong hui*) were professional business associations.

22. Wang, op. cit., pp. 310–314.

23. Chow, *op. cit.* p. 218.

24. Ibid., pp. 338–345.

25. Hu Shih et al., "Manifesto of the Struggle for Freedom," reprinted in the *Eastern Miscellany* (Shanghai) 17, No. 16 (Aug. 25, 1920), pp. 133–134.

26. Chow, op. cit., p. 248.

27. Wang, op. cit., p. 315.

28. See Hu Hua and Peng Ming, "Chen Tu-hsiu During the May Fourth Period," in Hu Hua, ed., *Historical Figures During the May Fourth Movement* (Beijing: China Youth Press, Nov. 1979), p. 107.

29. Benjamin I. Schwartz, *Chinese Communism and the Rise of Mao* (Cambridge: Harvard University Press, 1961), pp. 7–8.

30. "Redness" refers to loyalty to the leadership and devotion to the Communist cause.

31. *Chang-Chiang Jih-pao* [Yangtze daily] (Hangkow), July 13, 1957.

32. Zhou Enlai, *Report on the Question of Intellectuals* (Beijing: Foreign Language Press, 1956), p. 10.

33. Mao's *bai hua ji fang, bai jia zheng ming* is the rephrasing of an old term: A "hundred schools of thought contend" (*bai jia zheng ming*) is descriptive of the classical age, from about the sixth century to the third century B.C., when scholars were entirely free and many schools of thought, such as Confucianism, Taoism,

Moism, and Legalism, all coexisted. See Theodore H.E. Chen, *Thought Reform of the Chinese Intellectuals* (Hong Kong: University Press, 1960), p. 117.

34. *People's Daily*, June 13, 1956, p. 1.

35. *People's Daily*, March 25, 1957, p. 1.

36. Mao Zedong, "On the Correct Handling of Contradictions Among the People," *People's China*, No. 13 (1957), pp. 3–26.

37. For details, see Chu-yuan Cheng, *Scientific and Engineering Manpower in Communist China 1949–1963* (Washington, D.C.: National Science Foundation, 1965), pp. 258–259.

38. Nina Halpern, "Economists and Economic Policy-Making in the Early 1960s," in Goldman et al., op. cit., pp. 45–63.

39. For details, see Chu-yuan Cheng, "Power Struggle in Red China," *Asian Survey* 6, No. 9 (Sept. 1966), pp. 469–483.

40. *Peking Review* 11, No. 1 (Jan. 3, 1968), p. 14.

41. Chu-yuan Cheng, *China's Economic Development: Growth and Structural Change* (Boulder, Colo.: Westview Press, 1982), pp. 38–44.

42. Suzanne Ogden, *China's Unresolved Issues* (Englewood, N.J.: Prentice Hall, 1989), pp. 317–321.

43. *Peking Review* 21, No. 10 (March 10, 1978), p. 12.

44. *Hongqi* [Red flag], May 1, 1980.

45. *People's Daily*, Apr. 5, 1982.

46. *People's Daily*, July 14, 1979

47. Lynn T. White III, "Thought Workers in Deng's Time," in Goldman et al., op. cit., p. 259.

48. Carol Lee Hamrin, "New Trends under Deng Xiaoping and his Successors," in Goldman et al., op. cit., pp. 295–296.

49. Ibid., p. 298.

50. Qian Jiaju, *Qi Shi Nian de Jingyan* (Hong Kong: The Mirror Post Cultural Enterprises, 1986), p. 3.

51. Chu-yuan Cheng, *Taiwan's Experience and China's Reconstruction* (Taipei: Linking Press, 1989), pp. 316–318.

52. *China Daily* (Beijing), June 9, 1986, p. 4.

53. Quoted from Kyna Rubin, "Keeper of the Flame: Wang Ruowang as Moral Critic of the State," in Goldman et al., op. cit., p. 244.

54. Li's speech was published in *Pai Hsing* [The people] (Hong Kong), Aug. 15, 1987.

55. *People's Daily*, June 24, 1987

56. Dai Qing, "On China's Reform of the Political Structure—An Interview with Yan Jiaqi," *Xinhua Wenzhai* (Beijing), Sept. 1986, p. 9.

57. Su Shaozhi, "A Preliminary Study on the Reform of the Political Structure," *Xinhua Wenzhai*, Nov. 1986, pp. 12–15.

58. *World Economic Herald* (Shanghai), Nov. 24, 1986, p. 3.

59. *China Times* (Taipei), July 27, 1989, p. 9.

60. For details, see Chou Yu-sun, "Liu Pin-yen and Wang Jo-wang," *Issues and Studies* 23, No. 5 (May 1987), pp. 48–62.

61. *Ming Pao* (Hong Kong), May 1, 1981.

62. *He Shang* [River elegy], Part 4. My translation.

63. Ibid.

64. *People's Daily*, July 19, 1989, p. 2.

65. For details, see John Israel, "Reflections on the Modern Chinese Student Movement," in Seymour Martin Lipset and Philip G. Altbach, eds., *Students in Revolt* (Boston: Beacon Press, 1970), pp. 315–317.

66. Chang Chen-pang, "Student Protests in Mainland China," *Issues and Studies* 22, No. 1 (Jan. 1986), pp. 1–4.

67. Lowell Dittmer, "Reform, Succession, and the Resurgence of China's Old Guard," in Shao-chuan Leng, ed., *Changes in China* (New York: University Press of America, 1989), pp. 42–43.

68. Yu Yu-lin, "Resurgence of Student Movement in Mainland China," *Issues and Studies* 23, No. 1 (Jan. 1987), p. 2.

69. Dittmer, op. cit., p. 44.

70. Chou Yu-sun, "The Case of Fang Li-chih," *Issues and Studies* 23, No. 3 (March 1987), pp. 7–9.

5

Military and Politics

Since 1949, the role of the PRC's military has undergone many changes. First the instrument of revolution and the guardian of the state, it evolved into a gendarmerie of society and power broker of rival factions during the Cultural Revolution (1966–1976). After the Cultural Revolution, the Party leadership made strenuous efforts to disengage the army from politics by building a modern, professional, detached military force. Yet, when Premier Li Peng announced the imposition of martial law on May 20, 1989, and ordered a quarter of a million field troops into the capital, the world wondered whether the military would stay neutral in what seemed to be a power struggle between rival wings in the Party's hierarchy. The brutal massacre of unarmed civilians tarnished the image of the People's Liberation Army and left Deng's plan to construct a new pattern of Party-army relations in shambles.

This chapter will concentrate on the changing role of the PLA in Chinese politics. It will analyze the command structure of the PLA, its political role during various periods, Deng's efforts to reduce military involvement in politics, the military's resistance to Deng's agenda, and its reentry into the factional struggle in 1989.

The Command Structure

Official documents often refer to the Chinese People's Liberation Army as the "Great Wall" of the Chinese Communist Party. One of Mao's most famous axioms states: "The Party commands the gun, but the gun must

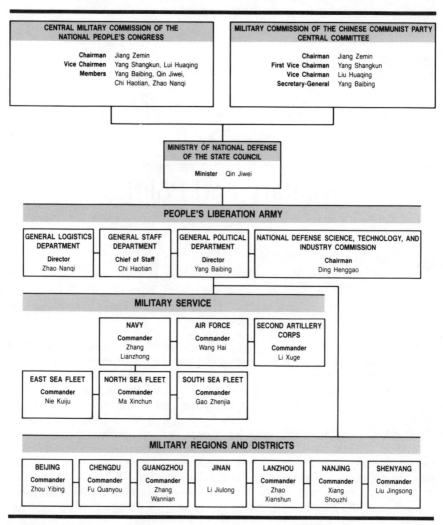

FIGURE 5.1
Military Organizations of the People's Republic of China (March 1990)

never be allowed to command the Party."[1] To put this axiom into effect, the CCP has established a highly formalized command structure, from the Party center down to provincial and subprovincial districts and covering all armed forces of the PLA (see Figure 5.1).

In terms of organization, the highest military decision-making body is the Party's Central Military Commission (CMC), an organ of the CCP Central Committee. In 1982, the Party created a State Military Commission (SMC) as a counterpart to the CMC for the state apparatus. The main function of the new organization was to coordinate the various ministries and commissions in charge of defense industries under the State Council. However, the Party CMC remains the final authority in military affairs.[2]

Prior to 1982, the Party chairman had always served concurrently as the chairman of the CMC. Yet, after the CCP's Twelfth Party Congress in 1982, in which Hu Yaobang became the new general secretary, Deng Xiaoping assumed the chairmanship of the CMC in his capacity as a member of the Politburo's Standing Committee. In 1987, to persuade the Party veterans to retire, Deng relinquished his membership in the Party's Central Committee and its Politburo, but retained his chairmanship of the CMC, thus creating an unique situation in which a rank-and-file Party member chaired the most powerful organization in the PRC. Deng also served as the chairman of the State Military Commission.

After the 1987 Thirteenth Party Congress, the entire military command system underwent a dramatic reshuffling. In the new CMC there were two instead of four vice chairmen. In April 1989, the military hierarchy was as follows:

- Chairman: Deng Xiaoping
- First vice chairman: Zhao Ziyang (general secretary, CCP)
- Executive vice chairman: Yang Shangkun (president, PRC)
- Permanent secretary-general: Yang Shangkun
- Deputy secretary-general: Hong Xuezhi and Liu Huaqin

Day-to-day affairs of the CMC are handled by the secretary-general, who runs the administrative office. In the past, the chief of staff of the PLA served concurrently as secretary-general; however, in recent years, these posts have been filled by two different people. Under the CMC, the country is divided into seven military regions (MR) and thirty military districts (MD) (see Table 5.1).

The backbone of the PLA is composed of 35 army corps, each consisting of 3 divisions and several small support units, about 45,000 men. The ground forces comprise 130 divisions, each consisting of 10,000 men. The corps account for two-thirds of the regular ground forces. The remainder are regional forces stationed in military regions and districts. In early 1989, the ground forces were deployed as follows: In north and northwest China, the Beijing and Shenyang MRs controlled 50 army divisions and 25 regional divisions. In northeast China, the Lanzhou MR controlled 15 army divisions and 3 regional divisions. In southeast China, the Jinan and Nanjing MRs controlled 32 army divisions and 30 regional divisions. In south China, the Guangzhou MR controlled 15 army divisions and 7 regional divisions. In southwest China, the Chengdu MR controlled 18 army divisions and 4 regional divisions.[3]

The army corps are dispatched to any region when necessary; the regional forces concentrate on defending their own localities in cooperation with the local militia.[4] Generally speaking, whereas regional forces are controlled by

TABLE 5.1
Military Regions and Districts in the PRC

Military Region	Commander	Political Commissar
Beijing MR	Zhou Yibing	Liu Chenhua
Hebei MD	Dong Xuelin	Zhang Chao
Inner Mongolia MD	Chai Ying	Lin Yiyuan
Shanxi MD	Yu Hongli	Luo Jinhui
Beijing MD	Yan Tongmo	Li Jinmin
Tianjin MD	Zheng Guozhong	Yan Baojin
Shenyang MR	Liu Jingsong	Song Keda
Liaoning MD	Wang Yuhan	Liu Dongfan
Jilin MD	Chen Xinyin	Wang Zhonghuan
Heilongjiang MD	Shao Zhao	Ma Chunwa
Guangzhou MR	Zhang Wannian	Zhang Zhongxian
Guangdong MD	Zhang Juhui	Xiu Xianghui
Guangxi MD	Li Xingliang	Xiao Xuchu
Hubei MD	Wang Shen	Zhang Xueqi
Hainan MD	—	—
Hunan MD	Jiang Jinliu	Gu Shanxie
Jinan MR	Li Jiulong	Song Qingwei
Shandong MD	Liu Yude	Cao Fansheng
Henan MD	Zhang Jinwu	Dong Guotang
Chengdu MR	Fu Quanyou	Wan Haifeng
Sichuan MD	Zhang Changyun	Gao Shuchun
Tibet MD	Jiang Hongchuan	Zhang Shaosong
Yunnan MD	Wang Zhushun	Zhao Gun
Guizhou MD	Zhao Bing	Qu Mingyao
Lanzhou MR	Zhao Xianshun	Li Xuanhua
Gansu MD	Zhou Yuechi	Wen Jingyi
Shaanxi MD	Wang Xilin	Kong Zhaowen
Qinghai MD	Qiu Fujian	Lu Baoyin
Ningxia MD	Liu Xueji	Wang Huanmin
Xinjiang MD	Gao Huancang	Tang Bingcai
Nanjing MR	Xiang Shouzhi	Fu Kuiqing
Anhui MD	Li Yuanxi	Zhang Linyuan
Jiangsu MD	Ying Shen	Yue Dewang
Zhejiang MD	Li Qing	Liu Xinzeng
Shanghai MD	Ba Zhongtan	Ping Changxi
Jiangxi MD	Wang Baotian	Wan Guande
Fujian MD	Zhang Zhongde	Chong Lizhi

Note: MR = military region; MD = military district
Sources: Zhonggong Yanjiu [Studies on Chinese communism monthly] 19, No. 7 (July 15, 1985), pp. 1–6; and Washington China Post, June 9, 1989.

military regions, army corps are controlled by the authorities in Beijing. The PLA's command hierarchy includes three departments: the General Staff Department, the General Political Department, and the General Logistics Department. Orders to army corps from Beijing are normally relayed through the military regions, but the central leadership has other direct means of communication as well.

The navy and air force are under central, not regional, control. The command of the air force is divided into six air districts, which generally do not coincide with the military regions. The three regional fleet headquarters—North, East, and South—command the PRC's naval forces. Representatives of the navy and air force are present in the military regions' headquarters to perform a liaison function.[5]

The Party maintains its control over the military through the dual Party-army leadership. Provincial military districts and the provincial Party committees are often very close-knit. The first political commissars of the military districts usually are the senior provincial Party secretaries. A 1966 directive from the PLA's General Political Department formalized this dual leadership system by stating, "The system of leadership by the military command and the local Party committee, under the unified guidance of the Party Central Committee, must be enforced."[6]

Despite a quite well-defined command structure, the power of command rests in the hands of about twenty top military leaders. Foremost among them (at the time of the Tiananmen massacre) was Deng Xiaoping, who not only controlled both the state SMC and Party CMC (Deng relinquished the latter post in November 1989) but also maintained personal connections with the commanders in the military regions and in the army corps. After resuming the position of chief of staff of the army in 1977, Deng, through continuous reshuffling of the military personnel, removed many commanders who opposed him and placed his own trusted men in key positions. Two of his longtime followers, Yang Shangkun and Qin Jiwei, were favorably affected by the reorganization of November 1987. Yang had administered day-to-day military affairs from July 1981, when he was appointed secretary-general of the CMC, until April 1988, when he became president of the PRC. His influence has grown considerably since the appointment in November 1987 of his younger brother, Yang Baibing (68), as director of the General Political Department of the PLA. Yang Baibing had been a political commissar of the Beijing Military Region. At the same time, Chi Haotian (60), Yang's close aide, was appointed as chief of staff, overseeing daily military operations. These two appointments made Yang Shangkun the second most powerful military leader after Deng Xiaoping. Qin Jiwei, another longtime associate of Deng and commander of the Beijing Military Region from 1980 to 1987, was appointed defense minister in 1987. Qin, a loyal supporter of Deng, has served under him since 1938.

Apart from these five power holders, several retired military leaders also exert great influence. Wang Zhen, a leading hard-liner and vice president of the PRC, has controlled the Xinjiang area for more than twenty years. He has also maintained wide connections among many regional commanders. Yu Qiuli, former head of the PLA General Political Department, also has influence in the PLA political system. On December 27, 1986, after the Beijing students' demonstration, Wang Zhen, Yu Qiuli, and Yang Shangkun joined the conservative leaders Peng Zhen, Bo Yibo, Hu Qiaomu, and Deng Liqun in going to see Deng Xiaoping to make their case against Hu Yaobang.

Faced with their combined pressure, Deng decided to remove Hu,[7] which revealed that as a group these old commanders still wielded substantial power.

In the moderate camp, three veteran generals—Yang Dezhi, Zhang Aiping, and Hong Xuezhi—reportedly expressed sympathy toward the 1989 student movement. Yang Dezhi served as chief of staff between 1980 and 1987 and strongly supported Deng's military modernization plan. Zhang Aiping, formerly a deputy chief of staff, headed the National Defense Science, Technology, and Industry Commission from 1975 to 1984 and was closely identified with the PRC's nuclear missile program. Zhang served as defense minister from 1982 until his resignation in April 1988. Hong Xuezhi, former director of the Department of Logistics of the PLA, served as deputy secretary-general of the CMC until November 1989. These three veterans all opposed martial law and the use of military force to suppress the students. They seem to have lost some influence as a result of the reshuffling of the CMC in November 1989 (see Figure 5.1). Those ten leaders, together with the new air force commander, Wang Hai (64), the navy commander, Zhang Lianzhong, the director of the General Logistics Department, Zhao Nanqi, the new vice chairman of the CMC, Liu Huaqing, and the seven military regional commanders constituted the top military hierarchy in the PRC at the end of 1989.

The Changing Role of the Army

Following Mao's military doctrine, the PLA was not merely a fighting force ready for combat but also a participant in economic reconstruction and an ideological role model for society. In the early years of Mao's rule, the PLA, besides engaging in the Korean War, actively performed many civilian duties, such as repairing the old railroad tracks and building new ones. Large-scale production and construction corps were established in the border regions—Xinjiang, Qinghai, Heilongjiang, and Inner Mongolia. The PLA also directly controlled most of the defense industry.

In 1955, when Defense Minister Peng Dehuai initiated a program to modernize the army, he intended to reduce substantially the army's role in production and concentrate on military training. Peng's ideas of professionalism were at odds with Mao's concept of members of the army as political functionaries and production assistants. In 1959 Mao dismissed Peng from the position of defense minister because of the latter's views and his opposition to the Great Leap Forward. That disastrous program brought great economic hardship to the rural areas and caused a loss of morale among most soldiers, who were of peasant origin. Lin Biao, after succeeding Peng Dehuai as defense minister, tried to transform the troops into ideological role models for society in an effort to boost their morale.

When, in 1964, Mao launched his Socialist Education Campaign to revive his radical line, he encountered stiff resistance from Party bureaucrats, led by Liu Shaoqi and Deng Xiaoping. To battle Liu and Deng, Mao turned to

Lin Biao and the PLA; soon, a nationwide campaign of "Learning from the PLA" was initiated. The Party media praised the PLA's work style as a model for the entire society to emulate. Each government organization was instructed to set up political departments fashioned after the PLA's political departments. Most of the new positions created were staffed by PLA officers and veterans.[8] For the first time in the CCP's history, the army, not the Party, functioned as the patriotic and spiritual leaders for the rest of society.

The PLA took on the role of political power brokers during the Cultural Revolution. By the end of 1966, the chaos created by the Red Guards had shattered most of the existing Party and state institutions. In the face of the resultant power vacuum, the PLA, with its disciplined command system, was the only viable force that could prevent total anarchy. On January 23, 1967, Mao issued his "Decision Concerning the PLA's Resolute Support of the Revolutionary Mass of the Left," calling for the PLA to intervene in the Red Guards' struggle and seize political power. Under the new guidelines, the missions of the armed force were supposed to be *san zhi liang jun* (three supports and two military tasks). The "three supports" referred to supporting the Maoist revolutionaries, agriculture, and industry. The "two military tasks" denoted the establishment of military control (or martial law) where necessary and the continuation of military and political training.[9]

To enforce Mao's instructions, hundreds of thousands of military personnel were dispatched throughout the country. They managed factories and schools, supervised the legal system, and conducted political indoctrination. These soldiers became the de facto rulers of society. In early 1967, most of the provinces were under military control and run by new government structures called revolutionary committees (*ge wei hui*). Where such committees were not established, the PLA ruled directly through military control committees (*jun guan hui*). According to CCP guidelines, the revolutionary committees were to be tripartite, composed of leaders of revolutionary mass organizations (Red Guards), representatives of local units of the PLA, and revolutionary leading cadres (Maoist radicals). In practice, the majority of the provincial-level revolutionary committees were dominated by the military. A survey showed that 19 of the 29 committee chairmen and 20 of the vice chairmen were PLA officers. In September 1968, of a total of 438 revolutionary committee members across the country, 205, or 46.8 percent, were PLA officers.[10] As *Hongqi* (Red flag), a Party organ, declared in March 1967, "The Great People's Liberation Army [is now] the mainstay of the dictatorship of the proletariat."[11]

The political role of the PLA reached its apex when the Ninth Party Congress convened in April 1969. Marshal Lin Biao, the head of the PLA, was named Mao's heir apparent. Moreover, the decision was written in the new Party constitution, an extraordinary action even by the standards of the Party's political history. Lin's loyal followers rode on his coattails to power. Of the newly elected Politburo members, 11 out of 21 had PLA backgrounds, including Ye Qun, Lin's wife.

Not only did the military dominate the Party center, but it also prevailed in the provincial Party committees. In the 29 provinces, autonomous regions, and special municipalities, 20 first secretaries and as many as 27 second senior secretaries and 60 percent of all provincial secretaries were senior military officers. Most of them concurrently served as chairmen or vice chairmen of revolutionary committees and first or second secretaries of the provincial Party committee. They were also the commanders or commissars of the provincial military districts. People called this phenomenon "three hats for one head." Since most of the Party's regional bureaus were demolished and government organizations destroyed, the regional commands of the PLA headquarters and their regional PLA Party committees became the only existing regional institutions and exercised enormous power over almost every aspect of social and political life. The PRC by mid-1971 had, in essence, become a garrison state.

The rapid rise of the military's power, especially that of the regional commanders, began to threaten the Beijing authorities. As early as July 1967, an independent division of the Wuhan Garrison Command helped to kidnap two important Beijing envoys of the Party's Central Committee's Cultural Revolution group (headquarters of the Maoist radicals), stunning the Maoist center. To rescue these two men, Beijing ordered one division of the 15th Army Corps and two warships from the East Sea Fleet to Wuhan. Locally stationed air force squadrons also gave additional support to quell this mutiny.[12]

In the wake of the "Wuhan incident," the CMC ordered the army corps to seize control of several military districts and run them directly. In early August 1967, four districts, Jiangsu, Hunan, Hubei, and Henan, were taken over by army corps, while another four provinces, Anhui, Zhejiang, Jilin, and Xinjiang, were also reorganized by army units. The use of centrally controlled units to supplant the administrative roles of regional forces was Mao's final ploy to keep the Cultural Revolution going. However, this action also caused a split within the army.[13]

In the Party center, the conflict between Lin Biao and the radical group headed by Mao's wife, Jiang Qing, began to intensify. Striking the first blow, the radicals instigated a secret campaign to downgrade the role of the PLA. From late 1970 through 1971, a series of press and radio reports criticized the PLA, accusing military personnel in nonmilitary posts of arrogance and "nonproletarian" conduct. Some of them, it was charged, harbored "bureaucratic airs" or "pursued special privileges."[14] The wind had quickly shifted from praising the PLA as the model of the society to denigrating it as "divorced from the masses."

The cracks between the Maoist Gang of Four and Lin Biao's group widened when Lin proposed in spring 1970 the reestablishment of the post of chairman of the PRC, a position that had been abolished after the fall of Liu Shaoqi in 1966. Lin's proposal, in Mao's eyes, was a step to usurp his ultimate authority; thus Mao rejected Lin's plan outright. The showdown came in the period August 23–September 6, 1970, when the Second Plenum of the Ninth Party Central Committee met at Lushan. At the session, Chen

Boda and several top military leaders supporting Lin launched a "surprise attack" on Mao's authority in the matter of the chairmanship post. After the conference, Mao struck back by appointing PLA officers loyal to him to the CMC, reorganizing the Beijing Military Region, and stepping up the criticism of the arrogance and complacency of the PLA.[15] The Mao-Lin conflict, as we have seen, culminated in Lin's abortive coup attempt and subsequent death. The sudden demise of Lin Biao, although eliminating Mao's formidable rival, dealt a devastating blow to the prestige of the PLA.

After the Lin Biao incident, Mao undertook a series of new measures to curtail the political power of the military. The first step was to eliminate Lin Biao's followers. The purge included Wu Faxian, commander of the air force, Huang Yongsheng, chief of staff of the army, and Qiu Huizuo, director of the Logistics Department. At least thirty-two key generals and sixty military regional and district commanders, commissars, and Party secretaries were removed. Second, Mao reemphasized military training instead of nonmilitary service and ideological affairs. Third, Mao thoroughly reshuffled eight regional military commanders by assigning them to different military regions. (There were a total of thirteen military regions in 1973.) In addition, he also ordered the interchange of cadres among the provincial military districts. The goal was to uproot factionalism by getting rid of the regional strongholds. The swapping of regional and district commanders at the end of 1973 proved to be a significant step in consolidating his control over the PLA. Although the PLA once again became Mao's vehicle, it remained a formidable political force. By 1973, commanders in twenty-three out of twenty-five military districts concurrently held Party and government posts. After five years of wielding power, many in the PLA were reluctant to relinquish their civilian positions. Some continued to intervene in the affairs of their original work units after being transferred to other places.[16]

At the CCP's Eleventh Party Congress, held in August 1977, twelve out of twenty-six members of the Politburo had military backgrounds. Those responsible for the arrest of the Gang of Four, a month after Mao's death, pledged their support to Hua Guofeng and made him the new Party chairman. That arrest was in essence a military coup, initiated by military leaders Ye Jianying, Xu Xiangqian, and Nie Rongzhen, with the support of Hua Guofeng and Wang Dongxing. The coup itself exemplified the army's ability to shape political affairs and demonstrated several facets of the PLA's unique role. First, although the PLA had the ability to initiate a coup on its own, it did not choose to do so. Instead, the army played the role of king maker rather than crowning itself. The army's behavior indicated that Maoist indoctrination regarding the proper roles of the army and the Party still guided the military leaders' actions. Second, Mao's axiom, "Political power comes from the barrel of a gun," is true for the PRC. Political upheavals have allowed the military to intervene in politics and consequently expand its strength. In 1989, the head-on struggle between Party conservatives and the moderates created another historical opportunity for the military to exert its muscle.

Decline in the Status of the Military

The rapid expansion of military power during and immediately after the Cultural Revolution undermined Mao's doctrine that the Party should control the gun. When Deng Xiaoping resumed power, he employed a wide range of strategies in his effort to reduce the influence of the military.

Under the rubric of modernization of the national defense, the Party redefined the role of the PLA. In the 1979 war with Vietnam, the combat weakness and poor equipment of the PLA became apparent. Deng believed that the PLA should devote time to basic training rather than engaging in political and ideological matters. Prior to the 1980 "Cherish the People and Army" campaign (an annual ritual to show the harmonious relationship between the army and the people), the *People's Daily* in an editorial indicated that "the three supports and two military tasks slogan of the Cultural Revolution period was no longer relevant."[17]

One step to reduce the PLA's responsibility was the transfer of its internal security function to public security organs. In 1981, the People's Armed Police (PAP), abolished during the Cultural Revolution, was revived. In January 1983, following a joint decision by the Party's Central Committee, the State Council, and the CMC, the Beijing Garrison Command handed over the maintenance of internal security in the capital to the Public Security Bureau, under the Ministry of Public Security.[18] In April 1983, a headquarters of the PAP was set up in Beijing. By 1985, the PAP had established 29 divisions, 564 regiments, and 1,029 battalions. The extensive size of this organization gives an indication of the scope of the PLA before the revival of the PAP.[19]

Furthermore, to decrease the nonmilitary role of the PLA, many of its previous functions were delegated to civilian departments. For example, authority over the PLA's Railway Engineering Corps, which had played a significant role in building the nation's railway system, accounting for about 43 percent of the PRC's new lines,[20] shifted to the Ministry of the Railways, under the State Council.

At the same time, many defense industries were also transferred to civilian departments. For instance, in early 1987, management of a major defense enterprise that had produced heavy tanks since 1970 and employed 17,000 was shifted to the China Trust Company, a joint state-private enterprise; it was transformed into an agricultural machinery plant.[21]

To increase efficiency, cut costs, and at the same time drive Maoist leftists from the army, Deng devised a series of steps to trim the size of the PLA. Between 1980 and 1984, under the plan of "streamlining administrations," approximately 1 million soldiers were demobilized. From May 23 to June 6, 1985, the CMC held an enlarged conference. On June 4, 1985, Deng announced that the conventional forces of the PLA would be reduced by 1 million men in 1985 and 1986, representing a 25 percent cut in the total PLA troop number.[22] Simultaneously, large numbers of older military officials were ordered to retire. According to Hu Yaobang, by the end of 1986, some 2 million military personnel and 70,000 to 80,000 senior PLA officers

TABLE 5.2
China's Defense Budget (1966–1989)

Year	In Millions of RMB (yuan)	As % of Total Budget
1966	10,101	18.7
1967	8,302	18.8
1968	9,409	26.1
1969	12,618	24.0
1970	14,526	22.4
1971	16,947	23.2
1972	15,939	20.8
1973	14,539	18.0
1974	13,339	16.9
1975	14,246	17.4
1976	13,445	16.7
1977	14,904	17.7
1978	16,784	15.1
1979	22,266	17.5
1980	19,384	16.0
1981	16,797	15.1
1982	17,635	15.3
1983	17,713	13.7
1984	18,076	11.7
1985	19,153	10.3
1986	20,075	8.6
1987	20,977	8.6
1988	21,796	8.2
1989	24,330	13.9

Note: RMB (Renminbi) Chinese currency: In 1989 one U.S. dollar equaled 3.7 yuan.
Sources: State Statistical Bureau, *Statistical Yearbook of China 1987* (Hong Kong: Longman Group Ltd., 1988), pp. 552–554; *China Times* (Taipei), January 24, 1990, p. 9.

underwent mandatory retirement.[23] Although the army reduction plan was not fully implemented, the size of the PLA shrank substantially. International sources listed the total size of the PLA at 4.75 million men in 1981–1982, decreasing to 3.9 million in 1985–1986.[24]

Cutting the defense budget represented another measure to reduce military influence. Since 1979, the growth rate of Chinese defense budget for each year has been below the expenditure for that year. Because the extra large budget for 1979 can be attributed to the war with Vietnam, the subsequent decline is not abnormal. However, that the share of the defense budget in total government spending has sharply declined year after year—from 26.1 percent in 1968 (Cultural Revolution) to 17.5 percent in 1979 (war with Vietnam) to 8.6 percent in 1986—incensed military leaders and clearly signaled the eclipse of the military's role (see Table 5.2).

In addition to spending cutbacks, after 1978 the Party also dissolved the revolutionary committees established during the Cultural Revolution, with their predominance of military personnel. Most military commanders had

TABLE 5.3
Interlocking Directorates in the PRC Military and Civilian Structure

Interlocking Roles	1973	1982
Political commissar/party	12	33
Political commissar/government	33	0
Political commissar/government/party	71	1
Commander/party	10	5
Commander/government	46	0
Commander/party/government	49	0
Party/government	224	34
Total dual positions	325	72
Total triple positions	120	1

Note: Political commissar and commander are military positions.
Sources: Monte R. Bullard, *China's Political-Military Evolution: The Party and the Military in the PRC, 1960–1984* (Boulder, Colo.: Westview Press, 1985), p. 143.

concurrently held several positions. The demise of the revolutionary committees eliminated the majority of those interlocking directorates, where Party, civil, and military powers had become the sole domain of one person (see Table 5.3). The linkage that remained in 1982—the same person as political commissar and Party secretary—was part of Deng's strategy to ensure the Party's control over the military. Since the second half of 1979, all Party committee secretaries at the provincial, district, municipal, and county levels have been appointed first commissars of their respective military units.[25]

To prevent the army from controlling the Party, Deng also took steps to reduce the percentage of the military in the Communist Party, thereby restricting the army's access to the Party apparatus and preventing its being used by opposition forces. According to various Chinese sources, the percentage of Party members in the PLA in the immediate post-Mao period had ranged from 50 to 80 percent, depending on military unit. Given an approximate army force of 4.5 million in 1978, this would amount to 2.25 to 3.5 million military Party members, or 5.6 to 8.7 percent of the total CCP Party members. In 1980, the CMC decided to limit Party membership in the PLA to graduates of military academies, which meant that future Party recruits would have passed the pro-Deng military educational system. It also directed that Party membership in the PLA be reduced to no more than 20 percent of total army personnel and took steps to prevent rushed application for Party membership in anticipation of the new restriction.[26] At the same time, the Party carried out a large-scale demobilization plan in 1978–1979 to eliminate those PLA Party members who had joined the Party during the Cultural Revolution and who still showed sympathy toward the Maoist radical views.[27]

However, the most conspicuous sign of military decline in influence was the dwindling membership of the military on the Party Central Committee

TABLE 5.4

Ratio and Percent of Military in the CCP Politburo and Central Committee (1956–1987)

	CCP National Congress					
	8th 1956	9th 1969	10th 1973	11th 1978	12th 1982	13th 1987
Politburo						
Member	7/17 (41.7)	13/25 (52)	6/21 (28.6)	12/23 (52.2)	11/28 (39.3)	2/17 (11.8)
Central Committee						
Member	30/97 (31)	85/170 (50)	52/195 (26.7)	61/201 (30)	50/210 (23.8)	32/175 (18.3)
Alternate	— —	55/109 (50)	25/124 (20.1)	39/132 (29.6)	25/138 (18.5)	23/110 (20.9)
Total	—	140/279 (50)	77/319 (24.1)	100/333 (30)	75/348 (21.5)	55/285 (19.3)

Sources: From 8th to 12th congresses, Yu Yu-lin, "Politics in Teng Hsiao-p'ing's Army-Building Strategy (1977–1984)," *Issues and Studies* 21, No. 10 (October 1985), p. 47. For the 13th Party Congress, Fang Hsueh-ch'un, "Analysis of the Personnel Elected at the CCP's Thirteenth National Congress," *Issues and Studies* 23, No. 12 (December 1987), p. 78.

and its Politburo. At the height of military power, the 1969 Ninth Party Congress elected 140 military personnel to the Central Committee, accounting for 50 percent of the 279 total members. Of the 25 members of the Politburo, 13 were from the army. However, after the Lin Biao affair, the influence of the army waned. When the Tenth Party Congress convened in 1973, the army won only 24 percent of the Central Committee seats and 29 percent of the Politburo. But after the successful coup in October 1976 to remove the Gang of Four, the army made a comeback, capturing 30 percent of Central Committee seats and 52.2 percent of the Politburo at the Eleventh Party Congress. In the wake of Deng's consolidation program, 60 ranking military officers were forced into the newly established Central Advisory Commission, a repository for Party veterans. Once again, the share of the military in the leading Party organizations fell sharply. The trend continued in the 1983–1987 period. By the time of the Thirteenth Party Congress in 1987, of the 285 members in the new Central Committee, only 55 came from the PLA; 32 of them were full members and 23 were alternates, and together they accounted for only 19.3 percent of the total, the lowest in the period since 1969. In the Politburo, only 2 of the 17 members had military backgrounds, representing only 11.8 percent, or less than one-fourth of the ratio in the preceding congress (see Table 5.4).

The changing composition of the CCP Politburo has often been regarded by outside observers as a barometer of power alignments. In the 1982 Politburo, senior military officers and regional commanders still occupied a dominant role. Besides Deng Xiaoping, military veterans Ye Jianying, Xu

Xiangqian, and Nie Rongzhen; regional commanders Wang Zhen, Li Desheng, and Yang Dezhi; and military functionaries Yu Qiuli, Song Renqiong, and Zhang Tingfa all held seats. A dramatic change occurred in September 1985 when ten members of the Politburo were replaced. With the exception of Deng Xiaoping and Yang Shangkun, most of the military oldtimers disappeared. A further eclipse in military representation occurred when the 1987 Central Committee included only Yang Shangkun and Qin Jiwei on the Politburo. On the surface, Deng's plan to reduce military influence appeared to have worked out well.

However, in reality, the military influence persisted. Many of the older military officers either attained new government posts, such as Wang Zhen (vice president of the PRC), or won control over regional forces through their old alignments, connections, and manipulation. The behind-the-scenes maneuvers of the senior military leaders have therefore replaced direct political involvement and have allowed them to continue to play a significant role.

Military Resistance to Reform

Deng's plan to modernize the army and his efforts to transform the role of the PLA encountered widespread resistance from within the military establishment. The resistance stemmed from the PLA's desire to maintain its power and interests and the military's ideological inclinations.

A large number of the CCP's 44 million members were holdovers from the Cultural Revolution, and many of them were unrepentant Maoists who regard Deng's reform policies as a betrayal of Maoist tenets. As Li Desheng, former commander of the Shenyang MR, indicated in an April 1984 article, the "leftists" feared that, since the Third Plenum of the Eleventh Party Central Committee, there had been a rightist trend in ideology that had violated basic tenets of Marxism-Leninism–Mao Zedong Thought. They were accustomed to understanding "class struggle as the key link" and believed that the surge in crime and social disorders in recent years was due to "casting off the key link." According to Li, "leftists" were also accustomed to egalitarianism in distribution, skeptical of the "open door" and the "enlivening" of the economy (two vital parts of Deng's reform program), and adamant in their belief that the economic reforms represented a deviation from socialism. They tended also to devalue the importance of knowledge and were prejudiced against the promotion of intellectuals in the PLA and the Party. They considered this new policy on intellectuals to be at the root of "bourgeois liberalism" in society and thought.[28]

Li's analysis summarized quite effectively the "leftist" ideological resistance to Deng's reform, which has been shared by a large number of PLA officers, including many leading figures. This mentality was severely challenged when the de-Maoization campaign launched by Hu Yaobang and his followers reached its high point in 1981. At that time, the most sensitive issue was how to evaluate Mao's "three supports and two military tasks" policy, which had brought the PLA into the factional struggle during the Cultural Revolution. Deng's followers and especially those who had been victimized during the Cultural Revolution argued that the PLA's support for the "leftists" was tantamount to a support for a faction. It contributed to the continuation of antagonistic class struggle in the PRC and participated in many theoretical errors that Mao had committed in his later years.[29] To prevent the army's future involvement in political struggles, Deng needed to negate this policy. Deng's camp insisted that the Party should openly repudiate it and that those who had committed crimes in the tumultuous period should openly apologize for their mistakes. But because large numbers of senior PLA officers had actively carried out the "three supports," they were reluctant to denounce their past activities and consequently lose face. As a result, Deng adopted a more conciliatory tone. In a talk with the leaders of the PLA in March 1981, Deng contended that had the PLA not acted as a mediator during the Cultural Revolution, the political and social situation would have deteriorated even further than it did. However, he added, by intervening in politics, the PLA also severely damaged the PRC's internal stability and its own reputation.[30]

The issue of the "three supports" contributed to the decision of many officers who had participated in the Cultural Revolution to impede Deng's program. However, the army's deep-rooted resentment probably stemmed more from the individuals' concerns over personal power and interests. Deng's rural reforms, while praised by economists as an important step for reviving the stagnant agricultural sector, encountered stiff opposition from many PLA personnel who were personally disadvantaged by the reform. Under the old system, the families of PLA soldiers and officers enjoyed a guaranteed income and food supplies from the commune. The new system of contract responsibility caused many difficulties for soldiers whose families, having less labor power, could not cultivate their contracted land. Moreover, under the new policy, peasants are permitted and even encouraged to get rich. Many peasant families became 10,000-yuan households, with annual incomes 50 to 100 times those of soldiers' families. The rising disparities in income distribution aroused deep hostility among soldiers and officers coming from the rural areas.

In accordance with the Maoist doctrine that the army should be a model of self-sacrifice, the soldiers' salaries have been meager. Over the past thirty years, when prices increased enormously, the soldiers' allowance remained at 6 yuan a month. In recent years, to compensate for the high rate of inflation, an additional allowance of 10 yuan was added to the monthly pay. The new allowance, however, hardly kept pace with rising prices. Many PLA officers found that their wives who were ordinary workers in the private sector earned much more than they did as soldiers. A survey by an artillery unit in the Shenyang Military Region on the income of the unit's officers disclosed that in 56 out of the 101 cases, the wives' income exceeded that of their husbands by 30 percent or more. The income of the rest was either slightly higher or was equal to their husbands'. The situation hurt the officers' self-esteem. Many were negative about their careers and considered themselves victimized by Deng's new economic policies.[31]

Deng's large-scale demobilization plan also created discontent. Likely candidates for demobilization included officers who were too old to meet the new age requirements for promotion. This included senior officers at the division level as well as younger company-level officers who were too old to be promoted to the regimental level (the age limit is forty years or younger), political commissars, PLA officers engaging in civil-military relations work, Vietnam veterans, and model soldiers. Those people slated for retirement faced uncertain futures. Not only would their connections in the PLA be severed but also they would enjoy few prospects for any employment because of their low level of education and scientific expertise. The problem of job placement for demobilized veterans is increasing as more soldiers are discharged each year. According to an article in the February 28, 1989, issue of Liberation Army Daily, there were, as of that date, 30 million demobilized veterans in the PRC, a number equal to the entire population of a medium-sized country.

In the cities, to improve efficiency and cut costs under Deng's reform program, each enterprise operates on the basis of a fixed number of employees and a fixed quota for hiring. Consequently, few job opportunities exist for retired veterans.[32] This huge throng of unemployed veterans not only constitutes a burden on society but has also created a horde of anti-Deng individuals.

Even the military officers who supported Deng's reform have not been entirely happy. They have viewed cuts in the defense budget as contradictory to Deng's defense modernization plan. A Liberation Army Daily article stated quite forcefully that the principal contradiction of military modernization was "between the objective needs of modern warfare and the relatively low level of the modernization expenditure of our army."[33] The article concluded that "it can be said that without the modernization of weaponry and equipment, modernization of national defense will be an empty phrase." A 1979 U.S. Defense Department study showed that the number of U.S. weapons needed to give the PRC a "confident capacity" for defense against a Soviet conventional attack would cost between $41 billion and $63 billion at 1977 prices. The PRC's published defense budget for 1978 was roughly $10.5 billion. U.S. experts believe that real expenditures for defense were about twice the published figures. Of the defense expenditures, 40 percent went for the purchase of weapons and equipment, meaning that in 1978 about $8.5 billion was earmarked for weapons procurement. But because expenditures for nuclear weapons took the lion's share, the budget for conventional weapons had to be rather limited.[34] The low defense budget has undoubtedly hindered the efforts of military professionals to improve military capabilities and modernize national defense.

Facing much bitterness and dissatisfaction, Deng and his associates adopted a two-pronged policy. In October 1983, Hu Yaobang announced the beginning of a three-year rectification campaign that would improve the Party units in the PLA by unifying thinking, reforming Party work styles, strengthening Party discipline, and purifying the Party organization. The campaign also aimed to ferret out "five kinds of people": (1) those who had risen to preeminence through revolt during the Cultural Revolution; (2) those whose thinking was along factional lines; (3) those who opposed the party line of the Third Plenum of the Eleventh Party Central Committee; (4) those who hit, smashed, and rioted; (5) those who broke the law and disturbed public order.

To provide a guiding ideology for the Party and the army, on July 1, 1983, the *Selected Works of Deng Xiaoping* was published. On the same day, the General Political Department of the PLA put out a notice ordering the entire army to study its contents seriously and to pass them along. Three days later, on July 4, the *People's Daily* carried an article on the *Selected Works* by Li Desheng, then commander of the Shenyang Military Region. On July 13 the same paper ran a long piece on the same subject by Yang Shangkun, then vice chairman of the CMC; and on July 26, Yu Qiuli, director of the General Political Department, published yet another long article on this subject. All of these articles praised Deng's work as "a fundamental guiding ideology; and the integration of the general tenets of Marxism-Leninism with the concrete reality of our country's military construction"—the same praise used for the works of Mao.[35] On July 12, the CCP Central Committee issued a notice urging the whole Party to study the *Selected Works*. The notice emphasized that "such study is an important ideological preparation for the overall Party rectification campaign to begin this fall and winter." It is clear that Deng had decided on an overall shakeup in the army and that the purpose of the *Selected Works* was to pave the ideological way for the purge.

In spite of the elaborate rectification campaign, the goal of getting rid of opponents and improving the work style of the army was not achieved. Nor did the campaign unify the ideology of the army and the Party. Conservative officers in the PLA used the broad rubric of "spiritual pollution" (*jingshen wuran*) to attack all forms of deviant behavior, most of which they attributed to Deng's economic and military reforms. For instance, it was said that officers in a Lanzhou artillery unit complained that their PLA uniforms were too rustic and demanded "more colorful" ones. These troublemakers allegedly read "vulgar" and "fantastic" novels and had long hair.[36] The neo-Maoists took advantage of such accusations to divert attention away from rectification, while the conservatives used the "spiritual pollution" issue as ammunition to challenge Deng and his followers.

Another form of resistance involved paying perfunctory attention to rectification and reforms but never carrying out the central policies. These surface obeyers openly proclaimed that "those above have their policies and those below have their countermeasures."[37] Because of the concerted opposition of local officers, hardly any of the reform plan was put into effect.

The greatest failure of Deng's rectification campaign has been the rampant corruption and profiteering in the army. As we have seen, the cuts in the defense budget, even as prices soared 10 to 30 percent a year, damaged military morale. After the introduction of a market economy and an open door, most army units, which had fewer responsibilities than before, opted to utilize their privileges and set up businesses. Some with special connections sold weapons to other Third World countries. Others engaged in smuggling and speculation. As mentioned in Chapter 2, the Hainan Island scandal, in which navy personnel used their vessels to assist civilian officials in shipping imported products to coastal ports on the mainland, where they reaped remarkable profits, was the most celebrated case of smuggling and profiteering.[38] In recent years, military speculation (*jun dao*) has been as widespread as official speculation (*guan dao*) and has become the root of social discontent. Many soldiers have been involved in moonlighting. In the first ten days of May 1988, in one army corp of Nanjing Military Region, thirty-six cases of moonlighting caused a breakdown in discipline.[39]

In view of these problems, Deng's grand plan to build a powerful, modern regular army has failed to materialize. By early 1989, not only had the PLA not disengaged from politics, but it had become drawn even deeper into factional contention. Its work style, instead of being improved, had become more corrupt. Deng described the army's image in July 1975 as "bloated, lax, conceited, extravagant, and inert."[40] Unfortunately, this image did not significantly improve in subsequent years.

Involvement in Factional Struggle

The PLA started out as an army that used guerrilla warfare tactics. As the army dispersed over a very wide area, each unit was led by men who shared many combat experiences and naturally formed a special clique. When the Long March reached Yanan in 1935, Mao launched a rectification campaign to eradicate factionalism and appealed to the whole army for unity. But for the purpose of conducting the civil war, the army was divided into four major field armies and the North China Field Army.[41] The 1st Field Army, commanded by Marshal Peng Dehuai in the 1950s (he was minister of defense between 1954 and 1959), played an active role in the Korean War in 1950. The entire northwest of the country lay under the control of the 1st Field Army. Prominent military veterans in this group included Huang Kecheng, who served as vice minister of defense and chief of staff of the army from 1954–1959, and Yang Dezhi, who became chief of staff in 1980. Many from this group were very active during the 1950s.

The 2nd Field Army, led by Marshals Liu Bocheng, He Long, and Deng Xiaoping when the PRC was established in 1949, controlled the southwest areas. Leading military leaders included Qin Jiwei, the present defense minister, Xian Zhouzhi, commander of the Nanjing Military Region, Liu Huaqing, vice chairman of the CMC, and You Taizhong, former commander of the Guangzhou Military Region. This group became influential after Deng returned to power.

The 3rd Field Army was led in 1949 by Marshal Chen Yi, who served as minister of foreign affairs in the early 1950s. Notable among this group were General Xu Yu, former vice minister of defense, and Tan Zhenlin, former vice premier of the State Council. The whole of eastern China area was under their sphere of influence, but they later became relatively inactive in the army.

The 4th Field Army, led by Marshal Lin Biao from 1946 until his death, controlled a part of Manchuria and most of the south China region. During the 1960s and 1970s, when Lin Biao assumed the helm of the PLA, many in the 4th Field Army were promoted to key positions in the PLA, including: Huang Yongsheng, chief of staff; Wu Faxian, deputy chief of staff and concurrently commander of the air force; Li Zuopeng, deputy chief of staff; Qiu Huizuo, deputy chief of staff and concurrently director of the General Logistics Department; and Han Xianchu and Yan Zhongchuan, both deputy chiefs of staff.

The North China Field Army was led in 1950 by Marshal Nie Rongzhen and controlled the Beijing areas. Important veterans included Yang Chengwu, deputy chief of staff from 1958–1968.

Between 1955 and 1966, the thirteen military regions were dominated by units and military leaders from these five field armies. In all cases, the units and elites concerned belonged to the same field army system.[42]

Before the Cultural Revolution, although the PLA was hardly monolithic, intra-army contentions focused on issues and were contained within a broader framework of unity. During this period, Mao exerted absolute power over the army. All factions showed loyalty to Mao and accepted his orders unconditionally. In 1959, when Marshal Peng Dehuai, Mao's devoted supporter and life saver, presented his 10,000-character letter criticizing Mao's Great Leap Forward policy, Mao had no qualms about purging him and labeling him the leader of the "rightist anti-Party clique." The factional struggle in this period centered on gaining Mao's favor.

The Cultural Revolution added new dimensions to intra-army struggle. First, during that period, Lin Biao, with Mao's support, purged all major leaders of the other three field armies. Peng Dehuai was purged by Mao in 1959 but was allowed to live peacefully until the Cultural Revolution. Peng suffered persecution and torture at the hands of the Red Guards until his death in 1969. The commanders of the 2nd and 3rd armies, He Long and Chen Yi, were also tortured to death. Deng Xiaoping was dismissed from all his posts and sent to labor reform, where he stayed until 1973. Lin Biao assumed control over the PLA by 1970. But because of a 1967 order calling for support of the leftists, and because of the splintering of the Red Guards, the PLA supported different groups and became split itself. During this period, the Party and army centers were controlled by Lin Biao and the Maoist radicals, but the military regions continued to be run by commanders who were more concerned with security than revolution. Factional contentions also developed between the center and the regions, as manifested by the "Wuhan incident." Therefore, factionalism no longer restricted itself to different field armies, but divided the "left" and "right" within the same army. The personnel and factional rivalries produced by this bitter period, and the strong desire to "settle accounts," split the entire army.[43]

Second, until the 1970s, Mao was able to play off one group in the army against the other, and no one dared to challenge his authority openly. The downfall of top leaders of three field armies completely changed the power game. As Mao had no other pawns, Lin Biao became the only person on whom he could rely to control the army. This greatly strengthened Lin's position and led to his later power struggle with Mao. After Lin's death, Mao had no choice but to rehabilitate Deng Xiaoping in August 1973 because Deng was the only person capable of unifying the army.

Deng's proposal to deal with army disunity involved a large-scale re-shuffling of commanders in military regions, districts, and in the various departments of the PLA in order to destroy their strongholds. In his first year after resuming the post of chief of staff, Deng transferred eight out of the thirteen commanders of military regions from one region to another. But the personnel exchanges failed to curb factional contention. In the post-Mao era, factionalism arose from two new elements: attitudes toward Deng's reforms and the struggle over Deng's successor.

Whereas most military leaders shared the view that the country's economic system needed reform, they differed greatly regarding its orientation, speed, and scope. Prior to the reform, Guangdong had been a relatively backward province. During the 1950s and 1960s, Mao considered Guangdong a national defense zone and reduced large-scale capital investment there for security reasons. The open-door policy and the establishment of three Special Economic Zones in Guangdong generated the economic boom of this southern province. As capital from Hong Kong and overseas Chinese flooded into Guangdong, its industrial output and foreign trade soared. By 1987, Guangdong ranked first in industrial output value, surpassing Jiangsu, the oldest industrial base in the PRC. In Zhao Ziyang's plan to develop the coastal areas, Guangdong was slated as "an advanced experimental area" for the open-door policy and a model for the country to emulate. Pleased about this new prosperity, military leaders in the Guangzhou Military Region as well as those in the Nanjing Military Region fully supported Deng's reform and Zhao's developmental strategy.

In contrast to the coastal areas, provinces in the interior, especially the vast underdeveloped northwest and southwest, hardly benefited from Deng's reform and open-door policy. During Mao's era, these two regions had been designated military bases in preparation for war with the Soviet Union. Large amounts of funds were allocated to military industry in these areas. The improvement of Sino-Soviet relations and the open door caused a substantial curtailment of state investment in the interior regions. At the same time, capital and professional manpower continued to outflow from these areas. Income distribution between interior and coastal areas became polarized. The gross industrial output value of sixteen counties in Guizhou, in the southwest, was smaller than the output value of one village in the delta area of Guangdong. The widening gap in income and standards of living aroused dissatisfaction toward reform and the open door in these internal areas.

The situation was exacerbated by Deng's large-scale army demobilization plan. In the economically underdeveloped provinces of Guizhou and Yunnan, where job opportunities were scarce, young people joined the army as an alternative. Consequently, those areas have more demobilized soldiers than the advanced areas. Each year, thousands of discharged soldiers returned to their hometowns only to face fewer job openings than when they had left. This vicious circle further depleted support for Deng's reform in these areas. During the 1985–1986 anti-bourgeois-liberalization campaign, the loudest voice of criticism came from economically backward provinces, such as Gansu, Shaanxi, Ningxia, Qinghai, and Xinjiang in the northwest; and Guizhou, Yunnan, and Tibet in the southwest. The economic factor weighed very heavily in rivalries among regional commanders who supported or opposed Zhao Ziyang.

The problem of Deng's succession undoubtedly has added to the factional contentions. When Deng passed the age of eighty-four—Mao's age the year he died and popularly regarded by Chinese as a critical year—struggle for Deng's succession intensified. Although he had appointed Hu Yaobang and then Zhao Ziyang as his heir apparent, the lack of either nominee's power over the PLA left people in the military hierarchy believing that the job was still open. In the wake of the Tiananmen massacre, Deng opted for balancing the power between conservatives and reformers and picked Jiang Zemin, the Party secretary of Shanghai, instead of Li Peng, the premier and the hard-liners' favorite, as the new Party general secretary. On the day he announced Jiang's appointment, Deng appealed to the Party hierarchy to abandon factional maneuvers and support the new Party chief. But as long as Jiang fails to establish his military power, his future as Deng's successor will be no brighter than that of his two predecessors. The contention for succession will escalate as Deng's health deteriorates.

The Military at the Crossroads

In the years following its formation in 1927, the PLA claimed to be an army of high morals that observed the Three Disciplinary Rules: obeying orders under all circumstances; not taking a single needle or piece of thread from the people; and handing over all booty to the government. The army's exemplary behavior won the hearts of the people and was a key factor in the Communists' victory over the KMT.

The army's model image has long since eroded as it moved from the rural to the urban environment and as most officers became government officials. But until the outbreak of the Cultural Revolution, the PLA had maintained its role of guardian of the Party and the state and had avoided direct involvement in politics. Mao's ordering the PLA to intervene in the factional struggle during the Cultural Revolution marked the turning point in the army's role. Ellis Joffe noted:

The Cultural Revolution was a great disaster for the PLA. It entangled the army in bruising factional fights and deeply divided the military leadership at all levels of the chain of command. It forced military commanders throughout the PLA to focus their concerns on political maneuvers rather than on military maneuvers. It diverted troops from routine tasks and severely strained their discipline. It threw the organization and regular procedures of the PLA into disarray. The Cultural Revolution, in short, effectively transformed the PLA from a professional military into a political force.[44]

Deng, when he was reappointed as chief of staff in 1975, painted an extremely dismal picture of the PLA:

The Army was thrown into a mess. A great many fine traditions have been cast off and the Army is over-staffed beyond endurance. The number of people in the Army has increased greatly. Military expenditures occupy an increasing proportion of the national budget, and a great amount of money is being spent on clothing and feeding personnel. More important, the Army has become bloated and not tightly knit; this will not do if war comes.[45]

Deng's ten-point prescription, as outlined by Yu Qiuli, former director of the Political Department, included: (1) undertaking a rectification campaign to purge heretics; (2) implementing the party line; (3) adopting the strategy of active defense (meaning not committing aggression against others); (4) making leadership more revolutionary, younger, knowledgeable, and professional; (5) reforming the military system; (6) improving military hardware; (7) raising the level of education and training of officers; (8) fostering a dual use of human resources for military and civilian purposes; (9) strengthening troop standardization; and (10) strengthening political and ideological works.[46] The thrust of these ten points was to disentangle the PLA from politics.

Deng made a grievous error when he ordered the June 4 crackdown on the demonstrators in Tiananmen Square. His precipitous decision contradicted his own ten-point plan and had serious ramifications. First, it demonstrated that the leadership was powerless to deal with a peaceful protest without resorting to force. This weakness was reflected in a commentary in the army newspaper, the *Liberation Army Daily*, entitled, "Without the Army There Is No Stability." The article bluntly pointed out: "If someone had talked about the importance of the army in peace time, he would have had few supporters. However, in the wake of the recent suppression of the rebellion in the capital, everyone would now accept [the issue] as very cogent."[47] The resurgence of the army has turned the clock back to the period of the Cultural Revolution.

Second, there are more than 200,000 troops stationed in the Beijing Military Region, adequate to suppress a military coup. Instead of relying on the local army, Deng's headquarters had to bring in army units from other parts of the country. This unusual action indicated that either the commanders of the Beijing unit refused to carry out orders, or different groups of troops were required to prevent a coup.

Third, by ordering the PLA to intervene in the student demonstrations, Deng repeated the error Mao had committed. He opened the way for the PLA to assume the role of king maker again. In the aftermath of the massacre, the *People's Daily* was taken over by the army. Shao Huaze, head of the propaganda division of the General Political Department, became editor-in-chief of the Party paper. In August 1989, the government stipulated that students entering Beijing University in fall 1989 had to undergo military training for as long as one year before they could begin their four-year study program.[48] Many government decisions after the June 4 bloodshed seem to be replays of the "three supports and two military tasks" of 1967.

The PLA, which reached a critical juncture at the end of 1989, has at least three sets of options confronting it. First, it must decide whether to ignore the spring 1989 intervention and continue its transformation into a modern army or to resume a political role similar to the one it played during the Cultural Revolution. Second, it must choose whether to follow Mao's axiom and be controlled by the Party or to force the government to accept the kind of military dictatorship prevalent in many Third World countries. Third, it must decide whether it will be a guardian of the state or become a pawn of several warlords contending for ultimate authority.

Although the PLA ranks among the largest armed forces in the world, the general consensus of Western military experts is that the Chinese conventional forces are inadequately armed, poorly equipped, out of date in communications, lacking in logistic support, and inadequately trained for complex operations. Of the 136 primary combat units in the main force armies, 121 are infantry, of which 12 are armored and 3 airborne. As Joffe commented, "The Chinese ground forces lacked all of the major attributes of a modern fighting force, such as firepower, mobility, advanced communication and logistics."[49] The technological backwardness of the PLA, however, is most acute in the air force and navy. The navy remains primarily a coastal defense force, lacking the capacity to operate at long distance from the coast. To make the PRC into a real military power in the twenty-first century, the PLA not only requires upgrading of its military hardware but, more important, also needs to build a professional military corps with a high level of education and strict discipline. Any deviation from this goal will only hinder the rise of the PRC's military status in the world.

Military commanders in modern China have sometimes tried to build their own spheres of influence into independent kingdoms. They were tempted to do this because of the vastness of the territory and the large populations in individual provinces (Sichuan has well over 100 million people and Guangdong, more than 60 million). Without a popularly supported central authority and a centrally controlled army, the potential exists for the PRC to relapse into the warlordism of the 1920s and 1930s. In the 1950s, Gao Gang, the former chairman of the Northeast Administration Government, attempted to build Manchuria into his own kingdom and provoked the first open power struggle in the PRC. In recent years, as the center has delegated more power to local governments, each province has become a self-contained unit. The key to the economic future of the country is in the hands of twenty or so military leaders.[50] The world will continue to monitor how these leaders handle the extremely delicate problems of the 1990s.

Notes

1. Mao Zedong, *Selected Military Writings of Mao Zedong* (Beijing: Foreign Languages Press, 1963), p. 272.

2. Alastair I. Johnson, "Changing Party-Army Relations in China 1979–1984" *Asian Survey* 24, No. 10 (Oct. 1984), pp. 1020–1021.

3. Based on intelligence information from Taiwan.

4. Harvey Nelson, "Military Force in the Cultural Revolution," *China Quarterly*, No. 51 (July–Sept. 1972), pp. 444–445.

5. Ibid.

6. John Gutting, "Army-Party Relations in the Light of the Cultural Revolution," in John Wilson Lewis, ed., *Party Leadership and Revolution Power in China* (Cambridge: Harvard University Press, 1970), pp. 387–388.

7. Lu Keng, "The True Story Behind China's Political Shakeup," *Pai Hsing* [The people] (Hong Kong), Apr. 1, 1987, p. 3.

8. Paul C. Marcks, "Two Steps Forward, One Step Backward: The Place of the Cultural Revolution in the Modernization of the PLA," *Issues and Studies* 25, No. 2 (Feb. 1989), pp. 80–82.

9. Ralph L. Powell, "The Military and the Struggle for Power in China," *Current History* 63, No. 373 (Sept. 1972), pp. 98–101.

10. Jurgen Domes, "The Role of the Military in the Evolution of Revolution Committees 1967–68," *China Quarterly*, No. 44 (Oct.–Dec. 1970), pp. 143–144.

11. "On the Revolutionary 'Three-Way Alliance,'" *Hongqi*, No. 5 (March 30, 1967).

12. For a detailed account of the Wuhan incident, see Thomas Robinson's article in the *China Quarterly*, No. 47 (July–Sept. 1971).

13. For details, see Harvey Nelson, "Military Forces in the Cultural Revolution," *China Quarterly*, No. 51 (July–Sept. 1972), pp. 444–474.

14. Powell, op. cit., p. 99.

15. Mao's statement appeared in a top-secret CCP document, "Summary of Chairman Mao's Talks to Responsible Local Commanders During His Tour of Inspection," mid-August to September 12, 1971, published in Y. M. Kau, ed., *The Lin Piao Affair* (White Plains, N.Y.: International Arts and Sciences Press, 1975), p. 62.

16. Deng Xiaoping, "Speech at a Plenary Meeting of the Military Commission of the Central Committee of the CCP," in Deng Xiaoping, *Selected Works 1975–1982* (Beijing: Foreign Languages Press, 1984), p. 98.

17. "Strengthen Unity Between Army and People, Promote the Four Modernizations," *People's Daily*, Dec. 23, 1979.

18. Ellis Joffe, *The Chinese Army After Mao* (Cambridge: Harvard University Press, 1987), p. 153.

19. Ibid.

20. New China News Agency, December 13, 1983.

21. New China News Agency, Jan. 5, 1987.

22. Wang Hsien, "Teng Hsiao-p'ing's Declaration to Cut Armed Forces by One Million," *Studies on Chinese Communism Monthly* 19, No. 7 (July 15, 1985), pp. 80–87.

23. *New York Times*, March 6 and Apr. 21, 1985.

24. June Teufel Dreyer, "The Reorganization and Streamlining of the PLA," in *Issues and Studies* 23, No. 5 (May 1987), pp. 32–33.

25. Yu Yu-lin, "Politics in Teng Hsiao-p'ing's Army-Building Strategy (1977–1984)," *Issues and Studies* 21, No. 10 (Oct. 1985), p. 531.

26. Alastair I. Johnson, "Party Rectification in the People's Liberation Army (1983–87)," *China Quarterly*, No. 112 (Dec. 1987), p. 603.

27. Johnson, "Changing Party-Army Relations in China," pp. 1031–1032.

28. Li Desheng, "Persistently Seeking Truth from Facts is the Key to Unifying the Thinking of the Whole Party," *People's Daily*, Apr. 30, 1984. (Li was a leftist himself; hence, this article represented a type of self-criticism.)

29. Johnson, "Party Rectification in the People's Liberation Army," p. 614.

30. Deng Xiaoping, "On Opposing Wrong Ideological Tendencies," *Selected Works*, p. 358.

31. Central People's Broadcasting Network, March 10, 1989, in *Inside China Mainland* (Taipei) 11, No. 5 (May 1989), pp. 20–21.

32. "Perspectives on the Work of Demobilization and Job Placement," *Jiefang Junbao* [Liberation army daily], Feb. 28, 1989, p. 1.

33. Pan Shiyang, "Thoughts about the Principal Contradiction in Our Country's National Defense Construction," *Jiefang Junbao*, Aug. 14, 1987.

34. Ellis Joffe, *The Chinese Army after Mao* (Cambridge: Harvard University Press, 1987), p. 51.

35. Yu Qiuli, "On the Direction of Military Construction During the New Period; Study the Discussions About Military Construction in the Selected Works of Deng Xiaoping," *People's Daily*, July 26, 1983.

36. Lanzhou Gansu Provincial Series, Nov. 11, 1983.

37. "A Thorny Path Lies Ahead for the Army," *Jiushi Niandai* [The nineties monthly] (Hong Kong), Jan. 1989, pp. 30–32.

38. *People's Daily*, Aug. 1, 1985, p. 2.

39. *Jiefang Junbao*, May 8, 1988, p. 1.

40. Deng, *Selected Works*, p. 32.

41. William W. Whitson, "The Field Army in Chinese Communist Military Politics," *China Quarterly*, No. 37 (Jan.–March 1969), pp. 1–30.

42. Ibid., p. 12.

43. Ellis Joffe, "The Chinese Army After the Cultural Revolution: The Effects of Intervention," *China Quarterly*, No. 55 (July-Sept. 1973), pp. 462–463.

44. Joffe, *The Chinese Army After Mao*, p. 19.

45. Deng, *Selected Works*, pp. 72–73.

46. Yu Qiuli, op. cit.

47. *Jiefang Junbao*, July 11, 1989.

48. *New York Times*, Aug. 15, 1989, p. 4.

49. Joffe, *The Chinese Army After Mao*, p. 95.

50. Wu Minzhi, "A Preliminary Analysis of Local Independence in Mainland China," *World Journal* (New York), June 5, 1989.

6

The Making of the Massacre

The Tiananmen prodemocracy demonstration started as a peaceful and orderly protest by several thousand Beijing University students. The protest, however, burgeoned into a people's movement that at one point drew more than a million residents to the streets of the capital and that involved hundreds of thousands more throughout the nation. The display of the power of the masses threatened the legitimacy of the regime, triggered a bitter intra-Party power struggle, brought down the Party's general secretary, and ended in horrible bloodshed.

The event revealed not only the public's enormous discontent with the government but also the Party gerontocracy's desperation to retain power. Although Western news media provided intensive coverage of the prodemocracy movement's evolution, many important issues require further elaboration. This chapter delves into the origins of the student campaign, identifies the factors that transformed the student protest into a mass movement, analyzes the behind-the-scenes power struggle within the Party hierarchy, and assesses the effects of martial law and the massacre.

Origins of the Student Protest

On June 9, 1989, in the wake of the military crackdown, the PRC's paramount leader, Deng Xiaoping, appeared on television surrounded by a group of Party hard-line military leaders. Addressing them, Deng claimed that the recent political storm had been determined by the international and domestic climate and would have happened sooner or later. According to Deng, the event "was independent of man's will."[1]

Changes within the Soviet Union, Poland, and Hungary had exerted a profound impact on intellectuals in the PRC. Mikhail Gorbachev's bold political reforms, involving contested elections and tolerance toward dissident intellectuals and outspoken non-Russian nationalists, had won him great admiration from the younger generation of Chinese. Poland's open elections had produced the first non-Communist government in four decades. The success of a people's revolution in the Philippines and the emergence of multiparty systems in Taiwan and South Korea had further inspired the Chinese intellectuals, who believed that democracy would be the mainstream form of government in the 1990s. These intellectuals asserted that for Chinese economic reform to continue, political reform was not only imperative but also inevitable.

The PRC's internal development had reinforced the public yearning for political changes. The economic crisis and galloping inflation in the prior two years had caused a continuous decline in income and living standards for one-third of the urban dwellers (see Chapter 2). The rapid rise in unemployment had created a 50-million-strong "fluid population," individuals without a job or a home. In contrast to the common people, the country's privileged class had been able to take advantage of the relaxation of controls and to engage in various illegal activities. The prevalence of *guan dao* (official profiteering) had widened the income disparities between various segments of the population and caused mounting social discontent.

The root of these social and economic maladies lies in the one-party totalitarian system, in which there is virtually no independent opinion nor checks and balances. Because political reform has been steadily postponed, remedies for the social and economic problems have been piecemeal. Those in charge have made little effort to consult the people or to take responsibility for measures enacted. Many Chinese view the government as arbitrary, unresponsive, and patronizing. Resentment against favoritism, corruption, and other forms of power abuse underscored the two previous student demonstrations, in 1986 and 1987. The large-scale demonstrations in 1989 may be considered to be a continuation of the earlier movements.

In spring 1989, in anticipation of the seventieth anniversary of the May Fourth Movement, the leading dissident Fang Lizhi wrote a letter to Deng Xiaoping calling for amnesty and the release of political prisoners, including Wei Jingsheng, who had challenged Deng's authority and advocated democratization in 1979 and had been sentenced to fifteen years imprisonment. Fang's letter, cosigned by thirty-three leading writers and scholars, gained immediate support from intellectuals inside and outside of the country. Within the PRC, forty-two prominent scientists and scholars presented an open letter to the CCP leadership, appealing for freedom of speech, release of political prisoners, and respect for human rights. Half of the cosignatories were Party members, several for more than fifty years. Among overseas Chinese, fifty-six noted scholars also published a joint statement in support of democratization and human rights.

Affected by the open appeals for democratic change, students at Beijing University began to set up "democracy salons" on campus to push for democratic change. Most democracy salons took the form of free discussions, with students gathered on the lawn carrying on debates and listening to lectures on major national issues. Topics included such sensitive subjects as "Neoauthoritarianism," "Commodity Economy and the Democratic Process," and "A Breakthrough in the Democratization of China." On several occasions, students invited famous dissidents to give lectures; most notable among these were Ren Wanding, a well-known figure in the 1979 democratic movement and former editor of *Human Rights in China*, who had been arrested and imprisoned in 1978 for providing an account of the history of the Democracy Wall, and Li Shuxian, the wife of Fang Lizhi. The democracy salons were viewed by the local Party leaders as signs of bourgeois influence that needed to be brought under strict control. Students who were active in the salons were interviewed by Party committees and were "persuaded" to cease their salon activities. To resist the pressure, students posted open letters of protest at Beijing University. In March 1989, fifty-seven students sent an open letter to the university authorities, demanding the elimination of all forms of censorship and asking that seminars and forums be allowed to take place on the lawn. The atmosphere within the university was volatile. Even without the death of Hu Yaobang, some form of student demonstration was bound to have occurred during early May when the country celebrated the seventieth anniversary of the May Fourth Movement.[2]

The heart attack and sudden death of Hu Yaobang on April 15 provided the excuse for students to stage large-scale demonstrations. Until his forced resignation in January 1987, Hu had been Deng's heir apparent, having served as the Party chief for six years. It was Hu who had pushed the PRC toward a market economy and a more open political system. Hu's respect for intellectuals and his tolerance of dissidents had won him student support. His fall from power in January 1987 came in the face of nationwide student protests calling for greater democracy. On the night of Hu's death, students at Beijing University immediately put up posters praising him as a heroic fighter for democracy and calling for large-scale demonstrations to mourn him. On April 18, two thousand students marched through the capital during the predawn hours, chanting democratic slogans and singing revolutionary songs. The students had three demands: (1) an official reappraisal of Hu's alleged mistakes that had led to his disgrace in 1987; (2) an open apology from the government for various mistakes made during the anti-spiritual-pollution campaign and anti-bourgeois-liberalization campaign; and (3) the resignation of some of the country's leaders. Later that day, other student leaders added further demands, such as democratic elections for the deputies of the National People's Congress, the release of political prisoners, and freedom of the press.[3]

With the student protests targeting the Party and the government, the demonstration became a source of embarrassment to the leaders who had forced Hu to resign two years earlier. The large-scale mourning was also reminiscent of the April 5, 1976, demonstration mourning the death of Zhou Enlai, the former premier. That event, which also took place in Tiananmen Square, had turned into a bloody antigovernment riot. Therefore, Party leaders were extremely sensitive about the new student unrest.

The student demonstrations gained momentum in the following days, as young people from other universities joined. On April 19, more than 10,000 people took over Tiananmen Square, defying an official ban. Several thousands then marched to Zhongnanhai, a walled compound, where CCP headquarters were and where most of the PRC's leaders lived and worked. The march to Zhongnanhai represented one of the boldest expressions of dissent since the height of the Cultural Revolution in the late 1960s. For two days, demonstrations continued outside Zhongnanhai. On April 20, the government dispatched thousands of police officers to disperse the crowd. Several protesters were beaten, and 150 to 200 demonstrators were removed.[4]

Despite the show of police force, the number of demonstrators snowballed. On the night of April 21, more than 100,000 people assembled in Tiananmen Square. Tens of thousands of university students camped out all night to foil government plans to close off the square. The sheer size of the crowd, combined with the high level of dissatisfaction expressed, alarmed Party authorities. The government called three divisions of the 38th Army Corps, stationed in Baoding, to reinforce the capital's police.[5]

After the conclusion of the mourning period on April 22, the student movement entered a new stage. The first change was the formation of a solidarity student union to unite all colleges and universities in the Beijing area. On April 23, the union issued a statement calling for a boycott of university classes. Second, the students' list of demands also lengthened. They also asked for public disclosure of the income and assets of the PRC's leaders and their children. Third, the students' slogans also were altered. Instead of the general calls for a more democratic political system, the students raised specific economic issues, such as inflation and speculation by officials. These issues struck a common chord with workers and city dwellers, propelling many workers to join in the rallies.

Although demonstrations in Beijing had been peaceful and nonviolent, large-scale rioting broke out in two interior provincial capitals, Changsha, in Hunan Province, and Xi'an, in Shaanxi Province. In both cities, clashes took place between the crowd and police, lasting more than seven hours in Changsha and more than twelve hours in Xi'an and causing much damage to public buildings. Although the violence was attributed to hoodlums rather than to the students, it nevertheless affected government policy toward mass demonstrations.

On April 24, the Beijing Municipal Party Committee urged Wan Li, in the absence of the Party general secretary, Zhao Ziyang—who was on an official visit to North Korea—to convene an enlarged meeting of the CCP Politburo Standing Committee that day. With Li Peng presiding, the committee concluded that the student demonstration was not an ordinary protest but an anti-Party and antisocialist political struggle and was being conducted in a planned and organized manner by a handful of persons. The committee then decided to establish a special group for ending the unrest. According to an official report by Chen Xitong, mayor of Beijing, Deng Xiaoping, after listening to the report, made "an incisive analysis of the nature of the turmoil" and concluded that "this was not a case of common student unrest, but a political turmoil, aimed at negating the leadership of the Communist Party and the socialist system."[6] Deng's verdict on the student movement set the tone for all subsequent governmental statements and determined the fate of the 1989 prodemocracy movement.

Under Deng's instruction, an editorial was prepared for the April 26 issue of the *People's Daily* and was broadcast in advance on the evening of April 25. It officially charged that the unrest was "a conspiracy to wrest power from the Communist Party" and "a grave political struggle." The editorial continued: "If we do not resolutely stop this unrest, our state will have no peace. Our reform and modernization will depend on this struggle, and the future of our state and nation will depend on it." Because of this editorial, many students and intellectuals predicted that a military crackdown was imminent.

From Student Demonstration
to People's Movement

The harshness of the *People's Daily* editorial failed to deter student actions. The next day, more than 150,000 university students—out of a student body numbering 160,000—defied the government's repeated warnings and ignored the concentration of troops, marching for fourteen hours throughout the capital. About half of the marchers were organized students carrying banners, and the rest were students taking part spontaneously and workers. For the first time, the prodemocracy student protest campaign drew enthusiastic support from the masses.

To back up their stern warnings, the Beijing authorities called in more army troops from surrounding areas. However, thousands of workers and residents encircled the soldiers and prevented them from approaching the student marchers. Sometimes workers pushed aside police barricades even before the students drew near and then joined the marchers in the four-mile-long parade, walking or cycling alongside. Including the onlookers who waved and cheered as the parade passed by, an estimated half million people participated.[7] The protest that had arisen from student discontent had evolved into a mass movement.

The transformation of the nature of the movement stems from several factors: (1) In the first ten days of the movement, Deng proved to be as intransigent as other hard-liners. Internal Party documents revealed that when the CCP Politburo raised the matter of student unrest, Deng answered the questions by saying that if necessary, some blood could be shed and that repression would not seriously harm the PRC's image in the world. Deng even asserted that "hundreds of thousands of students mean nothing since we have a 3-million-person army."[8] Deng's hostility toward the demonstration provoked the students and alienated millions of workers and residents. (2) To many workers, the students' slogan about eliminating corruption and inflation addressed their own dissatisfaction with the present system. At the April 27 march, crowds of cheering workers hailed the student marchers as a liberation army.[9] (3) Finally, despite a heavy police and military presence, no injuries or arrests were reported. The students decided to defy warnings and take to the streets. The police seemed to have been under instructions to avoid confrontation.

The April 27 rally and the overwhelming popular support it received prompted a stunned government to announce that it would meet the students' demand for a dialogue. In hindsight, however, the governmental concession proved to be a dilatory tactic prior to two international conferences scheduled to convene in Beijing—the Asian Development Bank annual meeting in early May and the Sino-Soviet summit in the middle of May. To avoid bloodshed within this period, informal talks served as a means of placating the students without offering them anything concrete. For a whole week between April 28 and May 4, the Beijing authorities alternated between the threat of a crackdown and partial concessions to the students' least threatening demands.

As student activities began to show signs of subsiding, the government's leading spokesman, Yuan Mu, made a provocative speech that not only rejected a student ultimatum on conditions for an official talk but also hinted at a crackdown later. In the speech, Yuan reiterated the government's stand and stated that "there are a handful of people behind the scenes engaged in political struggle against the leaders of the Communist Party." Yuan added: "We are not planning to take action against them yet. If we take action now, that would be too soon." Yuan's remarks revealed the government's lack of sincerity in carrying out a dialogue with the students. The students responded by calling a mass demonstration on May 4.[10]

That day was, of course, the seventieth anniversary of the first major student movement of modern times. Large numbers of nonstudent protest groups joined the student march. Several hundred journalists waved banners and shouted slogans criticizing governmental press policies and calling for the reinstatement of Qin Benli as editor of the Shanghai *World Economic Herald*. Qin's suspension on April 26 had made him the first victim of the suppression. In their first major expression of solidarity with the students, journalists from thirty organizations participated, including the *People's Daily*, the official Party newspaper, and Xinhua, the official press service.[11]

Zhao Ziyang's adoption of a conciliatory tone toward the student movement softened the stand of many students. In a speech to the governors of the Asian Development Bank meeting in Beijing on May 4, Zhao emphasized that the protests "are by no means opposed to our fundamental system. Rather they are asking us to correct mistakes in our work." He also indicated that "the reasonable demands from the students should be met through democratic and legal means." After Zhao's speech, student leaders announced plans to return to classes, thereby ending a two-week boycott, but stated they would continue their efforts to meet with government and Party leaders.[12]

As the students were preparing to end the strike, the intra-Party power struggle was raging with each side using the student unrest for its own purpose. Whereas Zhao and his associates cited the actions of the students to support their claim that more rapid reform was needed, the hard-liners pointed to the demonstrations to blame Zhao for pursuing a lax policy. Government delegates met repeatedly with student leaders, hoping to coax the students out of the square, but the hard-liners refused to accept any conditions set by the students. Consequently, several thousand students continued their occupation of the central square of the capital, and the protests continued. Had the Party leaders put aside their differences and modified their policy toward the student movement by acknowledging the patriotic motivation of the students and promising no penalty for their demonstrations, the student movement might have come to a peaceful end.

In the days prior to the Sino-Soviet summit on May 16, more than 1,200 journalists from an international press corps arrived in Beijing. The student movement became headline news for the world news media. Frustrated by the lack of governmental concessions, 2,200 students began a hunger strike on May 13. The number soon swelled to 3,000. They sat huddled in the center of the square, with more than 25,000 students crowded around them.

The hunger strike won popular sympathy and support. On the evening of May 16, some 300,000 workers, students, and onlookers, in one of the biggest displays of popular dissatisfaction that the capital has seen since the Communist revolution in 1949, turned the center of the capital into near pandemonium.[13] On May 17, as the Sino-Soviet summit meeting was in process, more than a million people took to the streets of Beijing, creating a situation similar to a general strike. The crowds took control of the capital, which by then had become a kaleidoscope of banners demanding the resignations of Deng Xiaoping and Li Peng and calling for greater democracy.

As the hunger strike entered its fifth day, many of the participants were extremely weak. Sirens wailed as ambulances sped by carrying hunger strikers to the hospitals. Volunteer doctors and nurses worked around the clock to save the lives of the strikers, who pledged to continue until death if the government refused to accept their demands. The demands concentrated on two points: a retraction of the April 26 *People's Daily* editorial with a proper appraisal of the student movement and a direct, televised dialogue with the leadership.[14] The hard-liners, however, turned down all demands.

The intransigence of the leadership and their indifference toward the loss of human life galvanized the Beijing residents to respond. Groups of workers rushed to help the students. These workers included not only auto mechanics and railroad employees but also staff members of some of the country's most respected and sensitive institutions, such as the People's Liberation Army, the Foreign Ministry, the Central Broadcasting Station, *People's Daily*, and even the office school of the CCP Central Committee. Most of the marchers were young people.[15]

The student movement had also gained wide support from prominent individuals and organizations. On the evening of May 13, several eminent social scientists, including Yan Jiaqi, Su Shaozhi, and Bao Zunxin, visited the hunger strikers in Tiananmen Square. They put up a poster at Beijing University urging intellectuals to take part in the demonstrations in support of the hunger strikers. On the following day, a joint statement by twelve well-known intellectuals appeared in the *Guangming Daily*, demanding that the student movement be declared a patriotic democratic movement and the student organization be legalized. They also expressed their willingness to take part in the hunger strike if these demands were ignored. Signers of the statement included: Yan Jiaqi, Bao Zunxin, Li Honglin (director, Fujian Academy of Social Sciences), Dai Qing (reporter for *Guangming Daily*), Yu Haocheng (director of the Masses Publishing House), Li Zehou (research fellow at the Philosophy Institute of the Chinese Academy of Social Sciences), Su Xiaokong (lecturer at the Beijing Broadcasting Institute and author of the noted television series "River Elegy"), Wen Yuankai (professor at the University of Science and Technology), and Liu Zaifu (director of the Literature Institute of the Chinese Academy of Social Sciences).

Echoing the appeal of these prominent intellectuals, the presidents of eight universities, the leaders of several minor "democratic political parties," the central committee of the Chinese Communist Youth League, the All China Youth Federation, and the All China Students' Federation openly appealed to the government to recognize the students' demands. After one month of struggle, the student campaign had been transformed from a student protest into a broad-based democracy movement.[16]

The conduct of the students during the events leading to the announcement of martial law on May 20 won the world's admiration. During the protests, students rarely alluded to their own poor living standards. Instead, they advocated greater democracy, press freedom, an end to corruption, and free elections to fill leading positions—aims that were shared by the masses. In contrast to other student demonstrations, the 1989 Chinese student movement was significant in the following ways:

First, the scale of the movement was the largest in history. Initiated by students of the 35 universities and colleges in the Beijing area, the movement soon spread across the entire nation. Official statistics revealed that between April 15 and early June, student protests occurred in more than eighty Chinese cities, involving 600 universities and colleges, with 2.8 million students participating. Almost all major institutes of higher learning joined the student movement.[17] Eventually, the movement embraced people from all walks of life, including educators, trade unionists, scientists and engineers, journalists, literary people and artists, as well as those from various social, Party, and governmental organizations. According to one official report, during the demonstrations more than 2,000 Party members, including some at the ministerial level, signed a petition to accept student demands.[18] In the demonstrations of May 17 and 18, a boisterous crowd of more than 1 million joined the march. Of the 6 million Chinese residents living in the adjacent British colony, Hong Kong, 1.5 million took part on May 29 in a parade, the largest demonstration in the island's history.[19]

Second, the campaign also appears to be the longest ever staged in Chinese history. From the day of mourning for Hu Yaobang to the day of the massacre, almost seven weeks elapsed. Although the movement underwent ebbs and flows, it never lost its vitality.

Third, unlike the radical student campaigns in South Korea and the Philippines, the Chinese student movement was completely nonviolent. From the beginning, the student leaders made it clear that their goal was to help the government correct its mistakes rather than to overthrow the government. The students chose to work for this goal through persuasion and dialogue. Although at an early stage of the protest, they did want the replacement of certain leaders, by mid-May their demands had been reduced to only two: an acknowledgment of their patriotic motivation and a promise of no penalty for their demonstration. The government could have granted both demands and ended the protest peacefully. Throughout the entire period, even when 1 million people were participating, students exercised disciplined restraint and avoided violence. On several occasions, they even formed a human fence to protect the Party leaders' compound from the possibility of being stormed by angry workers. On May 23, when three radicals from Hunan spilled paint over Mao's huge portrait in Tiananmen Square, students immediately handed them over to the police. When throngs of Beijing residents blocked the soldiers, students came to their rescue by persuading the masses to let the soldiers retreat. Without the June 4 crackdown, the 1989 demonstrations would have been remembered as a model of self-restraint for both the protesters and the government.

Fourth, the 1989 Chinese student movement also received the most universally televised coverage of any such demonstration. From the very beginning, the campaign had been widely reported in the Western world. When international reporters flocked to the PRC on the eve of Gorbachev's visit, the story of the hunger strikers overshadowed the Sino-Soviet Summit, thus making the protest an international event.

The Behind-the-Scenes Power Struggle

While student hunger strikers were languishing in Tiananmen Square, a direct confrontation between Zhao Ziyang, the Party general secretary, and Li Peng, the premier, took place. The power struggle had the extra dimension of Zhao's vehement disagreement with his mentor, Deng Xiaoping, over how to deal with the students.

The power contention between Zhao and Li had been going on for quite some time (see Chapter 3), but the change in the relationship between Deng and Zhao was a more recent development. The central issue was how to assess the nature of the student unrest. From the start of the movement, Zhao believed that the students were patriotic and harbored no intentions of overthrowing the government. His approach was to praise their patriotic

Students demonstrate in Tiananmen Square. The banners indicate participants from Qinghua University and China's People University. Photo by Grand Alliance for China's Reunification.

A student raises a sign for liberty. Photo by Grand Alliance for China's Reunification.

Students protest at the front gate of Xinhuamen at Zhongnanhai, headquarters of the Chinese Communist Party, in late April 1989. They have placed Zhou Enlai's photo on the sign and written "Li Peng, you let me down!" Photo by Grand Alliance for China's Reunification.

Students and workers demonstrate on April 27, 1989. The banner reads "Since the people do not fear death, there is hope for China." The building in the background is the Beijing Hotel. Photo by James Tu.

The sign reads "Long Live the Invincible Mao Zedong's Thought!" Photo by Grand Alliance for China's Reunification.

Students at Beijing University put up wall posters that "solemnly commemorate the seventieth anniversary of the May 4 movement." Photo by James Tu.

Student protestors in Tiananmen Square with victory signs. Photo by Grand Alliance for China's Reunification.

Workers participate in the demonstrations. They carry a banner that reads "The working class is a strong supporter of the patriotic student democracy movement." Photo by James Tu.

Student protestors in Tiananmen Square, May 15, 1989. Photo by *Global Views*.

Student protestors demand "Xiaoping Step Down!" Photo by James Tu.

Medical workers deliver medicine to the hunger strikers. The banner reads "We deliver medicine! The government is concerned only for power. The people will be reborn." Photo by James Tu.

Student demonstrators hold up a banner reading "Bloody evidence piled up like a mountain." Photo by Grand Alliance for China's Reunification.

Soviet leader Mikhail Gorbachev reaches out of the window of his automobile to shake the hand of a youngster as his motorcade departs Shanghai airport upon arrival May 18. Photo by Reuters/Bettmann Newsphotos, used by permission of the Bettmann Archive.

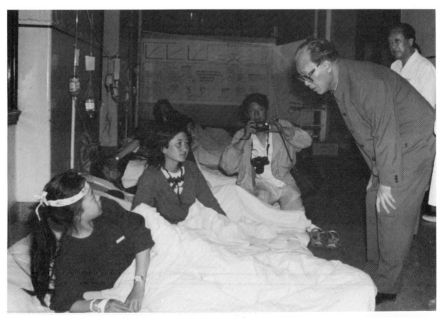

Zhao Ziyang, then general secretary of the CCP, visits the hunger strikers at a Beijing hospital in May 1989. Photo by *Global Views*.

A Chinese prodemocracy protestor gives a victory sign on Friday, May 19. Photo by Reuters/Bettmann Newsphotos, used by permission of the Bettmann Archive.

Students and PLA soldiers in confrontation. The building is the Mao Zedong Mausoleum. Photo by James Tu.

Beijing residents offer food to soldiers on a Beijing street early on Saturday, June 3, after barring them from reaching Tiananmen Square. Photo by Reuters/Bettmann Newsphotos, used by permission of the Bettman Archive.

Victim of the massacre. Photo by *Global Views*.

Military crackdown in process at Tiananmen Square. Photo by *Global Views*.

Crackdown in process on the morning of June 4, 1989, at Changan Street, near Tiananmen Square. Photo by *Global Views*.

After the crackdown on June 4. Photo by *Global Views*.

Victim of the June 4 massacre. Photo by Grand Alliance for China's Reunification.

Citizens walk and bicycle past Chinese People's Liberation Army trucks in the northeast section of the city on Monday, June 5. The sign above, which was put up by the citizens, translates "Blood must be returned with blood. Hang Li Peng and Yang Shangkun." Photo by Reuters/Bettmann Newsphotos, used by permission of the Bettmann Archive.

After the crackdown, a lone PLA soldier guards an empty Tiananmen Square. The building at the right is the People's Assembly Hall. Photo by *Global Views*.

zeal and to establish direct dialogue with them. Deng, a staunch Leninist, who deeply believed in the primacy of Communist Party control, found himself unable to tolerate any student challenge. Deng's personality and his close association with the army had shaped his approach to governing.

In 1957, after Mao had encouraged a brief outpouring of criticism of the Communists in the abortive Hundred Flowers Campaign (see Chapter 4), Deng, as the Party's general secretary, had helped lead a crackdown that exiled hundreds of thousands of professors, writers, and scientists to the countryside or labor camps for twenty years. Although Deng showed some amicability toward intellectuals in the wake of his second return to power (in 1978), his hostility toward political dissent remained unchanged. When Wei Jingsheng had criticized the government and called for democracy in 1979, Deng immediately sent him to prison. His disdain for critics was reflected in a comment he made to a group of Communist officials with respect to the suppression of intellectual dissidents: "We put Wei behind bars, didn't we? Did that damage China's reputation? We haven't released him, but China's image has not been tarnished by that. Our reputation improves day by day."[20] Deng's perception of the student unrest, his contempt for intellectuals, and his belief that supression was the best means to deal with such a crisis stiffened his stance. His insistence on labeling the student movement a "counter-revolutionary conspiracy" and his decision to use armed force to deal with the protesters led to the split between him and Zhao.

When Zhao returned from his official trip to North Korea, he attempted on several occasions to persuade Deng to change his position, but each time Deng rebuffed him. To detach himself from the hard-liners, Zhao made several gestures, each of which was subsequently given as evidence of his betrayal of Deng. Zhao's speech to the governors of the Asian Development Bank meeting on May 4 acknowledging the students' good intentions and rejecting the organized conspiracy accusations was interpreted by his rivals as an attempt to split the central leadership by openly airing a view diametrically opposed to Deng's. Deng also perceived the speech as Zhao's premature bid for ultimate power.[21]

After the hunger strike started on May 13, Zhao made another effort to persuade Deng to accept some of the students' demands, but once again he was ignored by Deng and other hard-liners. To further distance himself from Deng's policies and to ward off any backlash from the student crisis, during a televised meeting with Soviet President Mikhail Gorbachev, Zhao twice stated that Deng, although having relinquished his positions in the Central Committee and the Politburo, still held the ultimate power in the PRC and thus had the final word on major decisions. Zhao also mentioned that this was a state secret. Zhao's rivals interpreted his announcement of this well-known but never expressed fact as yet another power play, pointing out that the obstacle in negotiating a peaceful solution to the crisis was none other than Deng. When Zhao's remarks appeared in the news, Deng made final the decision to dismiss him as Party general secretary.[22]

Knowing that his position was shaky, Zhao went to Tiananmen Square before dawn on May 19 to visit the hunger strikers. With tears in his eyes, Zhao delivered a short but highly emotional speech: "We've come too late. You have good intentions. You want our country to become better. The problems you have raised will eventually be resolved. However, they are complicated, and there must be a process by which to resolve these problems." Zhao then bid farewell to the students, saying, "You are young and have a great future. We are old and do not matter."[23] Zhao's speech later was labeled by his rivals as an attempt to win support from demonstrators and to place blame on other leaders for adopting a hard-line stance.

Deng's decision to turn on his protégé and scrap his carefully laid plans for succession sprang from his deep-seated intolerance toward any form of social unrest or other political challenges to his authority. Two years before, on the eve of the previous crackdown on the student movement, Deng had said: "If our country were plunged into disorder and our nation reduced to a heap of loose sand, how could we ever prosper?" As one Western observer commented, "While Westerners have tended to think of China as under firm rule, Deng tends to see the potential for chaos, and may often feel the central government is hanging on by its fingernails."[24] With this kind of mentality, Deng tended to view bubbles of discontent not as a sign of the PRC's resilience but as a sign of its growing maladies and weaknesses. Whereas Zhao and his associates hailed the patriotic spirit of the young students, Deng and other veterans perceived the demonstration as being inimical to modernization.

For more than a decade, Deng had established himself as the nation's helmsman, a role previously assumed only by Mao. Zhao's May 4 speech constituted a direct challenge to Deng's authority because the speech had not been cleared by him in advance. It may be argued that there is a Western political tradition of respecting the lone dissenter, but in Deng's PRC, Zhao's persistent adherence to his own views was interpreted as impudence and treachery.[25]

As a result of Zhao's downfall, the political power balance shifted toward the hard-liners. In a last-ditch effort to reverse this, some opponents of Premier Li Peng were hoping to call an emergency meeting of the National People's Congress Standing Committee to veto the declaration of martial law and even to summon an emergency meeting of the full NPC to force the resignation of Li Peng as prime minister. However, the head of the NPC, Wan Li, was on an official trip to Canada and the United States. Both Zhao and Li had tried to contact him. Whereas Zhao urged Wan to cut short the trip and come back immediately, Li advised him to continue on.[26] Before Wan's return, many students had regarded him as a heroic figure destined to help Zhao. But instead of flying back directly to Beijing, Wan stopped in Shanghai—ostensibly for medical treatment, but in reality to assess his own political future. A veteran politician, Wan found himself torn by conflicting loyalties. On the one hand, he was Deng's old associate and bridge partner. On the other hand, Wan favored political liberalization and did not regard the student movement as serious enough to require a military crackdown. After days of deliberation, Wan finally expressed his support of Li Peng's hard-line policy, thus dashing Zhao's final hope to oust Li.[27]

After his ouster from his top Party position on May 19, Zhao was steadily attacked in the press and in meetings for his "serious mistakes," particularly his reputed support of the student-led protest movement. On June 16, Premier Li Peng delivered a lengthy report "on the mistakes committed by Comrade Zhao Ziyang during the Anti-Party, Anti-Socialist Turmoil" to the Fourth Plenum of the Thirteenth Party Central Committee. In this report, Li accused Zhao of the following offenses: (1) conspiring in the creation of the student-led turmoil during the April 15–22 Hu mourning period; (2) in his May 4th speech before the Asian Development Bank governors, deliberately disclosing the differences of opinion within the Party center and inspiring the demonstrations; (3) making public a Party secret in his disclosure to Gorbachev in order to place blame on Deng; (4) refusing to support martial law, splitting the Central Committee; (5) abandoning the Four Cardinal Principles. Li said that Zhao's involvement in bourgeois liberalization resulted in a surge of ideological attacks against socialism and the leadership of the Communist Party.[28]

Subsequently, in a 25,000-word report on putting down antigovernment riots, the Beijing mayor, Chen Xitong, held Zhao responsible not only for the student unrest but also for virtually all of the country's difficulties (see Appendix 3). The torrent of accusations was an attempt to set the stage for putting Zhao on trial, thus destroying his chance for a political comeback.

Preparation for the Crackdown

With Zhao immobilized, the way was open for the military crackdown. In a special telecast early in the morning of May 20, Li Peng announced that martial law had been imposed on some parts of the capital and that the government had called on the army to clear Tiananmen Square (see map 6.1). Li emphasized that he was speaking for both the government and the Party's Central Committee, thus implying that he was now the man in charge. He stated, "If we fail to put an end to such chaos immediately and let it go unchecked, it may very likely lead to a situation which none of us wants to see."

The first day of martial law, huge throngs of demonstrators and onlookers, numbering more than 1 million, took to the streets. They blocked troops from reaching the center of the capital, effectively preventing the crackdown planned by the government. Troops approaching Beijing on at least five major roads were halted or turned back by the largest crowds to have gathered so far. Students and ordinary citizens erected roadblocks. In one instance, an old woman street cleaner stopped a troop procession by lying down on the road in front of the army trucks. Immediately following her action, several hundred students dashed toward the convoy. The soldiers

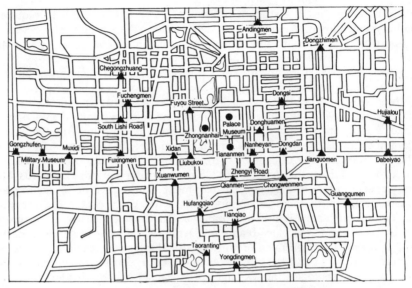

MAP 6.1   Sketch map of Beijing city center

found themselves surrounded by Beijing residents who not only showered them with questions about why they wanted to repress their fellow citizens but also provided them with breakfast and cold drinks. The soldiers were so moved by the people's appeals that they ended up retreating.[29]

There were several developments in the next three days. On May 21, seven top ex-commanders of the army wrote to Deng Xiaoping formally objecting to the governmental plan to bring troops into the capital to suppress the demonstrators. They asserted in their letter: "In view of the extremely serious situation, we as veteran soldiers demand that the People's Liberation Army not confront the population nor quell the population. The army must absolutely not shoot the people. In order to prevent the situation from worsening, the army must not enter the city of Beijing." The signers included Zhang Aiping, a former defense minister; Xiao Ke, a former deputy defense minister; Yang Dezhi, a former army chief of staff; Song Shilun, a former commandant of the Academy of Military Sciences; Chen Zaidao, a former commander of the Wuhan Military Region; Ye Fei, a former commander of the navy; and Li Jukui, a former commandant of the military academy. Collectively, they commanded great prestige and influence.[30] The letter's publication, therefore, dealt a blow to the crackdown plan. At the same time, forty top legislators, members of the National People's Congress, had agreed on a strategem to revoke martial law. All of these new developments created the false hope that Li Peng was on the way out and that Zhao would soon resume power.

In the midst of the demonstrators' exhilaration, the hard-liners were intent on carrying out the plan for a crackdown. Under the orders of the Central

Military Commission, troops from several regions were rushed to Beijing. In addition to ground armies, Deng also summoned several special military units, including airborne and armored divisions.[31] Most of the armed forces were stationed within the vicinity of Beijing. The four army units confirmed to be in the capital were the 27th, 16th, 38th, and 39th armies.[32]

The deployment of such a huge armed force to quell the unrest was a source of great puzzlement not only to the demonstrators but also to many foreign military experts. Some believed the goal was to intimidate the protesters. Others contended that some factional struggle may have developed within the army. Between May 25 and June 3, there were unconfirmed reports of tension between different military units. It was said that some units supported Li Peng and that others, such as the Beijing Garrison Command, were sympathetic to Zhao and for that reason refused to break up the demonstrators by force. The commanding officer of the 38th Army, which was normally stationed in the nearby city of Baoding, was reported to have refused an order from Deng to move troops to the capital. The 27th Army, stationed in Inner Mongolia, was then brought into Beijing to carry out the suppression.[33]

However, later developments showed that most of those rumors had been deliberately initiated by the army. Because the 38th Army was in the Beijing area, the military authorities had it play the role of the people's protector, and the 27th Army, far from the capital in Inner Mongolia, was assigned the role of suppressor. The plan was to have the 27th Army return to Inner Mongolia following the completion of the crackdown, leaving the 38th Army the job of rebuilding amity between the military and the masses.[34]

Ten days prior to the massacre, there were many signs indicating the imminence of the crackdown. First, there were visible relocations of tanks and gas and water cannons to the suburbs and certain areas of the city. Thousands of troops were in Beijing's main railroad station, a ten-minute march from Tiananmen Square, and also in subway stations. Even more ominous, hospitals in the capital were evacuating patients to make room for potential casualties of the confrontation.[35]

Second, enforcement of press restrictions presaged the impending crackdown. To prevent foreign access to military information, on May 21 Chinese officials abruptly halted the transmission of televised news reports from Beijing. They also barred foreign broadcasters from recording and transmitting news reports from the state-run network. Three days before the crackdown, the government announced even tougher new restrictions on foreign coverage, in effect preventing correspondents from writing any articles about the democracy movement. The new restrictions included bans on the print reporting, photographing, and videotaping of activities in Tiananmen Square prohibited by the martial law decrees. Because the decrees banned the demonstration, any press coverage of the protest movement would be in violation of the rules. Moreover, without approval, foreign journalists also could not write about, photograph, or videotape the troops enforcing martial law.

Third, while restricting foreign coverage of the demonstration, the hard-liners did not neglect control of the domestic mass media. Immediately after the announcement of martial law, Li Peng appointed a "working group" to take charge of propaganda. Editors-in-chief of the PRC's largest newspapers were summoned by the working group to a special meeting, in which they heard Zhao accused of inciting the student unrest. The leaders also announced that beginning on May 25, the *People's Daily* was obliged to submit proofs of each page to the working group before it could go to press.[36] Later, soldiers were dispatched to occupy the headquarters of several state-controlled news organs, including the official news agency Xinhua, the *People's Daily*, and the Central Broadcasting Station, whose journalists had clearly sided with the students. By May 25, the hard-liners had achieved almost complete control of the domestic mass media.

Li Peng, confident that preparations for the crackdown were nearing completion, declared on television on May 26 that his government was in full control. Li also said that "the troops will overcome the difficulties confronting them and will successfully enforce the martial law." Li's statement signaled that the military suppression was imminent. To ensure success and to lay down the groundwork for the postcrackdown cover-up, the martial law troop command devised several scenarios to deceive the protesters. One scheme involved dispatching 5,000 young, unarmed soldiers to clear Tiananmen Square during the late night hours of June 2. Most of the inexperienced soldiers rapidly retreated when confronted by the thousands of students and citizens. In retrospect, this was seen as a plot to reduce the vigilance of the protesters as well as to create an impression on the nation and the world that the demonstration was not a legitimate protest but a "counter-revolutionary rebellion."

Until the eve of the crackdown, it appeared that the army would continue to hold back. On several occasions, unarmed soldiers in shirtsleeves made only a desultory attempt at dispersing the crowds before quickly turning back. On other occasions, military vehicles were abandoned so that they could be destroyed by the protesters. According to Chen Xitong, over a period of several days, at least 1,280 military vehicles and police cars were wrecked, burned, or damaged. This destruction was carefully photographed by governmental agents for future evidence of the restraint and tolerance of the martial law troops and the violence of the protesters, thus chronicling the justification of a military crackdown.[37]

The Great Massacre

After two weeks of intensive preparations, the countdown time had finally arrived. At 2 A.M. on June 4, a convoy of fifty trucks accompanied by foot soldiers stormed through the crowded streets en route to Tiananmen Square. Advance troops torched barricades of buses and trucks to enable the convoy to proceed. Within a short period of time, soldiers of the PLA invaded the 100-acre square from side streets in a triple-pronged movement from the east, west, and south. Others advanced from the Forbidden City or were poised on the rooftops of the Great Hall of the People and Mao Zedong's mausoleum. With 10,000 soldiers, the army mounted a vicious assault. They randomly shot people on sight. As helmeted soldiers mounted their machine guns onto tripods facing the square, policemen with truncheons chased people from the sidewalks. The shooting became most intense by 2:15 A.M. Hundreds of PLA soldiers with AK-47s lined up in front of the Museum of the Revolution and fired into the helpless crowd. Panic-stricken people fell to the pavement or cowered behind the Imperial City's ornate stone lions. The scene was horrifying.[38]

The fighting soon spilled out of the Tiananmen area into other neighborhoods. Large numbers of tanks moved across the city, some of them firing indiscriminately. Beijing was transformed into a city of terror and bloodshed. By 5 A.M. on June 4, Tiananmen Square had been virtually emptied, and the dream of democracy lay shattered in the blood-stained debris (see Appendix 3: "A Student's Eyewitness Account of the Tiananmen Massacre"). The nation and the world were stunned. Questions arose concerning who had ordered the murderous military assualt, which army unit was reponsible for the bloodshed, and how many people had been killed in the massacre.

Deng's three-week long absence for unknown reasons had led many outside observers to conjecture at first that he might not have been aware of the situation. The man most likely to have been responsible for the massacre was considered to be President Yang Shangkun. Yang, in his May 24 speech to the enlarged meeting of the Central Military Commission, had indicated that the capital was out of control. He stated that "for every step we retreat, they advance." He then warned: "There's no way for us to retreat. To retreat means our downfall. To retreat means the downfall of the People's Republic of China and the restoration of capitalism." Yang thus viewed the democracy movement as a matter of life or death for the Communist Party. He further stated, "To safeguard public security and return to normal order in the capital, a group of the People's Liberation Army had to be transferred into the capital from outside Beijing."[39]

Yang's connections with the 27th Army, which was widely believed to have been the army responsible for the assault, sustained the theory that he had ordered the massacre. Chi Haotian, chief of staff of the PLA, and closely associated with Yang, had been the 27th Army's deputy political commissar and probably still retained close ties to it. For all of these reasons, Yang was popularly identified as the culprit.

A revelation in the *Beijing Review* has somewhat modified this view. According to this Party organ, the martial law enforcement troops were called to Beijing under orders of the Central Military Commission, of which Deng was chairman. On the evening of June 3, orders came from the martial law troop command to send the soldiers to Tiananmen Square.[40] Since Li Peng was a member of that command, he could have been the man who ordered the shooting. On June 8, before the reappearance of Deng Xiaoping,

Li Peng was the first top leader to appear on television and praise the attacking troops. These factors suggest that Li Peng may, in fact, have been the real culprit.

However, the man ultimately responsible for the whole tragedy was Deng Xiaoping. Deng was the one who determined that the nature of the democracy movement was a "counter-revolutionary rebellion." He was the one who refused to make any concessions to the students. Between May 16 and early June, Deng traveled to Wuhan, where he summoned the commanders of the seven military regions to persuade them to support his plan for the military crackdown. When he appeared on television on June 9, he expressed no remorse for the killings of thousands of citizens; instead he led the group in a minute of silence to honor the soldiers who had died in the fighting. Deng did not make the slightest conciliatory gesture to the millions of people around the nation who had supported the democracy movement. His harshness toward the demonstrators reveals his responsibility for the massacre. Thus one can conclude that Li Peng and Yang Shangkun initiated the crackdown but that Deng authorized the plan and permitted Li Peng to carry it out.

Immediately following the bloodshed, all the blame was focused on the 27th Army. Later information revealed the real story: On the night of June 3 and the morning of June 4, the soldiers that shot their way into Tiananmen Square were in fact a composite of several armies, including the 38th, the 63rd, and the 27th. The 15th Airborne Army, part of China's strategic reserves based in Wuhan, also participated.[41] Concentrating the blame on the 27th Army was part of the strategy to divert the people's resentment away from the army as a whole.

The true number of casualties from the bloodshed may never be known because the government forbade hospitals to report the numbers of dead or injured. Yuan Mu, government spokesman and Li Peng's closest aide, estimated on June 6 that only 300 people had been killed, among whom were soldiers, rioters, and civilians, including 36 university students. The number of wounded was put at 6,000 for the army and 3,000 for civilians.[42] On June 30, when Beijing Mayor Chen Xitong made a report to the Eighth Meeting of the Standing Committee of the Seventh NPC, he revised the casualty figures somewhat. Chen announced that more than 6,000 martial law soldiers, armed police, and public security officers had been injured, and the death toll was more than 10. More than 3,000 civilians had been wounded and over 200 had died, including 36 students.[43]

Unofficial estimates of the number of deaths ranged from several hundreds to several thousands. The Chinese Red Cross estimated that there were 2,600 fatalities of the night of June 4.[44] The student organization that coordinated the long protest movement estimated that 2,600 students had been killed. Several doctors in the Beijing hospitals indicated that based on their discussions with ambulance drivers and colleagues who had been in Tiananmen Square, at least 2,000 had died.[45] Residents in Beijing reported

MAP 6.2 Map showing Chengdu

that immediately after the massacre the troops sealed off Tiananmen Square and started a huge fire. The flames could be seen for miles around. They believed that the soldiers cremated the corpses in order to destroy the evidence.[46]

As time went on, a reassessment reduced the earlier unofficial estimates of the slaughter. Based on extensive interviews with eyewitnesses, Amnesty International in mid-August concluded that at least 1,000 civilians, most of them unarmed, had been killed and several thousands injured by troops firing indiscriminately into crowds in Beijing between June 3 and June 9, 1989. In addition to deaths in the capital, at least 300 people, according to Amnesty International, were also killed by troops and security forces on June 5 following student protests in Chengdu, the capital of Sichuan Province, in southwestern China (see Map 6.2).[47] Although the scale of the massacre in Chengdu did not equal that of Beijing's, its ferocity did. According to an eyewitness, the troops in Chengdu used concussion grenades, truncheons, knives, and electric cattle prods to attack the civilians. Even after having been knocked down to the ground, victims were beaten and stomped on by the troops; hospitals were ordered not to accept wounded students. On the second night of the attack, the police forbade ambulances from functioning.[48]

Although the number of deaths resulting from the military crackdown remains an unknown, common sense would suggest that if, even with their tanks, armored vehicles, and submachine guns, 6,000 soldiers were wounded and several dozens killed, the number of dead and wounded students and citizens must have been ten to twenty times greater. Amnesty International's estimates of 1,000 deaths in Beijing and 300 deaths in Chengdu may not be too far off the mark.

The Aftermath and Cover-up

Right after the June 4 massacre, the government began to arrest scores of people in the capital and major cities. These arrests, intended to destroy the democracy movement and to prevent organized resistance, were primarily of student leaders, activists in labor groups, and prominent intellectuals.

On June 7, large numbers of police, under orders of the martial law troop command, appeared on the streets of the capital and arrested student leaders and other activists who had led the protests. On June 8, Public Notice No. 10 of the Beijing municipal government and the Martial Law Enforcement Troops Command declared the Beijing Autonomous Federation of College Students and the Beijing Autonomous Federation of Workers illegal organizations and their leaders the "ring leaders" of the "counter-revolutionary rebellion." It called on them to surrender to the public security authorities, failing which they would be "brought to justice and punished severely." Public Notice No. 11, of the same authority, called on citizens to report on the "criminal activists of the counter-revolutionary rioters," stressing that "each and every citizen" in Beijing had the "right and obligation" to report and expose the rioters. It gave telephone numbers for people to use in making such denunciations. Similar notices and orders for the arrests of prodemocracy activists were issued later in provincial cities. Public warnings were repeatedly broadcast saying that citizens who failed to report people involved would themselves be liable to arrest and imprisonment. In some provinces, the militia and informal security agents were mobilized to search for wanted "counter-revolutionaries" and "rioters."

In a two-day period (June 10–11), the government announced that 1,000 were arrested in Beijing. For several days, Chinese national television showed people being taken into custody by security officers and held in a kind of airplane position. Many were handcuffed and squatting at gunpoint with heads bowed or were being frog-marched across a police courtyard. No attempt was made to conceal that the detainees had been severely beaten. The purpose of these television pictures presumably was to intimidate and deter the public from hiding or helping the protesters.

On June 13, the authorities issued warrants for the arrests of 21 student leaders on charges of inciting and organizing the "counter-revolutionary rebellions" in Beijing. Their photographs were shown on national television and detailed descriptions were published in newspapers and broadcast on state radio. By June 20, more than 1,500 people were officially reported to have been arrested throughout the PRC.

In mid-June, the government began executing people. On the two days of June 22 and 23, twenty-seven condemnees were shot in Beijing, including seven protesters. Besides intimidation, the arrests and executions served to counter the image displayed during the six weeks of student demonstrations of a weak and impotent government. But the large-scale executions attracted international attention. As international criticism mounted, Beijing altered its policy by quashing the publicity about such executions while continuing with them. By the middle of September, it was estimated that between

5,000 and 10,000 people had been arrested in Beijing and at least as many in other parts of the country.[49]

In the process of searching for students and workers on the wanted list, many methods used in the 1950s and 1960s were reemployed. The mobilization of street resident committees, located in every part of the cities, was one effective measure. Composed mostly of older women of low social status, these committees were very supportive of the public security departments. They closely watched the activities in their neighborhoods and reported the appearance of any strangers. The government created an atmosphere of fear by repeating its warnings day and night of the severe punishment for people hiding the protesters. In a case reminiscent of the human tragedy of the Cultural Revolution, Zhou Fengsuo, a twenty-two-year-old student leader, was turned in by his sister and brother-in-law.

The availability of modern technology also facilitated the nationwide manhunt. Throughout the two months of the prodemocracy movement, security agents or policemen had snapped pictures of student leaders, taken notes about them, and taped their speeches and conversations. Now these words came back to haunt the speakers. On many occasions, it was Western television footage that helped the police to identify the student protesters.

Soon, however, a concerted effort was made to win back the support of the people and to lure back foreign investors. Thus, in the wake of the bloodshed, the official propaganda machinery carried out an elaborate scheme for covering up the entire event. The first step in the cover-up involved offering the people a highly doctored account of the Beijing massacre. According to that account, on June 3 the troops that had been moved to Tiananmen Square to put down a "counter-revolutionary rebellion" were attacked and in some cases killed by "ruffians." Few civilians were harmed. When the soldiers arrived in Tiananmen Square about 4 A.M. on June 4, the protesting students who were camping out on the square withdrew quickly and after about only half an hour, the operation was complete. Television footage accompanying this account showed soldiers in the early morning peacefully clearing up the debris left over from the long occupation of the square. The campaign's greatest lie was that members of the People's Liberation Army were the heroic victims, not the perpetrators of violence. At a television press conference on June 6, Zhang Gong, deputy political commissar of the Beijing Military Region, declared that "troops did not kill or harm a single person, when we cleared Tiananmen Square."[50]

To sustain this account, the regime had to wage a massive propaganda blitz. State television broadcasted extensive clips from surveillance cameras and Western television network footage showing crowds stoning and burning military vehicles. The videotapes and sound tracks were edited to delete any evidence that soldiers had fired on demonstrators. On July 2, the television news announced that, at the behest of Deng Xiaoping, ten soldiers who died in Beijing when the army cracked down on the demonstration were being named "the defenders of the People's Republic of China" and inducted posthumously into the Communist Party. To convince the people that the army did not kill a single person in the Tiananmen Square, the government forced one leader of the hunger strikers who was arrested in June to declare that "he did not see any student, civilian or army man killed. Neither did he see anyone run over by military vehicles."[51]

To justify the military crackdown, the regime also attributed all the events from the day of mourning of Hu Yaobang to the large-scale demonstrations and hunger strikes to a conspiracy planned by a small group of counter-revolutionaries. This group was under the protection of Zhao Ziyang. In his report to the NPC, Beijing Mayor Chen Xitong traced the origin of the unrest to September 19, 1988, when Zhao met with U.S. economist Milton Friedman. According to Chen's interpretation, the meeting was part of a concerted plot by Zhao's "brain trust" to "topple Deng and to protect Zhao." The student movement was "exploited by organizers of the turmoil from the very beginning," and Zhao was the one who "supported the turmoil and split the party" and had "the unshirkable responsibility for the shaping and the development of the turmoil."[52] As attacks on Zhao and his associates escalated, the "turmoil" was later elevated to the status of "counter-revolutionary rebellion." On September 26, in his first press conference as the Party's new general secretary, Jiang Zemin, when asked by foreign reporters whether the "Tiananmen tragedy" could have been avoided, responded that "we do not believe that there was any tragedy in Tiananmen Square. What actually happened was a counter-revolutionary rebellion aimed at opposing the leadership of the Communist Party and overthrowing the socialist system."[53] Because the government determined the student protests to be "a counter-revolutionary rebellion," the use of the army to quell it was fully justified.

In creating a national consensus that the prodemocracy movement was a counter-revolutionary rebellion, the new leadership initiated another campaign requiring people in offices, institutes, schools, military installations, and factories all over the country to express their attitude (*biao tai*) toward the recent events. Weekly political study sessions for this purpose were resumed after a hiatus of several years. Under tremendous pressure, most people bowed to the official view by vowing their absolute support for the suppression of the counter-revolutionary rebellion. Almost all famous figures in the PRC—influential scholars, members of the NPC and the Chinese People's Political Consultative Conference (CPPCC), leaders of minor democratic parties—were requested to issue statements supporting the government actions against the students. Those who declined to make such statements, such as Wang Meng, the minister of culture, were relieved of their duties.

Other cover-up efforts included a tightening of control over the domestic news media and a fierce attack on foreign broadcasting. As part of the government indoctrination effort, newspapers continued under the tight control of a special propaganda committee formed after the declaration of martial law. The first pages of all newspapers printed whatever the committee dictated. Because official newspapers no longer reported news, transcripts of Chinese language broadcasts by the Voice of America (VOA) and the

British Broadcasting Company (BBC) became the only sources of information. During the demonstration and the crackdown, the Voice of America, despite being jammed, provided the most detailed accounts of the events, attracted a large audience, and became the primary source of unofficial news for most areas in the PRC. To discredit the VOA, television programs and newspaper articles publicized telegrams and letters from various provinces denouncing the U.S. broadcasters as "rumormongers." In mid-September, the *Beijing Review* published a six-page article, "Rumors and the Truth," to attack the credibility of the Voice of America.[54] The aim of the entire scheme was to silence the dissidents and to create a uniform view that followed the official line.

By employing terror, intimidation, and lies, the regime hoped to seal people's mouths and wash its own hands of the bloodshed. However, the scheme appears to have been only partially successful. Among the vast majority of the population that live in the countryside, where official television is the only source of information, the cover-up has won some converts who believed that the students rather than the government were to blame for the bloodshed. However, the witnesses in Beijing and around the world who had followed the events as they unfolded have viewed this rewriting of history as outrageous. The brutality shown on the screens of millions of television sets in the Western world has left an indelible impression, not easily eradicated by elaborate fabrications.

Nor has the large-scale manhunt for dissidents proved effective. Of the twenty-one student leaders wanted by the government, half have managed to flee the country. Included in the long list of exiles were Wuer Kaixi, a leader of the Independent Students Union, and Yan Jiaqi, one of the leaders of the Beijing Association of Intellectuals and the PRC's most influential political scientist. Other leading intellectuals who escaped from the country were Wan Runnan, head of the Stone Corporation, an extremly successful high-technology company in Beijing; Chen Yizi, the head of the government's Institute for Economic Structural Reform Research and the highest ranking officer to have taken refuge in the West; and Su Xiaokang, writer and film producer, whose credits include the controversial television series "River Elegy." By the end of September, more than 100 important dissidents had escaped the manhunt. The successful exodus of the dissenters indicated the existence of gaps in the public security net. It also reflected the widespread support of the intellectual leaders among the population and even among the public security officers. Without their assistance, it would have been extremely difficult for so many widely sought people to escape.

Because of the massacre and the cover-up, the Chinese Communist leadership not only was condemned worldwide for barbarism and deception but once again had alienated the country's intellectuals. As one veteran Western scholar observed, the regime has become a complete anachronism, losing its grip on reality and recycling the denunciatory clichés of the past. Such dusty and antiquated terms as "counter-revolutionary" and "anti-Party conspiracy" are now being used to describe the dissenters.[55] Whereas the people's memory of the massacre's brutality and terror may gradually fade with time, the impact of the bloodshed on the country's economy, national spirit, and foreign relations will be felt profoundly in the years ahead.

Notes

1. The English text of Deng's speech appeared in the *New York Times*, June 30, 1989, p. 4.

2. *Pai Hsing* [The people] (Hong Kong), May 1, 1989, pp. 14–15.

3. *New York Times*, Apr. 18, 1989, p. 3.

4. *New York Times*, Apr. 20, 1989, p. 60.

5. *Tiananmen 1989* (Taipei: Linking Press, 1989), pp. 58–59 (in Chinese).

6. Deng's comments are from Chen Xitong's report "Putting Down Anti-government Riots." English text in *China Daily* (New York), July 7, 1989, p. 4. See Appendix 3: "Report on Checking the Turmoil and Quelling the Counter-Revolutionary Rebellion."

7. *New York Times*, Apr. 28, 1989, pp. 1, 7.

8. *Tiananmen 1989*, p. 67.

9. *New York Times*, Apr. 28, 1989, p. 7.

10. *New York Times*, May 4, 1989, p. 6.

11. *Wall Street Journal*, May 5, 1989, p. A7.

12. Ibid.

13. *New York Times*, May 17, 1989, p. 1.

14. *Tiananmen 1989*, pp. 100–101.

15. *New York Times*, May 18, 1989, p. 8.

16. Ibid., p. 10.

17. *People's Daily*, Sept. 6, 1989.

18. *International Daily News* (Los Angeles), Aug. 30, 1989, p. 1.

19. *China Daily News* (New York), May 30, 1989, p. 10.

20. *New York Times*, May 21, 1989, p. 8.

21. For the hard-liners' interpretations, see Chen Xitong's report, op. cit.

22. Nicholas D. Kristof, "How the Hardliners Won," *New York Times Magazine*, Nov. 12, 1989, p. 68.

23. *People's Daily*, May 19, 1981, p. 1.

24. Nicholas Kristof, "Unrest Torments Deng," *New York Times*, June 1, 1989.

25. Ibid.

26. *International Daily News*, July 27, 1989.

27. For Wan Li's own account of his decision on May 27, see ibid.

28. The whole text of Li's report appeared in *World Journal* (New York), July 17, 1989, pp. 9, 34.

29. *New York Times*, May 20, 1989, p. 4.

30. *China Daily News*, May 22, 1989, p. 2.

31. Quoted from *World Journal*, May 25, 1989, p. 1.

32. *New York Times*, May 26, 1989, p. 5.

33. Ibid.

34. This plot was disclosed by someone who served in the 38th Army: *United Daily News* (Taipei), June 12, 1989, p. 1.

35. *Wall Street Journal*, May 22, 1989, p. 1.

36. *New York Times*, May 25, 1989, p. 6.

37. For a detailed description of the "counter-revolutionary activities," see Beijing Mayor Chen Xitong's report, op. cit., p. 6. For interpretations of the government's

plot, see *Tiananmen 1989*, pp. 174–175. Also see Chen Yizi's interview, *World Journal*, Sept. 9, 1989, p. 3.

38. This section is from a correspondent's report in *Time*, June 12, 1989, pp. 24–25.

39. Yang's speech appeared in *China Daily News*, May 30, 1989.

40. *Beijing Review*, Sept. 11–17, 1989, p. 24.

41. *Ming Pao* (Hong Kong), July 26, 1989.

42. *Beijing Review*, Sept. 11–17, 1989, p. 22.

43. Chen Xitong's report, op. cit., p. 6.

44. *Wall Street Journal*, June 5, 1989, p. A22.

45. *New York Times*, June 5, 1989, p. 7.

46. Ibid.

47. Amnesty International, *People's Republic of China—Preliminary Findings on Killings of Unarmed Civilians, Arbitrary Arrests and Summary Executions Since June 3, 1989*, Aug. 1989, New York, p. 1.

48. In a letter to the editor, Karl L. Hutterer, professor of anthropology, University of Michigan, noted that according to reliable sources 300–400 people were killed and 1,000 wounded. *New York Times*, June 23, 1989.

49. *New York Times*, Sept. 17, 1989, p. E3.

50. *Far Eastern Economic Review* (Hong Kong), June 22, 1989, p. 10.

51. *Beijing Review*, Sept. 11–17, 1989, p. 22.

52. Chen Xitong's report, op. cit., p. 4.

53. *New York Times*, Sept. 27, 1989, p. 8.

54. *Beijing Review* 32, No. 37 (Sept. 18–24, 1989), pp. 20–26.

55. Quoted from Simon Leys's interview, *Wall Street Journal*, June 6, 1989, p. A22.

7

The Impact of the Bloodshed

The brutal crackdown on the pro-democracy movement and the ensuing political oppression aroused worldwide repercussions. In response to the events in the PRC, the governments of the United States, Canada, and Western European countries immediately imposed economic sanctions against the Beijing regime. Although many of these measures were symbolic and transitory, they manifested the world's disapproval of a government's using force to crush its unarmed people in order to remain in power.

The reactions of Chinese communities around the world to the massacre and its aftermath was even more fervent. Many of the 56 million Chinese living abroad (including the 19 million in Taiwan) expressed their despair and rage. Putting aside differences in political beliefs, the overseas Chinese united in the common goal of supporting the prodemocracy movement.

The most profound impact of the crackdown, however, has been in the domestic economy of the PRC and in its educational and cultural development. As the hard-liners reasserted control over the economy, the reform suffered severe setbacks. The arrest or flight of the country's best minds have drained the country of the brain power it desperately needs.

International condemnation, economic sanctions, and intellectual disenchantment have put the PRC in a tenuous situation. This chapter surveys the world's reactions toward the bloodshed, assesses the effects on the loyalty of overseas Chinese to Beijing, evaluates the damages to its economic reforms and cultural development, and examines the ramifications on Beijing's plan to reunify the two sides of the Taiwan Strait.

The International Sanctions

On the morning after the June 4 bloodshed, President George Bush announced several sanctions against the Chinese government. Intended to strike a balance between preserving diplomatic relations and expressing the outrage of the American people, the White House's sanctions were rather limited in range: suspension of both government and commercial exports of weapons and suspension of military exchange visits between the United States and the PRC. In addition the president said that there would be a sympathetic evaluation of requests by Chinese students in the United States for extension of their visas, médical assistance through the International Red Cross for persons injured in the military crackdown, and a reevaluation of other aspects of Sino-U.S. relations in line with the development of events in the PRC.[1]

The Bush administration's actions were designed to preserve the relationship between the United States and the PRC, but there was strong sentiment in the U.S. Congress for harsher measures. On June 23, 1989, members of Congress introduced amendments that would severely curtail the export to the PRC of computers, weapons, and satellites and would cut financing. The legislators acted in response to public outrage about executions of prodemocracy demonstrators and disappointment with the Bush administration's timid response. The anger on Capitol Hill was highlighted in a vote of 418–0 in the House on June 29, adopting new sanctions against the Beijing government. The House package endorsed those moves adopted by the Bush administration but went a step further, adding suspension of trade and development programs, a ban on the sale of police equipment, and a limit on the transfer of high-technology and nuclear materials or components.[2]

In Western Europe, the French government also acted promptly. Inspired by the two hundredth anniversary of the French Revolution, Prime Minister Michel Rocard on June 6 announced that the government would freeze relations with the PRC at all levels, including contacts by the French president, prime minister, and other members of the government with Chinese leaders. In addition, the French diplomatic presence in the PRC would be reduced to a minimum. When the leaders of the world's seven most powerful democracies gathered in Paris on July 13, President François Mitterrand pressed the other participants—the United States, West Germany, Britain, Italy, Canada, and Japan—to condemn the Chinese government.[3]

Not all major countries followed the U.S. and French leads. As the United States and other Western countries imposed sanctions and condemned the PRC for its crackdown, Japanese officials sounded a note of caution, warning that such sanctions could backfire and deepen Beijing's "isolation" from the rest of the world. Among countries that provided aid, Japan has been the PRC's largest donor. Since the crackdown, Japan has criticized Beijing's actions in a far more muted tone than that of other countries. To protect its financial interests, Japan, in early June, suspended a $5.8 billion loan that had been announced in August 1988 by then–Prime Minister Noboru Takeshita. That loan was scheduled to begin in 1990. To maintain their business relations with Beijing, Japanese officials have hinted that the suspension of the new loan was only temporary and that the aid could be resumed if the PRC's economic liberalization program were restored, even if political freedom were not granted.[4]

By far, the most crucial sanction came from the World Bank. Under the pressure of the United States and Western Europe, the World Bank on June 8 announced the suspension of $780 million in loans to the PRC. Since 1981, the World Bank has been the PRC's chief financial provider, furnishing loans totaling $8.5 billion, of which $3.44 billion are interest-free and $5.09 billion are low-interest loans. One-third of the loans were used for the development of energy, transportation, communications, and industry; one-third for agriculture; and the remainder for education, culture, and social welfare. The suspension of these loans dealt a severe blow to the capital-starved Chinese economy.

Although it is still too early to assess the impact of international sanctions, fallout from them has been felt in several ways. Immediately after the crackdown and the U.S. sanctions, large-scale evacuation of U.S. and Western businesspersons occurred. Before the massacre, there were 950 U.S. business establishments in the PRC, of which 350 were sole proprietorships and 600 were joint ventures, with a total staff of 8,800. In the wake of the crackdown, U.S. businesspersons fled in droves. Big U.S. corporations, including IBM, Xerox, and Dow Chemical, pulled their non-Chinese employees out of Beijing or closed their offices. By June 20, only about 1,000 non-Chinese business-persons remained in the PRC. Representatives of other Western countries also left. By the end of June, of the 670 foreign companies that had been in Beijing, only 179 returned their representatives to the capital.[5] Many Western business executives face the question, In what kind of business environment will they operate in the near future? There are clear signs that the hard-liners, who have gained influence since they prevailed in the power struggle, may be trying to curtail the open-door policy. Many foreign executives believe that the long-term outlook for the economy is bleak. With the PRC's ultimate leadership still in doubt, the country's economic difficulties have been festering. Even if the situation stabilizes, it will become volatile again when Deng dies.[6]

Many companies associated with the PRC, in the face of enormous uncertainties, have reconsidered their future plans. Motorola, Inc., suspended its plans to build two new factories for semiconductor and mobile radio equipment, at least until the political situation settles down enough for the company to make a long-term assessment of the venture's prospects. The American Telephone and Telegraph Company has indefinitely delayed a joint venture it had agreed to in May 1989 to make optical fiber transmission equipment in Shanghai. Richard E. Gillespie, vice president of the U.S.-China Business Council, a Washington-based group that represents more than 300 U.S. companies that operate in the PRC, predicts no major new joint ventures and indicated that "China will be really hurt because they counted on foreign investment more and more each year."[7]

Nowhere is it more true that the suppression of the prodemocracy movement could stem the flow of foreign capital and technology crucial to modernizing the PRC's economy than in Hong Kong, whose mostly ethnic-Chinese population has invested more than any other country in the PRC. Hong Kong businessmen and economists seem unanimous in predicting a blow to the PRC from a near halt to new investment, at least for the short term. In Japan, businessmen and bankers also were taking a wait-and-see attitude. They indicated that they were continuing current projects but were also reconsidering and delaying plans for future projects until the situation sorts itself out.[8]

The U.S. sanctions have a direct bearing on the PRC's military renovation program. Since 1979, private companies in the United States have sold more than $748 million in weapons to the PRC. The United States also provided roughly 30 percent of the "dual use" technology that the PRC gets from the outside world. These are computers and other high-technology equipment that have military applications. This military hardware is critical to the PRC's economic and military modernization programs. The ban on the sale of military equipment imposed by President Bush also led to suspensions of work on about $600 million in foreign military sales (FMS)—government-to-government contracts—and almost $425 million worth of commercial sales on the munitions control list (MCL). The largest FMS contract, worth more than $500 million, is the F-8 fighter upgrade program, for which the Grumman Aerospace Corporation is the prime contractor. Other suspended projects include a U.S. Navy contract to supply the Chinese Navy with four Honeywell Mark 46 antisubmarine torpedoes and a General Motors/Hughes $60 million contract for four ANTPQ 37 antiartillery radars, only two of which have been delivered.[9]

Suspensions of military exports affected a number of nongovernment sales of military systems and hardware. According to U.S. experts, the impact will be felt even more by the PRC's air force, which is eagerly seeking Western technology to convert its Soviet MiG-19 and MiG-21 aircraft designs into a new generation of agile, extended-range fighter-interceptors. The U.S. military ban thus will stymie, at least temporarily, the PRC's plans for upgrading its armor capability and troop mobility.[10]

In the civilian sector, the foremost casualty of the crackdown and sanctions has been the burgeoning tourism industry. During the ten years of the open-door policy, tourism became the most rapid growth industry in the PRC. The number of foreign tourists rose from 4.2 million in 1979 to 31.7 million in 1988. Foreign-exchange revenue from tourism jumped from $448 million in 1979 to $2.2 billion in 1988. The massacre and martial law frightened off foreign visitors. Figures released by the Chinese National Tourism Administration (NTA) in early September reported that 22,000 foreigners (mostly journalists and businesspeople) visited the PRC in June— 81 percent fewer than in June 1988, and more than 90 percent of scheduled tour groups were canceled. After a decade of phenomenal growth, the recent numbers have dropped to the 1979 level, when the PRC first opened the door to foreign commercial tourism.

The drastic decline in the number of tourists affected hotels, restaurants, taxis, guided tours, and many other related businesses. At Beijing joint-venture hotels, the occupancy rates dropped to 15 percent after the crackdown. In many Chinese-managed hotels, the occupancy rate was 10 percent. In Xi'an, one of the major tourist spots in the Northwest, the number of tourists fell from 35,000 in June 1988 to only 5,500 in June 1989. The Bell Tower Hotel in Xi'an, run by the Holiday Inn, reportedly had only a 1 percent occupancy rate during the first week of July. In Shanghai, where the effect of the crackdown was moderate, the occupancy rate in June averaged 40 percent. Both Chinese and expatriate staff at all hotels have been considerably reduced, and pay has been cut for those remaining. At the International Hotel in Beijing, for instance, only 400 of the total 2,000 employees were working on any given day in August 1989.[11] Taxi companies and travel agencies are facing hard times. Employees have been dismissed, with only a certain percentage of the entire pool at work at any time. It was officially reported that the revenue of tourist business in 1989 was $1.8 billion, $400 million less than the previous year and $1.2 billion below the original target for 1989. Although martial law was lifted in January 1990, contact between Chinese and foreigners is still prohibited. The prognosis for any early return to the level of 1988 is poor.

Another major casualty of the crackdown and sanction has been the Chinese ability to raise investment funds. Between 1979 and 1988, foreign direct investment in the PRC totaled $12 billion.[12] At the same time, the country incurred a foreign debt of $42 billion. The suspension of the World Bank and Japanese loans and the postponement of foreign investment significantly curtailed the PRC's capital sources. The situation has been worsening as the country's trade deficit widens. Since 1980, the PRC has suffered a continuous trade deficit. In spite of the austerity policy, the trade deficit in 1988 reached $7.8 billion. In 1989, with strict control of imports, the country incurred a trade deficit of $6.6 billion. The continued incurrence of a trade deficit and the plunge in tourism revenue made Western bankers wary of the PRC's ability to repay its foreign debts. Although accurate figures are not available, Western financial analysts indicated that the PRC's debt payments will peak in 1991 or 1992. Estimates for the annual outlays range between $4.2 billion according to the World Bank and $8 billion to $10 billion according to Chinese financial experts. Clearly, the debt-service ratio is rising rapidly while the foreign-exchange reserves are not keeping pace. The State Administration for Foreign Exchange reported that at the end of March 1989, foreign reserves excluding gold were $17.49 billion, or more than three months of imports at projected rates for 1989. The number had dropped significantly by the end of June.[13] These two sets of figures suggest that the PRC may have difficulty repaying its foreign loans in the early 1990s.

The loss of foreign capital will inevitably hamper investment in infra-structure, the lack of which is a primary hindrance to Chinese economic growth. Recent official reports reveal that due to the shortage of investment funds, the plan to establish 120 new coal mines in 1989 had to be scrapped. The modernization of Bao Shan steel plant in Shanghai, one of the biggest in the PRC, was also postponed.[14] The time of foreign businessmen rushing to the PRC and competing for a niche in the Chinese market by offering preferential loans and seeking joint ventures is past.

Overseas Chinese Responses

The reaction of Westerners and their governments to the brutal crackdown stems mostly from humanitarian and economic concerns. The responses of the overseas Chinese involve a much more complex array of emotions—a mixture of tragedy, betrayal, and frustration. That the massacre was unnecessary and unjustified has generated anger and sadness; moreover, a rare solidarity emerged from the crackdown.

Since 1949, overseas Chinese communities, depending on their political affiliation, were generally split into two camps. Intellectuals from Taiwan and the leaders in the traditional clan associations, the mainstay of Chinatowns around the world, continued their support of the Nationalist government in Taiwan. Students from the PRC, recent immigrants to the United States, and individuals with economic ties to the mainland tended to support the PRC. Few connections existed between these rival groups. In recent years, as governments on the two sides of the Taiwan Strait adopted a more conciliatory gesture toward each other, a new air of amity began to emerge in the overseas Chinese communities. But the driving force in uniting the overseas Chinese was the prodemocracy movement in Beijing.

During the two months of student demonstrations, most overseas Chinese had been touched in some way by the events unfolding in the PRC. Believing that the students' demands represented the voice of the Chinese people, the intellectuals and community leaders in both camps formed several joint committees to support the student movement. They issued statements that appeared in major U.S. newspapers appealing to the Beijing authorities to conduct dialogues with students and avoid the use of force. Upset by the imposition of martial law on May 20, the overseas Chinese leaders and intellectuals stepped up their activities to avert bloodshed. Many famous scholars sent open letters to Chinese leaders, earnestly calling for restraint. Among those scholars are many who had consistently supported Communist causes in the past.

When the PLA initiated the bloodshed on June 4, the overseas Chinese communities were shocked. Large-scale demonstrations and mourning activities were staged throughout the world. In Hong Kong, thousands of students flocked to the local Red Cross to donate blood for the victims in Beijing. Scraps of black silk or cotton, symbols of mourning, fluttered on many of the colony's cars, taxis, trucks, and buses. Even Hong Kong's weathered fishing junks flew black flags from their masts to honor those who had died at Tiananmen Square.[15]

The frustration and rage over the brutality are fully reflected in an essay by I. M. Pei that appeared in the *New York Times*. Pei, a renowned U.S.

architect, had visited and worked in the PRC quite frequently during the previous decade. Believing that the country was gradually emerging from its long nightmare of war and repression and heading toward a more open and modern society, he was horrified by the events in Tiananmen Square. In the wake of the developments in Beijing, Pei wrote: "We were shocked beyond measure. The revulsion soon turned to anger, then sadness, for it was all so unnecessary." He lamented that "there was no justification for the use of force; a continued dialogue could have produced a peaceful outcome. . . . The government's killing of the students and citizens tore the heart out of a generation that carries the hope for the future of the country."[16] Pei's article reflected the views of most Chinese intellectuals both inside and outside the PRC.

Noteworthy during the prodemocracy movement had been the open defiance of the party line by three major Communist newspapers published in Hong Kong and New York. For more than four decades, both *Ta-Kung Pao* (Impartial daily) and *Wen Wei Pao* (Wen-hui daily), two major daily newspapers in Hong Kong, and *Huaqiao Ribao* (China daily news) in New York were devoted Communist mouthpieces. These newspapers had earnestly defended every government policy since the founding of the People's Republic—including the disastrous Great Leap Forward and the tumultuous Cultural Revolution. The student movement fundamentally altered their attitude. From the beginning of the demonstrations, these three papers carried extensive news reports, articles, and editorials urging the authorities to conduct sincere and forthright dialogue with the students in order to prevent the situation from deteriorating. After the imposition of martial law, these newspapers urged the authorities to exercise restraint. The change in their stance from loyally backing the CCP to outspokenly criticizing the Beijing regime led to an increase in their circulation. The daily circulation of *Huaqiao Ribao*, for instance, jumped from an average of 4,000 copies to 14,000 copies, an indication of its new popularity among overseas readers.

In the aftermath of the crackdown, all three papers immediately condemned the Beijing regime. An editorial entitled "The Judgment of the History will be Severe" in the Hong Kong *Ta-Kung Pao* said:

> Last night the gunfire broke out in Beijing's Tiananmen Square. These guns were fired by those who professed to be "the army of the people." . . . The cold hard fact is that the blood of Chinese people has flowed in Tiananmen Square . . . we can say that June 4th 1989 is the day that all the people of China cried out together for the tragedy. This day will be entered into the annals of Chinese history and those who committed this crime will be subject to the judgment of history.[17]

On the next day, the Hong Kong *Wen Wei Pao* published an editorial directly accusing Prime Minister Li Peng and PRC Chairman Yang Shangkun:

> June 4th will go down as the all too painful day known as The Beijing Massacre. The great offenses against humanity committed by the joint force

of Li Peng and Yang Shangkun are unforgivable. The bloody suppression of students and citizens resulted in a tragedy that claimed over a thousand lives, with the injured numbering in the tens of thousands. This grave situation, unfolding as it did before the very eyes of the Chinese people, goes beyond calls for resignation and must demand the public trial of these criminals. The people will never forgive the Li-Yang clique, for they were given opportunities but rejected them all.

The paper went even further, condemning the "insane savagery of the army" and denouncing Li and Yang as "thugs."[18]

The open condemnation of Beijing's government by these Communist newspapers inspired many left-wing organizations to defy the party line. From the PRC's enterprises in Hong Kong came some of the loudest voices raised against the Beijing regime. Officials of nearly all major central government concerns—including China Resources (Holdings) Co., the Bank of China group, and China Merchants Steam Navigation Company—placed one or more newspaper advertisements under their company name denouncing the violence. Two days after the June 4 massacre in Beijing, the Xinhua News Agency—the PRC's de facto embassy in Hong Kong—did not fly the PRC flag, as a gesture to mourn those killed in Tiananmen Square. Huge banners were draped across the Bank of China headquarters, the tallest building in Asia, denouncing the bloodbath. The open revolt of the Communist officials in Hong Kong was indeed unprecedented.[19]

In the United States, Canada, Japan, and Western Europe, students and scholars from the PRC staged demonstrations on campuses and in many capitals and other cities. On the day after the massacre, some 5,000 students from the Midwest gathered in Chicago for one of the largest student protests in that area. On June 10, several thousand students and overseas Chinese assembled in San Francisco for a candle-lit vigil mourning the deaths. In all the demonstrations, students from both sides of the Taiwan Strait participated. An anti-Beijing united front was gradually taking shape.

To show their resentment toward the Chinese Communist Party, on July 1, the sixty-eighth anniversary of its founding, more than 300 Chinese students and visiting scholars in the United States announced their resignation from the Party. Again, on October 1, on the fortieth anniversary of the PRC, another 360 renounced their Party membership. Most of them completely identified with the protesters in Beijing and vowed to devote their lives to the cause of the democracy movement.

As newspapers, students, and even government agencies openly defied the Beijing regime, Chinese diplomats stationed in the United States, Canada, Japan, and Western Europe confronted the problem of whether to maintain their loyalty to the government and face the wrath of their overseas community or to support the crushed democracy movement and thereby sever their ties with their homeland. A growing number of diplomats have chosen to seek refuge in the United States and other countries. In mid-June, ten days after the crackdown in their homeland, some twenty Chinese diplomats stationed abroad requested political asylum. By early September, the number had risen to over seventy.[20] Although most of the defectors have remained in seclusion, some have participated in parades, openly defying the Beijing government. Besides diplomats, other people have sought political asylum, including eight members of an opera troupe, dozens of visiting scientists, and members of various business groups. In August, a Chinese military representative stationed in North Korea sought asylum from South Korea, creating tensions between Beijing and Seoul. In early September, a Chinese air force pilot flew a MiG-19 to Quemoy (under Nationalist control), also drawing worldwide attention. All of these defectors indicated that they could no longer tolerate the actions of a government that lied about the shooting of demonstrators in Tiananmen Square.

The anti-Beijing climate in overseas Chinese communities provided a supportive environment for those dissidents who fled the mainland after the crackdown. On July 28, some 1,200 Chinese students from 200 schools gathered in Chicago to inaugurate the Federation of the Independent Chinese Student Unions in the United States. The function of the conference is to unify the independent student groups that represent the 40,000 Chinese students at the nation's universities.[21] Following the Chicago conference, a broader organization, the Federation for Democracy in China, was established in Paris to serve as an umbrella group for the coordination of worldwide opposition to the Beijing government. The inaugural meeting of this organization took place from September 22 to 24 and was attended by 167 Chinese exiles and opposition figures from around the world. It was by far the most important meeting of the Chinese opposition since the June 4 crackdown. The conference attendees elected Yan Jiaqi, a forty-seven-year-old political scientist who had been a close adviser to the deposed Party chief Zhao Ziyang, as president, and Wuer Kaixi, a twenty-one-year-old organizer of the student demonstration in Tiananmen Square, as vice president. Other founding members were Wan Runnan, one of the PRC's most prominent entrepreneurs, Su Xiaokang, a writer and intellectual, and Chen Yizi, a former adviser to Zhao and the highest-ranking official known to have gone into exile.

The main goal of the organization is to unite the 56 million Chinese living abroad. The federation's leaders hope to exert effective pressure on the PRC's government even though they are now outside the country. The founding manifesto asserted that the federation opposed a monopoly of power in the PRC and supported human rights, democracy, and an economy responsive to market forces. The federation recognized the link between property and liberty: "Taking away the property rights of the citizens in the name of the state is one of the important causes of economic stagnation and political dictatorship in all countries dominated by a communist party." The manifesto also pointed out that "returning society's wealth to the people and developing private enterprises is the only road that will let China find a way out of its difficulties and achieve modernization."[22]

Although the future of the federation remains uncertain, the organization represents a significant step toward a united front to counter the unpopular regime in Beijing. Many dissenters hope that the federation may someday develop into a political force parallel to the Solidarity movement in Poland.[23] According to Yan Jiaqi, the situation in the PRC will remain unstable. Communist rule has produced a corrupt, inefficient, and regressive regime, which will face yet another massive power struggle when Deng Xiaoping dies.[24] Wan Runnan has stated that he believes that economic problems will eventually bring down the current regime. Economic changes, he noted, effected during a decade of reform, already have provoked instability by creating inflation and disparities in income. He maintained that economic reforms were dead, and the new leaders had no alternative plan to bolster the economy. Serious stagnation would inflame resistance among the people, accelerate the internal power struggle within the Politburo, and create opportunities for liberalization, perhaps opening the door for the federation to participate in Beijing politics as the Solidarity movement did in Poland. The future of the federation therefore depends, to a great extent, on the Chinese economy, which has been seriously affected by the recent turmoil in Beijing.

Effects on the Domestic Economy

The impact of the crackdown was particularly profound on the domestic economy. Not only have the reform programs pursued by Zhao and his supporters been stalled or scaled back, the rapid growth of the economy during the 1980s seems likely to end.

Prior to the student movement, the reform programs had already lost momentum because of the mounting inflation and corruption. At a Party plenum in September 1988, price reform, the core of urban reform, was postponed and an austerity plan was adopted to curb the overheated economy. But the retrenchment was viewed as a temporary retreat. It was argued that once the economic situation had stabilized, more vigorous reform programs would resume.

The purge of the reformist leader Zhao Ziyang and a group of his advisers signaled the scrapping of radical reform. In mid-August 1989, the three influential "think tanks" of Zhao—the Rural Development Research Center; the Economic Structural Reform Research Institute; and the Economic, Technical, and Social Development Center—were all slated for abolition.[25] Most of the members of Zhao's brain trusts have either been placed under arrest or have fled the country.

One clear sign of policy change can be detected from a major speech by Jiang Zemin, the new Party general secretary. On September 29, 1989, two days before the PRC's fortieth anniversary, Jiang outlined the Party's new guidelines. Although Jiang promised continuation of the reform and open-door policy, his tone represented a complete departure from the policies enunciated by Zhao at the Party's thirteenth congress two years earlier. Jiang reemphasized "class struggle," the keystone of Mao's ideology, which had been out of favor for more than ten years. Jiang saw the recent upheavals as a "vital struggle" between two lines—the Four Cardinal Principles versus "bourgeois liberalism." According to Jiang, there were two diametrically opposite views on the issue of reform and the open door. The correct one, advocated by Deng and other veteran leaders, upheld the Four Cardinal Principles and would result in the modernization of the country and perfection of socialism. The erroneous line, proposed by Zhao and his followers, aimed at total Westernization and would "bring China into the orbit of the capitalist systems of the West." Jiang's statement implied that anyone who favored more aggressive changes patterned after Western countries was an agent of Western capitalism.[26] Jiang's speech has led many people to believe that as long as the hard-line leaders remain in power, reform programs are either on hold or headed for eventual dismantlement. In the second half of 1989, major changes could be discerned in five areas:

Price Reform. In the October 1984 Decisions on Economic Reform, the reform of the irrational price system was touted as the key to institutional transformation. Proponents of price reform argued that without it, the problems of artificial disparities of profit distributions among and within industries would remain unsolved and that under the existing multilevel price structure, corruption and profiteering by government officials could not be effectively checked. Thus they claimed that the most needed measure for rationalizing the economy was to allow prices to respond to market forces. In May 1988, with Deng's endorsement, Zhao proposed the bold solution of decontrolling prices. The populace responded with panic buying, which forced the government to rescind the policy. Since then, economic decision-making power has fallen into the hands of Li Peng and Yao Yilin, two protégés of Chen Yun, the leader of the conservative wing. In the first half of 1989, steps were taken to reimpose price controls for steel, copper, aluminum, and other basic materials. After the June 4 bloodshed, government officials reasserted centralized control over major segments of the Chinese economy. Although details have not been made public, it is known that a theme that prevailed in the Party's Fifth Plenum of the Thirteenth Party Central Committee in November 1989 was that recentralization was necessary.[27]

Stock Ownership. In fall 1988, when the hard-liners started the austerity drive, liberals, led by Zhao, tried to keep the reform program alive by proposing the sale of state enterprise stock to workers and employees. The plan, once hailed by economists as an innovative measure to foster workers' incentive and promote industrial efficiency, was condemned by the hard-liners as a betrayal of socialism. In fall 1989. Party newspapers even blamed proponents of the stock ownership idea for fueling the recent student unrest.[28] The plan is likely to remain in abeyance.

Private Business. Since the government reaffirmed the merits of individual business in 1980, the number of private businesses had grown by leaps and bounds, rising from 100,000 in 1978 to 14.5 million in 1988. Private business employed 23 million people and was one of the most dynamic sectors in the Chinese economy. After the conservatives took the helm, individual businesses began to dwindle. In the first half of 1989, their numbers fell by 2.4 million. Private enterprises in Beijing were deeply involved during the student demonstrations, providing demonstrators with funds, food, and equipment. To curb the influence of entrepreneurs, the new leadership has initiated an inspection program to regulate individual business. Government newspapers published many articles accusing the great majority of private businesses of evading taxes, engaging in illicit activities, and causing income disparities. Deng Xiaoping has ordered the closing of some rural factories because they diverted resources that should have gone to state companies.[29] The fate of the individual business is once again at stake.

Income Distribution. Under Mao's rule, the PRC adopted an egalitarian system of income distribution, which dampened individual incentive and motivation. When Deng launched the economic reform, he initiated a policy that would allow some people to become affluent before others. The new policy was responsible for the emergence of millions of 10,000-yuan families in the rural areas and tens of thousands of well-to-do businessmen in the cities. The rise of the new wealthy class inevitably increased disparities in income distribution. After Jiang Zemin became Party chief, he vowed to remedy this situation. Not only did he avoid mentioning Deng's policy of encouraging enrichment of a few first, but he also identified self-employed traders and peddlers as the source of rising income disparities.

Regional Autonomy. Under the original reform program, attempts were made to put an end to the practice of excessive central control and overrigid management by delegating some policy-making power to local government. Some provinces, such as Guangdong and Hainan, took advantage of this new local autonomy and achieved a measure of prosperity. In Zhao's coastal development strategy, Guangdong was designated as a province that would "boldly explore and seriously try the experience of various countries including the advanced management experience of the capitalist countries." Of the four Special Economic Zones, three were set up in Guangdong. The man who ruled Guangdong since 1985, Ye Xuanping, is the son of the late Marshal Ye Jianying, former chairman of the NPC, who paved the way for Deng's reemergence to power. Fully utilizing his personal relations with wealthy Hong Kong financiers, Ye Xuanping was able to attract huge overseas Chinese investment to finance development. Guangdong increasingly looked to capitalist Hong Kong, not Beijing, as its beacon of development. During the decade from 1978 to 1988, Guangdong's GNP grew at an annual rate of 12 percent, ranking it number one in the country. The province's $7.3 billion worth of exports in 1988 accounted for one-sixth of the nation's total.[30] The prosperity of Guangdong strengthened Ye's political position. During the student demonstrations, the governor showed tolerance toward dissidents, and there were no sweeping arrests in June and July. Many dissidents on Beijing's wanted list reportedly escaped abroad via Guangdong.

To eliminate Ye as a potential rival, the hard-liners in Beijing have used two tactics. One involved offering the governor a job in Beijing that would represent a promotion but would at the same time remove him from his power base. The other tactic would step up a drive aimed ostensibly at combatting graft but really geared toward the removal of officers who refused to follow the hard-line stance. Liang Xiang, the bold reformist governor of Hainan, was accused of abusing his office for personal gain and was dismissed in September. The fate of Governor Ye had not yet been decided at the end of 1989.[31] The campaign of removing officials who had been followers of Zhao's liberal economic reform and who flouted Beijing's directives represents another major effort toward recentralization.

Although these measures have helped the hard-liners to consolidate their power, they will inevitably generate negative effects on the economy. Suspension of price reforms perpetuates distortion of resources allocation. Because of the extremely low prices for petroleum, coal, and industrial raw materials, almost all of the major oil fields and coal mines in the country have been operating at a loss and required enormous state subsidies. The skewed price structure has encouraged trading companies to export underpriced commodities, such as raw materials and energy. In recent years, exports of pig iron, steel, coal, nonferrous metals, raw silk, and cotton all rose, even though domestic factories were reporting shortages of the same goods. Instead of exporting labor-intensive manufactured products, the PRC has become a resource-exporting country. Rapid export growth can only create more shortages in energy and raw materials and accelerate the rate of inflation.

Moreover, because the prices of grains, raw material, and energy are too low to stimulate their growth, without price reform, the PRC will be unable to boost grain production or encourage the development of energy and raw material resources to alleviate the imbalances in its economy. Furthermore, without additional reform in enterprises, industrial efficiency and labor productivity will lag. Beijing will experience more difficulties encouraging state enterprises to make responsible decisions regarding capital investment and salary and bonus increases.

The drastic curbs on individual business and the attempt to reassert control over the prosperous coastal provinces have dampened private incentive and hampered economic growth for the whole country. From the macro viewpoint, the June 4 bloodshed has significantly worsened the existing economic maladies. It has exacerbated the problems of the budget deficit, unemployment, and national debt.

Budget Deficit. During the years between 1979 and 1987, the state accumulated budget deficit totaled 160 billion yuan ($43 billion). It grew almost 50 percent in 1988, reaching $9.2 billion, and exceeded $10 billion in 1989. The spring upheavals forced the government to increase expenditure even as it suffered a decline in revenue: (1) Because the imposition of martial law and the use of armed force to suppress students strengthened the position of the military, the PRC's defense budget has begun to rise. In 1989, after a decade-long decline, defense spending rose 14 percent. According to an official report, the defense budget will increase 16 percent in 1990. (2) Because wages for urban workers have lagged behind the inflation rate for two consecutive years, resentment has been mounting. To prevent further unrest, the government may have to raise more income subsidies to workers and urban residents. (3) The dwindling of state investment in agriculture has underlain the stagnation of agricultural production. To remedy this situation, the state allocation to agriculture will also have to rise. (4) The crackdown markedly reduced state revenue from tourism. (5) Lower worker morale, which resulted in lower productivity, coupled with higher materials cost, further increased the losses incurred by state enterprises. In the 1989 budget, subsidies to bail out the bankrupt enterprises amounted to a staggering 52.1 billion yuan ($14 billion).[32] To finance the rising deficit, Beijing relied on issuing domestic bonds, assuming a greater foreign debt, and printing money. As foreign loans become more difficult to obtain, printing more money is almost inevitable.

Inflation. The government austerity plan failed to check inflation. Prices in 1989 still registered a 17.8 percent rise, only slightly lower than the 18.5 percent in 1988. The real inflation rate has been widely believed to be much higher than the reported rate. Because prices of raw materials have continued to surge, the demand-pull inflation might add the element of cost-push inflation, making the control of inflation even more difficult.

Unemployment. The 20 percent curtailment of state capital investment in 1989 and the slowdown of the growth rate of GNP from 11 percent in 1988 to only 3.9 percent in 1989 caused the rapid rise of urban unemployment. The official statistics reporting an unemployment rate of 3.5 percent were totally meaningless, for they substantially exaggerated the size of the work force and understated the unemployment problem.[33] The real unemployment rate in the urban labor force may have exceeded 10 percent in 1989.

National Debt. Ten years of rising budget deficits and six years of trade deficits have transformed the PRC from a debt-free to a debt-ridden state. Budget and trade deficits exceeded $10 billion a year in 1988 and 1989, and the cost to service domestic and foreign debt has been mounting.

The overall picture of the Chinese economy after the bloodshed has become much bleaker. The rising economic crisis is bound to fuel social and political unrest in the years to come.

Impact on Education and Culture

Another major casualty of the turmoil has been higher education and cultural activities. Until the crushing of the student movement, there had been a resurgence of academic and artistic freedom in the PRC. In the years between 1986 and 1988, a far wider variety of philosophy and literary works than before was published and several independent newspapers and magazines appeared. The appointment of Wang Meng, a noted novelist, as culture minister in 1986 had kindled hopes for a period of cultural renaissance.

After consolidating power, the hard-line leaders, who were convinced that the student unrest had been caused by a flourishing of bourgeois influence, immediately launched a nationwide campaign to intensify the indoctrination of university students. As the first step, all students that were to graduate in 1989 had to attend mandatory two-week-long political sessions. The functions of these sessions were to impose on the students the government view of the crackdown and to have them accept this view publicly. In each school, the students were divided into small groups to study the "important speech" attacking the student movement by paramount leader Deng Xiaoping. They also were required to watch an official videotape of the events of June 3 and 4. In that version, the only violence occurred when "ruffians" assaulted the PRC's "beloved soldiers."

After studying official documents, students had to participate in a group discussion about the unrest and to declare their stance publicly. The process of "self-confession" is one of the most frequently performed political rituals following a major political campaign. To pass the loyalty test, the participants must either blame themselves for supporting the "riot" or blame the already disgraced Party leaders who had misguided them. The easy way, of course, has been to blame everything on Zhao Ziyang, the deposed Party chief. No one dares to deviate from the party line. To do so would invite trouble and might result in one's being sent to labor camps. The entire process is a mutually deceiving game. The hard-liners, who had fabricated the notion of a "counter-revolutionary rebellion" as a pretext to attack their political enemies as well as to suppress the students, then compelled the students to accept the hard-liners' interpretations. The students who had been participants in the protest and knew the facts, gave lip service to the official lies.[34]

The hard-liners took several preventive measures to avoid future unrest among university students. First, they cut freshman enrollment for the 1989–1990 academic year by 30,000 to a total of 610,000. The cut was particularly deep for Beijing University, the nation's most prestigious school and the political center of the student movement. Before the turmoil, Beijing University had planned to enroll 2,100 freshmen, but after the crackdown the number was reduced to 784. Moreover, because many of the best-known student leaders were from the departments of philosophy, history, international relations, and public administration, the authorities ordered the closing of these four disciplines to new students.[35]

In an effort to combat bourgeois influence and to rekindle Communist values, new students in Beijing University were ordered to spend a full year in a military academy at Shijiazhuang, a city south of Beijing. One-third of the time would be allocated for military training and the remainder for intensive study of Communist ideology. In Tianjin, Shanghai, Xi'an, and Chengdu, 6 universities whose students had been active in the spring demonstrations were ordered to follow the Beijing University pattern. For students in the remaining 137 major universities, only eight weeks of military training would be required.[36] Most students graduating in summer 1989 were not allowed to be employed in cities but had to work in villages or factories for at least one year. Their behavior and thinking was to be scrutinized thereafter by Party officials to decide whether the students would be allowed to go back to school for graduate studies.[37]

Even those who had graduated three years before and were already experienced as government functionaries had to go to factories, mines, and villages to rectify themselves because of alleged bourgeois influence on their behavior. They have had to remain there until the leadership permitted them to return to their original work units.

These measures were devised to weed out from the rest of the student body those who had supported the prodemocracy movement during April and May. Those failing the loyalty test might have to stay in the villages or border regions for the rest of their lives. Such measures represented a return to the Cultural Revolution years, when education was employed as an instrument of politics and ideological indoctrination replaced the pursuit of knowledge.

To the intellectual community, the crackdown ushered in a period of new terror. In the two months following the massacre, the names of more than 2,000 intellectuals were placed on the government's wanted list. Most were dismissed from their positions and many were arrested. Their identifications have been transmitted to border-guard forces and customs services to prevent their fleeing the country. Mass campaigns have been staged by the hard-liners to criticize the leading intellectuals. Yan Jiaqi, the leader of the exiles, was accused of being the "black hand" behind Zhao's plot to usurp ultimate power. Su Xiaokang, principal scriptwriter of the television series "River Elegy," was condemned for having provided theoretical and emotional preparation for the unrest.[38] The dismissal of Wang Meng as culture minister in early September signaled the end of artistic freedom and the beginning of restriction and censorship.

Under the pretext of an "antipornography campaign," the hard-liners ordered a thorough scrutiny of all published works. Books by the intellectuals on the wanted list as well as literary and philosophical works containing liberal ideology were banned. On September 20, 1989, in a national conference on regulating newspapers, magazines, and publishers, the hard-liners announced that all newspapers, periodicals, and publishing houses that had in the recent past propagated bourgeois liberalization or promoted heretical views would be shut down and their licenses cancelled. Among those ordered to close were the three most influential periodicals: the Shanghai *World Economic Herald*, the *Economics Weekly Review*, and the *New Observer*, all of which had won high acclaim from students, intellectuals, and overseas Chinese.[39]

The crackdown exerted a profound impact on the life and future of the 70,000 students and visiting scholars studying in the United States, Japan, and Europe. Disillusioned with a government that had broken its own laws by shooting student protesters and then had used propaganda to conceal what had happened, many students began to doubt whether they had a role to play in the modernization of their homeland. The largest group of Chinese students studying overseas was in the United States. At the time of the Tiananmen bloodshed, there were 29,000 Chinese students studying at accredited U.S. colleges and universities—more than from any other country—and more than 10,000 Chinese who were visiting scholars or students at unaccredited universities. Most were clustered in graduate science and engineering departments at leading research universities, which generally were financing the Chinese students' education. Some received fellowships from the Chinese government. There were sixty-one Fulbright scholars, supported by the U.S. government.

During the high point of the Beijing protest movement, several thousand Chinese students took part in demonstrations in the United States in support of their fellow students in Tiananmen Square. Some even discontinued their studies and returned to the PRC to participate directly in the movement. After the massacre, many who remained in the United States used facsimile machines to send U.S. news articles and photographs to Chinese companies and agencies so that the people could learn what had really occurred in Beijing. The participation of those abroad in the prodemocracy movement made them the targets of government reprisal should they return to the PRC. Even those who did not join the demonstrations were also suspect because they knew the truth about the massacre. For all of these considerations, most Chinese students in the United States and Canada may decide to remain abroad.[40]

The alienation and possible loss of several tens of thousands of the best trained scientists, engineers, and scholars in the social sciences and humanities should be regarded as a catastrophe for the PRC's modernization drive. Yet, when Yang Shangkun, president of the PRC, was interviewed by a Chinese-American scholar in early July, he indicated that if the United States could employ all the Chinese students in the United States, the PRC would be happy to let them all remain.[41] Yang's remarks reflected the shortsightedness of the hard-line leaders, especially in their contempt toward intellectuals.

The impact on international cultural exchanges was equally disastrous. Since the resumption of diplomatic relations in 1979, there have been many exchanges of scholars between the PRC and major U.S. universities and research centers. From 1979 to 1983, a total of 19,000 Chinese students and scholars came to the United States. In the academic year 1983–1984, there were about 8,000 students and 4,000 scholars from the PRC in the United States. It was estimated that the number of Chinese scholars involved in studies abroad during the 1980s approached 10 percent of the total scientific and engineering research and development personnel in China.[42]

The crackdown on the prodemocracy demonstration and the resulting tension in Chinese-American relations have deterred many U.S. scholars from venturing to the PRC and also prevented many Chinese scholars from leaving their country. To protest the use of troops against demonstrators, the U.S. National Academy of Science suspended its three major exchange programs with the PRC, an act that affected about 200 U.S. and Chinese scholars. The academy urged 30 U.S. scholars in the PRC under its sponsorship to return home. It also postponed a symposium in Shanghai on gene research that would have had 15 speakers from the United States and 200 participants from all over the PRC. Scheduled conferences on Chinese religion and philosophy were also suspended.[43] The 49 organizations that handle direct exchange programs and the college offices that deal with thousands of Chinese students who come to the United States on their own also faced great uncertainty. Many exchange programs that had been firmly established have been unraveled by the Tiananmen tragedy.

During the ten years of extensive academic exchange with foreign countries, the PRC benefited immensely. The Cultural Revolution had suppressed the country's scientific research for a decade and had caused the country to lose pace with the rest of the world. Exchange programs with the United States helped the PRC to catch up. For instance, the Chinese scientists in Beijing's Institute of Microbiology, using biological engineering techniques borrowed from the West, were able to produce an attenuated strain of a virus, the cucumber mosaic, which devastates crops. The new strain immunizes pepper, tobacco, and some kinds of fruit against the virus. As a result, thousands of acres of crops have been saved. An interruption of the exchange program would severely impair modernization.

Although the leaders continue to claim support for an open-door policy, many signs point to the decline of cooperation with the West. Official denunciation of bourgeois influence makes the study of Western social science and philosophy pointless. The Chinese government has decided to reduce the number of students in the United States and France, which it has accused of supporting the prodemocracy movement, and is sending more to the Soviet Union and Eastern Europe.[44]

As long as the hard-liners remain in power, cultural exchange with the Western world cannot flourish. If the Cultural Revolution resulted in the deprivation of educational opportunity for a generation, the June 4 massacre may cause the PRC to lose the thinkers the country had cultivated for the prior one and one-half decades.

Effects on the Relationship with Hong Kong

The crackdown jeopardized the relationship between Hong Kong and the PRC. Since China ceded Hong Kong to the British in 1842, the colony has long been a haven for Chinese entrepreneurs and capital in times of great disturbances. During periods of turmoil, such as the Taiping Rebellion (1850–1864), the 1911 revolution, and the early stages of the Sino-Japanese War (1937–1939), Hong Kong continued to be an enclave that was immune to China's upheavals. The 1949 revolution drove large numbers of adventurous entrepreneurs and skilled laborers to Hong Kong. Chinese immigrants have created a reservoir of manpower that has kept wages flexible and responsive to external conditions. This has contributed significantly to Hong Kong's competitive edge in the world market.

During the past one and one-half centuries, Hong Kong has been the epitome of the classic economic model of laissez-faire. The British authorities adopted a free port policy; the English legal system guaranteed law and order, protected private property, and administered justice. The government also provided the social infrastructure for the economy while allowing the market mechanism to determine allocations of productive resources. Governmental nonintervention, coupled with a traditional work ethic on the part of the local Chinese population, created a very attractive environment for foreign investors. The continuous influx of foreign capital facilitated a high rate of capital formation. Like Japan and Taiwan, Hong Kong followed a strategy of export-expansion. Foreign trade was the driving force behind its growth. In 1984, Hong Kong's total trade (including re-exports) exceeded $55 billion, ranking it sixteenth in the world.[45]

The upward trend was disrupted in September 1982, when British Prime Minister Margaret Thatcher visited Beijing to initiate talks regarding Hong Kong's future status. Beijing's response was the announcement of its intentions to reclaim sovereignty over Hong Kong in 1997. This decision immediately touched off a chain reaction. Uneasiness about the region's political future sent local stock and property values plummeting. Many Chinese capitalists began transferring their assets abroad. In less than three years, the mood of the colony changed from euphoric to pessimistic. Because of Hong Kong's vital importance to the PRC's modernization, Beijing authorities attempted to dispel the people's fears by putting forward a series of programs. In October 1984, the Chinese and British governments reached an agreement. Six principles that would lead to restoring the Hong Kong people's confidence in the island's future were announced:

1. Hong Kong is to become a special zone of the PRC with a high degree of autonomy and with administration of the territory in the hands of the Hong Kong population.
2. The territory's socioeconomic system is to remain unchanged for the fifty years after 1997.
3. Hong Kong's present legal system is to continue.
4. The Hong Kong dollar is to remain an international currency.
5. In economic affairs, Hong Kong is to be allowed to deal freely with the rest of the world, although foreign policy is to be determined by the PRC.
6. The life-style in Hong Kong will not be altered.[46]

To further enhance the people's confidence in the special zone status, Beijing leadership advanced the concept of "one nation, two systems," emphasizing its desire for a longtime coexistence of socialist and capitalist systems. As one official put it, "The goal of China is to keep the capitalist economy of Hong Kong as a gateway to the international market, technology transfer, and management know-how."[47]

Since the announcement of these policies, Beijing has also stepped up direct investment in Hong Kong to replace the depleted British capital.

Moreover, to make Hong Kong more dependent upon the mainland market, the PRC has increased trade with Hong Kong and opened the Pearl River, or Canton Delta area, in neighboring Guangdong Province to Hong Kong's investors. These moves have helped stabilize the Hong Kong economy, which has enjoyed a steady recovery since 1984, registering double-digit growth in GNP in 1986 and 1987 and slowing down somewhat to 7.4 percent in 1988. As Beijing's developmental strategy shifted from import-substitution to export-expansion, trade between Hong Kong and the PRC rose phenomenally. During 1978–1988, trade grew at an annual rate of 30 percent. Since 1985, the PRC has been Hong Kong's most important trading partner, accounting for 29 percent of Hong Kong's total trade in 1988. As of 1987, Hong Kong was the PRC's largest trading partner, a status previously held by Japan.

In addition to increasing trade, Hong Kong has also played a vital role in foreign investment in the PRC. By the end of 1988, Hong Kong's direct investment in the PRC totaled $9 billion, accounting for 65 percent of all foreign investment there. Because of the growing shortage of labor and land, many Hong Kong manufacturers took advantage of the PRC's open-door policy by transferring their labor-intensive production to Guangdong, the province adjacent to Hong Kong. By the end of 1988, an estimated 25 to 30 percent of the total labor-intensive production had been transferred to the PRC. More than 2 million Chinese workers in the Canton Delta area are now working for Hong Kong manufacturers. A great degree of interdependence between Hong Kong and Guangdong has rapidly developed.[48]

Events up to the end of 1988 seemed to provide new hope for Hong Kong residents. The Beijing authorities seemed motivated to maintain Hong Kong's stability and prosperity. Not only has Hong Kong regularly provided about a third of the PRC's hard currency earnings, but it has also served as a highly convenient and effective source of capital funds, market information, managerial experience, and technological innovation. The growing PRC–Hong Kong nexus seemed to be a potentially powerful, mutually reenforcing engine of growth, if the PRC's modernization drive proceeded on course.[49]

Beijing's repression of the prodemocracy movement abruptly weakened the confidence of people in Hong Kong about the territory's scheduled reversion to the PRC in 1997. The bloodbath in Tiananmen Square provoked doubts about the PRC's becoming a predictable modernized state, caused a sharp drop in stock and real estate prices in Hong Kong, and spurred a new wave of emigration and capital flight. From May 18, the last stable trading day before the announcement of martial law, to June 5, the day after the massacre, the Hang Seng Stock Price Index (Hong Kong's Dow Jones Index) fell by 28 percent. During that period, not only were small investors dumping stocks, even foreign investors liquidated their stocks. The prices of real estate fell by 20 to 25 percent. The loss of stock and property value was estimated at $50 billion.[50]

The most visible expression of Hong Kong's weakened confidence has been the lines of visa seekers, which have increased exponentially since

June 4, outside most of Hong Kong's foreign consulates. Since the PRC's announcement that it would take over Hong Kong in 1997, the numbers leaving Hong Kong had increased every year. In 1988, 45,800 people left Hong Kong, more than double the average annual level in 1981–1986. A brain drain claimed many of Hong Kong's brightest and best-educated individuals, including managers, technicians, nurses, and secretaries, the kind of people Hong Kong needs most to maintain its prosperity. The Beijing bloodshed exacerbated the situation. The day after the massacre, more than 1,700 Chinese went to the Australian consulate for visas, compared with a normal average of 120 a day.[51] When these people left Hong Kong, they took their assets with them. In recent years, capital flight by the Chinese wealthy class has amounted to $5 billion a year.

One major impact on the PRC has been the suspension of Hong Kong's new investment in Guangdong. Many Hong Kong entrepreneurs used to think that the future of Hong Kong lay in its growing investment in the PRC. The bloodshed has left them scrambling for alternatives. The problem is not work unrest or official repression in Guangdong. While northern cities were embroiled in political crisis, production remained largely uninterrupted in south China. The trouble arose when overseas buyers, concerned with continuity of supply, began canceling orders. Many Hong Kong manufacturers felt that if they maintained their plants in the PRC, they would lose overseas clients. Thus many withdrew their investments, causing a further blow to the PRC's struggling economy.[52]

The most conspicuous effect probably was on the political forces in Hong Kong that had supported the Beijing government. For forty years, Beijing had assiduously built a political base in Hong Kong in left-wing labor unions, schools, newspapers, and more than 2,000 trading companies. Prior to the massacre, many wealthy capitalists and property owners, hoping to keep their assets in Hong Kong after 1997, had tended to support Beijing's stand. In 1988, about 200 prominent Hong Kong citizens were selected to help draft a set of laws to preserve Hong Kong's prosperity and stability after 1997. A group of influential business leaders supporting Beijing's view even produced a promotional video highlighting riots in South Korea to illustrate the negative consequences of political participation by the masses.

The pro-Beijing force has been knocked out by the bloodshed in Tiananmen Square. During the students demonstrations, many Communists working in Hong Kong openly sympathized with the prodemocracy movement. Xu Jiatun, then head of the Xinhua News Agency, visited Hong Kong students on a hunger strike in support of their fellow students in Beijing. Officials from the news agency openly joined a protest march of 600,000 people in front of the agency's building. In three months, the pro-Beijing force changed into an antigovernment vanguard. As hundreds of prodemocracy leaders escaped to Hong Kong, the hard-line leadership in Beijing issued warnings that Hong Kong had become a "base area for counter-revolution."

Faced with the new reality in the PRC, community leaders in Hong Kong have begun a campaign to press for better guarantees for the future. One important step was to try to persuade the British government to grant the 3.25 million Hong Kong residents eligible for British passports the right to live in Britain. Another step was to speed up the timetable for Hong Kong's first direct election, in hopes of establishing some form of local democracy before the PRC takes control. Many legislators and community leaders have also been advocating revisions in the draft of the Basic Law that will govern the territory after 1997. In the original draft, the PRC's National People's Congress would hold the right to interpret and amend the Basic Law and to determine what is treason and when to declare martial law. The PRC would also have the right to decide the number of PLA troops that would be sent to Hong Kong and where they would be stationed, a particularly worrisome provision after the massacre in Beijing.[53] Community leaders demanded that these rights be bestowed to the local legislative organization. Before the unrest in the PRC, Hong Kong legislators (who are currently appointed by the governor) had recommended that only 28 percent of legislators be directly elected by 1997, rising to 50 percent ten years later. Now the legislature is proposing that 50 percent of legislators be directly elected by the time the PRC assumes power, rising to 100 percent in 2003. The new demands have created tensions between Hong Kong and the PRC.

To boost the sagging confidence of the colony and to prevent a large-scale exodus of professional manpower, the British government made a proposal on December 20, 1989, to issue full British passports to 50,000 people considered essential to the colony, as well as to their families (225,000 people in all), to provide them a legal refuge. The move would encourage people with skills and property to take their chances on staying in Hong Kong, knowing that they had an insurance policy should the environment turn oppressive. At the same time, it would give the signal to Beijing that any repression could chase away the very people that the government most desires to remain in Hong Kong after the transfer. The British proposal has not yet been adopted by Parliament, where it is very controversial because of the fear of a wave of immigration. The move was attacked, however, by Beijing authorities as violating the 1984 agreement. On March 1, 1990, the Beijing Foreign Ministry issued a statement warning that it might not recognize foreign passports held by Hong Kong Chinese after the territory returns to the PRC in 1997. Beijing's response is likely to raise anxieties in Hong Kong and to accelerate the exodus.[54]

Whereas the British attempted to stabilize the Hong Kong situation, Chinese authorities sent mixed signals to the residents of Hong Kong. On the one hand, the Beijing authorities indicated that they would pardon those who participated in the May demonstrations in Hong Kong; however, on the other hand, the Standing Committee of the NPC on October 15, 1989, proposed a resolution forbidding antigovernment activities by Hong Kong residents after 1997. The committee also reaffirmed its authority to interpret the Basic Law, announce emergencies, and declare martial law. The NPC's statement constituted a total repudiation of the suggestions of Hong Kong's legislators.[55] The new conflict between Beijing and Hong Kong can only deepen the fears of the Hong Kong populace. As 1997 draws nearer, those with the ability to leave will migrate. If capital and professional manpower continue to drain away, the Hong Kong economy will decline. The century-long stability and prosperity of Hong Kong may become a thing of the past.

Impact on the Relationship with Taiwan

The bloodshed also dealt a blow to Beijing's effort to reunify the two sides of the Taiwan Strait, which Deng had put forward as one of the major goals he hoped to achieve in his lifetime. Since the Third Plenum of the Eighth CCP Central Committee, convened in December 1978, the Beijing authorities have launched many peace overtures to Taiwan. In its famous "message to compatriots in Taiwan" on January 1, 1979, Beijing proposed "three links" (san tong) and "four exchanges" (si liu).

The former means opening trade, transportation, and postal links; the latter refers to economic, cultural, scientific and technological, and sports exchanges between the two sides. Suspicious of Beijing's motivations and concerned with political implications, Taipei's response has been an outright rejection by proclaiming the "three no's" (san bu)—no contact, no negotiation, and no compromise. Thus, there has been no breakthrough that would resolve the political deadlock that has obtained between the two sides since the end of the civil war in 1949.

Despite the hard-line posture adopted by the Nationalist government, indirect trade between Taiwan and the PRC via Hong Kong has rapidly increased since 1979. In 1978, before Beijing's peace overture, products made in Taiwan and then exported through Hong Kong to the PRC amounted to $28,700. From this miniscule base, the volume surged 370-fold in 1979, followed by a 10-fold increase in 1980 and a 2-fold rise in 1981. Two-way trade reached $496 million in 1981. The upward trend was disrupted in 1982 and 1983, when Beijing slowed down its pace of economic growth, but recovered strongly in 1984 and 1985 when another Great Leap Forward was launched. In 1985, bilateral trade exceeded the $1 billion mark and has continued to rise, reaching $1.5 billion in 1987 and $2.7 billion in 1988, a 35-fold increase over the 1979 volume.

Taiwan-PRC relations entered a new stage on October 14, 1987, when the Nationalist government announced a partial lifting of the thirty-eight-year ban on personal contact with relatives in the PRC, by allowing residents to visit them after November 2, 1987. In response to Taiwan's gesture, Beijing announced a set of reciprocal policies for the reception of Taiwanese travelers. Although the Nationalist government maintained its official stance of "no contact, no negotiations, and no compromise," it had adopted a more flexible attitude toward nonofficial private contact. In a two-year period, more than 800,000 Taiwan residents visited their relatives in the PRC. The Taiwanese tourists spent a total of $1.4 billion on the mainland.[56]

The spending spree of the visiting Taiwanese and their generosity toward their relatives in the PRC aroused immense admiration for Taiwan's prosperity.

Study of the Taiwan experience became a popular topic in Chinese academia as well as among the common people. Beginning on July 26, 1988, the *People's Daily* published one short article daily for fifty consecutive days explaining aspects of Taiwan's life. *The Thirty Years of Taiwan*, a book analyzing Taiwan's experience in economic development, political reform, social and cultural changes, and international relations, appeared in Beijing in August 1988. In general it gave a quite positive assessment of Taiwan's achievements.

In Taiwan, people of the older generation rushed to be reunited with their families. The younger generation, harboring immense curiosity, was also eager to tour the PRC. Mainland merchandise ranging from traditional medicine to artistic products flooded the Taiwan market. For the first time in forty years, an atmosphere of amity had emerged between the two sides of the Taiwan Strait.

Realizing that personal exchange generated no damaging effect on the island, the Nationalist government decided to open the door wider. A series of new measures was adopted by the Taiwan government:

1. The government granted permission on April 18, 1988, for the indirect exchange of mail with the PRC, through Red Cross channels.
2. It allowed imports of academic, scientific, artistic, and literary publications from the PRC to Taiwan but restricted publications promoting communism.
3. It allowed indirect imports of forty kinds of raw materials from the mainland, including coal, cotton, and iron. The number initially announced by the Taiwan government on August 5, 1988, has since been raised to ninety.
4. It allowed athletes and scholars to go to the PRC to participate in sports and academic activities sponsored by international organizations.
5. It granted permission on November 11, 1988, for mainland Chinese to visit their seriously ill immediate family members or to attend the funerals of such people in Taiwan.
6. It granted permission on December 1, 1988, to outstanding PRC personnel, scholars, and students abroad to make short observation trips to Taiwan. As a result, a group of five mainland students who had been in the United States arrived in Taiwan on December 20, 1988, for a ten-day visit.

Taking advantage of the new mood, the Taiwan business community pressed the Nationalist government to lift the ban on direct trade and investment. Some adventurous Taiwanese entrepreneurs had already made investments in coastal cities of the PRC. Official statistics from Beijing disclosed that by the end of 1987, 238 enterprises financed by Taiwan capital were in operation in Fujian, a province opposite Taiwan. Most of them were small firms making labor-intensive products such as electronic components, sport shoes, garments, and toys. Total Taiwan investment was estimated at $200 million.[57] Other reports revealed that the Taiwanese have also been very active in Guangdong Province. In Guangzhou (Canton), the provincial capital, sixty Taiwanese entrepreneurs had invested a total of $200 million.[58]

To attract more investors from Taiwan, the government of Guangdong set up special zones between Canton and Shenzhen. In July 1988, on the eve of the KMT Thirteenth Party Congress in Taipei, the PRC State Council issued a twenty-two-article regulation intended to encourage further Taiwan investment. The regulation granted the Taiwan investors the same rights as foreign-funded companies: They could start private companies or participate in joint ventures or cooperative enterprises, supply materials for processing, purchase enterprise shares and bonds, and even buy land-use rights in PRC cities. In 1988, Taiwan investors set up 430 firms in the PRC, with a pledged investment of $600 million.

In spite of a Nationalist ban on direct trade, direct shipping has been going on between Taiwan and Fujian. Government sources in Taiwan revealed that there were six shipping routes linking the two sides, with ten medium-sized vessels plying the strait. Most of the vessels were smaller than 1,500 tons. By the end of 1988, there were eleven harbors on the coast of Fujian that were open to Taiwanese boats. A dramatic move was made in summer 1988 when several dozen KMT veteran members in a joint proposal suggested that the Taiwan government provide an interest-free loan of up to $10 billion to the PRC for developing private enterprises, if Beijing denounced the use of force to solve disputes and promised to adhere to Chinese culture.

The relationship between Taiwan and the PRC evolved further when, on April 6, 1989, the Taiwan government announced that a delegation headed by Shirley W.Y. Kuo, member of the Standing Committee of the KMT Central Committee and minister of finance of the Republic of China (ROC), would participate in the twenty-second annual session of the Asian Development Bank (ADB), to be held on May 4 in Beijing. The government also lifted the ban on Taiwan's news media personnel's travel to the PRC for news coverage, film shooting, and producing programs. Although Kuo went to the conference in her capacity as governor of the ADB, not as the minister of finance, her visit represented another step toward rapprochement. Many of Taiwan's big corporations began to map plans for large-scale investment in the PRC. If there had been no bloodshed in Tiananmen Square on June 4, a breakthrough in the political deadlock may have been forthcoming.

When Taiwan sent some one hundred reporters, filmmakers, and TV and radio personnel to Beijing to cover Kuo's participation in the ADB conference, the student demonstrations were at high tide. The extensive coverage of the student protests caught the attention of the people in Taiwan. On May 23, after Beijing authorities had imposed martial law, students and teachers from twenty-one colleges in Taiwan issued separate statements to support the prodemocracy movement. On May 31, approximately 100,000 students and young people took part in an islandwide rally to support their fellow students in Tiananmen. The participants joined hands along Taiwan's north-south superhighway, with the line of people stretching from the northern port city of Keelung to the southern port of Kaohsiung. Lee Teng-hui, chairman of the KMT and president of the ROC, had on several occasions shown his deep concern for the developments in the PRC and ordered all concerned offices to take effective measures to support the student movement. Taiwan's response was soon condemned by Beijing as provoking the "counter-revolutionary revolt."[59]

Taiwan's reaction to the Tiananmen massacre was less dramatic than people expected. Neverthelesss, the ruthless suppression of the peaceful demonstrations had destroyed the mood of amity the two sides had painstakingly built during the prior three years. The immediate effect was the halt of tourism, a plunge in bilateral trade, and disruption of the investment plans of many corporations.

In the wake of the bloodshed, the Beijing authorities pursued a carrot-and-stick policy. On the one hand, the hard-liners continued their attack on the Taiwan government, blaming them for supporting and financing "counter-revolutionary" activities inside and outside the PRC. To sustain their accusations, they arrested thirteen citizens on June 21 and charged them with being KMT's special agents. They were sentenced to long-term imprisonment. In early July, Beijing police arrested a Taiwanese reporter for attempting to help a student leader of the protest movement to escape. In August, the Beijing government adopted new measures to restrict the entry visas and activities of Taiwanese journalists. All these measures were designed to keep Taiwan from aiding the prodemocracy movement either inside or outside the PRC.

But on the other hand, confronted with the critical shortage of investment funds and mounting foreign debts, Beijing eagerly courted the cash-rich Taiwanese businessmen. In August, the Academy of Social Sciences of Fujian proposed a new strategy toward Taiwan, suggesting that the Beijing government use trade as a bait to attract Taiwan businessmen by offering them higher profit. The expansion of trade, the academy contended, would lead to the formation of an interest group in Taiwan that would exert pressure on the government for more direct contact with the PRC.[60] But as long as the hard-liners remain in power, the fear of suppression cannot be easily dispelled and business between the two sides may not soon return to normal.

In short, the bloodshed on June 4 has caused colossal damage to every aspect of Chinese life. The decade-long effort of Deng Xiaoping to break the stability-turmoil cycle has failed as miserably as his attempt to project the image of savior of the country. The massacre alienated a generation of the intellectual elite, shattered Deng's dream of building a modernized country through reform and open-door policies, and demolished his grand design to draw Taiwan and Hong Kong into the great Chinese orbit. The future of the PRC is now clouded with immense uncertainties, and no one knows which course the PRC will pursue. Although the damage to the country's long-term prospects need not be permanent, the immediate consequences of the massacre have left a pessimistic vision of the future.

Notes

1. *New York Times,* June 6, 1989, p. 1.
2. *New York Times,* June 30, 1989, p. 1.
3. *New York Times,* July 14, 1989, p. 4.
4. *New York Times,* June 22, 1989, p. 5.
5. *Wall Street Journal,* June 19, 1989, p. A8.
6. Ibid.
7. *New York Times,* July 3, 1989, p. 21.
8. *Wall Street Journal,* June 6, 1989, p. A19.
9. Richard E. Gillespie and Kelly Ho Shea, "The Military Sales Ban," *China Business Review,* Sept.–Oct. 1989, pp. 32–33.
10. Ibid.
11. Anne T. Thurston, "Back to Square One?" *China Business Review,* Sept.–Oct. 1989, pp. 36–41.
12. *People's Daily,* Feb. 28, 1990, p. 2.
13. *New York Times,* Aug. 14, 1989, p. 21.
14. *China Daily,* July 13, 1989.
15. *New York Times,* June 11, 1989, p. 9.
16. I. M. Pei, "China Won't Ever Be the Same," *New York Times,* June 23, 1989, op. ed. page.
17. Editorial, *Ta Kung Pao* (Hong Kong), June 4, 1989, p. 2.
18. Editorial, *Wen Wei Pao,* June 4, 1989.
19. *Wall Street Journal,* June 16, 1989.
20. *China Times,* Sept. 9, 1989, p. 6.
21. *New York Times,* July 31, 1989, p. 4.
22. *Wall Street Journal,* Sept. 27, 1989, p. A23
23. *New York Times,* Sept. 25, 1989.
24. *Wall Street Journal,* Sept. 27, 1989, p. A23.
25. *World Journal* (New York), Aug. 3, 1989, p. l.
26. *People's Daily,* Sept. 30, 1989, pp. 1–2.
27. *Wall Street Journal,* Nov. 28, 1989, p. A10.
28. *Wall Street Journal,* Sept. 26, 1989, p. A20.
29. *New York Times,* Sept. 26, 1989, p. 47.
30. *International Daily News* (Los Angeles), Sept. 7, 1989, p. 3.
31. *Wall Street Journal,* Sept. 19, 1989, p. A14, and *Beijing Review* 32, No. 39 (Oct. 2–8, 1989), p. 10.
32. *China Daily News* (New York), June 12, 1989, p. 6.
33. For the unreliability of unemployment statistics, see U.S. Central Intelligence Agency, *The Chinese Economy in 1988 and 1989: Reform on Hold, Economic Problems Mount* (Washington, D.C., Aug. 1989), pp. 19–20.
34. *Wall Street Journal,* July 20, 1989, pp. 1, 8.
35. *China Daily News,* July 22, 1989, p. 2.
36. *China Times* (Taipei), Oct. 9, 1989, p. 7.
37. *Ta Kung Pao,* Aug. 20, 1989, p. 2.
38. *People's Daily,* July 19, 1989, p. 2.
39. *World Journal,* Sept. 22, 1989, p. 32.
40. *New York Times,* June 17, 1989, pp. 1, 4.
41. *International Daily News,* July 18, 1989, p. 2.

42. O. Schnepp, "The Impact of Returning Scholars on Chinese Sciences and Technology," in Denis Fred Simons and Merle Goldman, eds., *Science and Technology in Post-Mao China* (Cambridge: Harvard University Press, 1989), pp. 175–176.

43. *New York Times*, June 28, 1989, p. 17.

44. *China Times*, Aug. 22, 1989, p. 6.

45. Chu-yuan Cheng, "Hong Kong's Prosperity: Foundations and Prospects," in Hungdah Chiu, ed., *Symposium on Hong Kong 1997* (Baltimore, Md.: University of Maryland School of Law, 1985), pp. 61–63.

46. *South China Morning Post* (Hong Kong), Oct. 24, 1984, p. 15.

47. *Liao Wang* [The outlook] (Beijing), Sept. 1984.

48. *International Daily News*, July 14, 1989, p. 4.

49. Y. C. Jao, "The 1997 Issue and Hong Kong's Financial Crisis," in Hungdah Chiu, op. cit, p. 53.

50. *International Daily News*, July 24, 1989, p. 6.

51. *New York Times*, June 18, 1989, p. 12.

52. *Wall Street Journal*, June 15, 1989, A10.

53. *New York Times*, June 18, 1989, p. 12.

54. *New York Times*, March 2, 1990, p. A3.

55. *World Journal*, Oct. 16, 1989, p. 1.

56. *China Daily News*, June 27, 1989, p. 6; and *World Journal*, Sept. 16, 1989, p. 32.

57. *China Daily News*, March 31, 1988, p. 2.

58. *International Daily News*, July 7, 1989, p. 6.

59. Shi Wei, "What Has Happened in Beijing?" *Beijing Review*, June 26–July 2, 1989, p. 15.

60. *International Daily News*, Aug. 28, 1989, p. 2.

8

The Road from Tiananmen

Over the decade ending in 1988, the PRC under Deng Xiaoping's leadership had been emerging as a land of promise. In the wake of the turbulent Cultural Revolution, the country had embarked on economic reform and had returned to the international community, seeking foreign investments and advanced technology. The world watched the development with high expectations, hoping that after a century of turmoil the PRC would eventually catch up with its East Asian neighbors. The June 4, 1989, bloodshed dashed these hopes. As the shock of the massacre gradually subsided, experts began considering what was underlying the event and seeking the real causes of the tragedy.

For many outside observers, the foremost question has been, What impelled Deng Xiaoping, a man reputed for his pragmatism, to undermine an elaborate program that had taken him more than a decade to achieve? Was the bloodshed inevitable, as the hard-line leaders asserted, or was it totally unnecessary, as many Chinese believed? From the long-range perspective, did the recent upheavals merely pose a temporary setback for the PRC on the road to greater material wealth and personal freedom, or was the preceding decade of relative relaxation and the open door simply an aberration in an era of repression and intolerance? What are the fundamental factors likely to shape the PRC's future, and on which path will the country tread in the decade ahead? Although no one possesses the answers to these questions, past experience and recent developments may serve as a basis for making conjectures.

The Causes of the Unrest

In retrospect, it has become fairly evident that the cycle of student protests and military crackdown involved four major factors: a spontaneous expression of popular discontent on the part of the students and Chinese people; the hard-line leaders' obsession with maintaining their absolute power and their intolerance of any criticism and challenge; an international atmosphere encouraging the students to harden their positions; and a fierce power struggle within the Party's top hierarchy.

Public discontent stemmed from social and economic problems (see Chapter 2), including inflation, unemployment, corruption, nepotism, and income disparities. Most of these social and economic woes, however, were not unique to the PRC but have been prevalent in most Third World countries. Large-scale demonstrations and student protests have occurred quite frequently in other Asian countries and in Latin American countries. The roots of the Tiananmen bloodshed rest more in the power structure and the mentality of the Chinese gerontocracy than in the economic disturbances.

As several social scientists have commented, the existing political system of the People's Republic of China is neither a "people's government" nor a "republic." It is a combination of a remnant feudal autocracy and a Stalinist totalitarian state. Under this system, the Party, government, economy, military, culture, and ideology all fuse together to form a pyramid-shaped power structure. The ultimate power rests in the hands of a few top leaders. In order to assert their authority, they do not tolerate dissenting views. Criticism of the leadership is often interpreted as a challenge to the regime's legitimacy.[1] Despite the decade-long reform and Party reshuffling, Deng has still maintained his grip on the ultimate power.[2]

The octogenarian leaders surrounding Deng share several attributes with him. They are very sensitive to any form of disorder and tend to interpret dissident demonstrations as an attack upon their authority. Since the founding of the PRC, the suppression of intellectual protests has been taken for granted. Deng, as CCP general secretary, helped Mao launch the antirightist campaign in 1957 in which some 400,000 higher intellectuals (professors, writers, scientists) were persecuted. Many of them were sent to labor camps for more than twenty years. In 1979, Deng ordered the crackdown on the Beijing Spring movement and sentenced several young dissidents to long-term imprisonment. In 1986, Deng sanctioned the suppression of student protests, and he dismissed Party General Secretary Hu Yaobang in early 1987 after Hu failed to carry out Deng's order. Deng's ironhanded policy and his abhorrence of chaos were reflected in his decision to crush several episodes of ethnic unrest. In 1975, after resuming the position as chief of staff of the army, Deng ordered a military crackdown on factional fighting in Sha Dian, a Muslim village in Yunnan, near the border of Vietnam. The army reportedly demolished the whole village, and the death toll was over 3,000.[3]

In the wake of these crackdowns, Deng received no explicit national or international reprimands. Suppression had become an established pattern in dealing with dissent and unrest. On December 30, 1986, during the first wave of student protests at dozens of Chinese universities, Deng maintained in a speech to Communist Party leaders: "Firm measures must be taken against any student who creates trouble in Tiananmen Square. When a disturbance breaks out in a place, it's because the leaders there didn't take a firm, clear-cut stand against bourgeois liberalization." Deng then reassured the Party leaders that suppression generated little ill effect on the PRC's international standing. "On the contrary, the prestige of our country is steadily growing."[4] Deng's past experiences seemed to have confirmed his belief that the use of force produced quick results without adverse consequences.

The intransigence of the hard-line leaders was countered by the increasing militance of the student body. Students' dissatisfaction toward nepotism in job assignments and widespread corruption had been reinforced by several developments. In February 1988, an article in the *World Economic Herald* called attention to the crisis facing the PRC. According to the journal, despite the advances made in the past decade, the country's international economic position was rapidly sinking. Not only was the gap between the PRC and the advanced countries widening in terms of technology and the state of the economy, but even developing countries, such as Thailand, South Korea, and Malaysia, were outpacing the PRC. In 1955, its GNP had accounted for 4.7 percent of the world's total. By 1980, its share had dropped to only 2.5 percent. In 1960, the GNP had been on a par with Japan's. By 1980, it accounted for only one-fourth of Japan's, and in 1985 it dropped further to one-fifth. In 1960, the U.S. GNP was $460 billion larger than the Chinese, but in 1980, the gap expanded to $3.68 trillion. According to the 1987 *World Development Report*, in terms of GNP per capita, the PRC ranked 105th of the 128 countries covered by the World Bank statistics. The *Herald* made the prediction that if the PRC could not catch up with the rest of the world, it would lose its membership in the international "club" of elite nations. The article aroused strong response from intellectuals, especially the young college students who have increasingly blamed the Maoists for the destructive effects of the Cultural Revolution and the conservatives for their snail's pace in political and economic reforms.

Students' resentment of the hard-liners deepened in 1988 after large numbers of Taiwanese had flocked to the PRC to visit their relatives. The material affluence and political liberalization of Taiwan convinced the students that industrialization and democracy were compatible with traditional Chinese culture and would be feasible with a more enlightened leadership in the PRC. They believed that the hard-line old guard and their protégés constituted the greatest hurdle to the country's progress. Because Li Peng was identified as one of the protégés, he was singled out as a target; because Deng sided with the hard-liners in dealing with the 1987 demonstration, he too became an object of the students' contempt.

The bloodshed might not have occurred had Zhao Ziyang and Li Peng not been engaging in a head-on struggle for succession. After the September

1988 Party plenum, there were reports from Beijing that the hard-line octogenarian leaders intended to make Zhao a scapegoat for the mounting economic crisis and had persuaded Deng to replace him.[5] When the student demonstration began, Zhao saw it as an expression of popular demand for reform that would strengthen his position. Li Peng, in contrast, viewed the unrest as an opportunity to win Deng's support and as an instrument to undermine Zhao. One week after the demonstration started, on April 23, Zhao left Beijing for a seven-day official visit to North Korea. Taking advantage of Zhao's absence, Li, at a Standing Committee meeting of the CCP Politburo on April 24, characterized the student movement as "anti-socialism turmoil." The next morning, Li conveyed to Deng the Standing Committee's support of Li's position. Without further investigation and consultation, Deng endorsed Li's interpretation of the event. Deng's hasty decision sealed the fate of the prodemocracy movement.[6]

On two occasions when Zhao was back in the PRC, the students decided to end the protests. But each time, the hard-liners goaded them into continuing. When Zhao spoke to the Asian Development Bank governors on May 4, 1989, he emphasized that "students who had staged demonstrations by no means opposed the fundamental system of China but rather wanted to have the errors of the party and government corrected." Zhao's speech won favorable student reaction because it demonstrated that a Party leader considered them patriotic, not manipulated by antigovernment elements. Student organizers immediately declared an end to their two-week class strike and called upon all striking students in Beijing to return to classes on May 5.[7] However, the hard-line spokesman Yuan Mu continued to voice the government's view of the protest as "a plot manipulated by a small group of people." Yuan's remarks nullified Zhao's efforts and provoked the students into continuing their class strike. The second chance was lost on May 19, after Zhao had made a predawn visit to the hunger strikers in Tiananmen Square and had delivered an emotional speech. The students were then on the verge of calling off the hunger strike. But Li Peng's announcement that night of the imposition of martial law hardened the student's resolve, making the crackdown unavoidable.

The Far-reaching Effects of the Massacre

The immediate effects of the bloodshed are discussed in Chapter 7. The long-term consequences deserve more consideration. One far-reaching effect has been the demise of the reform leadership. During the ten years of the reformers' stewardship, a new generation of social scientists emerged. Before 1980, all Chinese economists were trained in Marxian theory and had little knowledge of modern economics. The open-door policy and the dispatch of a large number of students to study in the West brought about drastic changes in economic studies. As modern economics replaced Marxian orthodoxy, young economists began to apply Western theories in formulating economic policies. The reform leaders, such as Zhao Ziyang and Hu Yaobang, appeared seriously interested in obtaining economists' advice. The three "think tanks" Zhao established in early 1980 employed several hundred economists, many of whom had received training in Western countries. In 1986 when economic reform was in full swing, Zhao, in a report on the Seventh Five-Year Plan (1986–1990) to the Fourth Session of the Sixth National People's Congress in March, invited Chinese economists to "boldly explore and seriously study the experience of various countries, including the advanced management experience of the capitalist countries." With this encouragement, many proposals to reform the system were presented by middle-aged and young economists. Notable among these were Liu Guoguang's proposal to transform the highly centralized planned economy into a commodity economy in which plan and market were well integrated;[8] Li Yining's proposal to reform ownership of state enterprises; Wu Jinglian's proposal to reform the price system; and Hua Sheng's and several young economists' proposal to privatize some state enterprises.[9]

In political science, Su Shaozhi and Yan Jiaqi advanced several incisive analyses of the Chinese political system and presented their reform proposals. Su called for a complete break with the feudal tradition and posited what was known in the PRC as the "Hungarian conclusion," that economic reform could not succeed without political reform. As Su saw it, the starting point of political reform was inner party democracy. He contended that "without inner party democracy, there can be no people's democracy, and it will be impossible to make the best democratic and scientific policy-decisions for reform."[10] Yan moved a step forward by calling for the establishment of a socialist political system with a high degree of democracy and a scientific decision-making structure. All of these reform proposals were innovative and constructive. The emergence of this group of reform-minded social scientists indicated that there was a spark of hope for the country.

With the purge of Zhao and his team, the PRC has been deprived of its principal proponent of reform. The Economic Structural Reform Research Institute of the State Council was suspended in October 1989. Of the 130 members of the institute, more than 20 went into exile, 8 high-ranking officers were arrested, and the remainder were either reassigned to other jobs or sent to labor camps, depending on how actively involved they had been in the prodemocracy movement.[11] As Lee Kuan Yew, prime minister of Singapore, observed: "It took Zhao Ziyang ten years to build a team of economists who understood how the Western economies work and now that team is part in exile, part being rusticated and part missing. Rebuilding that team, will take another 10 years. That's very sad for China and for Asia."[12]

The second far-reaching impact of the bloodshed has been the shattering of Deng's plan for an orderly power transition. Since the establishment of the first Communist state in the Soviet Union more than seventy years ago, transitions of power in Communist regimes have evoked struggle and instability. The prolonged infighting after the death of Lenin and Stalin and the succession struggles before and after Mao's death revealed a serious shortcoming of the system. Because of these bitter lessons, Deng, after his resumption of power, repeatedly underscored his intention to ensure policy continuity through the promotion of successors whose personal interests were geared to the reform policy.[13] To guarantee a smooth transition, Deng not only selected Hu Yaobang as Party general secretary and Zhao Ziyang as the prime minister but also started to build up what he called the "third echelon" of future leaders. Young leaders such as Tian Jiyun (vice premier), Li Peng (premier since 1988), Hu Qili (member of the Politburo between 1987 and June 1989) and Qiao Shi (member of the Politburo) were promoted to prominent positions as the potential successors to Hu and Zhao.

Deng's succession scheme proceeded quite successfully after the reshuffling of the Party Politburo in September 1985. On several occasions Deng reassured nervous foreign leaders that they need not worry about the PRC's reform policy after his passing because he had installed his own successors. "There is nothing to fear even if heaven should fall down. Hu Yaobang and Zhao Ziyang would be there to prop it up!"

The forced resignation of Hu Yaobang in January 1987 crippled Deng's succession plan. But many people still harbored the hope that Zhao Ziyang would eventually emerge as Deng's natural successor. The ouster of Zhao in May 1989 dismantled the entire succession plan, leaving Deng without a political heir. Although he quickly picked Jiang Zemin, a bland technocrat and former mayor of Shanghai, as his new successor, the latter has displayed little expertise or vision in economic matters. Nor has he any close connections with the military establishment. Although Deng made Jiang chairman of the Party's Military Commission in November 1989, most people believe that Jiang's tenure will not be longer than that of his two predecessors. The appointment of Jiang Zemin has done little to resolve the country's enduring political dilemma and has made a post-Deng power struggle almost certain.

The third far-reaching impact has been the rapid deterioration of the PRC's international status. Since 1979, China has broken its self-imposed isolation and made considerable strides in expanding diplomatic and economic relations with the rest of the world. The signing of the China-Japan peace treaty in 1972 and the normalization of diplomatic relations with the United States in 1979 had marked a new era in Beijing's international relations. Several dozen Latin American countries soon followed the U.S. step in recognizing Beijing as the sole government representing the whole of China. By the mid-1980s, the PRC had emerged as a respected regional power and played a balancing role between the two superpowers. The country had been able to attract sizable foreign capital, expand foreign trade, and develop scientific, educational, and cultural exchanges. During the 1978–1988 decade, foreign corporations had committed $28 billion to 16,000 enterprises (the actual amount invested was $12 billion), an infusion of capital that helped to double per capita income in ten years.

The bloodletting in June 1989 disrupted this progress. As Western countries imposed economic sanctions and banned direct contacts of high-level government officers, the PRC's relations with much of the developed world, especially the United States, soured. The U.S. government's reaction and countermeasures led to the most serious downturn in Beijing-Washington relations since Richard Nixon had begun the process of Sino-American reconciliation twenty years before.[14]

The PRC's new isolation was reflected in a rather embarrassing way when it celebrated its fortieth anniversary and invited all foreign diplomatic officials in Beijing to join them at the rostrum of Tiananmen for fireworks displays on the evening of October 1, 1989. None of the ambassadors from the major Western countries appeared. Moreover, the U.S. House and Senate worked out an agreement for legislative sanctions against the PRC. Temporary measures that were passed into law included a ban on military sales and exchanges, a suspension of high-level government contacts, and a halt of U.S. trade enhancement programs, such as the overseas Private Investment Corporation and the Trade Development Program. The enactment of these sanctions caused a further deterioration of the already strained relations.[15] Despite President George Bush's sending his close aides Deputy Secretary of State Lawrence Eagleburger and National Security Adviser Brent Scowcroft on a secret mission to the PRC after the crackdown, very little improvement of relations was achieved.

Even in the Third World, where Beijing has steadily tried to strengthen relations, its influence declined after the crackdown. In fall 1989, three Third World countries—Grenada (July), Liberia (September), and Belize (October)—switched their diplomatic recognition from the PRC to the ROC. As none of them is a major state, these changes will have only a marginal effect on Beijing's global standing. Yet, it undoubtedly signals a setback in the PRC's foreign relations.

The last but most significant impact is the alienation of the leadership from the people, particularly the generation of young intellectuals. Most leaders holding real power in the PRC are in their seventies and eighties. They live in the walled compound of Zhongnanhai and rarely set foot outside the compound. Their information about the student protests came largely from the hard-liners: Beijing Mayor Chen Xitong, Beijing Party Secretary Li Ximing, and Prime Minister Li Peng. These hard-liners apparently colored their reports to make the demonstrators appear to be advocating the overthrow of the system and directly attacking Deng.[16] Deng's loss of contact with the people and his unawareness of current developments were fully reflected in his remarks on June 9, 1989, after the military crackdown. In that speech Deng praised the soldiers for self-restraint and said, "If tanks were used to roll over people, this would have created a confusion between right and wrong among the people nationwide."[17]

The June crackdown and the attempt to cover it up destroyed the credibility of the government. The most ironic phenomena in the country today is the distrust of many people for their government. According to Simon Leys, the Chinese have so much contempt, distrust, and hostility for the Communist leadership that in their eyes, "whoever is in disgrace must be a hero and whoever is in power must be a scoundrel."[18] The leadership has continued to insist that it called in the troops to overcome a "counter-revolutionary" movement initiated by the infamous "handful" of conspirators. To support this contention, the government has forced intellectuals and Party members to endorse this account.[19] Resentment toward the government has by no means been confined to intellectuals. Even ordinary people feel the suppression is excessive and unjustified. After the crackdown, amid the large-scale manhunt for the dissidents, a young woman in Beijing's free-market clothing stall expressed her opinion about the *bao tu* ("ruffians" or "thugs"), the government's label for the demonstrators. She claimed that "they are students, workers, and ordinary people" and then added very seriously that if such were *bao tu*, "I am a *bao tu* too!"[20]

Factors Determining the PRC's Future

The June 4 crackdown disrupted economic reform and jeopardized the PRC's international relations. With the ascendancy of the hard-liners, the country's development reached a crossroads. Whether the PRC will continue on its reform track or turn back to the Maoist model of central control depends on several factors. Among them are the economic conditions in the next few years, the power realignment between the Party and the army, and Beijing's relationship with Taiwan and Hong Kong.

The Economic Factor

After a decade of rapid growth and several years of galloping inflation, the Chinese economy has been caught in a host of dilemmas: stability versus reform, efficiency versus unemployment, incentive versus income disparities, and open door versus regional imbalance. Economic reform entails a change in the status quo, causing instability. Price reform in the PRC would require the upward adjustment of prices for energy, transportation, and public services, which would exacerbate inflation. Increasing efficiency would require the closing of tens of thousands of marginal plants and would lead to large-scale unemployment. Balancing the national budget would mean cutting consumption and investment and causing the growth rate to decline. Many reform policies might violate the principle of equity. Weighing one policy goal against another is extremely difficult.

When Deng and his allies started the reform program in the late 1970s, their overriding goal was to gain popular support for reform. They believed that a high rate of growth was necessary because only such a growth rate could ensure high employment and provide people with more consumer goods. With this purpose in mind, Deng and Hu Yaobang set the target of quadrupling the annual gross output value of agriculture and industry by the year 2000, and the state dramatically increased capital investment. During 1980–1988, investment in fixed assets by state-owned enterprises increased at an annual rate of 17.4 percent, far exceeding the growth rate of the GNP.[21] To stimulate incentive, wages for employees and workers were increased steadily, at an annual rate of 10.5 percent. In 1979, government procurement prices for agricultural products also rose by more than 30 percent. All these measures have greatly increased the purchasing power of the Chinese consumer.

One major goal of the reform was to "enliven the economy." The institution of the contract system to individual farm households, the revival of individual businesses, the open door to foreign investors, and the encouragement for some of the population to become affluent were all intended to stimulate incentive and raise productivity. The implementation of these policies has produced several positive results.

1. The growth rate of the GNP was among the world's highest. The average annual growth rate during 1979–1988 was around 9.6 percent, higher than most of the developing nations.[22] It should be noted that the growth rate of the GNP appears very impressive in terms of Chinese yuan, but when converted into U.S. dollars, the growth rate becomes moderate. During the 1979–1988 period, the exchange rate between the Chinese yuan and the U.S. dollar depreciated by 58 percent: from $1 equaling 1.549 yuan to $1 equaling 3.7 yuan. During that period, the Chinese population increased by 9 percent. The combined effect of these two factors caused the GNP per capita in the PRC to remain almost unchanged in terms of dollars. According to the World Bank, the per capita GNP was $290 in 1980 and $310 in 1988, ranking the PRC among the bottom 22 of the 129 nations covered by the World Bank reports.

2. The increase in availability of consumer goods, especially household electric appliances, was very impressive. Almost nonexistent thirty years ago, the PRC's electronics industry produced 24.8 million television sets in 1988, of which 10.2 million were color. Output of refrigerators, washing machines, and bicycles also rose dramatically and made the country rank among the world's largest producers.[23]

3. Economic conditions in the coastal areas showed considerable improvement. The southern province of Guangdong, formerly a backward agricultural area, has become an advanced industrial center. During the decade of reform (1978–1988) Guangdong's GNP grew at an annual rate of 12 percent. In 1988, Guangdong's exports amounted to $7.3 billion, accounting for one-sixth of the PRC's total exports.[24]

The new policies, however, generated inflation and huge internal and external debts. Although the official inflation rate was 7.8 percent for 1987; 18.5 percent for 1988; and 17.8 percent for the first nine months of 1989, real rates were much higher. A study by the State Statistical Bureau revealed that the real inflation rate for 1987 was 35 percent.[25] Because both the 1988 and 1989 reported rates were higher than that of 1987, the real inflation rates for these two years must have exceeded 35 percent. Budget deficits were also significantly understated. Instead of counting internal and external debts as a part of the deficit, official reports counted them as revenues. For the 1979–1989 period, the actual budget deficit totaled 169.8 billion yuan, double the 75 billion yuan that was reported.[26]

Regional imbalances were aggravated by the open-door policy. The coastal areas raised most of the foreign capital, thereby accelerating their development at a rate much faster than that of the interior. A continuous outflow of capital and technical manpower from the interior to the coastal areas also widened the gap in growth between the two sectors of the PRC. With respect to the gross output value of agriculture and industry during the 1981--1985 period, the gap between the ten coastal provinces and the eleven interior provinces widened significantly, going from 256 billion yuan in 1981 to 436 billion yuan in 1985. The difference in per capita consumption of the coastal and the interior provinces increased from 7 yuan in 1981 to 137 yuan in 1985.[27] This has caused growing tension in the eastern and western provinces.

The most adverse effect of the reform policy, however, was the structural imbalance of the economy. As a result of the rapid increase in investment and consumption, the gap between aggregate supply and aggregate demand of the society widened from 26.5 billion yuan in 1983 to 224.3 billion yuan in 1988, underscoring the soaring inflation. The imbalance between industry and agriculture also worsened. From 1985 to 1988, the average annual growth rate of industry was 17.8 percent, while that of agriculture stood at only 3.9 percent. Output of food grains, cotton, and oil-bearing crops stagnated for five years, but during the same period the population increased by 15 million every year. Consequently, average grain output per capita dropped from 394 kg in 1984 to 362 kg in 1988; cotton output per capita dropped from 6.1 kg in 1984 to 3.9 kg in 1988, increasing the disparity between supply and demand.[28]

The problem within the industrial sector was particularly noticeable. The energy and raw material industries were not in balance with other industries, and the situation was worsening. The share of the energy industry in total industrial output declined from 14.1 percent in 1978 to around 10 percent in 1986–1988. The ratio between the raw material industry and the processing industries rose from 1:0.96 in 1978 to 1:1.67 in 1988. The critical shortage of energy and raw materials prevented further advancement within the processing industries[29] and became a hindrance to growth of the economy.

The structural imbalance led to deterioration in allocations of resources and has brought on a vicious cycle of more inputs, less outputs, and low efficiency. Losses incurred in state industrial enterprises rose from 3.4 billion yuan in 1984 to 10.56 billion yuan in 1988.[30] With many state enterprises on the brink of bankruptcy, the PRC's economy had reached a point by the end of 1988 where some sort of readjustment was imperative.

The policies adopted by the Third Plenum of the Thirteenth Party Congress in September 1988 shifted the focus from growth to stability. Important measures included: (1) curtailment of capital investment by 20 percent in 1989 and absolute restriction of public and private consumption; (2) suspension of price reforms and a reinstitution of price control; (3) recentralization of financial power from local government to the central authority; and (4) reorientation of development priorities. According to Liu Guoguang, vice president of the Academy of Social Sciences, excessive demand and credit expansion were the two villains behind the crisis. The tough new austerity policies "traded off" rapid growth for a stable and healthy economy.[31] The shift from growth to stability was partly a reaction to the escalation of inflation, which had underlain the popular discontent. It also stemmed from the severe shortage of energy and raw materials, making a high rate of growth unsustainable.

The new policies have not achieved major breakthroughs in resolving chronic supply-demand imbalances, but rather have pushed the Chinese economy into stagflation. Although the government has sharply reduced credit available for investment and ordered the suspension of thousands of building projects, aggregate demand has still exceeded aggregate supply and the inflation rate has continued to mount. In an effort to bring down inflation, the central bank enforced an extremely tight monetary policy, resulting in a net withdrawal of 5.3 billion yuan from circulation in the first half of 1989, compared with a net overissue of 8.9 billion yuan during the same period of 1988. The severe contraction in the monetary supply prompted a crunch in state-owned enterprises. Many of them delayed debt payment. Throughout the economy, there was a chain effect of bad debts among state enterprises. This phenomenon destroyed business confidence and obligated firms to deal with each other only in cash. Tight money supply and serious overstocking of unsold products created a market slump.[32]

At the same time, shortages of raw materials and electricity as well as of working capital forced many industrial enterprises to cut production. In October 1989, industrial output showed a negative growth of 2.1 percent. The situation worsened in January 1990, when industrial output fell 6.1 percent from a year earlier. This was by far the most serious monthly decline in the eleven years since Deng introduced the economic reform. As the economy weakened, unemployment escalated. Official estimates of unemployment ranged from 2 to 8 percent for the urban labor force, with the trend heading upward.

The situation caused the new leadership deep concern and prompted the calling of a Party Central Committee plenary session in early November 1989. The plenum decided to heighten austerity for another two to three years, reemphasized the importance of stability, and adopted a development strategy designed to shift priorities from regions to industries. Instead of emphasis on the development of the coastal region, as Zhao Ziyang had proposed in early 1988, the new strategy will grant preferential treatment to development of agriculture, raw materials, energy, and transportation. Efforts will be made to eliminate local trade barriers, encourage the formation of transregional corporations, and promote regional cooperation projects.[33] The new policies, when implemented, may help to ease inflation pressures but will create many new hurdles.

1. A slowdown in economic growth could mean huge losses at state-run factories and require a government bailout amounting to billions of dollars, further draining the depleted state coffers. In 1988, bailout subsidies rose 18 percent to 44.6 billion yuan ($12 billion), accounting for 58 percent of total subsidies and becoming a huge burden to the state budget.[34] In the

first half of 1989, the volume of losses from the deficit enterprises topped the total losses for 1988. Thousands of small semiprivate enterprises in the rural areas may go bankrupt because they have no state financial safety net and are at the mercy of available credit. A collapse in this sector could help create the country's largest-scale unemployment since the Communists took control in 1949.

2. The second difficult issue is the problem of unemployment. In the past, whenever the economy suffered a recession, unemployed laborers were sent back to rural areas. Today all land is contracted to individual households, so there is little room for the urban unemployed. The large number of unemployed will mostly add to the 50 million fluid population, moving from one place to another and becoming a potential anomic force in society.[35]

3. Third is maintaining the prosperity of the coastal areas. The development of the eastern coast was facilitated by policies that gave inducements to foreign investors. Without this preferential treatment foreign investors may look elsewhere and the prosperity may quickly fade away. The coastal areas contributed to most of the country's export trade and provided the lion's share of foreign exchange. Stagnation in this area will deal a severe blow to the national economy.

4. During the accelerating inflation in 1987–1989, urban dwellers bore the brunt of the high prices. Government reports showed that 34.9 percent of urban residents suffered a decline in real income in 1988.[36] In the second half of 1989, the central government lacked the cash it needed to pay workers at state enterprises, to pay farmers for their crops, and to pay off holders of a large number of treasury bonds due in subsequent months. To cover the shortfall, the government forced workers and employees to purchase bonds during the second half of 1989. Workers were furious because bond buying slashed their monthly income by one-third to two-thirds for one to four months.[37] The forced sale of bonds, if continued, may trigger new worker unrest.

As social and political pressures mount, policies may have to change again. Government policy reversals occurred several times in the past. In 1986, the government, fearing a recession and large-scale unemployment, discarded the retrenchment plan and began a new cycle of inflation. According to a study by the Chinese Academy of Sciences, the economy has been subject to cyclical fluctuations similar to Western business cycles. From 1950 to 1988, the economy passed through six cycles, each lasting an average of six years. The current cycle started in 1987, peaked in 1988, and may enter its contraction phase in 1990, to be concluded by 1991.[38] If this forecast is accurate, the belt-tightening measures of the hard-line leaders can only aggravate the contraction and push the economy into a deep recession.

If the nation's contradictory economic program is not untangled and people's incentive and productivity not revived, stagnation, inflation, and shortages will grow worse. Rising popular discontent may precipitate the downfall of the hard-line government and provide an opportunity for the return of the moderate reformers.

The Political-Military Factor

Although economic conditions may dictate the future path of development, policy changes still depend on who will be in charge of the Party after the octogenarian leaders leave the scene. The purge of Zhao and his associates precipitated a power realignment. Once again, Deng has illustrated his formidable ability of maneuvering to maintain a balance among rival factions. To keep his reform and open-door policy alive, Deng, instead of promoting the two hard-line front-runners, Li Peng and Yao Yilin, to the posts of Party general secretary and premier, picked the relatively obscure Jiang Zemin as his successor. When the Party convened its Fourth Plenum of the Thirteenth Central Committee on June 23–24, 1989, a new Standing Committee of the Politburo was formed. Zhao and his close associate Hu Qili were purged. Jiang Zemin, Li Riuhuan, the mayor of Tianjin, and Song Ping, head of the Party's organization department, became the new members, raising the number on the Standing Committee from five to six.

The Standing Committee of the Politburo then bore a strong conservative stamp. Yao Yilin, Li Peng, and Song Ping were disciples of Chen Yun, an eighty-four-year-old conservative economist, who has continued to rival Deng for influence. Chen was the man who helped Li Peng become minister of electric power in 1981 despite the opposition of both the Party chief, Hu Yaobang, and the premier, Zhao Ziyang. Yao and Song both had served at different times as Chen's aides in the state planning system. Chen was known for his concept of a "bird-cage economy," according to which the economy, like a bird, must operate within the "cage" of state central planning. Chen's view was discarded after Deng's reform but found its way back after Li Peng and Yao Yilin assumed policy-making power for economic affairs in September 1988.

To counter the conservatives, Deng promoted Jiang and Li Riuhuan for several reasons: Both of them supported economic reform and the open door but at the same time adhered to a firmer stance toward student unrest. They were more liberal than the triumvirate but more conservative than Zhao Ziyang and Hu Qili. Their records fit squarely into Deng's "economic liberal, political conservative" formula. In addition, both had not been directly involved in the Tiananmen massacre and were less hated than Li Peng by the population.

Qiao Shi has played a unique role on the Standing Committee. As the security czar of the Party, Qiao was a protégé of Peng Zhen, another conservative octogenarian. He supported reform on the one hand and favored stern measures toward dissenters on the other. Qiao might become the decisive player in the future power contention game.

Jiang's lightning elevation from Shanghai Party secretary to Party chief of course was not heartily supported by the conservatives. In terms of seniority, experience, and personal connections, Jiang not only could not match his two predecessors but could not even rival the triumvirate. A colorless technocrat, Jiang's record in Shanghai was generally seen as ineffective. He had no military experience and appeared to have no allies in the armed forces' leadership. Jiang's strength comes from his educational background. A graduate of one of the PRC's best engineering schools, Jiang is one of the few Communist leaders fluent in English and Russian. On November 13, 1989, Deng praised Jiang highly as "a very capable man" and said, "As an intellectual, he is more knowledgeable than I."[39]

Deng, aware of Jiang's weaknesses, adopted a series of tactics to build up his prestige. On May 31, 1989, Deng summoned Li Peng and Yao Yilin and persuaded them to support Jiang. Deng also warned them not to form any small cliques. On June 16, Deng met with eight party leaders and reiterated his decision to make Jiang "the core of the new leadership." After the June Party plenum, the CCP Propaganda Department launched a campaign to project Jiang's image as a "wise leader." On September 26, Jiang led other members of the Standing Committee of the Politburo to meet foreign correspondents and play the role of the Party's chief spokesman. On September 29, at a rally celebrating the fortieth anniversary of the founding of the PRC, Jiang delivered an important speech highlighting the major policies of the Party. Three days later, Yuan Mu, the hard-line spokesman of the State Council, openly praised Jiang's speech as the "political manifesto of the third echelon," indicating that Jiang had gained some support from the hard-liners and was gradually establishing his role as Party leader.

Jiang's political status received a major boost on November 9, when Deng resigned from his one remaining Party post, as the chairman of the Party's Central Military Commission, and named Jiang the new chairman. The decision ended months of inner contention that had delayed the opening of the Party's Fifth Plenum of the Thirteenth Central Committee.

Despite Deng's strenuous efforts to bolster Jiang's position, observers inside and outside the PRC have tended to view Jiang's political future as similar to that of Hua Guofeng, whom Mao had favored as heir and who had risen rapidly in the late 1970s, becoming both Party leader and head of the CMC. After Mao died, Deng wrested effective control from Hua and stripped him of both positions. In Chinese Communist history, no heir apparent has successfully succeeded his mentor.

Jiang's chief rivals were Premier Li Peng and President Yang Shangkun. Whereas Li Peng did not gain any new ground from the Party's fifth plenum, Yang further consolidated his control of the military headquarters. Although he did not replace Deng as the chairman of the CMC, Yang was named to succeed Zhao as that body's first vice chairman. Yang's former post as secretary-general of the commission was filled by his younger brother, Yang Baibing, who was also named to a post on the Central Committee's Secretariat, which is in charge of much of the Party's daily work (see Chapter 5). Since the founding of the PRC, this is the first time that two members of the same family served simultaneously on the military commission; thus the Yang brothers have become the most powerful team in the military hierarchy.

To balance the rising power of the Yang clique, Deng appointed Liu Huaqing as another vice chairman of the CMC. The seventy-two-year-old Liu, who has been Deng's close aide for more than four decades, may someday line up Deng's loyalists to support Jiang Zemin.[40]

Between the fourth plenum, held on June 23–24, and the fifth plenum, held on November 6–9, 1989, the hard-liners seemed to have achieved very little. Both Chen Xitong, the mayor of Beijing, and Li Ximing, the Party secretary of Beijing, two dominant figures in the crackdown, lost their bid for membership in the Standing Committee of the Politburo to fill the seats vacated by Zhao and Hu Qili. Prior to the fifth plenum, the conservatives had launched ferocious attacks on Zhao, giving the impression that a final indictment on Zhao was imminent. However, the communiqué of the plenum did not even mention Zhao's name. This indicated that the hard-liners were having difficulty winning support within the Central Committee, many of whose members had been selected by Zhao. Moreover, Deng himself has also changed his attitude toward Zhao. Internal Party documents circulating among senior officials disclosed that Deng has praised Zhao and Wan Li as two provincial leaders who initiated the rural reforms in the late 1970s, when Zhao served as Party secretary of Sichuan and Wan as Party secretary of Anhui. Their successful experiences became the models for nationwide reform. Deng therefore proposed that the decision on Zhao be postponed for two more years.[41] Deng's turnaround on Zhao and the absence of any open accusation against him in the plenum communiqué indicated that the political fate of the disgraced Party chief has not yet been sealed. A survey of Zhao's closest associates and allies who retained their original positions has further reinforced this impression. Influential figures surviving the postmassacre purge included:

- Wan Li—chairman, National People's Congress, a devoted reformer who supported Zhao's program.
- Tian Jiyun—vice premier, State Council, Zhao's close associate in the Politburo.
- Du Runsheng—director, Rural Development Research Center, State Council, Zhao's chief adviser on rural policy.
- Yang Rudai—Sichuan provincial Party secretary and member of the CCP Politburo, Zhao's ally in Sichuan.
- Wen Jiabao—director, CCP Central Committee general office, Zhao's close associate.
- Yan Mingfu—director, United Front Department, CCP Central Committee, Zhao's close aide, who met hunger strikers in Tiananmen Square.
- Li Changchun—governor, Liaoning Province, a reformer.
- Ye Xuanping—governor, Guangdong Province, a reformer.
- Li Hao—mayor, Shenzhen Special Economic Zone, a reformer.
- Wang Zhaoguo—governor, Fujiang Province, a reformer.
- Guo Shangzhuan—deputy director, State Economic Structural Reform Committee, Zhao's chief adviser on economic reform.
- Qin Jiwei—defense minister, reportedly a supporter of Zhao.[42]

In local Party committees as well as in PRC agencies in Hong Kong and overseas, Zhao's influence has still been profound. There has remained the possibility that Zhao might return to power at some point if the leadership changed.

The political and military alignment after the Party's fifth plenum entailed some new phenomena: Although Deng relinquished his final post, he has continued to serve behind the scenes as the ultimate arbiter of Party and government policy. It appeared that as long as Deng remains alive, Jiang would be the nominal leader of the Party and the army. But no one could be sure that Jiang would weather the bitter power struggles after Deng dies. Moreover, after Deng does die, a struggle will erupt between Jiang and the Li-Yao clique. This could create an opportunity for the Yang brothers to seize power and play the role of king or king maker. Finally, as long as Zhao remains unprosecuted, his chance of coming back cannot be totally ruled out.

The Taiwan–Hong Kong Factor

Apart from domestic political and economic conditions, the future of the PRC will also be dependent on its relations with Taiwan and Hong Kong, the two prosperous Chinese communities outside the mainland. Since 1949, Taiwan under Nationalist rule has been an independent political entity. Despite both the Nationalists' and Communists' adherence to a long-standing position of "one China," each continues to claim to be the sole legitimate representative of China. Prior to President Nixon's visit to Beijing in 1972, the Republic of China in Taiwan maintained full diplomatic relationships with more than seventy countries. Taiwan suffered a severe blow after the U.S. government shifted recognition from Taipei to Beijing in 1979. Since then, Beijing has gained recognition from the majority of nations, with only twenty-three countries retaining diplomatic relations with Taipei.

The diplomatic setback, however, has not impeded Taiwan's economic advance. Between 1978 and 1988, Taiwan's GNP grew at an average annual rate of 8 percent. Foreign trade jumped from $23.7 billion in 1978 to $110 billion in 1988, with an annual growth rate of 16.6 percent.[43] During those ten years, Taiwan's trade surplus totaled $77 billion. By the end of 1988, Taiwan's foreign-exchange reserves had grown to $75 billion, second only to Japan's. Per capita income in 1989 exceeded $7,200, compared with $350 on the mainland. This economic strength has boosted Taiwan's confidence, leading it to take the offensive.

As we saw in Chapter 7, the Nationalist government since 1987, partly because of economic strength and partly because of pressure from local residents, has dropped formal opposition to Taiwan residents visiting the mainland for family reunions. From 1987 to 1989, indirect trade between the PRC and Taiwan doubled and Taiwanese investments in the PRC tripled. The new initiative of the Taiwanese government constituted an effective countermeasure to Beijing's peaceful offensive and significantly increased Taiwan's influence on the populace of the PRC.

A more significant step adopted by the Nationalist leaders was the change of its diplomatic strategy. Under the name of "flexible diplomacy," the ROC government advanced a new concept of "one China—two governments," which would continue to support the principle of "one China" but would also recognize that there were two competing governments in China.

Beijing's reaction to Taipei's new diplomacy has been strong and bitter. The Foreign Ministry of the PRC charged that Taipei was intending to create "two Chinas," or "one China and one Taiwan," thus violating the "one China" principle. Taipei was also accused by Beijing authorities of ignoring the desire for reunification expressed by leaders on both sides of the Taiwan Strait.[44] Taipei's diplomatic offensive has made Beijing sensitive to its vulnerability in every diplomatic post around the world. Although the switch in diplomatic recognition from the PRC to the ROC by the three small countries mentioned above (Grenada, Liberia, and Belize) was due more to the failure of Beijing than to the successful diplomacy of Taipei, the Taiwanese considered it a breakthrough. As of the end of 1989, Beijing still enjoyed formal ties with 132 countries. But Taipei's victory posed a psychological threat to Beijing diplomats who had to worry about Taipei reeling in more countries.

The diplomatic competition for international recognition has strained the relationship between Beijing and Taipei. Beijing's future policy toward Taiwan will have a great bearing on China's future. If Beijing authorities decide to take a belligerent stance by renewing military threats or by using power plays to further isolate the ROC, the relationship between these two sides will quickly deteriorate. Taiwan may have to halt trade, investment, and all exchanges, making peaceful reunification impossible. In contrast, should Beijing follow the approach that worked in East and West Germany until the end of 1989 and recognize the fact that the ROC is an independent political entity that has formal diplomatic relations with 26 countries and trade relations with more than 100 countries, then economic cooperation between these two sides will be substantially enhanced. Taiwan's surplus capital might help tide the PRC over the economic crisis and lay the foundation for final unification.

Relations with Hong Kong are on a different schedule but will have great bearing on the PRC's modernization and unification prospects. Not only does Beijing have an important economic stake in Hong Kong, but also the merger of Hong Kong into the PRC will serve as a test case for Taiwan's reunification with the mainland in the future. The contribution of Hong Kong to the PRC's economy has been enormous. In 1988, this city of 6 million produced a foreign trade of $127 billion, ranking it the eleventh largest trading country in the world, surpassing both the PRC and the ROC. Per capita income reached $9,500—almost thirty times that of the PRC. Two-way trade with the PRC totaled $30 billion, surpassing the PRC's trade with Western Europe ($21.8 billion) and Japan ($19 billion). In recent decades, Hong Kong has in fact become the lifeblood of the PRC's foreign trade. Investment from Hong Kong accounted for 70 percent of total foreign capital in the PRC. For more than two decades, Hong Kong annually supplied the PRC with one-third of its foreign exchange and was a major gateway for the country for obtaining foreign technology and conducting overseas business.

The scheduled reversion to the PRC in 1997 has created the most serious crisis in confidence in the colony's 150-year history. The situation has been aggravated by the Tiananmen massacre. Until then, although many from the wealthy class had already sought emigration, most people hoped that the PRC would do its best to maintain the territory's stability and prosperity. After the Beijing bloodshed a new wave of emigration began. Although the absolute number of emigrants since 1984 has been relatively small, their concentration in the professional and upper classes has severely affected Hong Kong's economy. In 1988, the banking system in Hong Kong lost 12 percent of its total of about 700 executives, 60 percent through emigration. Similar problems have been noted across almost all sectors of the Hong Kong economy. Thus, although annual emigration represents less than 1 percent of the population, its effect is much larger. If Beijing authorities fail to adopt a conciliatory attitude toward Hong Kong's dissident population (1.5 million had participated in demonstrations supporting the prodemocracy movement in Beijing), the flight of capital and professional experience will accelerate. If this exodus causes Hong Kong to decline in prosperity, the annexation might turn into a liability for the PRC.

In short, both Taiwan and Hong Kong, under a proper arrangement, could become great assets to the PRC's modernization and industrialization, if these two "small dragons" of East Asia are allowed to continue their current pace of growth. However, their prosperity could be seriously disrupted if the hard-liners in Beijing resort to military solutions to expedite reunification. Although the chance of sparking a military conflict between Taiwan and the mainland is rather small, the prospect cannot be completely ruled out.

Alternative Scenarios

Even though the future of the PRC is difficult to predict, one thing is quite certain: The current situation cannot continue. The country is confronting the most serious political and economic crisis since the end of the Cultural Revolution. The Fifth Plenum of the Thirteenth Party Congress achieved factional compromise and brought some degree of normalcy to the country. But deep splits in the leadership persist. There is still a lack of consensus about how the country should be managed politically and economically. Based on the three factors discussed in preceding sections, several possible scenarios will be explored here.

Hard-Line Dominance

It is possible that the domination of the hard-liners will continue for another three to five years. Under this scenario, the personnel arrangement made by the fifth plenum is assumed to remain unchanged and both Deng Xiaoping and Chen Yun will remain active and continue their involvement in politics during this period. The ruling power will consist of two groups: First, the six Standing Committee members of the CCP Politburo plus Yang Shangkun, the state president, and Wan Li, the chairman of the NPC. The other group, the eight octogenarians—Deng Xiaoping, Chen Yun, Li Xiannian, Peng Zhen, Bo Yibo, Deng Yingchao, Song Renqiong, and Wang Zhen— will still pull the strings. Because three of the six Standing Committee members, Li Peng, Yao Yilin, and Song Ping, are loyal disciples of Chen Yun, Chen's influence will prevail. A combination of Deng's open door and Chen's "bird-cage economy" may guide the regime.

Under this scenario, the regime will take the form of a collective leadership with a strongly conservative character. Li Peng and Yao Yilin will be in charge of economic and foreign affairs; the Yang brothers will control the army; Song Ping and Qiao Shi will supervise organization and security; and Jiang Zemin and Li Ruihuan will be in charge of party affairs. The new leadership will have to solve a series of crucial problems: (1) how to continue the economic reform as the leaders pledged, (2) how to save the faltering economy from collapse, (3) how to settle the schism involving Zhao Ziyang and his associates, and (4) how to deal with the rising challenges from Hong Kong and Taiwan. Some conjectures, based on post-Tiananmen speeches of Deng, Jiang, and Li Peng, can be made about future policy directions.

Economic Reform. Radical economic reform as defined in September 1984 is dead. Price reform will be replaced by price control. Delegation of power to local governments will be replaced by recentralization of power in the central planning bureaucracy. The scope of rationed commodities may be extended if the shortage of necessities develops. (Since the beginning of 1988, salt, pork, sugar, eggs, and cooking oil have been rationed in many major cities.[45]) Recent U.S. government information indicates that the PRC is starting to recollectivize its farms, especially in the northeast region, because collectivization makes it easier for Party officials to reassert control over the 800 million peasants.[46] Should this become a national trend, it would represent a great leap backward from Deng's reform and a step forward toward Chen Yun's "bird-cage economy."

Development Policy. The overriding goal of the development policy is to bring the real inflation rate down from 40 percent to below 10 percent. Capital investment will be further curtailed and public and private consumption reduced. Higher priorities in resource allocation will be accorded to agriculture, basic industry, energy, and transportation. Consumer goods manufacturing, particularly of durable consumer appliances, will be limited. In regional development, western provinces will receive new attention and growth in coastal areas will be scaled down.

Power Contention. To enlarge Jiang Zemin's power base, Deng may have to rehabilitate a number of Zhao's supporters who have been purged. This may make the hard-liners resentful and spur them on to demand Zhao's public trial. Power contention between the hard-liners and the moderates will intensify.

Ideological Indoctrination. Both Deng and Jiang have claimed that the neglect of ideological education was responsible for the student unrest. Since June 1989, the speeches of leaders have again become the basis of study. This indoctrination program is reminiscent of what was once a daily routine for schools, factories, army, and government organizations, a routine that had virtually disappeared for more than a decade.

Policy Toward Taiwan and Hong Kong. The hard-liners adopted a two-faceted policy toward Hong Kong and Taiwan. Politically, they pursued a stern policy, accusing Hong Kong of being an anti-Communist base and Taiwan of violating the "One China" principle. But economically, they launched a campaign to lure Taiwanese businesspeople by offering them all kinds of preferential treatment. The invitation extended to W. C. Wang, chairman of the Taiwan Plastics group, the number-one enterprise in Taiwan, to explore possible sites for the construction of huge petrochemical plants on the mainland represented a new strategy toward Taiwan.

The return to a hard-line regime may silence the dissenters and bring down the inflation rate. It may nevertheless also sow the seeds of greater disturbances.

Large-Scale Unemployment. The three-year retrenchment plan is bound to add at least 30 million people into the existing army of the unemployed. As we have seen, the old solution of sending urban unemployed back to rural areas is no longer feasible. The unemployed simply move from one city to another, creating a large fluid population. Failure to solve the problem of unemployment may ignite widespread unrest.

Mounting Losses of State Enterprises. One-third of the state enterprises have suffered chronic losses. The cost of bailing out these industries reached 60 billion yuan in 1988. The rapid rise of production costs and the shrinkage of demand will push many more into bankruptcy.

Rising Internal and External Debts. The 168-billion-yuan internal debt ($46 billion) and the $42 billion external debt will be an unbearable burden for the hard-line government. Unless Western countries and Japan lift economic sanctions, the debt repayment in the forthcoming years will exacerbate the economic crisis.

East European Influence. Even as Chinese hard-liners regress to past policies, Communist regimes in Eastern Europe have undergone an earth-shaking transformation. In a short span of three months, the hard-line regimes of Erich Honecker of East Germany and Todor Zhivkov in Bulgaria were both forced to step down. On August 24, former solidarity activist Tadeusz Mazowiecki became the first non-Communist prime minister of Poland. On October 7, Hungary's Communist Party reconstituted itself as the Hungarian Socialist Party. On November 9, East Germany opened the Berlin Wall. On December 3, the entire leadership of the East German Communist Party resigned under public pressure. On December 10, a "velvet revolution" swept away the Communist government of Czechoslovakia. In a new cabinet of twenty-one, there were eleven non-Communists. But the most dramatic event was a massacre in Romania that triggered the downfall and the execution of Nicolae Ceausescu and his wife on December 25, ending their twenty-four years of tyrannical rule.

The downfall of Ceausescu was a shock to the PRC's hard-line leaders because Beijing's top security chief, Qiao Shi, had visited Romania just the week before, reaffirming the PRC's ties to the dwindling fellowship of die-hard Communist regimes. Moreover, Ceausescu was the only Eastern European leader who tried the "Chinese solution" of ordering an army assault on demonstrators. In Romania, however, the troops eventually joined the popular revolt.[47] In the short span of one week, following the events in Romania, the CCP held four sessions of the Standing Committee of the Politburo, one session of all members of the Politburo, and one enlarged session, attended by first secretaries of provinces and autonomous regions.[48] Like a wind sweeping over the entire Communist bloc, the Eastern European revolution is bound to shake the ideological foundation of the hard-line regime in Beijing.

All of these new developments have undermined the economic base and superstructure of the hard-line leadership. Once the octogenarians die, the regime may crumble quickly. When change finally comes, it is likely to be very rapid. The Maoist political hierarchy and economic systems collapsed only two years after Mao died. When Deng and his colleagues join Mao, sweeping change may well ensue.[49]

The Reformist Resurgence

An alternative scenario could emerge if the hard-line regime were replaced by a moderate one prior to the death of Deng and the other octogenarians. In early 1990, there were signs indicating that Deng was eager to improve the international image of the PRC and to revive the faltering economy. Both Li Peng and Yao Yilin were slated for replacement. According to unconfirmed reports, Deng proposed that Li Ruihuan become the premier and Zou Jiahua chairman of the State Planning Commission. The hard-line leaders agreed to Zou's appointment but insisted that Li Peng retain his current position to maintain policy continuity. A later report suggested that Deng might "promote" Li Peng to the state presidency and thus deprive him of control of the State Council.

Should the moderates return to power, they may pursue more fundamental changes in political and economic systems after they consolidate their control. Prior to the 1989 spring student unrest, social scientists in Zhao's camp had contemplated many novel proposals to revamp the political and economic systems. Some of them may be revived and become the blueprint of the reformers.

Economic Reform. Following the pattern of changes in Eastern Europe, reform in price formation and ownership of state enterprises may become the two focal points. Zhao in summer 1988 had proposed decontrol of major industrial prices. In the beginning of 1989, several young economists with close ties to Zhao had openly called for the end of state ownership of industry, to be accomplished by transferring state-owned companies to shareholders, which would include individuals, universities, institutions, and local governments. Many economists suggested that a new definition of socialism was needed, one focusing on broad issues of social justice, such as equality of opportunity, instead of on public ownership of the means of production. The proposal of moving toward a system of shareholder ownership had gained endorsement from the Communist Party under the leadership of Zhao[50] and might be revived by the reformers.

To eliminate the huge budget deficit and to stimulate peasant incentive, the sale of farmland to the tillers is another measure the reformers could adopt. At a price of 500 yuan per *mu* (one mu = 0.1647 acre), the 1.6 billion *mu* of farmland would be worth 800 billion yuan. Under a ten-year installment payment plan, the state would receive up to 80 billion yuan annually from the peasant households. The land-sale revenue could help phase out the budget deficit and reduce inflation. In recent years, because of the shortage of consumer goods, peasants have accumulated sizable savings. Government statistics showed that household savings at the end of 1989 had reached a record high of 513 billion yuan. A part of these savings could be used to pay for the purchase of land.

Developmental Policy. To tackle the problem of widespread unemployment and to revive the sagging economy, expanding the private sector and attracting more overseas investment are two methods. A burgeoning private sector would create new job opportunities for the unemployed, generate tax revenues for the state coffers, and increase incentive for the producers. Privatization and internationalization could help the PRC out of its predicament.

Political Reform. Realizing the interdependence of economic development and political liberalization, the reformers would be likely to undertake the dismantling of the corrupt, entrenched bureaucracy and the Stalinist totalitarian state. The reformers would have to deal with the separation of Party and state; the division of power among legislature, judiciary, and executive; the direct election of deputies to the NPC; and the protection of basic human rights. With these basic reforms, the PRC would then evolve into a democratic and pluralistic society.

Policy Toward Taiwan and Hong Kong. Both Chinese communities could become enthusiastic participants in the reform, if the leaders adopted appropriate policies. Instead of threatening the security of these two communities, Beijing's new leaders should renounce the use of force to settle disputes and repeal the provision allowing the stationing of troops in Hong Kong after 1997. If Beijing were to treat Taipei as an equal partner rather than as a local government, mutual trust could eventually develop and large-scale economic cooperation could be promoted.

Although the reformers would undoubtedly encounter an array of tormenting problems, the country could march forward again, with the support of the populace and the overseas Chinese. This occurred once, in 1931–1936, after the collapse of the warlords and again, in 1978–1985, after the conclusion of the Cultural Revolution.

The Rise of Regional Independence

The worst-case scenario would be the disintegration of the central authority after a prolonged power struggle in the Party hierarchy and a breakdown of the major military command. Ambitious provincial governors or powerful regional military commanders would develop their territories into independent or semi-independent strongholds, reviving the warlordism of the 1920s.

During the 1916–1927 period, the lack of a strong power holder generated a period of chaos and upheaval. Competition between the warlords, each of whom occupied one or several provinces with the support of foreign powers, rendered this period the darkest in the history of republican China.[51] With the advent of communism, the Party controlled the armed forces and eradicated the warlords. Both Mao and Deng adopted a policy of continual shuffling of commanders in military regions in order to destroy their strongholds. But during the Cultural Revolution, the rise of the military's power, especially that of the regional commanders, began to threaten the Beijing authorities and caused the Wuhan Incident in July 1967 (see Chapter 5).

In recent years, the delegation of economic power to local authorities has led to the emergence of economic regionalism. To increase their tax base, each locality has taken measures to protect its own interests by restricting or banning movement of raw materials and consumer goods out of its territory. Localities have even set up checkpoints along their peripheries to collect duties for goods delivered to other localities.[52] The incipient economic regionalism may lay the foundation for regional independence, for it provides the ambitious regional commander with a financial base.

Of the PRC's thirty provinces, municipalities, and autonomous regions, six have a strong enough historical background and economic potential to become independent. They are Guangdong, in the south, the most dynamic province; Sichuan, in southwest China, with a population of 110 million; Xinjiang, on the Soviet border, with one-seventh of the country's territory; and the three northeast provinces, Liaoning, Jilin, and Heilongjiang, together known as Manchuria, where most of the PRC's heavy industry is located.

The southern province of Guangdong was the original base of the 1911 revolution. Guangdong has also been the birthplace of most overseas Chinese, including the majority of the 6.5 million residents in Hong Kong and Macao. Historically, the Cantonese have had a strong tendency to defy orders of inept or corrupt government authorities. In the ten years of the open door, Guangdong has emerged as the PRC's most developed area. In 1988, Guangdong was the PRC's top exporter.

Before moving to Sichuan, Zhao Ziyang had served as Party secretary in Guangdong for several years. As a result, Zhao has many supporters in Guangdong, Hong Kong, and Hainan. Should the central authorities crumble, Guangdong could be the first province to defy Beijing's order. Together with Hong Kong, Macao, and Hainan, Guangdong could become a formidable political and economic force to be reckoned with.

The second potential candidate for independence probably would be Sichuan, the most populous province—it has 10 percent of the nation's total—with an area double the size of Guangdong. Sichuan was the base of the Nationalist government during the Sino-Japanese War. Since 1949, Sichuan has been developed into a new industrial area. Zhao Ziyang served as Party secretary there before he was named premier and has retained connections and influence in this province.

Other potential independent regions include Xinjiang, in the far west, bordering the Soviet Union, and Manchuria in the northeast. Both areas historically were strongholds of warlords. During the 1920s and 1930s, warlords in Xinjiang, with Soviet-backed armed forces, attempted unsuccessfully to build the area into an independent state. Between 1932 and 1945, the three northeast provinces under Japanese manipulation became the puppet state of Manchukuo (the Manchu State). Although few people expect that the PRC will break apart, the rapid rise of economic regionalism—if combined with military power—could render the Beijing authorities impotent and hamper the Four Modernizations.

Toward a Greater Chinese Common Market

The best scenario would be for the reformers to move toward the Taiwan–Hong Kong model and to unite the four Chinese communities—the PRC, Taiwan, Hong Kong, and Singapore—to form a common market, thus laying a foundation for national reunification in the future.

It seems likely today that in the twenty-first century the world economy will be dominated by three major economic forces, North America, Western Europe, and Japan. If separate, the PRC, Taiwan, Hong Kong, and Singapore will only be peripheral states. By uniting, the four Chinese communities could constitute a formidable economic bloc. Based on 1988 statistics, they had a combined population of 1.12 billion—the PRC, 1.084 billion; Taiwan, 19.5 million; Hong Kong, 5.6 million; and Singapore, 2.6 million. The Chinese common market would account for one-fifth of the world's population. In terms of GNP, the 1988 gross national products of these four Chinese communities totaled around $524 billion. Compared to the United States, Western Europe, and Japan, the GNP appears rather small. But the share would increase rapidly if all four exhibited above-average growth rates in the next two decades.

The strength of the Chinese common market rests on its exporting capacity. Embracing three of the four "small dragons" of East Asia, total foreign trade for these four Chinese communities in 1988 amounted to $430 billion, almost equaling Japan's total trade in the same year. The developmental potential of this common market is enormous. The PRC possesses unparalleled manpower and natural resources. Taiwan has the world's second largest foreign-exchange reserve. Hong Kong is the world's third largest financial center, and Singapore is the most important trading center in Southeast Asia. The combined economic force of these four would rival Japan's in the Far East.

However, as the two parts of China are still politically antagonistic to each other, the formation of such a common market promises to be a difficult task. Several preconditions are required.

1. The PRC would first have to renounce the use of force to solve disputes and would have to continue its economic and political reforms to narrow the gap between the two sides of the Taiwan Strait.
2. Taiwan would have to abandon the existing "three no's" policy and remove barriers for direct trade, investment, and personal exchanges.
3. The PRC would have to keep its promise to maintain Hong Kong's existing social, economic, and legal systems after the 1997 reversion.

If trade and investment relations were improved, mutual trust could be gradually established and political dialogue between the two governments could then be opened. Thus, the formation of a common market not only could put the economic potentials of the four Chinese communities into full play, it could also lay a solid foundation for China's future reunification.[53] The idea of a greater Chinese Common Market is still an academic concept rather than a reality, but it has been greeted enthusiastically by economists and government officials in Taipei, Hong Kong, and China.[54]

In reality, the scenarios outlined above may not exhaust the many possibilities. In the next five to ten years the most likely would be the first or second. Scenario three is less likely, and scenario four represents an idealist's solution.

Although the road from Tiananmen is littered with obstacles, the long-term prospect (let us say, thirty to fifty years) for the PRC's becoming a world economic power is still possible. The success stories of Taiwan, Hong Kong, and Singapore testify to the ingenuity and vitality of the Chinese people and point the PRC in the right direction. With the passing of the hard-line veterans, a change in leadership may bring about a radical alteration in political and economic systems, which could usher in a period of stability and prosperity. If the two sides of the Taiwan Strait eventually become united, Taiwan's capital, technology, and managerial skills, combined with the PRC's manpower, material resources, and market, may rebuild China into a modern industrial state. The 1989 "June Fourth Movement," as one Western scholar called it, like the 1919 "May Fourth Movement," may become a major turning point in Chinese history.[55]

Notes

1. These are the views of several famous scholars who fled the PRC after the massacre. See for instance, Su Shaozhi, director of the Institute of Marxism, Leninism, and Mao Zedong Thought at the Chinese Academy of Social Sciences, "The Origins and Effects of the 1989 Democracy Movement," *Ming Pao* (Hong Kong), Sept. 5, 1989, p. 3.

2. Yan Jiaqi, "China Is Hardly a Republic," *Ming Pao*, July 23–24, 1989, p. 6.

3. "The Causes and Consequences of the Beijing Incident," by a high-ranking Party official, *World Journal* (New York), Sept. 12–13, 1989, p. 33.

4. Quoted from *Wall Street Journal*, June 16, 1989, p. 4.

5. *New York Times*, Sept. 26, 1988, p. 7, and Nicholas D. Kristof, "How the Hardliners Won," *New York Times Magazine*, Nov. 12, 1989, p. 41.

6. For other inside information on Deng's decision, see *China Daily News* (New York), May 23, 1989, p. 1. In a public speech at Columbia University, Chen Yizi also disclosed similar information. See *World Journal*, Sunday Supplement, Oct. 29, 1989, p. 6.

7. *Beijing Review*, May 15–21, 1989, pp. 10–11.

8. Liu Guoguang, "Major Changes in China's Economy," *Beijing Review* 29, No. 49 (Dec. 8, 1986), p. 17.

9. Li Yining, "Possibilities for China's Ownership Reform," *Beijing Review*, 29, No. 52 (Dec. 27, 1986), pp. 17–19.

10. Quoted from *Massacre in Beijing: China's Struggle for Democracy* (New York: Time, 1989), p. 120.

11. *Wall Street Journal*, Oct. 30, 1989, p. 31.

12. Karen Elliott House and Barry Wain, "Singapore's Prime Minister Lee Kuan Yew Surveys Asia," *Wall Street Journal*, Nov. 1, 1989, p. A15.

13. Deng Xiaoping, "The Primary Task of Veteran Cadre Is to Select Young and Middle-aged Cadres for Promotion," in *Selected Works of Deng Xiaoping (1975–1982)* (Beijing: Foreign Languages Press, 1984), p. 361.

14. For a detailed discussion of the PRC's foreign policy in the 1990s, see Robert G. Sutter, "China's Foreign Policy in the 1990s and Its Implications for the United States," paper presented at the 31st Annual Meeting of the American Association of Chinese Studies, Aug. 23–25, 1989, at the University of Wyoming.

15. *Wall Street Journal*, Oct. 26, 1989, p. A11.

16. See Chen Yizi's speech at Columbia University, p. 6.

17. See Deng's speech to military leaders, *New York Times*, June 30, 1989, p. 4.

18. "Chinese Despotism's Death Throes," *Wall Street Journal*, June 6, 1989, p. A11.

19. Frederic E. Wakeman, Jr., "The June Fourth Movement in China," *Items* (Social Science Research Council) 43, No. 3 (Sept. 1989), p. 64.

20. "All Fire and Vengeance, the Dragons are Loose," *New York Times*, June 24, 1989, p. 4.

21. State Statistical Bureau, PRC, *Statistical Yearbook of China 1987* (Hong Kong: Longman Group, 1988), p. 404; and "Communique for 1988 Economic Development," *People's Daily*, March 1, 1989, p. 3.

22. *People's Daily*, Sept. 30, 1989, p. 1.

23. *China Reconstructs* 38, No. 10 (Oct. 1989), pp. 33–41.

24. *World Journal*, Sept. 7, 1989, p. 33.

25. *Zhongguo Tongzi* [China's statistics] (Beijing), May 1989, p. 24.

26. The 169.8 billion yuan figure is from *Beijing Review*, Sept. 4–10, 1989, p. 26. The 75 billion yuan figure is from *Wen Wei Po* (Hong Kong), Aug. 24, 1989, p. 1.

27. *Pei-mei Daily* [North American daily] (New York), Oct. 26, 1987, p. 4.

28. For details see State Statistical Bureau, PRC, "Economic Structural Imbalance: Its Causes and Correctives," *Beijing Review*, Sept. 4–10, 1989, pp. 22–28.

29. Ibid.

30. Ibid.

31. Liu Guoguang, "Economic Reform Faces New Challenges," *Beijing Review*, March 27–Apr. 12, 1989, pp. 20–22.

32. *Beijing Review*, Oct. 30–Nov. 5, 1989, p. 21.

33. *World Journal*, Nov. 2, 1989, p. 32.

34. *People's Daily*, July 5, 1989, p. 1.

35. *China Times* (Taipei), Aug. 11, 1989, p. 7.

36. State Statistical Bureau, "Communique on 1988 Economic Development," *People's Daily*, March 1, 1989, p. 3.

37. *New York Times*, Oct. 8, 1989, p. 1

38. *People's Daily*, Nov. 3, 1989, p. 3

39. *New York Times*, Nov. 14, 1989, p. 4.

40. This is the view of experts in Taiwan and Hong Kong. See *China Times*, Nov. 10, 1989, p. 3.

41. *China Times*, Oct. 31, 1989, p. 9.

42. *New York Times*, June 14, 1989, p. 9, and *China Times*, Oct. 4, 1989, p. 7.

43. Council for Economic Planning and Development, ROC, *Taiwan Statistical Data Book 1989* (Taipei, 1989), p. 208.

44. Commentator's article, *People's Daily*, Oct. 28, 1989, p. 1.

45. *New York Times*, Sept. 26, 1988, p. 7.

46. This information was provided by the U.S. ambassador to China, James Lilley, in a talk delivered in early November 1989 in Hong Kong. See Editorial, *Wall Street Journal*, Nov. 10, 1989.

47. Claudia Rosett, "The Powderkeg That Is China," *Wall Street Journal*, Dec. 28, 1989.

48. *World Journal*, Dec. 29, 1989, p. 1.

49. This view is held by many Western and China observers. See Kristof, op. cit., p. 71.

50. *New York Times*, Jan. 10, 1989, pp. 1, 4.

51. Immanuel C.Y. Hsu, *The Rise of Modern China*, 3d ed. (New York: Oxford University Press, 1983), p. 482.

52. Commentator's article, *People's Daily*, Nov. 1, 1986, p. 1.

53. The idea of a greater Chinese Common Market was initiated by this author. See Chu-yuan Cheng, "Toward a Greater Chinese Common Market," *China Times*, June 9, 1988, p. 2.

54. The director and deputy director of the Institute of Taiwan Studies under the Chinese Academy of Social Sciences in Beijing have echoed this idea with some modifications. See Li Jiaquan, "More on Reunification of Taiwan with Mainland," *Beijing Review*, Jan. 16–22, 1989, pp. 26–30. The *World Economic Herald* openly endorsed the concept. See *World Economic Herald* (Shanghai), Dec. 19, 1988, and Jan. 16, 1989. Chen Ping, president, Chinese Young Economists Association in America, hailed the proposal as the key to China's modernization. See Chen Ping, "The Future of Pacific Basin and China's Global Policy," *Forum of Chinese Young Economists* (Austin, Tex.), Summer 1988, pp. 44–45.

55. Wakeman, op. cit., pp. 57–64.

Appendix 1: Chronology
(April 15–July 15, 1989)

April 15	Hu Yaobang dies. Students at Beijing University put up posters praising him and indirectly criticizing his opponents, who forced his resignation after student demonstrations in 1986–1987.
April 17	Thousands of students march in Beijing and Shanghai shouting, "Long live Hu Yaobang! Long live democracy!"
April 18	About 2,000 students from Beijing head into Tiananmen Square by bicycle, continuing the protest, and hold a sit-in at the Great Hall of the People. They demand freedom of the press, release of political prisoners, repudiation of past official campaigns against liberalism, more money for education, abolition of regulations against demonstrations, and an apology from the government for various unspecified mistakes. They also want leaders to reveal their incomes and reevaluate Hu Yaobang.
April 19	More than 10,000 people take over Beijing's central square in front of the Communist Party headquarters in a rally for democracy. The police break up the protest.
April 20	At least 10,000 defy a ban on political protests and march on Communist Party headquarters for the second time. Students again demand a reappraisal of Hu, a repudiation of past crackdowns on intellectuals, and freedom of the press. Two thousand police file out of several nearby buildings to disperse the student demonstrators.
April 21	More than 100,000 gather in Tiananmen Square to mourn Hu. The *People's Daily* publishes a fierce criticism of the students: "Those who take advantage of the mourning for Comrade Yaobang and charge, smash, rob, or set fire to offices of the Communist Party or the government will be condemned by history." Tens of thousands of students camp all night in the square to prevent the government from closing off the area.
April 22	Students defy police orders to leave the square. Tens of thousands join them on the square, while official memorial ceremonies are held for Hu. Chinese leaders going to the memorial observe the demonstrations from behind a wall of soldiers. Riots break out in Xi'an and Changsha. In Changsha, rioters smash and rob twenty-four shops. In Xi'an, crowds attack the provincial government headquarters, burning several buildings, twenty houses, and ten vehicles.

April 23	University students plan class boycotts, which they say will continue until their demands are met. They demand public disclosure of the income and assets of the PRC's leaders and their children.
April 24	The Communist Party bans an issue of the *World Economic Herald*, which had printed bold criticism of the Party. Jiang Zemin, Party leader in Shanghai, gives order that the *Herald* cannot be distributed. Tens of thousands of students at Beijing universities begin a class boycott, demanding a dialogue with the government.
April 25	The Communist Party calls the student unrest "a grave political struggle." The CCP charges that the unrest was a conspiracy to wrest power from the Party. Students gather at Beijing University to discuss strategy. Mood is defiant.
April 26	An editorial in the *People's Daily* states that the students' purpose is to poison people's minds, create national turmoil, and sabotage the nation's political stability. It claims that the protest is a planned conspiracy which, in essence, aims at negating the leadership of the party and the socialist system. Qin Benli, editor-in-chief of the *World Economic Herald* in Shanghai, is suspended and his paper put under censorship. The Party summons an urgent meeting of 20,000 Communist Party officials in Beijing and Shanghai. There are unconfirmed reports that at least 10,000 troops from the 38th Army have been moved from Hebei Province to Beijing.
April 27	Demonstrators numbering 150,000, with wide support from people on the street, surge past police lines and fill Tiananmen Square, chanting slogans for democracy. Students promote populist themes like official corruption and inflation. The government responds in the evening by agreeing to the students' demand for discussions with officials.
April 29	Government officials meet with student leaders, but independent student groups vow to continue a class boycott.
April 30	Wang Dan, a twenty-year-old Beijing University history student and the movement's best-known leader, is singled out by the CCP for attack in anonymous wall posters. Wuer Kaixi, a twenty-one-year-old from Chinese Turkestan, emerges as chairman of the illegal student group that organized the protest movement.
May 1	Students gather at Beijing University to discuss plans for expanding the prodemocracy movement.
May 2	Tens of thousands of university students in Shanghai demonstrate for democracy. They demand that Qin Benli be reinstated as editor-in-chief of the *World Economic Herald.*
May 3	Zhao Ziyang delivers an address on the topic, "Carry the Spirit of the May Fourth Movement Further in the New Era of Reform and Construction." He emphasizes the importance of stability and calls upon his listeners to take a clear stand in opposing disorder. Yuan Mu, the government spokesman, hints at a crackdown later, saying that now was not an appropriate time for arrests. Yuan also suggests that Fang Lizhi played a role in the unrest. Wuer Kaixi denies Fang's involvement.
May 4	About 100,000 students and supporters march on Tiananmen Square to celebrate the seventieth anniversary of the May Fourth Movement. State-employed journalists participate, including many from the *People's*

Daily and the Xinhua News Agency. The journalists call for the reinstatement of Qin Benli and protest the false and biased reporting of the student protests. Thousands of workers defy the government warning of dismissal if they attended the march, and cheering onlookers line the streets. Demonstrations are held in Shanghai, Nanjing, and other cities. In Shanghai, 20,000 march. In Changchun, 8,000 to 10,000 student demonstrators gather at the provincial headquarters. Zhao Ziyang adopts a conciliatory tone urging in a speech that the "reasonable demands from the students should be met through democratic and legal means." Students start returning to classes.

May 6   Five student leaders present a petition to the Central Committee of the Chinese Communist Party, the Standing Committee of the National People's Congress, and the State Council requesting that a dialogue be arranged as soon as possible.

May 9   Thirty representatives present a petition signed by more than 1,000 journalists calling for talks about the independence of the press, broader coverage of the student demonstrations, and the dismissal of Qin Benli.

May 10   More than 5,000 students parade on bicycles to show support for journalists who have called for greater press freedom. At a meeting with a delegation from the Communist Party of Bulgaria, Zhao Ziyang declares that "unless we carry out a reform of the political system, there will be no way to overcome our economic difficulties."

May 13   More than 2,000 students begin a hunger strike in Tiananmen Square. Thousands flock to the square a day later to back the students. The number fasting rises to 3,000. Li Peng maintains in a speech to workers that the PRC is in need of "a political situation of stability and solidarity."

May 14   Twelve well-known intellectuals draft a joint "Urgent Appeal" urging Zhao Ziyang and Li Peng to open a dialogue with the students and persuade them to leave Tiananmen Square.

May 15   Welcoming ceremony for Mikhail Gorbachev near Tiananmen Square is moved to airport as thousands fill the square. Citizens show organized participation in the movement. Hunger strikers demand direct talks with government officials, a favorable reevaluation of the student movement, and a retraction of the April 26 editorial in the *People's Daily*. A crowd of 150,000 protesters and spectators rally to show support for the hunger strikers. Yuan Mu declares that the April 26 editorial in the *People's Daily* was not directed at most of the students. He concedes that the editorial failed to distinguish between a very small number of conspirators and the great majority of patriotic students.

May 16   About 300,000 workers, students, and onlookers occupy Tiananmen Square. Many wave banners calling for Deng Xiaoping's retirement. Gorbachev's visit to the Monument to the Heroes of the People is cancelled because of demonstrations. Journalists and intellectuals join the protest, including the presidents of thirty universities, who issue an open letter urging that the government meet with the students. Gorbachev and Deng meet and jointly announce that PRC-Soviet ties are in the process of being normalized. At a meeting between Gorbachev and Zhao Ziyang, Zhao states that since 1978 Deng has been the leader of the PRC. A resolution passed by the First Plenum of the Thirteenth Party Central Committee declares that Deng is to make all decisions on matters of great importance.

May 17   Zhao's predawn plea for students to leave is rejected by students. More than 1 million Chinese take to the streets to support calls for more democracy. On the fifth day of the strike, 3,000 hunger strikers galvanize support in Beijing. Demonstrations in support of hunger strikers are held in twenty-one other cities. In Shanghai and Tianjin, nearly 30,000 students rally. Presidents of eight universities, leaders of small "democratic political parties," and the central committees of the Chinese Communist Youth League call on the government to heed the students.

May 18   About 1 million people, including many workers, again take to the streets to show their support for the hunger strikers. Government arranges a nationally televised meeting between Li Peng and the student leaders of the prodemocracy movement. Li sternly lectures student leaders during the meeting.

May 19   A tearful Zhao makes a predawn visit to weakened hunger strikers, urging them to end the strike. Li also visits briefly with students. Students decide to end the hunger strike.

May 20   Premier Li Peng calls for "resolute and powerful measures to curb turmoil." He states that "if we fail to put an end to such chaos immediately and let it go unchecked, it will very likely lead to a situation which none of us want to see." The State Council issues a decree that as of ten o'clock on that day, martial law will be in effect in Beijing. The government calls troops into the capital, ordering a crackdown on the democracy movement. Tens of thousands of ordinary Chinese immobilize a convoy of twenty-one trucks, carrying 1,000 troops. Zhao Ziyang is stripped of all power but retains his title as general secretary of the Party. The commanding officer of the 38th Army reportedly refuses an order from Deng to move the troops to the capital. Troops from the 27th Army in nearby Hebei Province are summoned instead. Huge throngs amounting to over 1 million people defy martial law and prevent troops from reaching the center of the capital. Half a million people demonstrate in Shanghai; Xi'an is brought to a standstill by 300,000 protesters; rallies occur in at least a half-dozen other cities.

May 21   Troops arrive from the military regions of Jinan, Shenyang, Chengdu, and other regions surrounding Beijing. Throngs continue to clog the intersections along roadways leading to Beijing's central square. Students continue their sit-in in Tiananmen Square. In Hong Kong 400,000 to 500,000 take to the streets to show their support of the prodemocracy movement.

May 22   Workers and students block new advances by army convoys, preventing a military crackdown. Tanks turn back when thousands of citizens block their way and refuse to move. Several dozen top legislators begin preparing a strategy to revoke martial law. The Central Advisory Commission and the Central Discipline Inspection Committee of the CCP send a joint letter to the Central Committee supporting the use of troops to crush the student movement. A television newscast states: "The public-order situation is probably going to get worse. The army must fulfill the Government's command. We have the duty to resort to any effective means to change the situation."

May 23   After meeting with President Bush, Wan Li, the chairman of the Standing Committee of the National People's Congress, announces that he will cut short his visit to the United States and return to the PRC.

May 24   Military and Party leaders of the seven military regions overwhelmingly express their support for the stand taken by Li Peng.

May 25   Li Peng appears on television and expresses the hope that "the troops will overcome the difficulties confronting them and successfully impose martial law." Wan Li returns from a trip to the United States but stops in Shanghai for medical treatment. Li suggests that Zhao was using the disturbances to seize power. A spokesman for the Ministry of Foreign Affairs declares that Zhao is still general secretary of the Central Committee of the CCP. About 100,000 workers and students hold new demonstrations in Beijing to demand Li's resignation.

May 27   Wan Li issues a written statement declaring his support for Li Peng's speech of May 19 and the resolution passed by the Standing Committee of the Politburo of the CCP Central Committee to suppress the upheavals firmly.

May 28   Students vote to stay in the square until a June 20 meeting of the Standing Committee of the National People's Congress. The World Bank moves out of its Beijing office and suspends all negotiations for any further loans.

May 30   Students erect a thirty-foot-high Statue of Liberty in Tiananmen Square. Only 10,000 students still occupy the square.

June 1   The Beijing Colleges and Universities Association and the Tiananmen Square Headquarters in a joint statement put forth four preconditions to dialogue: (1) lift martial law; (2) withdraw the troops; (3) give assurances that no form of retaliatory measures will be taken against anyone who had taken part in the democracy movement; (4) discontinue news censorship.

June 2   Unarmed soldiers make a half-hearted pass at dispersing the crowd but quickly retreat. An article in the *People's Daily* points out that the statue in Tiananmen Square flagrantly violates laws and regulations and urges that it be pulled down.

June 3, 2 P.M.   Troops hurl tear-gas shells and beat up people trying to stop them from moving into the center of Beijing. Students hold fast and with civilian help surround the 1,200 troops again. Soldiers retreat. PLA Martial Law Enforcement Troops issue the announcement that if those people impeded the troops from executing their maneuvers, that would give the troops the right to adopt means to "force compliance."

June 4, 2 A.M.   A convoy of fifty trucks with foot soldiers barrel along the crowded streets that lead to the square. Advance troops torch barricades of buses and trucks. Ten thousand strong, the soldiers level their AK-47 assault rifles and begin to fire away at the mobs. Huge streams of people flee along Changan Avenue. By 5 A.M. Tiananmen is emptied of almost all protesters. In Chengdu, violent clashes take place.

June 5   The army tightens its hold on the center of Beijing. Outraged citizens continue to attack and burn army vehicles. The death toll rises to at least several hundred. President Bush announces the suspension of arms sales and the discontinuation of nongovernmental exports of military hardware to the PRC.

June 6   Clashes between military units are reported. The shooting of civilians continues. A man blocks a convoy of tanks for a few minutes. In Nanjing 10,000 people gather to mourn the deaths of Beijing civilians. Fang Lizhi and his wife enter the American Embassy in Beijing for personal safety. Yuan Mu, spokesman for the State Council, announces that 6,000 troops were wounded and nearly 300 soldiers and rioters died. In Shanghai, a train runs over a crowd blocking the track, killing 6 people and wounding 6 more. The crowd burns the train cars in retaliation.

June 7   The government denies reports of fighting between military units. Public security officers begin a complete search and arrest of people involved in the democracy movement.

June 8   A major convoy of tanks and trucks returns to the capital. Firing at diplomatic compounds occurs. Premier Li Peng and Vice President Wang Zhen reappear and visit with the troops and officers of a martial law enforcement unit. The army tightens its grip on Beijing. Bush bars normal ties with the PRC. A government spokesman claims that 300 are dead and 7,000 injured.

June 9   Deng appears on Chinese television and praises the soldiers: "Facing a life-threatening situation, our troops never forgot the people, never forgot the Party, never forgot the country's interest." Tens of thousands of students rally in Shanghai. The government names Fang Lizhi as the real culprit behind the unrest.

June 10   Chinese authorities arrest 400 in Beijing, including several leaders of student and labor organizations, for engaging in "counter-revolutionary riots." The Beijing Public Security Bureau issues warrants for the arrest of Fang Lizhi and his wife, Li Shuxian.

June 11   The total number of arrests reaches 1,000. Border troops and public security units are put on alert to guard against student protesters leaving the country.

June 12   The government bans unofficial prodemocracy organizations and gives police the right to shoot rioters. Official broadcasts state that "Fang Lizhi and Li Shuxian together engaged in counter-revolutionary propaganda and instigation." The *Beijing Daily News* attacks the Voice of America (VOA) for "fabrications." U.S. Secretary of State James A. Baker meets with the Chinese ambassador, Han Xu, in an effort to solve the Fang Lizhi issue.

June 13   Moderates appear on TV, easing fears of wholesale purge. A wanted list for twenty-one student leaders, including Wuer Kaixi, Wang Dan, and Chai Ling, is issued.

June 14   The PRC orders the expulsion of two Beijing-based U.S. journalists, including one from the Voice of America. Two student leaders—Zhou Fengsuo and Xiong Yan—are arrested. Chai Ling is nominated for the 1990 Nobel Peace Prize by two lawmakers in Norway.

June 15   Three workers accused of wrecking traffic tools and equipment in Shanghai are sentenced to death. The government accuses the VOA of reports that distort the facts.

June 16   Yuan Mu, spokesman for the State Council, states that no casualties occurred during the martial law troops' clearing of Tiananmen Square,

	no one was killed, and that the foreign impression of a military bloodbath at Tiananmen is false.
June 17	The Beijing Intermediate People's Court sentences eight people who participated in the "counter-revolutionary riots" to death.
June 18	Liu Binyan predicts that the maximum life expectancy of the current regime is two years.
June 19	The General Political Department of the PLA requests that all military officers study the main points of Deng Xiaoping's "Uphold the Four Basic Principles, and Reject Bourgeois Liberalization."
June 20	The U.S. government formally appeals to Chinese leaders to deal more leniently with those sentenced to death and to stop the widespread arrests.
June 21	Three men who set a Shanghai train on fire are executed. Beijing authorities make new visa arrangements to prevent those who participated in the democratic movement from going abroad.
June 22	National television and radio announce the arrest of thirteen spies allegedly working for the rival government in Taiwan to foment unrest during the student democracy movement.
June 23	Beijing public security personnel arrest seventeen teachers and students at Beijing University of Medicine and other universities.
June 24	The Fourth Plenum of the Thirteenth Party Central Committee concludes and issues a communiqué condemning Zhao Ziyang for "supporting the revolt and dividing the Party." Jiang Zemin is appointed the new general secretary of the Party.
June 25	Yan Jiaqi, a well-known political scholar, and his wife escape to Hong Kong.
June 27	The European Economic Community's twelve member nations appeal to the PRC to stop executing members of the democracy movement and put into effect a ban on selling military weapons to the Beijing government.
June 29	The eighth meeting of the Standing Committee of the Seventh National People's Congress convenes, with Wan Li, committee chairman, presiding. Wan stresses that the PRC will continue to develop its socialist democracy and legal system.
June 30	The Standing Committee of the Seventh National People's Congress dismisses Zhao Ziyang from his position as vice chairman of the state Central Military Commission. Beijing Mayor Chen Xitong reports that during the "counter-revolutionary riot" more than 6,000 military and police personnel were injured and more than 10 died, and 3,000 civilians were injured and 200 died, including 36 students.
July 1	On the sixty-eighth anniversary of the founding of the CCP, an editorial in the *People's Daily* calls for rigorous enforcement of ideological conformity and punishment for those who deviated from the official line.
July 2	Jiang Zemin, CCP general secretary, tells revolutionary veterans that a thorough shake-up is needed at every level within the party to resolve serious problems.
July 3	Wang Dan, a history student at Beijing University who led the student protests, is arrested.
July 4	Yan Jiaqi and Wuer Kaixi, two leaders of the prodemocracy movement who escaped from the PRC, announce in Paris the formation of an

	international exile organization to continue their campaign for liberty in the PRC.

July 5   Official newspapers in Beijing report nearly 50 new arrests in the nationwide crackdown on protesters. The newly reported arrests add to the over 2,500 people already taken into custody in the nationwide sweep.

July 6   Two more people are sentenced to death for rioting in the southwestern city of Chengdu.

July 7   The seventh session of the Standing Committee of the CPPCC Seventh National Committee approves the "Report on the Mistakes of Comrade Zhao Ziyang Committed During the Anti-Party and Anti-Socialist Turmoil," delivered by Li Peng.

July 8   The Chinese government orders the expulsion of Mark Hopkins, correspondent for the Voice of America, for violating his visa status and the terms of martial law.

July 9   The *People's Daily*, in a lengthy editorial, assails the United States and "anti-Communist international capitalists" for trying to subvert socialism in the PRC.

July 10   The *Beijing Daily* reports that more than 2,000 graduating students at Qinghua University have been required to attend political reeducation sessions.

July 11   Yuan Mu, spokesman for the State Council, blames Zhao Ziyang for growing corruption and indicates that a continuing investigation would determine whether Zhao would stand trial.

July 12   Wuer Kaixi and Li Lu, two student leaders, reappear in public in Paris accompanied by a French government minister.

July 13   Chinese authorities execute two more men linked to the prodemocracy protests in June and issue a ten-year jail sentence for a "rumormonger" who was caught after being interviewed on U.S. television.

July 14   The U.S. Senate votes 81 to 10 to impose economic sanctions against the PRC and to urge President George Bush to take even harsher measures.

Appendix 2:
Profiles of Fifty Major Figures

Bao Tong (b. 1932) Reform leader. Bao was chief policy adviser to Zhao Ziyang. A member of the CCP Thirteenth Central Committee, he was appointed in February 1989 to head the Party's Political Structural Reform Research Center. Bao was identified by Beijing mayor Chen Xitong as the author of Zhao's May 4, 1989, speech delivered to the Asian Development Bank meeting. This speech was denounced by the hardliners and Bao was arrested on June 3, 1989. On July 7, he was accused in the Party newspaper of being a member of the "anti-Party and antisocialist group."

Bao Zunxin (b. 1937) Prodemocracy leader. A renowned historian and thinker, Bao served as an associate research fellow at the Institute of Chinese History of the Chinese Academy of Social Sciences. He served concurrently as the editor of *Du Shu* (Study) magazine. On April 21, 1989, he persuaded forty-seven noted intellectuals to publish a joint letter to the CCP Central Committee, the Standing Committee of NPC, and the State Council, praising Hu Yaobang as a symbol of the PRC's democratization and expressing their full support of the student demonstrators. He also helped to found the Beijing Autonomous Intellectual Union. Bao was arrested and expelled from the Party in early July 1989.

Bo Yibo (b. 1908) Hard-line octogenarian leader. Vice chairman, CCP Central Advisory Commission. He joined the CCP in 1926 and was elected to the CCP Seventh Central Committee in 1945–1946. Bo served as vice chairman of the North China People's Government, 1948–1949; political commissar, North China Military Region, 1948; minister of finance, 1949–1953; chairman, State Construction Commission, 1954–1956; State Economic Commission, 1956; member, CCP Eighth Central Committee, 1956; vice chairman, State Planning Commission, 1962. Purged during the Cultural Revolution, he was rehabilitated in 1978. Bo became vice premier in 1978, member of the State Council and vice chairman of the State Economic Structural Reform Committee in 1982; member of the CCP Central Advisory Commission (CAC) in 1983; and vice chairman of the CAC in 1987.

Chai Ling (b. 1966) Student leader. Chai Ling graduated from Beijing University and was a graduate student in child psychology at Beijing Normal University. Chai joined her husband, Feng Congde, in the April 27 demonstration and the May hunger strike; she became commander of Tiananmen Square on May 22. Before the massacre began, she pleaded with fellow students to leave the square. On June 8, her emotional eyewitness account of the massacre was broadcast on Hong Kong television stations.

She was among the twenty-one people on the government's most-wanted list. In early April 1990, she and her husband escaped to the West.

Chen Xitong (b. 1930) Hard-line leader. Mayor of Beijing. He graduated from Beijing University. Before becoming the vice mayor of Beijing in December 1979, he served in different local Party capacities. In August 1981 he became secretary of the CCP Beijing committee. He was elected member of the Twelfth and Thirteenth Central committees in 1982 and 1987. Since 1983, he has been mayor and director of the Planning and Construction Committee of Beijing. He has also been a State Council member since January 1988. Chen's report "Checking the Turmoil and Quelling the Counter-revolutionary Rebellion," delivered to the Standing Committee of the NPC on June 30, 1989, provided an official version of the massacre.

Chen Yizi (b. 1940) Reform leader. Chief adviser of Zhao. A graduate of Beijing University and director of the Economic Structural Reform Research Institute of the State Council, Chen was recognized as the architect of many of Zhao's reform programs. On May 19, 1989, knowing that Zhao had lost, Chen proposed the convening of a special session of the NPC and a special congress of the CCP to resolve political crisis. Having been on the most-wanted list, he hid for several weeks before fleeing to France.

Chen Yun (b. 1905) Leading figure of the hard-line octogenarians. He is chairman of the CCP Central Advisory Commission and widely regarded as the second most powerful man in the CCP. He began his career as one of the organizers of the "May Thirtieth Movement" in 1925. Joining the CCP in 1925, he sat on seven CCP central committees—from 1931 until 1987. In 1934, he became a member of the Politburo. After participating in the Long March in 1934–1935, he returned to Shanghai to develop the Party's underground network. He subsequently went to Moscow, where he worked as a member of the CCP delegation to the Comintern. Returning to Yanan in 1937, he became head of the Organizational Department of the CCP Central Committee and was in charge of the financial and economic affairs of the Shaanxi-Gansu-Ningxia border area. His work in these positions and as deputy head of the Northwest Financial and Economic Affairs Office of the CCP Central Committee started his long career in economics. Chen became one of the principal leaders of the Party, government and army in northeast China during the civil war. After the People's Republic of China was founded, he was appointed vice premier and minister in charge of the central government Financial and Economic Commission. He became a member of the Secretariat of the CCP Central Committee in 1950 and was one of the top decision-makers of the Party. By 1956, he had become the Party's vice chairman. Removed from his posts during the Cultural Revolution, he was reelected to the Politburo, Central Committee, and Central Commission for Discipline Inspection of the Party in 1978. In 1982, he was reelected a Standing Committee member of the Politburo and first secretary of the Discipline Inspection Commission.

Chi Haotian (b. 1929) Military leader. As chief of staff of the PLA, Chi is the senior officer overseeing daily military operations. He joined the PLA in 1944 and fought against the Japanese. His career progressed as follows: company commander of the 27th Army (1949); fought against U.S. forces in North Korea and promoted to battalion commander (1950); major and vice commander of his regiment (1959); regiment commander (1964). In October 1975, he became assistant editor-in-chief for the Beijing military region. Became deputy editor-in-chief of the *People's Daily* in 1977 and a member of the Twelfth Central Committee of the CCP in 1982. In June 1985, he was appointed political commissar for the military region of Jinan. Elected as a member of the Thirteenth National Party Congress, he was appointed to position of chief of staff in November 1987.

Dai Qing (b. 1946) Prodemocracy writer and a noted columnist for the *Guangming Daily.* She grew up as the adopted daughter of Marshal Ye Jianying, the former chairman of the NPC. She made her reputation by reporting many inside stories of top leaders. She also interviewed Fang Lizhi and other leading intellectuals. On June 4, after the massacre, she publicly resigned from the Communist Party in protest against the crackdown. She was arrested on July 14, 1989.

Deng Xiaoping (b. 1904) Paramount leader of the PRC. He studied in France, where he joined the Communist Youth League in 1922 and the Chinese Communist Party in 1924. After continuing his studies in the Soviet Union in 1926, he returned to China to lead two uprisings in Guangxi Province, in Bose (1929) and Longzhou (1930), which led to the formation of the 7th and 8th Red Armies as well as the establishment of Communist bases along the Zuojiang and Youjiang rivers. Serving as secretary-general of the Party Central Committee, he participated in the Long March in 1934–1935. During the Sino-Japanese War, he and Liu Bocheng led several major campaigns. The Liu-Deng army was the vanguard in the PLA's full-scale counteroffensive against the KMT. In one of the biggest campaigns of the civil war—the Huaihai Campaign—they dealt the KMT a crushing blow. Deng served as political commissar of a field army and in 1949 assumed the positions of vice chairman of the National Defense Council, chief of staff of the PLA, and vice chairman of the Central Military Commission. In the political sphere, he became a member of the Party Central Committee in 1945, member of the Politburo in 1955, and general secretary of the Party Central Committee from 1955–1966. During the Cultural Revolution, he was purged by Maoist radicals and sent to Jiangxi Province to do manual labor. Reinstated in 1973 by Zhou Enlai, he once again lost all of his positions in 1976 when Mao recommended his dismissal. In 1977, Hua Guofeng restored him to his former standing. Seeking to undermine Hua's "two whatevers" policy, Deng announced in May of 1978 that "practice is the sole criterion of truth" and that the Party "seeks truth from facts." These two principles lay behind the sweeping reforms and open-door policy, which he initiated in December 1978. In late August and early September 1980, Deng resigned from his major posts in order to force Hua's resignation, which Hua duly submitted. By 1982, Deng had fully consolidated his power and was elected to membership in the Politburo and the chairmanship of the Central Advisory Commission. In 1985, he resigned from all important positions except the chairmanship of the Central Military Commission and the State Military Commission. He relinquished those two posts in November 1989 and March 1990, respectively. While no longer an official member of the top political hierarchies, he possesses almost absolute control over the CCP, government, and military.

Ding Guan-gen (b. 1929) Alternate member of the Politburo and secretary of the Central Secretariat of the CCP Central Committee. He joined the CCP in July 1956. Graduated from the transport department of Jiaotong University in Shanghai in August 1951. After 1975, he worked as an engineer and deputy section head of the foreign affairs bureau, assistant to the director of the planning bureau, and director of the education bureau of the Ministry of Railways; after 1983, worked as deputy secretary-general of the Standing Committee of the National People's Congress and member of the leading Party members' group in the NPC; after 1985, worked as minister of railways and secretary of the leading Party members' group in the ministry. He became an alternate member of the Politburo in 1987 and secretary of the Central Secretariat in June 1989; he has also served as director, Office of Taiwan Affairs, State Council.

Fang Lizhi (b. 1936) Leading astrophysicist and the PRC's best-known dissident, whom the government labeled the instigator of the student unrest. He and his wife took refuge at the U.S. Embassy following the Tiananmen massacre. A physics and nuclear physics major at Beijing University, he graduated in 1956. He then entered the Modern Physics Research Institute of the Chinese Academy of Sciences and married his classmate Li Shuxian. Branded a rightist in the 1957 antirightist campaign, he was expelled from the CCP for the first time. During the Cultural Revolution, he was once again subjected to persecution, spending a year in a "cow pen" from 1968 to 1969. Fang came to national prominence while serving as vice president of the University of Science and Technology in Hefei. He promoted greater democracy and his ideas were widely discussed. Fang was expelled from the Party on January 17, 1987, after Hu Yaobang's fall, and transferred to Beijing to work as a professor in the Beijing Observatory. In February 1989, when Fang was denied entry to a party to which he had been invited by President Bush when the latter was visiting the PRC, Fang's name was again in international headlines. Early in 1989 he wrote a letter to Deng Xiaoping, petitioning the release of Wei Jingsheng, a political prisoner. His appeal was widely endorsed by other intellectuals and became the prelude of the 1989 prodemocracy movement.

Hu Jiwei (b. 1916) Prodemocracy leader. He graduated from Huaxi (West China) University in 1938. In 1961, he was appointed deputy editor-in-chief of the *People's Daily* but was suspended during the Cultural Revolution. In December 1976, he became editor-in-chief and in May 1982 publisher. In April 1988, Hu was elected a member of the Standing Committee of the NPC. After Li Peng announced martial law in May 1989, Hu initiated a letter-writing campaign among NPC members to call an emergency session to resolve the country's political crisis and possibly dismiss Li Peng as premier. His effort did not succeed, and he became a target of hard-liners' attacks after the crackdown.

Hu Qili (b. 1929) Reform leader. Close associate of Zhao Ziyang and former member of the Standing Committee of the Politburo. He joined the Party in 1948 and graduated from Beijing University in 1951 with a degree in mechanical engineering. After graduation, he began a career in youth work and served as president of the All-China Students' Federation and alternate member of the Secretariat of the Communist Youth League Central Committee. During the Cultural Revolution, he was sent to work in Xiji County and Guyuan Prefecture, the Ningxia Hui Autonomous Region, one of the poorest areas in the PRC. This experience sparked his concern about the country's underdeveloped regions. In 1977–1978, he was Qinghua University's vice president and a member of the Secretariat of the CYL Central Committee; 1978–1980, president of the All-China Youth Federation; 1980–1982, mayor of Tianjin; and 1982–1983, director of the General Office of the Communist Party Central Committee. Hu was purged with Zhao Ziyang in June 1989.

Hu Yaobang (1915–1989) Reform leader. Hu served as Party general secretary from 1982–1986 and was Deng's heir apparent but was blamed for the student unrest of December 1986 and removed from his position by Deng in early 1987. His death on April 15, 1989, triggered the student protests. He joined the CYL in May 1930, was admitted into the CCP in November 1933, participated in the Long March, and served in many youth-related positions. After 1946, Hu was political commissar of a column (an army grouping) and director of a political department in the PLA. In 1950, Hu became secretary of the North Sichuan Regional Party Committee and chairman of the regional administrative office; later he was political commissar of the military area. After being secretary and first secretary of the Central Committee of the Youth League, he became first secretary of the Shanxi Provincial Party Committee. Persecuted during the Cultural Revolution, he was sent to a cadre school to do physical labor. Positions after 1975: head of the Organization Department of the CCP Central Committee, third secretary of the Central Commission for Discipline Inspection, general secretary of the CCP Central Committee and concurrently head of the Propaganda Department of the Central Committee; member of Eighth, Eleventh, Twelfth and Thirteenth Party Central committees; Standing Committee member, chairman of the Politburo of the Eleventh Party Central Committee; and Politburo Standing Committee member and general secretary of the Twelfth Party Central Committee.

Jiang Zemin (b. 1926) Moderate reformer. Named general secretary of the CCP Central Committee at the Fourth Plenum of the Thirteenth Party Central Committee (June 1989) and chairman of the Central Military Commission at the fifth plenum. He joined the CCP in April 1946. In 1947 he graduated from the electrical machinery department of Jiaotong University in Shanghai. Between the revolution and 1980, he worked in engineering and industrial-related positions in Shanghai and Moscow. After 1980, he became vice chairman and secretary-general of the State Administration Commission on Import and Export Affairs and State Administration Commission on Foreign Investment. After 1982, he headed the Ministry of Electronics Industry. In 1985, he became deputy secretary of the Party committee and mayor of Shanghai. In 1988, he became Party secretary of the CCP Shanghai Committee. As Party secretary, he cracked down on the outspoken *World Economic Herald*. Following Zhao Ziyang's removal from the position of general secretary, Jiang assumed his current position.

Li Honglin (b. 1925) Prodemocracy leader. Li joined the Communist Party in his early twenties. An influential theoretician, Li was trained as an economist and served as a researcher and adviser to the Party's Central Committee in the 1950s. He was sent into rural exile during the Cultural Revolution. Rehabilitated in the mid-1970s, he did research and then became president of the Fujian Academy of Social Science. In 1986, he was a visiting professor at Princeton University and published an article in which he summed up his views on the PRC's politics, "No Democracy, No Modernization." During the 1987 anti-bourgeois-liberalization campaign, Li was dismissed as president of the academy. In February 1989, he was among the thirty-three intellectuals who signed a petition asking for the release of political prisoners. He was arrested in mid-July 1989.

Li Peng (b. 1928) Hard-line leader. Premier of the State Council. He joined the Communist Party in 1945 before undertaking his studies at the Moscow Power Institute in 1948. Upon his return to the PRC in 1955, he worked as a chief engineer and director of two power plants. After 1966, he served as director of the Beijing Electric Power Administration. From 1979 to 1983, he was vice minister and minister of electric power and first vice minister of water resources and electric power. In 1982, he was elected to the Politburo and in 1985 to the Secretariat. He assumed the position of vice premier of the State Council in 1983 and became premier in 1988. His being the foster son of Zhou Enlai helped his meteoric rise.

Li Ruihuan (b. 1934) Moderate reformer. New member of the Standing Committee of the Politburo and member of the Secretariat in charge of propaganda; served several years as mayor of Tianjin. He joined the CCP in September 1959, was a member of the secretariat of the CYL and vice chairman of the All-China Youth Federation (1979); a member of the Standing Committee of the CCP of Tianjin, deputy mayor, and acting mayor of Tianjin (1981–1984); deputy secretary of the Party committee and mayor of Tianjin (1984–1987); after 1987, he was appointed Party secretary and concurrently mayor of Tianjin; was a member of the Twelfth Party Central Committee and became a member of the Politburo of the Thirteenth Party Central Committee (1987). He was named to his present posts at the Fourth Plenum of the Thirteenth Party Central Committee in June 1989.

Li Tieying (b. 1936) Politburo member and councillor of the State Council in charge of education. He joined the CCP in April 1955. After studying physics in Czechoslovakia (1955–1961), he worked in research-related positions. In 1983, he became the secretary of the CCP Liaoning Provincial Committee and concurrently secretary of the Haicheng County Party Committee. In 1985, he was the minister of electronics industry and secretary of the leading Party members' group in the ministry. After March 1987, he took charge of the State Commission for Restructuring the Economy. He was elected to the Twelfth and Thirteenth Party Central committees.

Li Xiannian (b. 1909) Hard-line octogenarian leader. Former state president and chairman of the Chinese People's Political Consultative Conference (CPPCC). He joined the CCP in 1927. Li became political commissar of the 30th Army, 1935; deputy commander, 4th Field Army, 1949; chairman, Hubei Provincial People's Government, 1949; vice premier of the State Council, vice chairman of the Financial and Economic Affairs Committee, and minister of finance, 1954; member of the Eighth, Ninth, Eleventh, and Twelfth Party Central committees and member of the Politburo. He served as president of the PRC, 1984–1988, and became chairman of the CPPCC in 1988.

Li Ximing (b. 1926) Hard-line party official. Secretary of the CCP's Beijing Committee. He joined the CCP in March 1948. Li studied civil engineering at Qinghua University. He organized the CYL at the Shijingshan Power Plant (1949); served as secretary of the CCP general branch of the Shijingshan Power Plant (1952–1970) and chairman of the revolutionary committee of the plant until 1975. Li worked in the Ministry of Water Resources and Electric Power and the Ministry of Power Industry until 1982. In 1984, he assumed the position of secretary of the Beijing Municipal Party and became a member of the Twelfth and Thirteenth Party Central committees. He played a vital role in the June massacre. It was his report that prompted Deng Xiaoping to conclude that the student movement was "turmoil" instead of "unrest."

Liu Binyan (b. 1926) Prodemocracy leader. He first won a prize for a short story when he was thirteen. Liu began to participate in Communist underground activities in 1943, becoming a member in 1944, and serving on the editorial board of the *China Youth Daily* in 1951. In 1957, Liu was labeled a "rightist." During the Cultural Revolution, he was dispatched to May 7 Cadre School for labor reform and was not rehabilitated until October 1976. He then worked at the *People's Daily* as a reporter and played a role of social investigator and articulator of popular grievances. His works included *Ren Yao Zhi Jian* (Between people and monster) and *Di Er Zhong Zhong Cheng* (The second kind of loyalty), and he was the most prominent Chinese writer of the 1980s. After serving on the Board of Directors, he became vice president of the Chinese Writers Association in 1985. He was expelled from the Party during the 1987 anti-bourgeois-liberalization campaign. In 1988, he was granted a one-year stint as a Nieman Fellow at Harvard University. He joined the overseas Chinese Democratic Front after the June 4 massacre.

Liu Huaqing (b. 1916) Military leader, vice chairman of the Central Military Commission, and one of Deng's close aides in military affairs. Liu served as military commissar in the Central Plains Field Army, 1946; vice commissar in the 2nd Field Army, 1948; transferred to navy, 1950; studied in the Soviet Union and obtained rank of rear admiral in 1955; appointed vice commissar of China's South Sea Fleet, 1963; vice commissar of the Chinese Navy, 1965; transferred to serve as vice chairman of the National Defense Committee for Science and Industry, 1967. From 1967 to 1977, he served as deputy chief of staff of the navy and deputy secretary-general of the Chinese Academy of Science. He became assistant to the chief of staff of the army, 1979; deputy chief of staff, 1980; member of the Twelfth Party Central Committee, 1982; and commander of the navy, 1982. Elected to the Thirteenth Party Central Committee in 1987, he was appointed deputy secretary-general of the Central Military Commission and became vice chairman of the CMC in November 1989.

Peng Zhen (b. 1902) Hard-line octogenarian leader. Former chairman, Standing Committee of the NPC. He joined the CCP in 1926. Peng served as director, CCP North Bureau, 1936; political commissar of Nie Rongzhen's force, 1937; principal, CCP Central Party School, 1938–1942; member, Seventh Party Central Committee, 1945; secretary, CCP North Bureau, 1945; member, Central People's Government, 1949; vice chairman, Political and Legal Affairs Committee, 1949; mayor of Beijing, 1951–1965; member of the Politburo and secretary, Central Secretariat, Eighth Party Central Committee, September 1956. Purged in 1965, he was rehabilitated in 1977 and became a member of the Eleventh Party Central Committee and of the Politburo in 1978. He served as chairman of the Legal System Committee, NPC, and vice chairman of the NPC in 1979. Peng was a member of the Twelfth Party Central Committee and of the Politburo in 1982. From 1983 to 1988, he was chairman of the NPC.

Qiao Shi (b. 1924) Member of Standing Committee of the Politburo and chairman of the Central Commission for Discipline Inspection, protégé of Peng Zhen. He joined the CCP in Shanghai in 1940. After 1945, he was one of the organizers of the students' movement in Shanghai. Following the 1949 revolution, Qiao did Party, political, and technical work. From 1954 through 1962 he was technical division chief of a construction company under the Anshan Iron and Steel Works. Later he served as director of the Design Institute of Jiuquan Iron and Steel Company, a new iron and steel enterprise in Gansu Province. Transferred to the International Liaison Department of the CCP Central Committee in 1963, he worked there until 1982. In 1982, he became an alternate member and a member of the Secretariat of the CCP Central Committee, director of the General Office of the Central Committee, head of the Organizational Department of the Central Committee, and secretary of the Political and Law Committee under the Central Committee. In 1985, he was elected to the Politburo; and in 1986, was appointed vice premier of the State Council. His wife's family suffered during the antirightist campaign beginning in 1957. His daughter has studied in the United States, his son, in Norway.

Qin Benli (b. 1918) Prodemocracy leader. Qin was editor-in-chief of Shanghai's *World Economic Herald*. He served also as Party secretary of the Research Institute of World Economy, Shanghai Academy of Social Science. A man of vision and conviction, Qin has been an influential journalist in the PRC. He visited the United States in 1988. After the death of Hu Yaobang, the *Herald* published a series of articles demanding reappraisal of Hu's role. He was suspended as editor-in-chief in early May by Jiang Zemin, who was then Shanghai Party secretary, for refusing to print a retraction of the demands in those articles.

Qin Jiwei (b. 1914) Moderate military leader. Minister of defense and only army officer on active duty on the Politburo. He joined the Red Army in August 1929 and the CCP in April 1930, served as division commander of the Red Army, and took part in the Long March. Qin served under Deng Xiaoping from 1938 to 1950 as commander of a guerrilla detachment and commander of the second branch of the Taihang Military Area, deputy brigade commander of the 129th Division of the 8th Route Army, and commander of the first branch of the Taihang Military Area. Qin became commander of the 15th Army of the 4th Army Group of the PLA. After studying at the Nanjing Military Academy (1950), he commanded the 15th Army of the Chinese People's Volunteers in Korea. In 1973, he became commander and Party secretary of the PLA Chengdu Units and first political commissar of the PLA Beijing Units. He commanded the Beijing military region from 1980 to 1988. His troops were among the first to carry out Deng's military modernization policies.

Rui Xingwen (b. 1927) Reform leader. Rui was one of Zhao's close aides in charge of propaganda. He joined the CCP in 1945 and served as vice minister of Aerospace Industry, State Council. In 1984, Rui became vice chairman of the State Planning Commission and later minister of urban reconstruction and environmental protection. Elected to the Twelfth and Thirteenth Central committees in 1985 and 1987, Rui joined the Party Secretariat and became a supporter of Zhao. On May 18, 1989, he went with Zhao and Li Peng to visit hunger strikers at several hospitals. He was dismissed from the post along with Zhao during the Fourth Plenum of the Thirteenth Party Central Committee.

Song Ping (b. 1917) Hard-line leader. New member of the Standing Committee of the Politburo. He joined the CCP in December 1937 while he was studying at the Agricultural College of Beijing University (1934–1938). Positions that he held from 1938–1972 include: secretary-general of the editorial department of the Chongqing-based *Xinhua Daily*, political secretary of Zhou Enlai, and member of the State Planning Commission. After 1972, he became first secretary of the Party and chairman, Revolutionary Committee of Gansu Province. After 1981, he worked as minister of the State Planning Commission. Song was elected to the Eleventh, Twelfth and Thirteenth Party Central committees. He acquired his present post during the Party reshuffle in June 1989.

Song Renqiong (b. 1909) Military leader and vice chairman of the CCP Central Advisory Commission. He joined the CCP in 1926. Song served as political commissar of a regiment in Lin Biao's army, 1930; participated in the Long March, 1934–1935; became an alternate member of the Seventh Party Central Committee, 1945; political commissar, 4th Army Group, 1949; deputy political commissar, Southwest Military Region, 1950; deputy general secretary, CCP Central Committee, 1955; member, Eighth Party Central Committee, 1956; minister of the Third Ministry of the Machine-Building Industry, 1958; minister, Second Machine-Building Industry, 1959. Purged during the Cultural Revolution, he was rehabilitated in 1977 as vice chairman of the CPPCC; he became Minister of the First Machine-Building Industry in 1978; director, Department of Organization of the CCP Central Committee, 1979; secretary, CCP Central Secretariat, 1980; member of the Twelfth Party Central Committee and Politburo; he was assigned his present post in 1987.

Su Shaozhi (b. 1923) Prodemocracy leader. Former director of the Research Institute on Marxism-Leninism and Mao Zedong Thought of the Chinese Academy of Social Sciences. Su had been the most respected authority in the PRC on Marxist-Leninist theory. He graduated from Chongqing University around 1950 and received graduate training at Nankai University. A strong advocate of political modernization, he lost his position as director after Hu Yaobang was dismissed in early 1987. On April 19, 1989, in a seminar in Beijing, Su proposed reversing the verdict on Hu Yaobang and openly supported student demonstrations. He was on the wanted list of the government but had fled to the United States via Europe; he was a visiting professor at Marquette University in 1989.

Su Xiaokang (b. 1949) Prodemocracy leader. He was lecturer of broadcasting at Beijing University and a principal author of "River Elegy" (*He Shang*), a television documentary series that shocked Chinese intellectuals in 1988. An influential writer, Su was a member of the Standing Committee of the Central Committee and of China's Democratic League, one of the minor political parties in China. After the June 4 massacre, "River Elegy" was under severe attack and Su joined other exiled dissidents in Paris.

Tian Jiyun (b. 1929) Reform leader. Vice premier in charge of agricultural affairs, State Council. He joined the CCP in May 1945. In 1981, he was deputy secretary-general of the State Council. After 1983, he became vice premier and secretary-general of the State Council. He was elected to the Politburo and a member of the Secretariat of the Twelfth and Thirteenth Party Central committees. He had been a close aide of Zhao Ziyang, but he retained his position after Zhao's fall.

Wan Li (b. 1916) Moderate leader. Chairman of the National People's Congress. He joined the CCP in May 1936 and graduated from a normal school that year. After doing underground work in Dongping County, he served as member and general secretary of the Party committee of Hebei-Shandong-Henan in 1947. After 1949, he held the positions of minister of industrial department and minister of construction; he was secretary of the Beijing municipal Party committee and deputy mayor of Beijing before being persecuted during the Cultural Revolution. Rehabilitated in 1973, he became first secretary of the CCP Anhui Committee in 1977, where he started rural reform and gained great success. He was promoted to vice premier of the State Council after 1980. He also held the positions of chairman and secretary of the leading Party group of the State Agricultural Commission and member of the financial and economic leading group of the CCP Central Committee. During the students' hunger strike, Wan was on an official visit to North America. He expressed the need to respect the patriotism of the students but also demanded the maintenance of social order. When he returned from the United States to Shanghai on May 27, he openly endorsed Li Peng's and Deng's decision to label the student movement "turmoil."

Wan Runnan (b. 1946) Prodemocracy leader. Chairman of the Stone Corporation, the most successful private computer firm in the PRC, set up in the open-door era. He was the son-in-law of the former state president Liu Shaoqi. During the student demonstrations, Wan was deeply involved and heavily financed the student movement. He was on the most-wanted list but escaped to Paris and helped organize the Chinese Democratic Front. Elected secretary-general of the organization, he visited Taiwan in December 1989 in an effort to raise funds for Democratic Front activities.

Wang Dan (b. 1965) Student leader. Wang Dan was a freshman at Beijing University, from which both his parents had graduated. His father is an associate professor of geology. In spring 1989, Wang Dan and several students formed the "Democracy Salon" to discuss the PRC's political reform. During the student demonstrations, Wang Dan became a prominent leader in the Autonomous Student Union of Beijing Universities, which led the protest and hunger strike. After the June 4 crackdown, Wang Dan was number one on the government most-wanted list. Following an unsuccessful attempt to escape from the country, he returned to Beijing. In early July 1989, while seeking a Taiwanese journalist's help to flee, Wang was arrested by the secret police.

Wang Hai (b. 1925) Military leader. Commander of the air force. He joined the CCP in 1945 and became an air force hero in the Korean War. Wang became commander of the 3rd Division of the Air Force in 1959; led the air force in its support of North Vietnam in the Vietnam War in the 1960s; became the air force commander of Guangzhou Military Region in the 1970s and vice commander of the air force in 1983. In 1985, he was promoted to commander.

Wang Ruowang (b. 1918) Prominent writer. He became a member of the CCP in 1937. After the revolution, he served as the assistant head of the propaganda department of the All China Federation of Trade Unions and manager of the Shanghai Diesel Engine Factory. In 1955, he became an editor of the *Literary Monthly* (*Wenyi Yuebao*). Attacked for his writings during the antirightist movement, he was eventually dismissed from his positions and expelled from the CCP. Rehabilitated in 1962, he published the novel *The Story of a Big Plot,* which attacked the Communist leadership. Imprisoned during the Cultural Revolution, he was not released until 1979. On January 13, 1987, Wang lost his Party membership for the second time.

Wang Zhen (b. 1908) Hard-line octogenarian leader. State vice president. Wang joined the CCP in 1927 and the Red Army in 1929. He became political commissar of the regiment in 1930 and of the division in 1932; commander, 6th Red Army, 1937; alternate member, Seventh Party Central Committee, 1945; chief of staff, Central Plains Military Region, 1946; first vice commander, Xinjiang Military Region, 1949; commander, 1st Army Group, 1949; secretary of the CCP Xinjiang Bureau; commander, Xinjiang Military Region, 1950; deputy chief of staff, PLA, 1955; vice premier, State Council, 1975–1980; principal, Central Party School, member, Eleventh and Twelfth Party central committees and Politburo, 1978–1985. He served as vice chairman of the Central Advisory Committee, 1985–1987; he attained his present office in 1988.

Wuer Kaixi (also known as Werkesh Daolat) (b. 1968) Student leader. An ethnic Vighuer, he was a student at Beijing Normal University. He led students sitting in front of Zhongnanhai, headquarters of the CCP Central Committee, on April 20, 1989, and set up the Autonomous Student Union in Beijing Normal University. At the end of the month, he became president of the Autonomous Student Union of Beijing Universities. On May 18, as one of the student leaders in a television confrontation with Li Peng, he articulated two demands: government recognition of the student protests as a patriotic democratic movement and government legalization of the Autonomous Student Union of Beijing Universities. He fled to France after the June 4 crackdown. In September 1989, he was elected vice president of the Chinese Democratic Front. He was then enrolled as a special student at Harvard University.

Yan Jiaqi (b. 1942) Prodemocracy leader. Yan originally was a student majoring in physics. He graduated from the University of Science and Technology in 1964 but switched to social science. At forty-five, Yan became the youngest director of the Institute of Political Science, a new organization under the Chinese Academy of Social Sciences. In 1986, Yan and his wife, Gao Gao, coauthored the most comprehensive history of the Cultural Revolution. The two-volume *Ten-Year History of China's Cultural Revolution* became an instant best-seller. In 1987, he published another major work, *On Top Leadership,* which also drew nationwide acclaim. During the student demonstrations, Yan, joined by other influential intellectuals, appealed to the Communist leaders to acknowledge that what had been proposed by the students was positive and democratic. He also participated in demonstrations in Tiananmen Square. After the June 4 massacre, Yan was accused by the Party newspapers of being the "behind-the-scenes" schemer who had incited the students. He and his wife fled to France and helped launch the Chinese Democratic Front. In September 1989, he was elected president of the organization.

Yan Mingfu (b. 1931) Reform leader. His father was a high official in the Nationalist government. In the late 1940s Yan Mingfu learned Russian at the Harbin Foreign Language Institute and he studied in Moscow in the 1950s. In 1957, he worked in the general office of the CCP Central Committee. When Khrushchev visited the PRC in 1959, Yan served as an interpreter. During the Cultural Revolution, he was imprisoned for seven-and-one-half years. Rehabilitated in 1978, Yan became deputy secretary-general of the Standing Committee of the NPC in 1985. In 1987, he was elected to the Thirteenth Party Central Committee and was appointed director of the CCP United Front Department, an organization in charge of Taiwan-PRC relations. On May 16, 1989, he went to Tiananmen Square to persuade hunger strikers to return to their campuses. In June 1989, he lost his post as member of the Party Secretariat.

Yang Baibing (b. 1920) Hard-line military leader. Secretary-general of the CMC and director of the General Political Department, PLA. He is the younger brother of Yang Shangkun. He was not well known until 1985 when he was appointed commissar of the Beijing Military Region. He was elected in October 1987 to the Thirteenth Party Central Committee. In November 1987, he got his General Political Department post, in November 1989, his CMC post and membership in the Central Secretariat.

Yang Rudai (b. 1926) Reform leader. Member of the Politburo of the CCP Central Committee. He received an education equivalent to senior high school. He joined the CCP in August 1952 and worked in different capacities in Fangjia District, becoming Party secretary of Renshou County (1954–1970). He served as deputy governor and secretary in charge of day-to-day work of the Provincial Party Committee of Sichuan. After 1983, he worked as secretary of the Sichuan Provincial Party Committee. Yang was elected to his present post in 1987.

Yang Shangkun (b. 1907) Hard-line military leader. State president and first vice chairman of the Central Military Commission. Yang joined the Communist Youth League in 1925 and the CCP in 1926 and took part in student and workers' movements in Chengdu, Chongqing, and Shanghai. He studied at Sun Yat-sen University in Moscow. He served as editor of *Red China* and *Struggle* (1933) and participated in the Long March. Yang became secretary-general of the Military Commission of the CCP Central Committee (1945). He was persecuted during the Cultural Revolution. After 1978, he headed the Guangzhou city Revolutionary Committee. He served as vice chairman and secretary-general of the Standing Committee of the Fifth NPC (1980) and was a member of the Eighth, Eleventh, Twelfth and Thirteenth Party Central committees, becoming a member of the Politburos of the Twelfth and Thirteenth Party Central committees. From July 1981 to April 1988, he administered day-to-day military affairs as secretary-general of the Central Military Commission. Yang became president of the PRC in April 1988 and got his CMC post in November 1989.

Yao Yilin (b. 1917) Hard-line leader. Vice premier in charge of economic affairs and widely regarded as the chief economic planner; member of the Politburo Standing Committee since 1985. Yao graduated from Qinghua University and joined the CCP in 1935. He was one of the organizers of the Beijing students' patriotic movement against Japanese aggression. From 1946 to 1949, he was the deputy director of the Financial and Economic Office of the Shanxi-Chahar-Hebei Border Region Government and head of the Department of Industry and Commerce of the North China People's Government. In the years following 1949, he was vice minister of trade, vice minister of commerce, and deputy director of the Office in Charge of Finance and Trade under the State Council. Dismissed during the Cultural Revolution, he regained his positions in 1973 and served successively as first vice minister of foreign trade, minister of commerce, minister in charge of the State Planning Commission, head of the Leading Group of Economic and Financial Affairs, and deputy general secretary and director of the General Office of the CCP Central Committee. He has been vice premier since 1978. He became a full member of the Eleventh Party Central Committee in 1977 and a member of the Secretariat. He was elected to the Politburo at the committee's fifth plenum in 1985.

Yuan Mu (b. 1928) Hard-line official. Yuan is the official spokesman of the State Council. In September 1983, he was appointed deputy secretary-general of the State Council. Later he became deputy secretary-general of the Leading Group of Economic and Financial Affairs, CCP Central Committee. In October 1988, he assumed the position of director, Research Office of the State Council. During the student unrest, Yuan played important roles as government spokesman and as participant in dialogues with the student leaders.

Zhang Lianzhong (b. 1931) Military leader. Commander of navy. Zhang is a specialist in submarine warfare. He entered the PLA Navy in 1947. In 1960 he was appointed vice commander of a battleship. In 1968, he became commander of an escort vessel in the North China Sea Fleet and in 1984, commander of the navy base at Port Arthur. He was named vice commander of the navy in March 1986 and became an alternate member of the Thirteenth Party Central Committee on November 1, 1987. On January 31, 1988, he received his present command.

Zhao Nanji (b. 1929) Military leader. Director of the General Logistics Department, PLA. He became the Party secretary of the autonomous Korean nationality prefecture of Yanbian, Jilin Province, and chairman of its revolutionary committee in 1978. Served as lieutenant governor of Jilin in 1980; first secretary of Yanbian in 1980; member of the Twelfth Party Central Committee, 1982; deputy director of the General Logistics Department and deputy political commissar, 1985. He became director of the department in November 1987.

Zhao Ziyang (b. 1919) Reform leader. Served as premier, 1980–1986, and Party general secretary between 1987 and late May 1989. Zhao joined the Party in 1938. Before the Sino-Japanese War, he had served as a local Party leader at the county and prefectural levels in central China. In the early 1960s, he became the first Party secretary of Guangdong Province and a member of the Secretariat of the Central-South Bureau of the Party Central Committee. When the Cultural Revolution broke out, he was purged and sent to work in a factory. Rehabilitated in 1971, he undertook the leadership of Inner Mongolia, Guangdong, and Sichuan provinces. Because of his achievements in Sichuan, the most populous province, he was named to the Party Central Committee at the Tenth Party Congress in 1973. In 1980, he became premier of the State Council. In 1982, at the First Plenum of the Twelfth Party Central Committee, he was elected to the Standing Committee of the Politburo. His appointment to the position of general secretary of the Party came in the wake of Hu Yaobang's fall in January 1987, following student unrest in December 1986. In May 1989, Zhao's conciliatory approach to massive student demonstrations cost him his job. He is currently being held responsible for the student unrests and has been under house arrest since late May 1989.

Bibliography

China Daily News (New York), June 26, 1989, p. 3.

"China's Military Hierachy," *New York Times*, May 23, 1989, p. 5.

Institute for International Relations, ed. *Chung-Kung Jen-min Lu* [Who's who in Communist China]. Taipei: Institute for International Relations, 1978.

Morrison, Donald, ed. *Massacre in Beijing, China's Struggle for Democracy*. New York: Time, Inc., 1989, pp. 262–267.

"Profiles of the Party's Leaders." *Beijing Review* 32, No. 28 (July 10–16, 1989), pp. 21–25.

Rosett, Claudis, "Last in the Chinese Gulog," *Wall Street Journal*, August 8, 1989, editorial page.

The 13th Party Congress and China's Reform. Beijing: Beijing Review, 1987, pp. 83–113.

The Truth of Fire and Blood: A Documentary on the Pro-Democracy Movement in Mainland China in 1989. Taipei: Institute for the Study of Chinese Communist Problems, 1989.

Union Research Institute. *Who's Who in Communist China.* Hong Kong, 1966.

Yang, Ann Stevenson. "China's New-Look Leadership." *China Business Review,* September–October 1989, p. 5.

Appendix 3: Documents

"It Is Necessary to Take a Clear Stand
Against the Disturbances"*

Among the activities of mourning in connection with the passing away of Comrade Hu Yaobang, the great majority of Communist Party members, workers, farmers, intellectuals, cadres, soldiers in the People's Liberation Army and young students expressed their feelings of grief in all sorts of ways and also demonstrated a determination to transform grief into strength in order to carry out the Four Modernizations and devote vigorous efforts to the revival of China.

During the period of these activities of mourning, a number of abnormal situations also emerged. A very small number of people took advantage of this opportunity to spread rumors, to attack by name leaders of the Party and the government and to seduce the masses into attacking Xinhuamen in Zhongnanhai, the site of the headquarters of the Central Committee of the Chinese Communist Party and the State Council. Some people even went so far as to shout reactionary slogans such as "Down with the Communist Party!" etc. In Xi'an and Changsha, incidents occurred in which lawless elements carried out serious crimes such as beating, smashing, robbery and arson.

Out of consideration for the feelings of grief and mourning felt by the great majority of the masses, with regard to a number of inappropriate words and actions carried out by young students in a state of excitement, the Party and the government adopted an attitude of tolerance and containment. On April 22, the day on which a great funeral ceremony was held in honor of Comrade Hu Yaobang, with regard to a number of students that had gathered in Tiananmen Square ahead of time and who refused to clear the square in advance of the funeral ceremony as is customary, the authorities merely asked them to maintain order and decorum in obedience to law and join in the general funeral ceremony for Comrade Hu Yaobang. In this way, through the concerted efforts of all concerned, we were able to ensure that the funeral ceremony was carried out smoothly in an atmosphere of dignity and solemnity.

However, after the ceremony was finished, a small number of people with ulterior motives continued to take advantage of the grief felt by these young students at the passing of Comrade Hu Yaobang to promulgate all sorts of rumors, to corrupt the minds and hearts of the people, to use large-character and small-character posters to attack the leaders of the Party and the government with vicious lies and wild

---

*This editorial appeared in the *People's Daily,* April 26, 1989, p. 1.

accusations. In clear violation of the Constitution, they aroused opposition to the leadership of the Communist Party and the system of socialism. In some institutions of higher learning they established illegal organizations which "usurped power" from the student organizations. Some even went so far as to establish campus broadcasting centers. In some institutions of higher education they urged students to carry out a boycott of classes, urged the teachers to go on strike and in some cases even went so far as to use force to prevent students from attending classes. Usurping the name of labor organizations, they distributed reactionary leaflets and they spread out in all directions, hoping to create even wider disturbances.

These events demonstrate clearly that this small number of people were not carrying out mourning activities in honor of Comrade Hu Yaobang. They were not acting to promote the advance of a socialist democratic system of government. Nor were they merely proclaiming various private grievances. They ran up the banner of democracy in order to destroy the democratic legal system. Their purpose was to confuse the hearts and minds of the people, to disrupt the entire country, to destroy the political situation of stability and solidarity. This was a conspiracy with a definite plan. It was an incitement to upheaval. Its true nature was a basic negation of the leadership of the Chinese Communist Party and a negation of the socialist system. This was a serious attempt to stir up political strife aimed at the entire Party and at all the people of the nation regardless of their ethnic background.

If we take a tolerant and relaxed attitude to this upheaval and allow it to go on unchecked, the result will be to bring about a situation of severe chaos. Programs on which the highest hopes of all the people of our country, including the great majority of young students, are placed, programs such as the reform and the opening to the outside world, regularization and rectification, construction and development, regulation of prices, improvement of the standard of living, opposition to the phenomena of corruption, the construction of democracy and a system of law will all vanish into thin air. It is even possible that the great results already achieved in ten years of carrying out reforms will be lost and will all come to nothing. The great hopes of reviving China which have been so ardently cherished by all the people of our country will be hard to fulfill. A China that is filled with hope and that is looking forward to a great future will be transformed into a chaotic land where there is no peace, a land with no hope for the future.

The entire Party and all the people of our country must fully recognize the serious nature of this struggle. They must all rise up in solidarity and take a clear stand in opposition to agitation for upheaval. We must resolutely safeguard the political situation of stability and solidarity which has not been easy to bring about. We must safeguard the Constitution, safeguard socialist democracy and the system of law. We must not by any means allow the establishment of any illegal organizations. We must firmly put a stop to any action on any pretext that would infringe on the rights and privileges of the legal student organizations. With regard to those who harbor suspicions, foment rumors and spread slander, we must investigate their criminal responsibility in accordance with the law. We must put a stop to illegal marches and demonstrations. We must forbid them from establishing contacts in factories, in agricultural villages and on college campuses. With regard to those who are guilty of striking, smashing, robbing and burning, they must be punished by law. We must protect the students' just right to attend classes. We must carry out on a larger scale the aspirations of the students to do away with corruption and implement democracy. That is what the Party and the government are also striving for. These aspirations can only be achieved under the leadership of the Party, through a strengthening of regularization and rectification, through positive promotion of ough the construction and perfection of socialist democracy and a

des throughout the Party and our fellow countrymen throughout
all clearly recognize that if we do not firmly put a stop to this
upheavals our country will have no peace. This struggle will affect the
success of the reforms, the opening to the outside world and the Four Modernizations,
it will affect the future of the people of our country. Members of Communist Party
organizations at all levels, the great majority of Communist Party members, members
of the Communist Youth League, all the democratic parties, patriotic people of
democratic persuasion, and all the people of our country must clearly distinguish
right from wrong. We must take positive action. We must resolutely struggle to
swiftly put a stop to this agitation for upheaval.

A Student's Eyewitness Account
of the Tiananmen Massacre*

In the predawn hours of June 4, I was sitting on the steps of the Monument to
the People's Heroes. I saw with my own eyes what happened when the army opened
fire on the students and citizens quietly sitting in the square.

At midnight, after two armored vehicles sped down the side of the square from
the front gate, the tension mounted. Shrill loudspeakers barked out repeated "no-
tifications." Thick formations of soldiers in steel helmets were moving into the square
from all sides. In the dark, we could make out machine gun placements on the roof
of the History Museum. The students crowded back around the Heroes Monument.

At 4 A.M. Sunday the lights on the square were suddenly extinguished. Through
the loudspeakers, we again heard orders to "clear out." A sudden wave of anxiety
passed through me, and a voice in my head said over and over, "The moment has
come."

Then, Hou Dejian (Taiwan pop singer) and other hunger strikers negotiated with
the army for a peaceful retreat of the students. But just as we were about to move,
at 4:40 A.M., a barrage of red flares shot into the sky. Immediately, the square was
brightly illuminated. I saw that the front of the square was full of soldiers. From
the Great Hall of the People, a squadron of soldiers rushed out, dressed in camouflage,
carrying assault rifles, and wearing helmets and gas masks.

The first thing that the charging soldiers did was to erect a row of 10 or more
machine guns right in front of the Heroes Monument. The machine gunners took a

---

*When the Chinese Army began its crackdown in Beijing in the predawn hours of June 4,
student demonstrators in Tiananmen Square were the focal point. A Hong Kong newspaper,
Wen Wei Pao, later published a firsthand account of the assault, given by a twenty-year-old
student at Qinghua University, whose identity the paper withheld. An excerpt from that article
was published in the *China Times* on June 10, 1989. This was one of the earliest eyewitness
reports to surface in the aftermath of the massacre. Since it was first published, other witnesses
have come forward with different, conflicting accounts. Such disagreements are perhaps to be
expected, given the chaos of developments in various locations around Tiananmen Square at
different times during the night of June 3 and the early morning hours of June 4. We can
neither confirm nor deny the view of events presented here. Reprinted by permission of the
China Times (weekly), New York, No. 224 (June 10, 1989), pp. 24–25.

—*Chu-yuan Cheng*

prone position, with their backs to the Gate of Heavenly Peace. As soon as the placements were established, a huge number of soldiers and military police appeared.

They were all holding electric cattle prods and rubber truncheons, and some special-purpose weapons that we did not recognize. They charged at us, breaking apart the formation in which we were sitting, beating us with all their might. Our ranks were broken into two groups, and they forced their way through the middle to the third tier of the monument. I saw about 50 students who were so badly beaten that blood completely covered their faces.

At that moment, the armored vehicles and additional forces that had been waiting on the square closed in on us, and we were completely surrounded by rows and rows of vehicles, leaving only a small gap in the direction of the museum.

At the same time, the soldiers and military police who had reached the third tier went about smashing all of the students' printing and broadcasting equipment and dragged the students down from the steps. Even then we remained seated, holding hands and singing the "Internationale" and shouting "The People's Army will not hurt the people!" But unable to resist the kicking and clubbing of such a large number of attackers, the students sitting on the third tier were forced down.

When they reached the ground, machine guns erupted. Some soldiers opened fire from a kneeling position, their bullets flying over our heads, but the gunners splayed on the ground were shooting right at the chests and heads of the students. When this happened, we could only retreat up the back of the monument. Then the machine guns stopped. But the beating of the soldiers above forced us back down. Then the machine guns started again.

At this time, workers and citizens, putting their own lives aside, took up bottles, sticks or anything that could be used as weapons, and rushed across to fight the soldiers.

The Student Association urged everyone to get out of the square.

At that point a large number of students tried to get out through the gap in the armored vehicles. But even this exit was sealed off. Thirty armored cars came crashing into the crowd. Some students died under the wheels, and even the flagpole in front of the monument was knocked down.

I never thought that the students could be so courageous. One group went to try to turn over the vehicles, but were repulsed by bullets. Then a second wave, stepping over the bodies of those in front, rushed at the vehicles again, managing to topple one of them. Three thousand students, myself included, rushed out amid flying bullets through this opening toward the History Museum.

Those who survived joined citizens outside the museum who were running north. Seeing flashes of gunfire from the trees ahead, we turned around and ran south.

Tears streamed down our faces as we ran. We could see a second group of students trying to escape under fire, many of them falling. We all wept and, weeping, we ran. Just as our group reached the front gate of the city, we were met by a large contingent of soldiers, all running from the direction of the Jewelry Market. When we met, they didn't shoot, but began beating us madly with huge wooden clubs.

At this point, a crowd of citizens came rushing up the front gate and started fighting ferociously with the soldiers, they did this to protect us as we tried to break through in the direction of the railway station. The soldiers pursued us. By 5 A.M., the gunfire in the square was dying away. Afterward I ran into a friend at the International Red Cross, and he told me that by 5 A.M. anyone who could escape had done so.

I will never be able to forget what happened when the students were shot down, and others rushed to save the wounded and carry away the bodies. Some of the women tore off their clothes to bandage wounds until they had nothing more to take off.

A Qinghua University friend of mine from Jiangsu Province was bleeding heavily but still running with us until he could keep up no longer. He fell against my shoulder, saying, "Can you help me?" I was already supporting two injured women students so I couldn't get to him right away. He fell on the ground and the crowd trampled him. I still have the stains of his blood on my back.

After we reached the train station, two other students and myself went back to the square. It was now 6:30 A.M. We followed a huge crowd of civilians to the Mao Zedong Mausoleum. There, armored cars and a wall of soldiers blocked the way. We climbed up the trees on the side of the road, and saw that soldiers were collecting corpses in plastic bags on the square. The bodies were piled on top of each other and covered with canvas.

There I ran into a student from my department. He was among those who broke out [of the square] with the second group. He told me that the death toll was enormous. Soldiers had kept Red Cross ambulances from getting to the wounded.

Around 7:20 A.M., I went back to the square again to find out more. I talked to some elderly people who said that the people on the walkways around the square had died all bunched together. The soldiers had draped the area from the sight of the Beijing people with canvas sheets. They also said that many military trucks had come in and carried the wounded off to an unknown destination.

How many people died altogether? I don't really know.

Am I pessimistic? No, I'm not at all pessimistic. Because I have seen the will of the people. I have seen the hope of China. Some of my friends died. Even more are now bleeding. I am a survivor, and I know how to live my life from now on. I will never forget the students who lost their lives. I also know for sure that all decent people in the world will understand and support us.

Deng's Talk on Quelling Rebellion in Beijing*

You comrades have been working hard.

First of all, I'd like to express my heartfelt condolences to the comrades in the People's Liberation Army (PLA), the armed police and police who died in the struggle—and my sincere sympathy and solicitude to the comrades in the army, the armed police and police who were wounded in the struggle, and I want to extend my sincere regards to all the army, armed police and police personnel who participated in the struggle.

I suggest that all of us stand and pay a silent tribute to the martyrs.

The Nature of the Storm

I'd like to take this opportunity to say a few words. This storm was bound to happen sooner or later. As determined by the international and domestic climate, it

---

*On June 9, five days after the crackdown, Deng Xiaoping delivered an address in Beijing to military commanders. The address has emerged as a key document setting out the Party line in the crackdown on the prodemocracy movement, and the Chinese authorities have urged citizens to study it. This is a transcript of the speech, which was translated into English and appeared in the *Beijing Review*, July 10–16, 1989, pp. 18–21. It is followed by explanatory notes by this author.

was bound to happen and was independent of man's will. It was just a matter of time and scale. It has turned out in our favor, for we still have a large group of veterans who have experienced many storms and have a thorough understanding of things. They were on the side of taking resolute action to counter the turmoil. Although some comrades may not understand this now, they will understand eventually and will support the decision of the Central Committee.

The April 26 editorial of the *People's Daily* classified the problem as turmoil. The word was appropriate, but some people objected to the word and tried to amend it. But what has happened shows that this verdict was right. It was also inevitable that the turmoil would develop into a counter-revolutionary rebellion.

We still have a group of senior comrades who are alive, we still have the army, and we also have a group of core cadres who took part in the revolution at various times. That is why it was relatively easy for us to handle the present matter. The main difficulty in handling this matter lay in [the fact] that we had never experienced such a situation before, in which a small minority of bad people mixed with so many young students and onlookers. We did not have a clear picture of the situation, and this prevented us from taking some actions that we should have taken earlier.

It would have been difficult for us to understand the nature of the matter had we not had the support of so many senior comrades. Some comrades didn't understand this point. They thought it was simply a matter of how to treat the masses. Actually, what we faced was not just some ordinary people who were misguided, but also a rebellious clique and a large quantity of the dregs of society. The key point is that they wanted to overthrow our state and the party. Failing to understand this means failing to understand the nature of the matter. I believe that after serious work we can win the support of the great majority of comrades within the party.

The nature of the matter became clear soon after it erupted. They had two main slogans: to overthrow the Communist Party and topple the socialist system. Their goal was to establish a bourgeois republic entirely dependent on the West. Of course we accept people's demands for combatting corruption. We are even ready to listen to some persons with ulterior motives when they raise the slogan about fighting corruption. However, such slogans were just a front. Their real aim was to overthrow the Communist Party and topple the socialist system.

A Severe Test

During the course of quelling the rebellion, many comrades of ours were wounded or even sacrificed their lives. Some of their weapons were also taken from them by the rioters. Why? Because bad people mingled with the good, which made it difficult for us to take the firm measures that were necessary.

Handling this matter amounted to a severe political test for our army, and what happened shows that our People's Liberation Army passed muster. If tanks were used to roll over people, this would have created a confusion between right and wrong among the people nationwide. That is why I have to thank the PLA officers and men for using this approach to handle the rebellion.

The PLA losses were great, but this enabled us to win the support of the people and made those who can't tell right from wrong change their viewpoint. They can see what kind of people the PLA are, whether there was bloodshed at Tiananmen, and who were those that shed blood.

Once this question is made clear, we can take the initiative. Although it is very saddening that so many comrades were sacrificed, if the event is analyzed objectively, people cannot but recognize that the PLA are the sons and brothers of the people.

This will also help people to understand the measures we used in the course of the struggle. In the future, whenever the PLA faces problems and takes measures, it will gain the support of the people. By the way, I would say that in the future, we must make sure that our weapons are not taken away from us.

In a word, this was a test, and we passed. Even though there are not so many veteran comrades in the army and the soldiers are mostly little more than 18, 19 or 20 years of age, they are still true soldiers of the people. Facing danger, they did not forget the people, the teachings of the party and the interests of the country. They kept a resolute stand in the face of death. They fully deserve the saying that they met death and sacrificed themselves with generosity and without fear.

When I talked about passing muster, I was referring to the fact that the army is still the People's Army. This army retains the traditions of the old Red Army. What they crossed this time was genuinely a political barrier, a threshold of life and death. This is by no means easy. This shows that the People's Army is truly a great wall of iron and steel of the party and country. This shows that no matter how heavy the losses we suffer and no matter how generations change, this army of ours is forever an army under the leadership of the party, forever the defender of the country, forever the defender of socialism, forever the defender of the public interest, and they are most beloved of the people.

At the same time, we should never forget how cruel our enemies are. For them we should not have an iota of forgiveness.

Some Questions Worth Thinking About

The outbreak of the rebellion is worth thinking about. It prompts us to calmly think about the past and consider the future. Perhaps this bad thing will enable us to go ahead with reform and the open-door policy at a more steady, better, even a faster pace. Also it will enable us to more speedily correct our mistakes and better develop our strong points. I cannot elaborate on this today. I just want to raise the subject here.

The first question is: Are the line, goals and policies laid down by the Third Plenum of the 11th Central Committee, including our "three step"[1] development strategy, correct? Is it the case that because this riot took place there is some question about the correctness of the line, goals and policies we laid down? Are our goals "leftist"? Should we continue to use them for our struggle in the future? These significant questions should be given clear and definite answers.

We have already accomplished our first goal for doubling the gross national product. We plan to use 12 years to attain our second goal of doubling the GNP. In the 50 years after that we hope to reach the level of a moderately developed country. A two-percent annual growth rate is sufficient. This is our strategic goal.

I don't believe what we have arrived at is a "left" judgment. Nor have we set up an overly ambitious goal. So, in answering the first question, I should say that our strategic goal cannot be regarded as a failure. It will be an unbeatable achievement for a country with 1.5 billion people like ours to reach the level of a moderately developed nation after 61 years.

China is capable of realizing this goal. It cannot be said that our strategic goal is wrong because of the occurrence of this event.

The second question is this: Is the general conclusion of the 13th Party Congress of "One Center, two basic points" correct?[2] Are the two basic points—upholding the four cardinal principles and persisting in the open policy and reforms—wrong?

In recent days I have pondered these two points. No, we haven't been wrong. There's nothing wrong with the four cardinal principles. If there is anything amiss, it's that these principles haven't been thoroughly implemented—they haven't been used as the basic concept to educate the people, educate the students and educate all the cadres and party members.

The crux of the current incident was basically the confrontation between the four cardinal principles and bourgeois liberalization. It isn't that we have not talked about such things as the four cardinal principles, worked on political concepts, and opposed bourgeois liberalization and spiritual pollution. What we haven't done is maintain continuity in these talks—there has been no action and sometimes even hardly any talk.

The fault does not lie in the four cardinal principles themselves, but in wavering in upholding these principles, and in the very poor work done to persist in political work and education.

In my Chinese People's Political Consultative Conference talk on New Year's day 1980, I talked about four guarantees,[3] one of which was the enterprising spirit of hard struggle and plain living. Promoting plain living must be a major objective of education and this should be the keynote for the next 60 to 70 years. The more prosperous our country becomes, the more important it is to keep hold of the enterprising spirit. The promotion of this spirit and plain living will also be helpful for overcoming corruption.

After the People's Republic was founded we promoted plain living. Later on, when life became a little better, we promoted spending more, leading to wastage everywhere. This, in addition to lapses in theoretical work and an incomplete legal system, resulted in backsliding.

I once told foreigners that our worst omission of the past 10 years was in education. What I meant was political education, and this doesn't apply to schools and students alone, but to the masses as a whole. And we have not said much about plain living and the enterprising spirit, about what kind of a country China is and how it is going to turn out. This is our biggest omission.

Is there anything wrong with the basic concept of reforms and openness? No. Without reforms and openness how could we have what we have today? There has been a fairly satisfactory rise in the standard of living, and it may be said that we have moved one stage further. The positive results of 10 years of reforms must be properly assessed even though there have emerged such problems as inflation. Naturally, in reform and adopting the open policy, we run the risk of importing evil influences from the West, and we have never underestimated such influences.

In the early 1980's, when we established special economic zones, I told our Guangdong comrades that on the one hand they should persevere with reforms and openness, and on the other hand they should deal severely with economic crimes, and carry out ideological and political education.

Looking back, it appears that there were obvious inadequacies—there hasn't been proper coordination. Being reminded of these inadequacies will help us formulate future policies. Further, we must persist in the coordination between a planned economy and a market economy. There cannot be any change in this policy.

In the course of implementing this policy we can place more emphasis on planning in the adjustment period. At other times there can be a little more market adjustment so as to allow more flexibility. The future policy should still be a marriage between the planned economy and market regulation.

What is important is that we should never change China back into a closed country. Such a policy would be most detrimental. We don't even have a good flow of information. Nowadays, are we not talking about the importance of information? Certainly, it is important. If one who is involved in management doesn't possess information, he is no better than a man whose nose is stuffed and whose ears and eyes are shut. Again, we should never go back to the old days of trampling the economy to death. I put forward this proposal for the consideration of the Standing Committee. This is also an urgent problem, a problem we'll have to deal with sooner or later.

In brief, this is what we have achieved in the past decade: Generally, our basic proposals, ranging from a developing strategy to policies, including reforms and openness, are correct. If there is any inadequacy, then I should say our reforms and openness have not proceeded adequately enough. The problems we face in implementing reforms are far greater than those we encounter in opening our country. In political reforms we can affirm one point: We have to insist on implementing the system of the National People's Congress and not the American system of the separation of three powers. The U.S. berates us for suppressing students. But when they handled domestic student unrest and turmoil, didn't they send out police and troops, arrest people and shed blood? They were suppressing students and the people, but we are putting down counter-revolutionary rebellion. What qualifications do they have to criticize us? From now on, however, in handling such problems, we should see to it that when a trend occurs we should never allow them to spread.

What Should Be Done in the Future

What do we do from now on? I would say that we should continue, persist in implementing our planned basic line, direction and policy. Except where there is a need to alter a word or phrase here and there, there should be no change in the basic line or basic policy. Now that I have raised this question, I would like you all to consider it thoroughly. As to how to implement these policies, such as in the areas of investment, the manipulation of capital, etc., I am in favor of putting the emphasis on capital industry and agriculture. In capital industry, this calls for attention to the supply of raw materials, transportation and energy—there should be more investment in this area for the next 10 to 20 years, even if it involves heavy debts. In a way, this is also openness. Here, we need to be bold and have made hardly any serious errors. We should work for more electricity, work for more railway lines, public roads, shipping. There's a lot we can do. As for steel, foreigners judge we'll need some 120 million tons a year in the future. We are now using some 60 million tons, half of what we need. If we were to improve our existing facilities and increase production by 20 million tons we could reduce the amount of steel we need to import. Obtaining foreign loans to improve this area is also an aspect of reform and openness. This question now confronting us is not whether the policies of opening and reforming are correct or not or whether we should continue with these policies. The question is how to carry out these policies, where do we go and which area should we concentrate on?

We have to firmly implement the series of policies formulated since the Third Plenary Session of the 11th Party Central Committee. We must conscientiously sum up our experiences, persevere in what is right, correct what is wrong, and do a bit more where we lag behind. In short, we should sum up the experiences of the present and look forward to the future.

That's all I have to say on this occasion.

Notes

1. Deng, in his speech, mentioned several terms that require explanations: The "three-step developmental strategy" refers to a plan that calls for the doubling of

the gross national product in ten years. The second step calls for the doubling of GNP again. The third step will see China reach the level of a "moderately developed" country within fifty years.

2. "One Center" means a focus on economic construction. "Two basic points" refers to economic reform and the open-door policy.

3. "Four guarantees:" (1) It is necessary to unswervingly implement the Party's political line; (2) It is imperative to maintain a political situation of stability and unity; (3) It is necessary to carry forward the enterprising spirit of hard struggle and plain living; and (4) It is necessary to train a contingent of cadres who adhere to the Socialist road and have professional expertise.

"Checking the Turmoil and Quelling the Counter-Revolutionary Rebellion"*

Chairman, Vice-Chairman and Committee Members,

During late spring and early summer, namely from mid-April to early June, of 1989, a tiny handful of people exploited student unrest to launch a planned, organized and premeditated political turmoil, which later developed into a counter-revolutionary rebellion in Beijing, the capital. Their purpose was to overthrow the leadership of the Chinese Communist Party and subvert the socialist People's Republic of China. The outbreak and development of the turmoil and the counter-revolutionary rebellion had profound international background and social basis at home. As Comrade Deng Xiaoping put it, "This storm was bound to happen sooner or later. As determined by the international and domestic climate, it was bound to happen and was independent of man's will." In this struggle involving the life and death of the Party and the State, Comrade Zhao Ziyang committed the serious mistake of supporting the turmoil and splitting the Party, and had the unshirkable responsibility for the shaping up and development of the turmoil. In face of this very severe situation, the Party Central Committee made correct decisions and took a series of resolute measures, winning the firm support of the whole Party and people of all nationalities in the country. Represented by Comrade Deng Xiaoping, proletarian revolutionaries of the older generation played a very important role in winning the struggle. The Chinese People's Liberation Army, the armed police and the police made great contributions in checking the turmoil and quelling the counter-revolutionary rebellion. The vast numbers of workers, peasants and intellectuals firmly opposed the turmoil and the rebellion, rallied closely around the Party Central Committee and displayed a very high political consciousness and sense of responsibility as masters of the country. Now, entrusted by the State Council, I am making a report to the Standing Committee of the National People's Congress on the turmoil and the counter-revolutionary rebellion, mainly the happenings in Beijing, and the work of checking the turmoil and quelling the counter-revolutionary rebellion.

---

*This is an abridged version of the speech authorized by the State Council and delivered by Chen Xitong, mayor of Beijing and concurrently a state councillor, at the Eighth Session of the Seventh NPC Standing Committee on June 30, 1989. This version is adapted from the *Beijing Review*, July 17–23, 1989.

1. *The turmoil was premeditated and prepared for a long time.*

Some political forces in the West have always attempted to make the socialist countries, including China, give up the socialist road, eventually bring these countries under the rule of international monopoly capital and put them on the course of capitalism. This is their long-term, fundamental strategy. In recent years, they stepped up the implementation of this strategy by making use of some policy mistakes and temporary economic difficulties in socialist countries. In our country, there was a tiny handful of people both inside and outside the Party who stubbornly clung to their position of bourgeois liberalization and went in for political conspiracy. Echoing the strategy of Western countries, they colluded with foreign forces, ganged up at home and made ideological, public opinion and organizational preparations for years to stir up turmoil in China, overthrow the leadership of the Communist Party and subvert the socialist People's Republic. That is why the entire course of brewing, premeditating and launching the turmoil, including the use of varied means such as creating public opinion, distorting facts and spreading rumors, bore the salient feature of mutual support and coordination between a handful of people at home and abroad.

This report will mainly deal with the situation since the Third Plenary Session of the 13th Central Committee of the Chinese Communist Party. Last September, the Party Central Committee formulated the policy of improving the economic environment, straightening out the economic order and deepening the reform in an all-round way. This policy and the related measures won the support of the broad masses and students. The social order and political situation were basically stable. A good proof of this was the approval of Comrade Li Peng's government work report by an overwhelming majority (with a mere two votes against and four abstentions) at the National People's Congress in the spring of this year. Of course, the people and students raised many critical opinions against some mistakes committed by the Party and the government in their work, corruption among some government employees, unfair distribution and other social problems. At the same time, they made quite a few demands and proposals for promoting democracy, strengthening the legal system, deepening the reform and overcoming bureaucracy. These were normal phenomena. And the Party and government were also taking measures to solve them. At that time, however, there was indeed a tiny bunch of people in the Party and society who ganged up together and engaged in many very improper activities overtly and covertly.

What deserves special attention is that, after Comrade Zhao Ziyang's meeting with an American "ultra-liberal economist" on September 19 last year, some Hong Kong newspapers and journals, which were said to have close ties with Zhao Ziyang's "brain trust," gave enormous publicity to this and spread the political message that "Beijing is using Hong Kong mass media to topple Deng and protect Zhao."

Collaboration between forces at home and abroad intensified towards the end of last year and early this year. Political assemblies, joint petitions, big- and small-character posters and other activities emerged, expressing fully erroneous or even reactionary viewpoints.

All this prepared, in terms of ideology and organization, for the turmoil that ensued. A *Ming Pao Daily News* article commented: "The contact-building and petition-signing activities for human rights initiated by the elite of Chinese intellectuals exerted enormous influence on students. They had long ago planned a large-scale move on the 70th anniversary of the May 4th Movement to express their dissatisfaction with the authorities. The sudden death of Hu Yaobang literally threw a match into a barrel of gun-powder." In short, as a result of the premeditation, organization and engineering by a small handful of people, a political situation already emerged in which "the rising wind forebodes a coming storm."

2. Student unrest was exploited by organizers of the turmoil from the very beginning.

Comrade Hu Yaobang's death on April 15 prompted an early outbreak of the long-brewing student unrest and turmoil. The broad masses and students mourned Comrade Hu Yaobang and expressed their profound grief. Universities and colleges provided facilities for the mourning on the part of the students. However, a small number of people took advantage of this to oppose the leadership of the Communist Party and the socialist system under the pretext of "mourning." Student unrest was manipulated and exploited by the small handful of people from the very beginning and bore the nature of political turmoil.

This turmoil, from the very beginning, was manifested by a sharp conflict between bourgeois liberalization and the Four Cardinal Principles. Of the programmatic slogans raised by the organizers of the turmoil at the time, either the "nine demands" first raised through Wang Dan, leader of an illegal student organization, in Tiananmen Square or the "seven demands" and "ten demands" raised later, there were two principal demands: one was to reappraise Comrade Hu Yaobang's merits and demerits; the other was to completely negate the fight against bourgeois liberalization and rehabilitate the so-called "wronged citizens" in the fight. The essence of the two demands was to gain absolute freedom in China to oppose the Four Cardinal Principles and realize capitalism.

Echoing these demands, some so-called "elitists" in academic circles, that is, the very small number of people stubbornly clinging to their position of bourgeois liberalization, organized a variety of forums during the period and indulged in unbridled propaganda through the press.

This turmoil also found expression in the fact that, instigated and engineered by the small handful of people, many acts were crude violations of the Constitution, laws and regulations of the People's Republic of China and gravely running counter to democracy and the legal system. They put up big-character posters en masse on the campuses in disregard of the fact that the provision in the Constitution on "four big freedoms" (speaking out freely, airing views fully, holding great debates and writing big-character posters) had been abrogated and turning a deaf ear to all persuasion; they staged large-scale demonstrations day after day in disregard of the 10-article regulations on demonstrations issued by the Standing Committee of the Beijing Municipal People's Congress; late on the night of April 18 and 19, they assaulted Xinhuamen, headquarters of the Party Central Committee and the State Council, and shouted "down with the Communist Party," something which never occurred even during the "cultural revolution"; they violated the regulations for the management of Tiananmen Square and occupied the square by force several times, one consequence of which was that the memorial meeting for Comrade Hu Yaobang was almost interrupted on April 22; ignoring the relevant regulations of the Beijing Municipality and without registration, they formed an illegal organization, "solidarity student union" (later changed into "federation of autonomous student unions in universities and colleges"), and "seized power" from the lawful student unions and postgraduate unions formed through democratic election; disregarding law and school discipline, they took by force school offices and broadcasting stations and did things as they wished, creating anarchy on the campuses.

This turmoil was marked by another characteristic, that is, it was no longer confined to institutions of higher learning or the Beijing area; it spread to the whole of society and to all parts of China. After the memorial meeting for Comrade Hu Yaobang, a number of people went to contact middle schools, factories, shops and villages, made speeches in the streets, handed out leaflets, put up slogans and raised money, doing everything possible to make the situation worse. The slogan "Oppose the Chinese Communist Party" and the big-character poster "Long live class boycott and exam boycott" appeared in some middle schools. Leaflets "Unite with the workers and peasants, down with the despotic rule" were put up in some factories. Organizers and plotters of the turmoil advanced the slogan "Go to the south, the north, and east and the west" in a bid to establish ties throughout the country. Students from Beijing were seen in universities and colleges in Nanjing, Wuhan, Xi'an, Changsha, Shanghai and Harbin, while students from Tianjin, Hebei, Anhui and Zhejiang took part in demonstrations in Beijing. Criminal activities of beating, smashing, looting and burning took place in Changsha and Xi'an.

Reactionary political forces in Hong Kong, Taiwan, the United States and other Western countries were also involved in the turmoil through various channels and by different means. Western news agencies showed unusual zeal. The Voice of America, in particular, aired news in three programmes beamed to the Chinese mainland for a total of more than ten hours everyday, spreading rumors, stirring up trouble and adding fuel to the turmoil.

Facts listed above show that we were confronted not with student unrest in its normal sense but with a planned, organized and premeditated political turmoil designed to negate the Communist Party leadership and the socialist system. It had clear-cut political ends and deviated from the orbit of democracy and legality, employing base political means to incite large numbers of students and other people who did not know the truth. If we failed to analyze and see the problem in essence, we would have committed grave mistakes and landed ourselves in an extremely passive position in the struggle.

3. People's Daily's *April 26 editorial was correct in determining the nature of the turmoil.*

From the death of Comrade Hu Yaobang on April 15 to the conclusion of the memorial service on April 22, Comrade Zhao Ziyang all along tolerated and connived at the increasingly evident signs of the turmoil during the period of the mourning, thus facilitated the formation and development of the turmoil. In the face of the increasingly grave situation, many comrades in the central leadership and Beijing municipality felt that the nature of the matter had changed, and repeatedly suggested to Comrade Zhao Ziyang that the central leadership should adopt a clear-cut policy and measures to quickly check the development of the situation. But, Zhao kept avoiding making a serious analysis and discussion on the nature of the matter. At the end of the memorial meeting for Comrade Hu Yaobang, comrades in the central leadership again suggested to Zhao that a meeting be held before his visit to the Democratic People's Republic of Korea on April 23. Instead of accepting this suggestion, Zhao went golfing as if nothing had happened. Because of his attitude, the Party and the government lost a chance to quell the turmoil.

On the afternoon of April 24, the Beijing Municipal Party Committee and People's Government reported to Comrade Wan Li. At his proposal, members of the Standing Committee of the Political Bureau met that evening, presided over by Comrade Li Peng, to analyze and study seriously the development of the situation. A consensus was reached that all signs at that time showed we were confronted with an anti-Party and anti-socialist political struggle conducted in a planned and organized way and manipulated and instigated by a small handful of people. The meeting decided that a group for quelling the turmoil be established in the central leadership, requiring at the same time the Beijing Municipal Party Committee and People's Government to mobilize the masses fully, to win over the majority so as to isolate the minority and to strive to put down the turmoil and stabilize the situation as soon as possible.

On the following morning, Comrade Deng Xiaoping made an important speech, expressing his full agreement and support for the decision of the Political Bureau Standing Committee and making an incisive analysis of the nature of the turmoil. He pointed out sharply that this was not a case of ordinary student unrest, but a political turmoil aimed at negating the leadership of the Communist Party and the socialist system. Deng's speech greatly enhanced the understanding of the cadres and increased their confidence and courage in quelling the turmoil and stabilizing the overall situation.

The *People's Daily* editorial on April 26 [see "It Is Necessary to Take a Clear Stand Against the Disturbances"] embodied the decision of the Political Bureau Standing Committee and the spirit of Comrade Deng Xiaoping's speech, and pointed out the nature of the turmoil. At the same time, it made a clear distinction between the tiny handful of people who organized and plotted the turmoil and the vast number of students. The editorial made the overwhelming majority of the cadres feel reassured. It clarified the orientation of their activities, thus enabling them to carry out their work with a clear-cut stand.

The clear-cut stand of the April 26 editorial forced the organizers and plotters of the turmoil to make an about-turn in strategy. Before the publication of the editorial, large numbers of posters and slogans were against the Communist Party, socialism and the Four Cardinal Principles. After the publication of the editorial, the illegal Beijing Federation of Autonomous Student Unions in Universities and Colleges issued on April 26 "No. 1 Order of the New Student Federation" to change their strategy, urging students to "march to Tiananmen under the banner of supporting the Communist Party" on April 27. The designated slogans included "Support the Communist Party," "Support Socialism" and "Safeguard the constitution." It also, at the suggestion of Fang Lizhi, changed their subversive slogans as "Down with the Bureaucratic Government," "Down with the Corrupt Government," "Down with the Dictatorial Rule," etc. into those like "Oppose bureaucracy, Oppose Corruption and Oppose Privilege," and other slogans that could win support from people of various circles.

4. Comrade Zhao Ziyang's speech on May 4 was the turning point in escalating the turmoil.

When the turmoil was about to subside, Comrade Zhao Ziyang, as General Secretary of the Chinese Communist Party, adopted a capricious attitude of going back on his words. At first, when members of the Political Bureau's Standing Committee solicited his opinion during his visit to Korea, he cabled back and explicitly expressed "full agreement with the policy decision made by Comrade Deng Xiaoping on handling the current turmoil." After he returned on April 30, he once again expressed at a meeting of the Political Bureau's Standing Committee his agreement with Comrade Deng Xiaoping's speech and the determination of the nature of the turmoil as made in the April 26 editorial, and maintained that the handling of the student unrest in the previous period was appropriate.

A few days later, however, when he met with representatives attending the annual meeting of the Asian Development Bank on the afternoon of May 4, he expressed a whole set of views diametrically opposed to the decision of the Political Bureau's Standing Committee, to Comrade Deng Xiaoping's speech and to the spirit of the editorial. First, as the turmoil had already come to the surface, he said "there will be no big turmoil in China"; secondly, when a host of facts had proved that the real nature of the turmoil was the negation of the leadership of the Communist Party and the socialist system, he still insisted that "they are by no means opposed to our fundamental system. Rather they are asking us to correct mistakes in our work"; thirdly, although facts had shown that a tiny handful of people were making use of the student unrest to instigate turmoil, he merely said that it was "hardly avoidable" for "some people to take advantage of this," thus totally negating the correct judgment of the Party's Central Committee that a handful of people were creating turmoil.

This speech of Comrade Zhao Ziyang's was prepared by Bao Tong beforehand. Bao asked the Central Broadcasting Station and CCTV to broadcast the speech that very afternoon and repeat it for three days running. He also asked the *People's Daily* to front-page the speech the following day and to carry a large number of positive responses from various sectors. Differing views were held up and not even allowed to appear in confidential materials. Comrade Zhao Ziyang's speech, publicized through the *People's Daily* and certain newspapers, created serious ideological confusion among the cadres and the masses and inflated the arrogance of the organizers and plotters of the turmoil.

Egged on by Comrade Zhao Ziyang and a few others, leaders of the Autonomous Student Unions of Beijing University and Beijing Normal University declared a resumption of the class boycott that night. Many other universities followed suit and organized "pickets" to prevent students from going to class.

After that, a new wave of demonstrations surged ahead. On May 9, several hundred journalists from more than 30 press units took to the streets and submitted a petition. About 10,000 students from a dozen universities including Beijing, Qinghua and People's universities, Beijing Normal University and the University of Political Science and Law staged a demonstration, supporting the journalists, distributing leaflets and calling for continued class boycott and a hunger strike.

Henceforth, the situation took an abrupt turn for the worse and the turmoil was pushed to a new height. Influenced by the situation in Beijing, the already calmed down situation in other parts of China became tense again. Shortly after Comrade Zhao Ziyang's speech, a large number of student demonstrators assaulted the office buildings of the Shanxi Provincial Party Committee and Provincial Government in Taiyuan on May 9 and 10. They also assaulted the ongoing International Economic and Technological Co-operation Fair, the Import and Export Commodities Fair and the Folk Arts Festival. The above incidents exerted very bad influence both at home and abroad.

5. The hunger strike was used as coercion to escalate the turmoil.

Good and honest people asked if the lack of understanding, consideration and concession on the part of the government had brought the students to make so much trouble.

The facts are just the opposite.

From the very beginning of the turmoil, the Party and government fully acknowledged the students' patriotism and their concern about the country and people.

Their demands to promote democracy, promote reform, punish official profiteers and fight corruption were acknowledged as identical with the aspirations of the Party and government, which also expressed the hope to solve the problems through normal democratic and legal procedures.

But such good aspirations failed to win active response. The government proposed to increase understanding and reach consensus through dialogues of various channels, levels and forms.

The illegal student organization, however, put forward very strict conditions as terms of the dialogue. They demanded that their partners in the dialogues "must be people holding positions at or above the Standing Committee member of the Political Bureau of the Party Central Committee, vice-chairman of the NPC Standing Committee and vice-premier"; "a joint communique on every dialogue must be published and signed by both parties"; and dialogues should be "held in locations designated in turn by representatives of the government and students."

These bore nothing like a dialogue but stage-setting for political negotiations with the Party and government. Facts revealed time and again that the very small number of organizers and plotters of the turmoil were determined to oppose us to the very end and that the problem could not be solved even with tolerance on 1,000 occasions and 10,000 concessions. It needs to be pointed out in particular that Comrade Zhao Ziyang did not do what he should have done when the situation quickly deteriorated, but instead stirred up the press with wrong guidance for public opinion, making the deteriorated situation more difficult to handle.

In his May 6 meeting with Comrades Hu Qili and Rui Xingwen, both then in charge of propaganda and ideological work in the Central Committee, Comrade Zhao Ziyang said, the press "has opened up a bit and there is no big risk to opening up a bit by reporting the demonstrations and increasing the openness of news." He even said: "Confronted with the will of the people at home and the progressive trend worldwide, we could only guide our actions according to circumstances."

Here, he even described the adverse current against the Chinese Communist Party and socialism as "will of the people at home" and "progressive trend worldwide."

His instructions were passed on to major news media units in the capital the same day and many arrangements were made afterwards.

As a result, the *People's Daily* and many other national newspapers and periodicals adopted an attitude of full acknowledgement and active support of the demonstrations, sit-in and hunger strike, devoting lengthy coverage with no less exaggeration. Even some Hong Kong newspapers expressed their surprise over this unique phenomenon.

Under the wrong guidance of public opinion, the number of people who took to the streets to support the students increased day by day as their momentum grew after May 15. The number of people involved grew from tens of thousands to a hundred thousand in addition to the 200,000 students who came from other parts of the country to show their support for the fasting students.

For a time, it looked as if refusal to join in the demonstrations meant "un-patriotic" and refusal to show support was equal to "indifferent to the survival of the students."

Under such circumstances, the fasting students were put on the back of the tiger and found it difficult to get off.

As the situation became increasingly serious Comrade Zhao Ziyang used the opportunity of meeting Gorbachev on May 16, deliberately directing the fire of criticism at Comrade Deng Xiaoping and making the situation even worse.

Right at the beginning of the meeting, he said: "Comrade Deng Xiaoping's helmsmanship is still needed for the most important issues. Since the 13th National

Party Congress, we have always reported to Comrade Deng Xiaoping and asked for his advice while dealing with the most important issues." He also said that this was "the first" public disclosure of the "decision" by the Communist Party of China.

On the following day, Yan Jiaqi, Bao Zunxin and others published their most furious and vicious "May 17 Declaration." They made such assertions as: "because the autocrat controls the unlimited power, the government has lost its own obligation and normal human feelings"; "despite the Qing dynasty's death 76 years ago, there is still an emperor in China though without such a title, a senile and fatuous autocrat." "General Secretary Zhao Ziyang declared publicly yesterday afternoon that all decisions in China must be approved by this decrepit autocrat." They said without any disguise in their hoarse voices, "Gerontocratic politics must end and the autocrat must resign."

Against the backdrop of such screams, slogans smearing Comrade Deng Xiaoping and attacking Comrade Li Peng were all around. Some demanded "Deng Xiaoping step down" and "Li Peng step down to satisfy the people." Meanwhile, slogans like "Support Zhao Ziyang," "Long live Zhao Ziyang" and "Zhao Ziyang should be promoted to be chairman of the Central Military Commission" could be seen and heard in the demonstrations and at Tiananmen Square.

Plotters of the turmoil attempted to use the chaos as an opportunity to seize power. They distributed leaflets, proclaiming the founding of the Preparatory Committee to the People's Conference of All Circles in Beijing to replace the Municipal People's Congress. A call was made to establish "Beijing regional government" to replace the legal Beijing Municipal People's Government. They attacked the State Council, which was formed in accordance with the law, as "pseudo-government." They also made up rumors saying the Ministry of Foreign Affairs and a dozen other ministries had already "declared independence" from the State Council and that about 30 countries in the world broke diplomatic relations with our country. After the rumor that "Deng Xiaoping has stepped down" was heard, some went to demonstrations carrying a coffin, burned Comrade Xiaoping's effigy and set off firecrackers on Tiananmen Square to celebrate their "victory."

The situation in Beijing became increasingly serious, with anarchism viciously spreading and many areas sinking into complete chaos and white terror. If our Party and government did not take resolute measures under such circumstances, another vital chance would be missed and further irredeemable, great damages could be done. This would by no means be permitted by the broad masses of the people.

6. The government had no alternative but to take the correct measure of declaring martial law in parts of Beijing.

To safeguard social stability in the city of Beijing, to protect the lives and property of the citizens and ensure the normal functioning of the Party and government departments at the central level and of the Beijing Municipal Government, the State Council had no alternative but to declare martial law in parts of Beijing as empowered by Clause 16 of Article 89 of the Constitution of the People's Republic of China and at a time when police forces in Beijing were quite inadequate to maintain the normal production, work and living order. This was a resolute and correct decision.

The decision on taking resolute measures to stop the turmoil was announced at a meeting called by the central authorities and attended by cadres from the Party, government and military institutions in Beijing on May 19. Comrade Zhao Ziyang, persisting in his erroneous stand against the correct decision of the central authorities, neither agreed to speak at the meeting together with Comrade Li Peng, nor agreed to preside over the meeting. He even didn't agree to attend the meeting. By doing so, he openly revealed his attitude of separating himself from the Party before the whole Party, the whole country and the whole world.

Under the extremely urgent circumstances, the Party Central Committee and the State Council decided resolutely to declare martial law in parts of Beijing, starting from 10 A.M., May 20, to prevent the situation from worsening and grasp the initiative to stop the turmoil so as to give support to the broad masses who were opposed to the turmoil and longed for stability. However, as the organizers and schemers of the turmoil had learnt of our decision before it was implemented, there were tremendous difficulties and obstacles to the troops' entry into the city.

On the eve of declaring the martial law and in the first two days after it was declared, all major crossroads were blocked. More than 220 buses were taken away and used as roadblocks. Transportation came to a standstill. Troops to enforce the martial law were not able to arrive at their designated places. The headquarters of the Party Central Committee and the State Council continued to be surrounded. Demagogic speeches could be heard everywhere on the street. Leaflets spreading rumors could be seen everywhere in the city. Demonstrations, each involving thousands of people, took place in succession and Beijing, our capital city, fell into total disorder and terror. In the following few days, the martial law troops managed to enter the city by different ways. Meanwhile, the armed police and security force continued to perform their duties by overcoming tremendous difficulties. Urban and suburban districts organized workers, residents and government office workers, as many as 120,000 people altogether, to maintain social order. The outer suburban counties also sent out militiamen. The concerted efforts of the troops, police and civilians helped improve the transportation, production and living order in the capital and people felt more at ease. But the very small number of people never stopped for a single day their activities to create turmoil and never changed their goal of overthrowing the leadership of the Communist Party. Things were developing day by day towards a counter-revolutionary rebellion.

One of the major tactics of the organizers and schemers of the turmoil after martial law was declared was to continue to stay on the Tiananmen Square. They wanted to turn the square into a "center of the student movement and the whole nation." Once the government made a decision, they planned a "strong reaction" at the square and formed an "anti-government united front." These people had been planning to stir up blood-shedding incidents on the square, believing that "the government would resort to suppression if the occupation of the square continues" and "blood can awaken people and split up the government."

7. How did a small minority of people manage to stir up the counter-revolutionary rebellion?

After the announcement of martial law in some areas of the capital May 20, the troops, despite repeated obstructions, were mobilized to march towards the city proper in accordance with a deployment plan and by different ways to take up appointed positions.

The handful of organizers and plotters of the rebellion were well aware that they would not be able to continue their illegal and counter-revolutionary activities and their conspiracy would come to nothing if the martial law troops took up positions in the center of Beijing. Therefore, they started to create trouble deliberately and did their best to aggravate the unrest, which eventually developed into a counter-revolutionary rebellion.

On June 1 the Public Security Bureau detained a few of the ringleaders of the illegal "Federation of Autonomous Workers' Unions." The agitator of the rebellion then took advantage of this opportunity to incite some people to surround and attack the offices of Beijing Municipal Public Security Bureau, the Municipal Party Committee and Government and the Ministry of Public Security.

On the evening of June 2 a police jeep on loan to the Chinese Central TV Station was involved in a traffic accident in which three people died. None of the victims was a student. This was deliberately distorted as a provocation by martial law troops. The conspirators attempted to seize the bodies and parade them in coffins, stirring up the people and making the atmosphere extremely tense. After this incitement and uproar they lit the fire of the counter-revolutionary rebellion.

As the situation rapidly deteriorated, the instigators of the upheaval became more vicious. At about 5:00 P.M., the ringleaders of the illegal "Beijing Federation of Autonomous Student Unions of Universities" and "Colleges and Federation of Autonomous Workers' Unions" distributed knives, iron bars, chains and sharpened bamboo sticks, inciting the mobs to kill soldiers and members of the security forces. In a broadcast over loudspeakers in Tiananmen Square, the "Federation of Autonomous Workers' Unions" urged the people "to take up arms and overthrow the government." It also broadcast how to make Molotov cocktails and how to wreck and burn military vehicles.

A group of rioters organized about 1,000 people to push down the wall of a construction site near Xidan and stole tools, reinforcing bars and bricks, ready for street fighting.

They planned to incite people to take to the streets the next day, a Sunday, to stage a violent rebellion in an attempt to overthrow the government. At this critical juncture, the Party Central Committee, the State Council and the Central Military Commission decided to order troops poised on the outskirts of the capital to enforce martial law and quell the counter-revolutionary rebellion.

8. How did the counter-revolutionary rebels injure and kill People's Liberation Armymen?

During the enforcement of martial law in Beijing, the martial law troops heading for Beijing proper tried their best to avoid conflicts, exercising great restraint in accordance with instructions of the Party Central Committee. After the June 3 riot happened and before the troops entered the city, the Beijing municipal government and the headquarters of the martial law enforcement troops issued an emergency announcement at 6:30 P.M., which said, "All citizens must heighten their vigilance and keep off the streets and not to go to Tiananmen Square as of the issuing of this notice. Workers should remain at their posts, and other citizens must stay at home to ensure their security." The announcement was broadcast over and over again on TV and radio.

About 10 P.M. on June 3, most of the martial law troops heading for Beijing proper from various directions had been halted at barricades set up at the main crossroads. Even so, the troops were still quite restrained, while the counter-revolutionary rioters took the opportunity to beat and kill soldiers, to seize military materials and burn military vehicles.

The mobs also murdered soldiers in various bestial ways. About dawn on June 4, some mobs beat up soldiers with bottles and bricks at Dongdan crossroad. In Fuxingmen, a military vehicle was surrounded and 12 soldiers were dragged off the vehicle. They were searched and severely beaten. Many of them were badly injured.

In Liubukou, four soldiers were surrounded and beaten up, and some were beaten to death. In the Guangqumen area, three soldiers were severely beaten. One was rescued by some bystanders and the other two have not been found yet. In Xixingsheng Lane of the Xicheng District, more than 20 armed policemen were beaten up by mobs; some were badly injured, and the others' whereabouts are unknown. In Huguosi, a military vehicle was halted, and soldiers on it were beaten up and detained as hostages. Submachine guns were snatched. A truck full of bricks was driven from Dongjiao Minxiang to Tiananmen Square, and people on the truck shouted "if you are really Chinese, attack the soldiers."

In the several days of the rebellion, more than 1,280 military vehicles, police cars and public buses were wrecked, burned or otherwise damaged. Of the vehicles, over 1,000 were military vehicles, more than 60 were armored personnel carriers and about 30 were police cars. More than 120 public buses were destroyed as well as more than 70 other kinds of motor vehicles. During the same period, arms and ammunition were stolen. More than 6,000 martial law soldiers, armed police and public security officers were injured and the death toll reached several dozens. They sacrificed their blood and even their precious lives to defend the motherland, the Constitution and the people. The people will remember their contributions.

Such heavy losses are eloquent testimony to the restraint and tolerance shown by the martial law troops.

In order to quell the counter-revolutionary rebellion and to avoid more losses, the martial law troops, having suffered heavy casualties and been driven beyond forbearance, were forced to fire in the air to open the way forward after repeated warnings.

During the counter-attack, some rioters were killed. Because there were numerous bystanders, some were knocked down by vehicles, some were trampled on or were hit by stray bullets. Some were wounded or killed by ruffians who had seized rifles.

According to the information we have so far gathered, more than 3,000 civilians were wounded and over 200, including 36 college students, died during the riot. Among the non-military casualties were rioters who deserved the punishment, people accidentally injured, and doctors and other people who were carrying out various duties on the spot.

During the whole operation no one, including the students who refused but were forced to leave, died. Tales of "rivers of blood" in Tiananmen Square and the rumor-mongers themselves "escaping from underneath piles of corpses" are sheer nonsense. The counter-revolutionary rebellion was put down with Tiananmen Square returning to the hands of the people and all martial law enforcement troops taking up their assigned positions.

Due to the turmoil and the counter-revolutionary rebellion, Beijing has suffered heavy losses in its economy and losses in other fields cannot be counted with money. Workers, peasants and intellectuals are now working hard to retrieve the losses. Now, order in the capital has fundamentally returned to normal and the situation throughout China is also tending to become calm which shows that the correct decision made by the Party Central Committee has benefitted the Chinese people of all nationalities. Yet, the unrest and the rebellion are not completely over, as a handful of counter-revolutionary rioters refuse to recognize defeat and still indulge in sabotage, and even dream of staging a comeback.

In order to achieve thorough victory, we should mobilize the people completely, strengthen the people's democratic dictatorship and spare no effort to ferret out the counter-revolutionary rioters. We should uncover instigators and rebellious conspir-ators, and punish the organizers and schemers of the unrest and the counter-revolutionary rebellion, that is, those who obstinately stuck to the path of bourgeois liberalization and conspired to instigate rebellion, those who colluded with overseas and other foreign hostile forces, those who provided illegal organizations with top secrets of the Party and state, and those who committed the atrocities of beating, smashing, grabbing and burning during the disturbances. We should make a clear distinction between two different types of contradictions and deal with them accordingly, through resolute, hard and painstaking work. We must educate and unite people as much as possible and focus the crackdown on a handful of principal culprits and diehards who refuse to repent. On this basis, we will retrieve all the losses suffered in the unrest and the counter-revolutionary rebellion as soon as possible. For this, we must rely on the people, try to increase production, practice the strictest economy and struggle arduously.

Index